Literary Approaches to the Bible is a tour de force! It gives readers a much needed and enjoyable tour of the history of literary approaches in biblical studies up to their most recent developments. Highlighted sections and annotated bibliographies in each chapter create ease for reading and give a path for further study to interested readers. Covering canonical, narrative, rhetorical, structural, and poststructural criticisms alongside topics of intertextuality and inner-biblical interpretation, this book will be a rich and insightful resource for scholars and students alike for years to come!

—Beth M. Stovell, associate professor of Old Testament, Ambrose University; author, *Mapping Metaphorical Discourse in the Fourth Gospel*

This collection provides an excellent introduction to various methodologies utilized in literary interpretation of the Bible. Each essay gives a definition and explanation of the method being presented, examples of its application to the biblical text, and a balanced assessment of its advantages and limitations. Students and practitioners of biblical interpretation will find this a very helpful introduction to various literary methods of interpretation, which are not presented as the means of interpreting the Bible, but rather one tool to be utilized alongside others to assist the interpreter in grasping the meaning and significance of the text.

—David R. Beck, associate dean of biblical studies and professor of New Testament and Greek, Southeastern Baptist Theological Seminary

T0282943

LITERARY APPROACHES TO THE BIBLE

LEXHAM METHODS SERIES

LITERARY APPROACHES TO THE BIBLE

—

Edited by Douglas Mangum & Douglas Estes

LEXHAM PRESS

Lexham Methods Series: Volume 4: Literary Approaches to the Bible
Copyright 2017 Lexham Press

Lexham Press, 1313 Commercial St., Bellingham, WA 98225
Lexhampress.com

Print ISBN 9781577996668
Digital ISBN 9781577997078

Lexham Editorial Team: Claire Brubaker, Abigail Stocker, Danielle Thevenaz, and Joel Wilcox
Design: Brittany Schrock
Typesetting: ProjectLuz.com

CONTENTS

SERIES PREFACE

T he Lexham Methods Series introduces a variety of approaches to biblical interpretation. Due to the field's long history, however, the coverage is necessarily selective. This series focuses on the major areas of critical biblical scholarship and their development from the 19th century to the early 21st century. While we recognize that theological approaches to interpretation have played an important role in the life of the Church, this series does not engage the wide variety of hermeneutical approaches that arise from specific theological readings of the biblical text.

The methods discussed here include the broad movements in biblical criticism that have helped define how biblical scholars today approach the text. Understanding the basics of textual criticism, source criticism, form criticism, tradition history, redaction criticism, linguistics, social-scientific criticism, canonical criticism, and contemporary literary criticism (rhetorical, structural, narrative, reader-response, post structural) will help illuminate the assumptions and conclusions found in many scholarly commentaries and articles.

Each approach to biblical interpretation—even those that are not explicitly theological—can be defined according to a guiding presupposition that informs the method.

- **Textual criticism**: Reading the text to identify *errors in transmission* and determine the best text

- **Source criticism**: Reading the text to find the *written sources* the author(s) used

- **Form criticism**: Reading the text to find the *oral traditions* the author(s) used

- **Tradition-historical criticism**: Reconstructing the *historical development of the traditions* identified by form criticism

- **Redaction criticism**: Reading the text to understand *how it was put together* and what message the text was meant to communicate

- **Canonical criticism**: Reading the final form of the text *as Christian Scripture*

- **Rhetorical criticism**: Analyzing the text for the *rhetorical effect of the literary devices* the writers used to communicate and persuade

- **Structural criticism**: Analyzing the text *in terms of contrast and oppositions*, recognizing that contrast is believed to be the essence of meaning within a cultural, linguistic, or literary system

- **Narrative criticism**: Reading the text *as a narrative* and paying attention to aspects including plot, theme, and characterization

- **Linguistic approach**: Analyzing the text *using* concepts and theories developed by *linguistics*

- **Social-scientific approach**: Analyzing the text *using* concepts and theories developed in the *social sciences*

The Lexham Methods Series defines these approaches to biblical interpretation, explains their development, outlines their goals and emphases, and identifies their leading proponents. Few interpreters align themselves strictly with any single approach. Contemporary Bible scholars tend to use an eclectic method that draws on the various aspects of biblical criticism outlined above. Many of these methods developed in parallel, mutually influenced each other, and share similar external influences from literary theory and philosophy. Similarly, ideas and questions arising from one approach often directly influenced the field as a whole and have become common currency in biblical studies, even though the method that generated the concepts has been radically reshaped and revised over the years.

In introducing a variety of methods, we will address each method as neutrally as possible, acknowledging both the advantages and limitations of each approach. Our discussion of a particular method or attempts to demonstrate the method should not be construed as an endorsement of that approach to the text. The Lexham Methods Series introduces you to the world of biblical scholarship.

ABBREVIATIONS

REFERENCE WORKS

AEL   *Ancient Egyptian Literature.* M. Lichtheim. 3 vols. 1971–1980.

ANET   *Ancient Near Eastern Texts Relating to the Old Testament.* J. B. Pritchard. 1954.

AYBD   *Anchor Yale Bible Dictionary* (formerly *Anchor Bible Dictionary*). D. N. Freedman. 1992.

BDAG   W. Bauer, F. W. Danker, W. F. Arndt, and F. W. Gingrich. *A Greek-English Lexicon of the New Testament and Other Early Christian Literature.* 3d ed. 1999.

BDB   *Enhanced Brown-Driver-Briggs Hebrew and English Lexicon.*

BEB   *Baker Encyclopedia of the Bible.* W. A. Elwell. 2 vols. 1988.

BHRG   *A Biblical Hebrew Reference Grammar.* Christo van der Merwe, Jackie Naudé, and Jan Kroeze. 1999.

COS   *The Context of Scripture.* W. W. Hallo and K. L. Younger. 3 vols. 1997–2003.

DCH   *Dictionary of Classical Hebrew.* D. J. A. Clines. 1993.

DDD   *Dictionary of Deities and Demons in the Bible.* K. van der Toorn, B. Becking, and P. W. van der Horst. 1995.

DJG   *Dictionary of Jesus and the Gospels.* J. B. Green and S. McKnight. 1992.

DLNT   *Dictionary of the Later New Testament and Its Developments.* R. P. Martin and P. H. Davids. 1997.

DPL   *Dictionary of Paul and His Letters.* G. F. Hawthorne and R. P. Martin. 1993.

DNTB	*Dictionary of New Testament Background*. S. E. Porter and C. A. Evans. 2000.
EDB	*Eerdmans Dictionary of the Bible*. D. N. Freedman. 2000.
EDNT	*Exegetical Dictionary of the New Testament*. H. Balz and G. Schneider. 1990–1993.
GKC	*Gesenius' Hebrew Grammar*. E. Kautzsch (ed.) and A. E. Cowley (trans.). 1910.
HALOT	*The Hebrew and Aramaic Lexicon of the Old Testament*. L. Koehler, W. Baumgartner, and J. J. Stamm. 1994–1999.
IBHS	*An Introduction to Biblical Hebrew Syntax*. B. K. Waltke and M. O'Connor. 1990.
IGEL	*An Intermediate Greek-English Lexicon*. 1888.
ISBE	*International Standard Bible Encyclopedia*. Revised ed. G. W. Bromiley. 4 vols. 1979–1988.
JM	*A Grammar of Biblical Hebrew*. P. Joüon and T. Muraoka. Rev. English ed. 2006.
LBD	*Lexham Bible Dictionary*. John D. Barry. 2012.
LEH	J. Lust, E. Eynikel, and K. Hauspie. *A Greek-English Lexicon of the Septuagint*. Revised ed. 2003.
L&N	J. P. Louw and E. A. Nida. *Greek-English Lexicon of the New Testament: Based on Semantic Domains*. 1989.
LSJ	H. G. Liddell, R. Scott, and H. S. Jones. *A Greek-English Lexicon*. 9th ed. with rev. supp. 1996.
MM	J. H. Moulton and G. Milligan. *The Vocabulary of the Greek Testament*. 1930.
NBD	*New Bible Dictionary*, 3rd ed. D. R. W. Wood. 1996.
NIDNTT	*New International Dictionary of New Testament Theology*. C. Brown. 4 vols. 1975–1985.
NIDOTTE	*New International Dictionary of Old Testament Theology and Exegesis*. W. A. VanGemeren. 5 vols. 1997.
OTP	*Old Testament Pseudepigrapha*. J. H. Charlesworth. 2 vols. 1983–85.
ODCC	*The Oxford Dictionary of the Christian Church*. F. L. Cross and E. A. Livingstone. 2nd ed. 1983.
TDNT	*Theological Dictionary of the New Testament*. G. Kittel and G. Friedrich. 10 vols. 1964–1976.

TLNT	*Theological Lexicon of the New Testament*. C. Spicq. 3 vols. 1994.
TLOT	*Theological Lexicon of the Old Testament*. E. Jenni and C. Westermann. 3 vols. 1997.
TWOT	*Theological Wordbook of the Old Testament*. R. L. Harris and G. L. Archer Jr. 2 vols. 1980.
ZEB	*The Zondervan Encyclopedia of the Bible*. Moisés Silva and M. C. Tenney. 5 vols. 2009.

COMMENTARIES

ACCS	Ancient Christian Commentary on Scripture
AYBC	Anchor Yale Bible Commentary (formerly Anchor Bible Commentary)
BCBC	Believers Church Bible Commentary
BKC	Bible Knowledge Commentary
BNTC	Black's New Testament Commentaries
CCS	Continental Commentary Series
FOTL	The Forms of the Old Testament Literature
IBC	Interpretation: A Bible Commentary for Teaching and Preaching
ICC	International Critical Commentary
ITC	International Theological Commentary
K&D	Keil, C. F., and F. Delitzsch. *Commentary on the Old Testament*. 1857–1878. Reprint 1996.
NAC	New American Commentary
NICNT	New International Commentary on the New Testament
NICOT	New International Commentary on the Old Testament
NIGTC	New International Greek Testament Commentary
NIVAC	The NIV Application Commentary
OTL	Old Testament Library
PNTC	The Pillar New Testament Commentary
TNTC	Tyndale New Testament Commentaries
TOTC	Tyndale Old Testament Commentaries
UBCS	Understanding the Bible Commentary Series (formerly the New International Biblical Commentary)
WBC	Word Biblical Commentary

| ZIBBCNT | Zondervan Illustrated Bible Backgrounds Commentary (New Testament) |
| ZIBBCOT | Zondervan Illustrated Bible Backgrounds Commentary (Old Testament) |

JOURNALS

ATJ	Ashland Theological Journal
BA	Biblical Archaeologist
BAR	Biblical Archaeology Review
BBR	Bulletin for Biblical Research
BSac	Bibliotheca sacra
CBQ	Catholic Biblical Quarterly
CurBS	Currents in Research: Biblical Studies
CurTM	Currents in Theology and Mission
EQ	Evangelical Quarterly
HUCA	Hebrew Union College Annual
JAAR	Journal of the American Academy of Religion
JBL	Journal of Biblical Literature
JETS	Journal of the Evangelical Theological Society
JHS	Journal of Hebrew Scriptures
JNES	Journal of Near Eastern Studies
JNSL	Journal of Northwest Semitic Languages
JSOT	Journal for the Study of the Old Testament
JSNT	Journal for the Study of the New Testament
JSSR	Journal for the Scientific Study of Religion
JR	Journal of Religion
MSJ	The Master's Seminary Journal
NovT	Novum Testamentum
PRSt	Perspectives in Religious Studies
RevExp	Review and Expositor
RBL	Review of Biblical Literature
Them	Themelios
TS	Theological Studies
TynBul	Tyndale Bulletin
USQR	Union Seminary Quarterly Review
VT	Vetus Testamentum

WTJ   *Westminster Theological Journal*

BIBLE VERSIONS

AMP   The Amplified Bible. 1987.
ASV   American Standard Version. 1901.
BHK   *Biblia Hebraica.* R. Kittel. 1905–1973.
BHS   *Biblia Hebraica Stuttgartensia.* K. Elliger and W. Rudolph. 1977–1997.
BHQ   *Biblia Hebraica Quinta.* A. Schenker. 2004–.
CEB   Common English Bible. 2011.
CEV   Contemporary English Version. 1995.
DRB   Douay-Rheims Bible.
ESV   English Standard Version. 2001.
GNT   Good News Translation. 1992.
HCSB   Holman Christian Standard Bible. 2009.
JPS   Jewish Publication Society. 1917.
KJV   King James Version.
LEB   Lexham English Bible. 2012.
LES   Lexham English Septuagint. 2012.
LHB   Lexham Hebrew Bible. 2012.
LXX   Septuagint
MT   Masoretic Text
MSG   *The Message.* 2005.
NA27   Nestle-Aland *Novum Testamentum Graece.* 27th edition. 1993.
NA28   Nestle-Aland *Novum Testamentum Graece.* 28th edition. 2012.
NAB   New American Bible. 1970.
NASB   New American Standard Bible. 1995.
NCV   New Century Version. 2005.
NET   New English Translation. 2005.
NIV   New International Version. 2011.
NIV84   New International Version. 1984.
NJPS   *Tanakh.* Jewish Publication Society. 1985.
NKJV   New King James Version. 1982.
NLT   New Living Translation. 2007.
NRSV   New Revised Standard Version. 1989.
RSV   Revised Standard Version. 1971.

SBLGNT   Greek New Testament: SBL Edition. 2011.
TNIV   Today's New International Version. 2005.
UBS4   United Bible Societies' *Greek New Testament*. 4th edition. 1998.

1

INTRODUCTION: THE LITERARY APPROACH TO THE BIBLE

Douglas Estes

> The Teacher was full of wisdom, and he taught the people
> with knowledge. He carefully considered many proverbs
> and carefully arranged them. The Teacher sought to find
> delightful words, and he wrote what is upright—truthful
> words. [Ecclesiastes 12:9–10 LEB]

1.1 A BRAVE NEW LITERARY WORLD

In a few short decades in the latter half of the twentieth century, the interpretation of the Bible underwent a notable shift such as has happened only occasionally over the last few thousand years. During this time the focus in biblical interpretation began to shift from what the text can teach us about the past to also include what the text can teach us about the text (and ourselves). Increasingly, the Bible began to be viewed and read not just as a religious or historical document but also as a literary text. Bible scholars speak broadly of this shift as being from a *historical-critical method* of biblical interpretation toward a *literary-critical method* of biblical interpretation. This shift was not wholesale; it was felt more in some areas of biblical studies than others.[1] This description also does not tell the whole

---

1. Even to speak of "biblical studies" includes a large field with many interests and many groups; some subfields of biblical research have made an almost wholesale shift from

story—there is much more involved here than simply the inclusion of a new method (which, in some cases, also largely replaced an older method).[2] The growth of the literary approach to the Bible was and is *philosophical* more than theological or anything else.

This shift in biblical interpretation correlates strongly with the sea change that took place in the Western world during the twentieth century. During this century, there are clear examples of change in areas such as science and technology, in which the telegraph and the Pony Express were completely eclipsed by the mobile phone and the space shuttle. We describe these changes as surface changes because they occurred on the surface of our world, fully visible and understood as dramatic changes by any observer. However, below these surface changes, this century also brought rapid change (by historical standards) to the Western worldview. Yet, below even these changes there were deeper changes in the most fundamental understanding of how people know, learn, exist, and interact. These fundamental shifts set in motion the shifts in biblical studies, through a long process of cause and effect.[3] As a result, for a beginning student, it can be challenging to ask, "How and where did the literary approach to the Bible get started?" since each answer reveals more answers (and questions) lurking below the surface. Therefore, instead of trying first to pinpoint an inexact origin, let us begin with a different type of answer: *The shifts in biblical interpretation in the late twentieth century have little or nothing to do*

---

historical-critical to literary-critical methods, but in others, any literary-critical influence has been much more muted.

2. One question that arises is: What is the relationship between the historical-critical method and the literary-critical method? How one answers depends a great deal on a number of factors, including: (1) what subfield of biblical studies one is in, (2) whether one is more oriented toward singular or diverse models of interpretation, (3) what groups one associates with, and (4) when one "came of age" in the formal study of the Bible. Let me offer one anecdotal example: The Library of New Testament Studies is a major monograph series for the study of the NT. Surveying the books published in that series over the last two-and-a-half-year period reveals that studies heavily influenced by literary-critical ideas outnumber the studies heavily influenced by historical-critical ideas by a factor of almost three to one. Most importantly, the slight majority of the studies during that timeframe are probably best described as being in dialogue with both approaches. This is only one series, but it seems indicative of the larger world of biblical studies.

3. Most likely the surface changes and the deep changes are symbiotic; that is, they occurred together because one inadvertently affects the other. The mobile phone affects the Western worldview, which affects the underworking philosophy of the day, which affects the mobile phone, which affects the Western worldview, on and on.

with the Bible itself. Instead, they have everything to do with the changes occurring in Western thought and culture.

To give us a taste for these shifts, let us mention a number of them in passing. The meaning of "literature" changed—moving from the more narrow poetic type to signifying almost any text type (including the Bible). Romanticism, as it had been applied to literature, completely fell out of favor. The science of language moved from a "soft" philology to a "hard" linguistics. Modernism, that incredibly powerful structure of Western thought prevailing for more than three centuries, cracked and began to crumble. The Cartesian basis for the identity of individuals began to be rejected. Disciplines such as psychology and phenomenology were launched. Old disciplines such as history and literary criticism were largely reinvented. New ideologies such as naturalism, Marxism, and feminism supplanted or complemented previous ideologies. Two world wars, the end of colonialism, and a sexual revolution formed the backdrop for the "narrative turn" in the study of world literature. There were many more factors than we can possibly mention here. Yet, few have anything to do with the Bible itself.[4]

By acknowledging this up front, we can gain a positive perspective on the literary approach to the Bible. It is just one philosophical approach. It is useful in the era in which we live. One day, it will be eclipsed by another approach. The approach that preceded the literary approach is also just one approach. It was useful in the era in which it was most prominent. It too became eclipsed by another approach. One day, it will probably be found useful again (though in a different form with a different name). If we can recognize that the various historical and literary approaches, with their respective methods, are simply tools in an interpreter's toolbox, we can faithfully use those tools without fear or blame. Some of these new literary tools—like deconstruction—can seem daunting and unusual at first to

---

4. The few words of this introduction can do little justice to the movements contributing to the philosophical shifts that influenced biblical studies in the second half of the twentieth century. For more detailed treatments of the development of literary criticism, see M. A. R. Habib, *Literary Criticism from Plato to the Present: An Introduction* (Malden, MA: Wiley Blackwell, 2011); and volumes 6 through 8 of *The Cambridge History of Literary Criticism*. Furthermore, this introductory chapter will only highlight a few key thinkers, but even they were building on the work of the many people who preceded them.

beginning students of the Bible, but it is just a tool like any other.[5] In any situation, one tool will work better than another, but the skilled interpreter understands that most every tool has its proper use.

Thus it is both true and not true that the literary approach to the Bible goes back to the time of the early church. One chapter in this volume will introduce you to the ancient art of rhetoric. This interpretive method existed long before the writing of the NT, and it comprises one of the modern literary approaches to the Bible. At the same time, one chapter in this volume will introduce you to the variegated methods of poststructuralist thought. These methods are almost completely distinct from ancient interpretive techniques. But both rhetorical criticism and poststructuralism are examples of the many methods that comprise the literary approach to the Bible.

We should clarify a few terms at the outset. This volume of the Lexham Method Series is called *The Literary Approach to the Bible*. By "literary approach," a very general and nontechnical term, Bible interpreters mean reading the Bible with an eye for any method that could fit into any literary theory (new or ancient, conventional or radical). In contrast, when we speak of "literary criticism," we are talking about a specific consideration and analysis of a literary text by means of a literary method. Therefore, a literary approach is a general way of speaking of some type of literary criticism. In contrast, "literary theory" describes a philosophical consideration of the many possible methods and meanings that a reader may be informed of by the text.[6] Or, to put it another way, we could describe literary criticism as the practical application of some form of literary theory. In this chapter, even though there will be some "theory" considered, what we are working through is some highlights of literary criticism, far more than literary theory. Literary theory, especially after the shifts in the late twentieth century, tends to be—for the average reader—philosophically dense and often not too interested in the texts themselves.[7] The literary approach to the Bible is meaningful, because the Bible is literature—but "literature" is a term describing any text that can be read and interpreted;

---

5. See David Seeley, *Deconstructing the New Testament* (Leiden: Brill, 1994), 19.

6. Mario Klarer, *An Introduction to Literary Studies*, 2nd ed. (London: Routledge, 2004), 77.

7. That literary theory is this way both is a barrier to its acceptance and usefulness in biblical studies and, in some cases, brings about concerns or criticisms for its influence within biblical studies; see §1.5 Limitations of the Literary Approach.

it no longer refers only to a particular subset of Western writings. Further, we use the word "modern" to denote primarily the thinking and ideology of the classical-to-late modern periods, roughly synonymous with the time between the mid-eighteenth century and the mid-twentieth century; and we use the word "postmodern" to refer to the period beginning from the fall of modernity, which roughly started in the late mid- to late twentieth-century.[8]

The confusion over these literary foundations has led to the rise of a number of inaccurate assumptions about the literary approach to the Bible. Here we mention the most frequent objections to the literary approach to the Bible:

- *The Bible is not literature.* The problem with this statement is what one means by "literature."[9] Usually this statement implies that literature is a specific group of fictional works that range from Milton to Hemingway. However, the term "literature," while traditionally used to mean "to designate fictional and imaginative writings—poetry, prose fiction, and drama," now means "any other writings (including philosophy, history, and even scientific works addressed to a general audience) that are especially distinguished in form, expression, and emotional power."[10] The former definition is closer to what literary critics mean when they use the term "(literary) canon." As we rely on current definitions of the word "literature," the Bible is literature.

- *The literary approach is new and therefore anachronistic.* The first known occurrence of literary criticism in the West dates

---

8. Modernity can be broken down into three phases: early, middle (or classical), and late. Depending on how modernity is measured, it may have lasted a full six centuries. As a result, its stamp on Western culture is insurmountable—it is really quite impossible for anyone born in the late modern period to understand the thinking of premodern writers without making a large number of assumptions.

9. For a lengthier discussion of the problems with the word "literature," see Peter Widdowson, *Literature*, The New Critical Idiom (London: Routledge, 1999), 1–25; and Terry Eagleton, *Literary Theory: An Introduction*, anniversary ed. (Minneapolis: University of Minnesota Press, 2008), 1–16.

10. M. H. Abrams and Geoffrey Galt Harpham, *A Glossary of Literary Terms*, 9th ed. (Boston: Wadsworth, 2009), 177–78.

back to the production of Aristophanes' *Frogs* in 405 BC.[11] After this, Aristotle (384–322 BC), Longinus (*fl.* late first century AD), and Dionysius of Halicarnassus (*fl.* late first century BC) produced works on literary theory and criticism that are still extant today, not to mention that the Teacher in the book of Ecclesiastes mentions at least one aspect of literary criticism (Eccl 12:9–10). While some of the individual methods within the broad umbrella of the literary approach to the Bible are new and could be used anachronistically, the approach itself is not new and actually predates the NT (and some parts of the OT as well). Further, some methods within other approaches (such as the historical-critical approach, the most notable predecessor to the literary approach) are also new and can also be used anachronistically. Therefore, anachronism is always a concern for interpreters of ancient texts, regardless of approach and method.

- *The literary approach has no final "answer" in interpretation or endpoint—many different interpretations are equally valid.* This claim is partly true and partly false, but it only has a little to do with the literary approach itself.[12] Differences in interpretation have existed from the moment of creation of any biblical text. In past generations, it was not the method that provided an end to interpretive discussion but rather an authority (such as a council, a church, a church leader, or a consensus). It is true that one of the results of recent literary theory is a proliferation of different methods (and as a result, interpretations), but this is more a result of the proliferation of ideologies in

---

11. Habib, *Literary Criticism from Plato to the Present*, 10.

12. Many beginning students of the Bible will find that they have already been exposed to one literary theory within the literary approach to the Bible, whether realizing it or not—the author-focused interpretive strategy. This is a traditional strategy but also was popularized by E. D. Hirsch Jr., a literary critic, whose work contrasted with the direction of much of postmodern literary theory. Those uncomfortable with recent literary theory have often rallied around Hirsch's works, which is where author-focused strategy can enter into biblical interpretation; see also Daniel J. Treier, *Introducing Theological Interpretation of Scripture: Recovering a Christian Practice* (Grand Rapids: Baker, 2008), 134.

the Western world in the last century than it is of any movement or expectation in the field of biblical studies.

- *The literary approach is not scientific or rigorous (as the historical approach is).* This argument depends a great deal on who
the interpreter is and whether an appropriate tool is selected.
Every approach to Scripture will have less rigorous examples and more rigorous examples, regardless of the approach.
Further, "scientific" and "rigorous" are modern ideals that
earlier interpreters of Scripture may not have held to be
extremely important (as they were not influenced by the
modern worldview).

- *The literary approach is not historical/avoids historical concerns.*
This last objection is the most frequently noted by those
critical of the literary approach. It is true that many literary approaches to Scripture avoid or ignore historical questions and concerns. But it is not true in all cases. Furthermore,
applications of the literary approach to the Bible are often
ahistorical, but rarely *anti-historical.*[13] In other words, when
an interpreter takes a tool from a literary method out of their
toolbox, they are letting the reader know that they are focusing on literary concerns more than historical concerns. The
same is true when an interpreter decides to employ the historical approach—that interpreter typically is not trying to
avoid literary questions; rather, it is just not their focus in this
situation. Currently, biblical scholars are using the literary
approach to focus on the text, but increasingly they are not
shunning historical concerns and questions when appropriate for their interpretive goals.

There is one specific situation where the literary approach to the Bible
did arise and become predominant in biblical studies because of an issue in
biblical studies. As noted above, many confluences brought about the sea

---

13. For further discussion, see Douglas Estes, *The Temporal Mechanics of the Fourth Gospel:
A Theory of Hermeneutical Relativity in the Gospel of John* (Leiden: Brill, 2008), 25–27.

change in the Western world in the twentieth century. Romanticism was on the decline, and there was a greater call for more exacting strategies to read literature. With the advent of linguistics and intense interest in texts, the literary movement called Formalism took hold in the beginning of the twentieth century. The most notable group of Formalists was the Russian Formalists (1920s–1930s), who believed a text could be broken down into discrete structures and was interpretable as such. Formalism was soon followed by New Criticism (1940s–1960s), a literary movement starting in the southeastern US and affirming a very narrow, text-focused model of interpretation. After a few decades, structuralism (1960s–1970s) ascended to the top of the literary theory pile, followed soon after by poststructuralism (1980s–onward). During this latter time there was a rapid proliferation and acceptance of ideology-based literary theory. By the late 1970s, these developments began to slowly leach into the world of biblical studies. One reason for this was the failure of the modern historical-critical approach to reach the definitive answers it suggested was possible. In a way, the modernized historical approach had reached a dead end. Poignantly popularized—and its death knell signaled—by Albert Schweitzer in his book *The Quest of the Historical Jesus* (1906), the modern scientific approach to the Bible, the reigning emperor of interpretive method, was seen to have no clothes.[14]

This crisis in biblical studies, coupled with the rapid changes occurring in the outside world, propelled OT scholars to start exploring a postmodern, literary approach to the Bible (1970s). Soon becoming popular with NT scholars (1980s), the literary approach was partially something new and partially a way out of the artificial gridlock of the modernized historical approach. In some ways, this shift continued to open up Pandora's interpretive box, as at the beginning of the twenty-first century, modern literary theory encompasses a hodgepodge of complementary and competing theoretical methods, including deconstructionism, feminist theory, Bakhtinian criticism, poststructuralism, new historicism, queer theory, postcolonialism, narratology, Marxist theory, and reader-response theory,

---

14. Albert Schweitzer, *The Quest of the Historical Jesus*, trans. W. Montgomery (Mineola, NY: Dover, 2005).

among many more. These, on top of biblical interpreters who still prefer to use Romantic or (traditional) historical approaches, have dramatically increased the work of the beginning student of the Bible to understand the myriad methods now available for reading Scripture. Where once, perhaps, a person could read a commentary on a biblical book and only need to know a little about the religious background of the author to grasp the "where" of the commentary, today the student must be familiar with numerous theories to appreciate the "where" of the commentary, in order to best integrate the world of secondary *literature* on the Bible with the student's own growth and appreciation of sacred Scripture.

1.2 THE RELATIONSHIP OF AUTHOR, TEXT, READER, AND CONTEXT

As the tumultuous twentieth century was under way, literary theorists became more aware that the meaning of a text could come from more than one source, traditionally understood as "what the author meant." The first awareness of this came as a result of the Formalist focus on the text itself, apart from the author. This brought a clear distinction between those who interpreted literature through a reconstruction of the authorial intent and those who ignored everything except the text itself.[15] As a result, literary theory had created an author-focused approach to interpretation and a text-focused approach to interpretation. This bifurcation resulted in questions about the reader, and the subsequent development of a reader-focused approach. These three approaches represent the basic triad of reading: the creator of the text, the text, and the reader of the text. By the end of the twentieth century, some literary theorists believed there was more to reading than just these three; there was the context of the author/ text/reader that must be taken into consideration, and this resulted in the start of the context-focused approach to interpretation.

Klarer distinguishes these four types in this way:

> The *text-oriented* approach is primarily concerned with questions
> of the "materiality" of texts, including editions of manuscripts,

---

15. This awareness was also rising in the field of philosophy, where a renewed interest in hermeneutics and epistemology inaugurated a new search for meaning and truth.

analyses of language and style, and the formal structure of literary works. *Author-oriented* schools put the main emphasis on the author, trying to establish connections between the work of art and the biography of its creator. *Reader-oriented* approaches focus on the reception of texts by their audiences and the texts' general impact on the reading public. *Contextual* approaches try to place literary texts against the background of historical, social, or political developments while at the same time attempting to classify texts according to genres as well as historical periods.[16] [*emphasis added*]

While all four of these types fall within the umbrella of the literary approach, each type has different interests that do not always intersect. One way to understand each of these types is to ask, where does the interpreter look when employing these types? Chart 1 answers this question by detailing where each type looks for its interpretation:

TYPE OF APPROACH	WHERE IT LOOKS
Author-Focused	Behind the Text
Text-Focused	At the Text
Reader-Focused	In Front of the Text
Context-Focused	To the Side of the Text

FOCI OF LITERARY APPROACHES

Another way to understand these four approaches is to see what methods and critical tools line up under each approach. Chart 2 breaks these approaches down via method:

---

16. Klarer, *Introduction to Literary Studies*, 78.

TYPE OF APPROACH	KEY EXAMPLES OF METHODS
Author-Focused	Traditional Criticism(s), Biographical Criticism, Psychoanalytic Criticism, and Phenomenological Criticism
Text-Focused	Rhetoric, Narratology, Deconstruction, Semiotics, and New Criticism
Reader-Focused	Reader-Response Criticism and Reception History
Context-Focused	Literary History, Marxist Literary Theory, Feminist and Gender Studies, and Cultural Criticism

METHODS OF LITERARY APPROACHES

With the growing attention paid to the literary features of the Bible in the early twentieth century, the literary approach to the Bible began to reflect the interest of literary critics in the world at large. Biblical scholars began to draw new lines around their interpretations with these tools. We will look at each of these different literary foci in turn.

1.2.1 AUTHOR-FOCUSED APPROACHES

Author-focused approaches to interpretation stem from the traditional idea that the author is the final arbiter of meaning in the text. Prior to the twentieth century, the author-focused approach was the customary approach used by literary theorists. Or, put a little differently, prior to this point critics viewed the meaning of a text straightforwardly, as an extension of the author's original intent in writing the text.[17] Thus, when a biblical interpreter prior to the twentieth century read the Letter to the Romans, the interpreter would discuss what Paul wrote and what Paul meant.

Although this idea started to fall out of favor quickly as the twentieth century progressed, by midcentury the attacks on the author reached a fever pitch. As an example, philosopher Hans-Georg Gadamer extensively dismantled the idea that the thoughts of the author could be known by

---

17. The beginning of the twentieth century serves as a marking point for the first of many questions raised against this approach.

a reader.[18] Shortly afterward, Roland Barthes declared the death of the author. Barthes, speaking against the author-focused approach, argued that the creation of the text eliminates all of the thoughts that preceded it, as the act of "writing is the destruction of every voice, of every point of origin."[19] Against this perspective, literary theorist E. D. Hirsch Jr. wrote a defense of the author-focused approach in *Validity in Interpretation* (1967). In this work, Hirsch finds that to remove the author from consideration is "to reject the only compelling normative principle that [can] lend validity to an interpretation."[20] Even though Hirsch's work did not prove particularly popular in literary and philosophical circles, it did gain a larger following among some segments of biblical scholars.[21] There are several reasons for this, but at the beginning of the twenty-first century, biblical scholars (as a whole) seem to be more open to author-focused approaches than their literary counterparts. While the future viability of the author-focused approach is debatable among biblical scholars, it is still the most common approach among educated lay readers.

1.2.2 TEXT-FOCUSED APPROACHES

Text-focused approaches to the interpretation of literature consider the text, and only the text, when reading and interpreting. The idea for this approach really has at least two points of origin. First, the concerns over Romantic psychologizing of traditional literary criticism turned critics toward the text, especially through early twentieth-century movements such as Russian Formalism and New Criticism. Second, the importance of focusing on the text above all else (even in literary circles) is a fallout from the hermeneutical practices of reading Scripture after the Protestant Reformation. As Gadamer suggests, the text-focused approach was essentially the view of Martin Luther.[22] These kinds of comments led Hirsch, critical of the turn to the text without the author, to call it a "shift toward

---

18. Hans-Georg Gadamer, *Truth and Method*, trans. Joel Weinsheimer and Donald G. Marshall, 2nd rev. ed. (London: Continuum, 2004), 209–10.

19. Roland Barthes, *Image, Music, Text*, trans. Stephen Heath (New York: Hill and Wang, 1977), 142.

20. E. D. Hirsch Jr., *Validity in Interpretation* (New Haven, CT: Yale University Press, 1967), 5.

21. For example, Robert H. Stein, "The Benefits of an Author-Oriented Approach to Hermeneutics," *JETS* 44, no. 3 (2001): 451–66.

22. Gadamer, *Truth and Method*, 176.

exegesis," instead of the traditional practice of literary criticism.[23] Yet to biblical interpreters, the idea of reading the text with a focus on the text is widely accepted; where this differs from more traditional biblical interpretation is that it focuses on the text with little or no appeal to outside issues.[24] For example, if a biblical interpreter tries to read Romans with a text-focused approach, the interpreter will not (much) consider Paul or Paul's intent in writing, or try to guess what Paul may have meant by a word or idea.[25] To engage in such speculation would be to commit an *intentional fallacy* (in the eyes of proponents of text-focused approaches; see below).

The text-focused approach was very popular in literary criticism by the mid-century mark, and certain methodological offshoots still tend to be well used in literary circles. One attractive aspect of the text-focused approach is that it allows the interpreter the feeling of precision by engaging the text in a *close reading*, with a minimum amount of guessing about the author's intent or the reader's perspective. Within biblical studies, the text-focused approach proved to be highly popular. By far the most important text-focused method in biblical studies today—and maybe the most influential method of any approach in biblical studies today—is narrative criticism.[26] At the beginning of the twenty-first century, the text-focused approach remains extremely popular in Bible interpretation, with speculation of its impending death at the end of the twentieth century greatly exaggerated.

1.2.3 CONTEXT-FOCUSED APPROACHES

The newest approach to interpreting texts in the postmodern liter ary approach is the context-focused approach. Unlike the other three approaches, which arose out of centuries-old struggles over interpreting the text, the context-focused approach came about more as a new way

---

23. Hirsch does not object to increased interest in exegesis per se, just an increased focus on the text at the expense of the author (and recall that he is a literary critic, not a biblical scholar, for whom exegesis is not a typical approach); see Hirsch, *Validity in Interpretation*, 2.

24. Of course, this is not always the case in practice.

25. This is because the text-focused reader will not be able to ask Paul what he meant by his writing; the only thing the text-focused reader knows about Paul is what is contained in the text itself.

26. Narrative criticism is something of a biblical studies invention; users of this method base it almost completely on the literary theory narratology. These terms are not exactly synonymous, but biblical scholarship uses them almost interchangeably.

to read older texts. Also unlike the other three approaches, the context-focused approach is not easily systematized as a distinct approach, but is better understood as an umbrella term for a variety of related methods.[27] As a result, the methods that make up the context-focused approach are much more a loose group of divergent methods with similar strategies for interacting with the text—and these similar strategies are what unites the different methods in this approach.

To put it another way, context-focused methods are a "heterogeneous group of schools and methodologies which do not regard literary texts as self-contained, independent works of art but try to place them within a larger context."[28] Here the word *context* does not mean "background"; it means the parameters by which a text can produce meaning.[29] So when we speak of context-focused approaches, we are speaking still of the quest for the meaning of a text—but instead of the meaning coming from the intent of the author, the literal words themselves, or the reaction of the reader, context-focused approaches find meaning in the parameters placed on the text in its world-environment. As an example, two major methods within the context-focused approach is Marxist criticism and queer criticism.[30] The goals and interests of these theories are not the same, but they approach the text in a similar way. At the beginning of the twenty-first century, context-focused approaches are gaining in popularity within biblical studies. This is largely in part due to the changing, dynamic nature of the global world in which we live. In this world, truth is more fragmented, and different groups want to be able to understand a work of literature (such as the Bible) in relation to notable cultural and philosophical contexts. This fragmentation creates additional challenges for the biblical interpreter.

---

27. For example, see the opening thoughts in the special Context edition of the *Journal of Literary Theory* 8, no. 1 (2014).

28. Klarer, *Introduction to Literary Studies*, 94.

29. See also Nils Erik Enkvist, "Context," in *Literature and the New Interdisciplinarity: Poetics, Linguistics, History*, ed. Roger D. Sell and Peter Verdonk (Amsterdam: Rodopi, 1994), 47.

30. As a simple example, an interpreter using Marxist theory accomplishes this by taking the theories developed by Karl Marx and reading the Bible in light of, and often as a response to, those theories.

1.2.4 READER-FOCUSED APPROACHES

The abandonment of traditional, Romantic criticism in the early twentieth century, coupled with the intense interest in the text—and only the text—by midcentury, eventually led critics to express concern over the Lepidus, or the ignored third, of the literary triumvirate: the reader. Just as *the text* rose to prominence over *the author* by midcentury, *the reader* began to rise in prominence in some areas of literary theory toward the end of the century. As with the growth of the text-focused approach, it is also quite possible to locate a second point of origin for the reader-focused approach—that second point being within text-focused Formalist practice, in which attempts to understand the text led theorists to imagine the effects of the text on potential readers.[31] However, reader-focused methods were not willing to stay in the shadow of text-focused methods for long. By the mid- to late twentieth century, reader-focused approaches moved into the mainstream by way of several methods, most notably reader-response criticism. Instead of looking to the intent of the author or the words of the text itself, reader-focused approaches turn to the meaning received by the reader to the point where the goal became to make "the text disappear."[32] In fact, reader-focused approaches argue that during the process of reading and interpretation, it is not the author who speaks to the reader; it is not the text that speaks to the reader; it is the *reader* who speaks to the reader.[33]

By the late twentieth century, reader-oriented theorists and critics became prevalent in both literary and biblical interpretation circles. Reader-focused methods such as reader-response criticism are most concerned with answering three questions:

1. Do different reader responses create the same (or different) meanings from the text?

2. Is the number of valid meanings only limited by the number of valid readers?

---

31. Jane P. Tompkins, ed., *Reader-Response Criticism: From Formalism to Post-Structuralism* (Baltimore: Johns Hopkins University Press, 1980), x.

32. Stanley E. Fish, "Interpreting the 'Variorum,'" *Critical Inquiry* 2, no. 3 (1976): 468, 485.

33. Roland Barthes, *S/Z*, trans. Richard Miller (Oxford: Blackwell, 1990), 151. We see a glimpse of this whenever we observe someone "reading into" a text (at least from our perspective).

3. Is one interpretation more valid than another interpretation?[34]

In the area of biblical studies, reader-response criticism and other reader-focused approaches open up a whole new set of issues and concerns that do not occur in literary theory. The reason, of course, is that the meaning(s) applied to a biblical text tends to cause more debate than the meaning(s) applied to a literary text.[35] At the same time, the questions of meaning and the reader are extremely important for biblical scholars to address. This is also true because the question of meaning and text has been a part of Christian discourse for two millennia, and of Israelite discourse for at least a millennium before that. Biblical interpretation, more so than the interpretation of fictional literature, is vitally aware of the Wirkungsgeschichte that lies between the text and the current reader.[36] At the beginning of the twenty-first century, reader-focused approaches are not the most popular of the literary approaches, but they do continue to hold great value for future interpreters.

1.3 INFLUENTIAL CONCEPTS
FROM LITERARY STUDIES

From these approaches, there are a number of important and influential concepts from literary theory that biblical scholars have adapted as part of the literary approach to the Bible. Sometimes, when a word leaves literary theory and enters biblical studies, it takes on a different nuance. While not exhaustive, this list highlights some of the most important concepts that students may come across.

---

34. This list is adapted from Todd F. Davis and Kenneth Womack, *Formalist Criticism and Reader-Response Theory*, Transitions (New York: Palgrave, 2002), 51.

35. As a simple example, if two readers read one of Shakespeare's sonnets and, using reader-response criticism, come away with two (very) different meanings for the sonnet, there may only be some small discussion but no large-scale debates. This would not be the case if two readers read a biblical text and, using reader-response criticism, came away with two very different meanings, to say nothing of the fact that neither of these meanings could be privileged or favored and that both would be considered (to some degree) eisegetical interpretations.

36. Books often translate Wirkungsgeschichte as "reception history," meaning the history of how a text is received, but the word has different nuances in different situations. As it is a word coined by Gadamer, it is probably best understood as "history of influence"; for more details, see Mark Knight, "Wirkungsgeschichte, Reception History, Reception Theory," JSNT 33, no. 2 (2010): 137–46.

1.3.1 TEXT AND CANON

In recent decades, much discussion has occurred over the use of *canon* within literary studies. This idea originated in the field of biblical studies but became useful for literary theory. There are, in fact, at least three major definitions for the word "canon."[37] The first use is in the religious sense, meaning the canon is the "standard" or selection of texts that constitute the norm for Scripture. Thus the canon of Scripture is composed of the authoritative texts. The second way "canon" is used is to refer to a specific set of literary texts to distinguish those texts as normative or standardized. Thus literary theorists can speak of the "Shakespearean canon," and this refers to the main works of Shakespeare, while excluding spurious (that is, illegitimate) works. The third, and perhaps most widely used, definition of "canon" in literary theory is to signify the most important literary works of the Western world, as decided by unofficial consensus of critics due to age, pedigree, and privilege of the texts. Since the 1960s, coupled with the rise of poststructuralism and globalism, literary theorists and critics have heavily debated (and at times attacked) the merits of a literary canon. One concern is that a literary canon is subjective and unofficial, selected by an elite group of insiders (such as literary theorists in prestigious academic posts).[38] Another concern is that the concept of a canon, since there is no beginning and end, becomes a self-fulfilling circle, in which only those texts that fit theorists' methods for literary work are included—in other words, only texts that appear canonical can become canonical.[39] Therefore, if not careful, the literary canon becomes "a set of texts deemed suitable for reading and studying by students and academics, [that] is effectively a setting up of a virtual, idealized world of literature, excluding many of the texts produced in the real world, which break the rules."[40]

---

37. One of the leading beginner's resources for literary theory, Abram's and Harpham's *Glossary* gives a fuller explanation of all three major uses; see Abrams and Harpham, *A Glossary of Literary Terms*, 38–41.

38. These concerns with the literary canon have also bled over into recent attacks on the biblical canon, for very similar reasons.

39. Peter J. Rabinowitz, "Against Close Reading," in *Pedagogy is Politics: Literary Theory and Critical Teaching*, ed. Maria-Regina Kecht (Urbana: University of Illinois Press, 1992), 233.

40. David Birch, *Language, Literature and Critical Practice: Ways of Analysing a Text* (London: Routledge, 1989), 36.

One of the challenges for literary theory is the interpretive danger associated with the canonical cycle. The cycle works like this: A literary text is deemed canonical by "the consensus." Often, the texts awarded this status are not due to popularity, but more to their fit within the existing group. As a result, when literary critics turn to these texts—over and over again, because the canon is limited—a canonical reading emerges whereby the meaning and interpretation of a text becomes fixed.[41] The meaning also becomes unchangeable because it is reprinted over and over again in the books that introduce the canon.[42] As more books are added to the canon, or considered for the canon, these books (and their interpretation) are considered alongside of the canonical books (and their canonical interpretation). As a result, the meaning of a poem or story can become artificially fixed and limited, which damages the power and significance of literature as it was meant to be read. Students of the Bible can see the same thing happen in the interpretation of the Bible; it is possible for a "consensus" to emerge on the interpretation of a passage, to the point where even new evidence to the contrary is unable to effect an adjustment to the consensus. Therefore, students of the Bible must be able to differentiate the canon of Scripture (its meaning and importance) from the canonical formulations of texts and interpretations that recent literary theory has so clearly exposed.

1.3.2 CLOSE READING

It is quite common in biblical scholarship today to see the words "close reading" mentioned in passing, often used by interpreters to signify a more detailed and focused reading of a biblical text (without much consideration for the world around it).[43] However, close reading as it is most often used in biblical studies is an idea that was popularized with New Criticism, and it has several shades of meaning beyond the common use of the term. Simply defined, close reading is a method of reading that

---

41. Paul de Man, *The Rhetoric of Romanticism* (New York: Columbia University Press, 1984), 83–92.

42. See also Wolfgang Iser, *The Range of Interpretation* (New York: Columbia University Press, 2000), 17, 39.

43. See for example, Gianni Barbiero, *Song of Songs: A Close Reading* (Leiden: Brill, 2011); and Lyle Eslinger, *Kingship of God in Crisis: A Close Reading of 1 Samuel 1–12* (Sheffield: Almond, 1985). The phrase is also widely used in literary theory (see Rabinowitz, "Against Close Reading," 230).

focuses intently on the words on the page, especially in relation to the figures and meanings that the text itself creates, and it does not allow any information about the author or audience to affect the reading. It is a reading method that shuns the so-called *affective fallacy* (reading while being influenced emotionally by the text) and *intentional fallacy* (reading while being influenced by the author's context and intentions; see below) in interpreting the text.[44] Thus the text should become the one and only indicator of meaning for the reader.

Close reading as it is meant today started in the 1930s with the insights of literary critics William Empson and I. A. Richards, who questioned the prevailing tendency to read texts with an inattention to details.[45] F. R. Leavis and Cleanth Brooks followed shortly after and further popularized the idea. It is often tied closely to Formalism (of the New Critical variety) and is similar to the French literary concept of *explication de texte* ("explanation of text"). It also often dovetails well with the text-based aims of structuralism and narratology, and it is regularly used in poststructuralist interpretations (such as deconstruction). The great strength of close reading is its resolve "in catching the details and nuances of literary expression."[46] Since it focuses on the details, as if using a microscope, close reading is sometimes depicted as a more scientific approach to texts than the more traditional artistic readings from the eighteenth and nineteenth centuries.[47] Performing a close reading requires the reader to account for all of the details of the text—each word, phrase, and clause is considered in relation to the rest of the text, including other words, phrases, and clauses, but also characters, point of view, plot, style, and tone. A close reading is slow and laborious, so that the reader will have no detail unaccounted for. As a literary technique, close reading has several appealing features for biblical interpreters. First, it allows the reader to approach the text without solving all of the historical quandaries presented by the text. Second,

---

44. Klarer, *Introduction to Literary Studies*, 85–86.

45. William Empson, *Seven Types of Ambiguity* (London: Chatto and Windus, 1930); and I. A. Richards, *Practical Criticism: A Study of Literary Judgment* (London: Kegan Paul, Trench, Trubner, 1930).

46. Paul de Man, *Blindness and Insight: Essays in the Rhetoric of Contemporary Criticism*, 2nd ed. (Oxford: Oxford University Press, 1971), 27.

47. As a general example, see I. A. Richards' book *Science and Poetry* (1926).

it puts the focus on the text itself, rather than historical reconstructions. Third, it encourages the reader to look more closely at the text than they may otherwise look. One downside of close reading for biblical interpreters is the tendency to ignore historical details that can help shed greater light on the meaning of a text. Another is that the focus required renders it an unnatural approach to reading.[48] The future of close reading seems uncertain; likely, the general idea will remain useful while literary theory moves on to newer types of reading.[49] When approaching the text, interpreters need to remember that there are numerous reading strategies, each with their own strengths and weaknesses.[50]

1.3.3 READING FALLACIES

Literary critics maintain that there are a number of major *reading fallacies* that may disrupt or mislead the reader in trying to understand the text. Typically, the word "fallacy" means "an incorrect or erroneous belief," but the use of the word here should be taken with some leeway. Certain reading fallacies are only fallacies in the eyes of certain critics and theorists, and none of the reading fallacies is universally accepted. The two most important reading fallacies are the *intentional fallacy* and the *affective fallacy*. Many (but by no means all) literary critics view these situations as fallacies as they include mistaken beliefs that can cause a reading or interpretation to go off track. The acceptance of these fallacies is most closely associated with methods within the text-focused approach.

The *intentional fallacy* holds that readers who try to discern the intent of the author in composing the text will be misled in their interpretation of the text, since "the design or intention of the author is neither available nor desirable as a standard for judging the success of a work of literary

---

48. Rabinowitz, "Against Close Reading," 239.

49. For example, Dan Shen, "What Narratology and Stylistics Can Do For Each Other," in *A Companion to Narrative Theory*, ed. James Phelan and Peter J. Rabinowitz, Blackwell Companions to Literature and Culture 33 (Oxford: Blackwell, 2005), 147; and Michael Wood, "William Empson," in *The Cambridge History of Literary Criticism*, vol. 7, *Modernism and the New Criticism*, ed. A. Walton Litz, Louis Menand, and Lawrence Rainey (Cambridge: Cambridge University Press, 2000), 219.

50. Rabinowitz, "Against Close Reading," 232.

art."[51] "Intention" refers to the intent of the author of the work, both conscious (specific design) and unconscious (background interaction). It was first noted as such by William Wimsatt and Monroe Beardsley in 1946.[52] Prior to this, critics no less than T. S. Eliot and C. S. Lewis had noted the need to focus on the text itself first rather than any reconstructed information.[53] Wimsatt and Beardsley highlighted the intentional fallacy to combat Romantic reading tendencies. The fallacy forces a reader to struggle with the text instead of treating the author as an all-knowing "oracle" who can solve any textual problem.[54] One result of the influence of the intentional fallacy is the creation of the idea of the *implied author*, in the sense of the remnants of the real author that are still discernible from the pages of the text.[55]

The *affective fallacy*, also noted by Wimsatt and Beardsley, states that readers misinterpret a text if they evaluate the text by the way the text affects them (especially emotionally).[56] It "is a confusion between the poem and its *results* ... by trying to derive the standard of criticism from the psychological effects of the poem and ends in impressionism and relativism."[57] The danger of the affective fallacy is that a critic may replace the intended cultural or emotional perspective inherent in the text with their own emotional perspective, which may mislead future readers of the text.[58] As with the intentional fallacy, Wimsatt and Beardsley aim to turn the interpreter away from subjective readings and toward objective criticism. By the 1970s, the growing popularity of reader-focused approaches caused sympathetic literary critics to heavily criticize the affective fallacy.

---

51. W. K. Wimsatt, *The Verbal Icon: Studies in the Meaning of Poetry* (Lexington: University of Kentucky Press, 1982), 3. Readers may understand that in literary works the author is not "available," but may find it strange that the author's view is also not "desirable." This is a complicated issue, but in the case of literary works, the author's perspective may end up different from what can be discovered in the text itself. This can be true with biblical works, but discussion of this introduces a number of hypothetical philosophical and theological elements related to inspiration.

52. Wimsatt, *Verbal Icon*, 3–18.

53. Peter Lamarque, "The Intentional Fallacy," in *Literary Theory and Criticism: An Oxford Guide*, ed. Patricia Waugh (Oxford: Oxford University Press, 2006), 177.

54. Wimsatt, *Verbal Icon*, 18.

55. David Herman, *Basic Elements of Narrative* (Oxford: Wiley-Blackwell, 2009), 69.

56. Wimsatt, *Verbal Icon*, 21–39.

57. Wimsatt, *Verbal Icon*, 21.

58. Wimsatt, *Verbal Icon*, 39.

The intentional fallacy and the affective fallacy received a great deal of attention when first recognized and quickly became a standard rule in literary criticism.[59] However, as with much late twentieth-century criticism, literary critics soon assailed these fallacies to the point where their acceptance is on the wane in some circles. More significantly, recent work by critics in author-focused, reader-focused, and context-focused methods sometimes overtly reject these fallacies as being too narrow.

1.3.4 TEXT AS OBJECT

The origin of the *text as object* idea predates its modern usage as it is found in Aristotle's *Poetics*. In his work, Aristotle likens a text (in this case, a tragedy) to an object that is complete and self-contained, and that has a determinable size and structure.[60] He also points out that the size and shape of the tragic object should not be either too large/complex or too small/simple. Taking this a step further, starting with the Russian Formalists, the text moved away from being perceived by literary critics as a Romanticized dynamic splendor of art and was increasingly viewed as a fixed, static object composed of identifiable structures and devices.[61] Thus the *text as object* concept refers to the idea that the text is a closed system of identifiable components. Famous anthropologist Claude Lévi-Strauss once famously described this as "an object endowed with precise properties, that must be analytically isolated, and this work can be entirely defined on the grounds of such properties ... it is as an object which, once created, had the stiffness—so to speak—of a crystal."[62] From Lévi-Strauss' description, a literary text can be simply taken by the interpreter as the sum of its parts. Scholars from outside the text-focused field have criticized this perspective.[63] With the demise of structuralism, even critics favoring the

---

59. For example, Peter Swirski believes Wimsatt and Beardsley's essay on the intentional fallacy to be one of the two "most influential textualist manifestos" in literary criticism; Peter Swirski, *Literature, Analytically Speaking: Explorations in the Theory of Interpretation, Analytic Aesthetics, and Evolution* (Austin: University of Texas Press, 2010), 46.

60. Aristotle, *Poetics*, 7.

61. Terry Eagleton, *The Event of Literature* (New Haven, CT: Yale University Press, 2012), 189.

62. Claude Lévi-Strauss, from an interview, as quoted in Umberto Eco, *The Role of the Reader: Explorations in the Semiotics of Texts* (Bloomington: Indiana University Press, 1979), 3-4.

63. An example of a criticism is that a text does not have meaning until the reader infuses the text with meaning through the reading process; see, Eco, *Role of the Reader*, 5.

text-focused approach have not continued with some of the idea's reductionist tendencies.

1.3.5 THE ROLE OF THE READER

Greater scrutiny toward the role of the text also resulted in a greater scrutiny toward the *role of the reader*. In approaching most texts, the text is obvious and the author is identifiable, but the reader's role is much less clear cut. Are all readers the same? Are readers passive or active in the interpretation of a text? Clearly, the reader is as vitally important to interpretation as the author and the text.[64] However, the role of the reader goes far beyond just reading. When a text is created, there is not just an author (creator), and the text (creation), but also a reader (createe) conceived—the author is aware of the reader who will read.[65] Furthermore, when a reader goes to read the text, the open and dynamic nature of texts allows the reader to create meaning from the text. As Roland Barthes explains, "The goal of literary work (of literature as work) is to make the reader no longer a consumer, but a producer of the text."[66] What the reader produces is the *text*—what is meant by what the text means. Theorists often describe this shorthandedly by saying that the role of the reader is to determine the meaning of the text, and that what the text means does not come from the author or the text itself. At first glance, this may seem problematic: Won't different readers come up with different meanings? However, when a critic evaluates a text, the information from the author and from the text can also be different and used differently by different readers—thus the role of the reader is to clarify what the text means from the myriad possible meanings (something the author and the text itself cannot do).[67]

1.3.6 INDETERMINACY OF MEANING

Experience teaches that two different people can read the exact same text and come away with two very different, even incompatible, meanings.[68]

---

64. Peter Brooks, *Reading for the Plot: Design and Intention in Narrative* (Cambridge, MA: Harvard University Press, 1992), 14.

65. Eco, *Role of the Reader*, 3.

66. Barthes, *S/Z*, 4.

67. Fish, "Interpreting the 'Variorum,'" 468.

68. See also W. V. Quine, *Word and Object* (Cambridge, MA: MIT Press, 1960), 27.

How is that possible from the same text? Is one reader just wrong? Or could both be right? As we read texts, our eyes see the printed words on the page first—but those printed words are not the same thing as meaning. They are just printed words. Somewhere between the printed words on the page and our brains, our minds generate meaning during the reading process. Just because we can see the words on the page does not entail that we know what those words mean (for example, think of an ancient text written in an unknown language; we can see the words but we cannot tell anyone what it means). These questions over meaning play an important role in twentieth-century philosophy. As a key example, philosopher W. V. Quine argues in his *Word and Object* that it is entirely possible to translate a text in two different ways, each compatible with the text, but not compatible with each other. One possible result of this argument is the question of whether a text can even *have* meaning, and whether text statements can ever be declared true or false with certainty.[69] These discussions over meaning have involved many famous thinkers of the twentieth century, from W. V. Quine to Ferdinand de Saussure to Martin Heidegger.

Within literary theory, these philosophical discussions have affected the methods for literary interpretation by recognizing the *indeterminacy of meaning* that comes as a byproduct of the reading process.[70] In fact, reading meaningful texts (literature) draws the greatest contrast between the text and the question (and problem) of meaning.[71] In *Seven Types of Ambiguity*, William Empson raises a number of questions about how uncertainty in the text can create more than one valid interpretation.[72] This type of discussion on ambiguity was a precursor to the

---

69. For more details of this argument, see Gabriel Segal, "Four Arguments for the Indeterminacy of Translation," in *Knowledge, Language and Logic: Questions for Quine*, ed. Alex Orenstein and Petr Kotatko (Dordrecht: Springer, 2000), 131–39.

70. Wolfgang Iser, *Prospecting: From Reader Response to Literary Anthropology* (Baltimore: Johns Hopkins University Press, 1989), 7.

71. Jonathan Culler, *The Pursuit of Signs: Semiotics, Literature, Deconstruction* (London: Routledge, 2001), 39.

72. William Empson, *Seven Types of Ambiguity* (London: Chatto and Windus, 1930). There is some debate as to the relationship between ambiguity and indeterminacy; while these ideas are not synonymous, there can be a high degree of overlap. For more information, see Gerald Graff, "Determinacy/Indeterminacy," in *Critical Terms for Literary Study*, ed. Frank Lentricchia and Thomas McLaughlin, 2nd ed. (Chicago: University of Chicago Press, 1995), 165.

way poststructuralists, especially deconstructionists, would utilize the indeterminacy of meaning within texts to undermine conventional or assumed interpretations. Therefore, when literary theorists speak of *indeterminacy of meaning*, they do not mean a situation where a text is confusing, unclear, or hard to understand with precision; instead, they mean a situation where they recognize that, as there is no absolute or exact meaning, a text may have variant meanings that are valid yet incompatible, and that there is no simple way to determine a "correct" meaning. With biblical interpretation, it is tempting to suggest that the meaning of any given text is "what the author meant," or "what the text literally says," but neither of these two arguments is very successful against the challenge of indeterminacy of meaning. However, this should not prevent the interpreter from making a sustained argument for a "better" or even "best" interpretation, even when they encounter situations where two or more valid interpretations are at play.[73]

1.3.7 MODEL FOR NARRATIVE COMMUNICATION

Among texts, a *narrative* is a specific type of text that is defined by its telling of a sequence of events.[74] The meaning of narrative is similar to the way we use the word *story* in English. Since a narrative tells a sequence of events, novels are narrative, but many poems are not. Therefore, not all examples of literature are narrative. Because narrative tells a story, it is communicating events to the reader. As interest in narrative grew in the mid-twentieth century, literary theorists began to realize there are different levels of narrative communication. In essence there are three levels, with a teller and a receiver on both ends: *real author, real reader; implied author, implied reader;* and *narrator, narratee.* The model for narrative communication can be depicted as:

---

73. An elementary example of this comes in a number of Jesus' parables, such as the parable of the Prodigal Son. It is "valid" to argue that the younger son is the prodigal son, but is it the best interpretation of that parable? When I teach biblical interpretation, students naturally gravitate to picking the prodigal that most resembles their own perspective—not to mention that both of the sons are, in a sense, prodigals.

74. Gerald Prince, "Narrative Analysis and Narratology," *New Literary History* 13, no. 2 (1982): 179; Shlomith Rimmon-Kenan, *Narrative Fiction: Contemporary Poetics* (London: Routledge, 1994), 2; and Estes, *Temporal Mechanics*, 6–10.

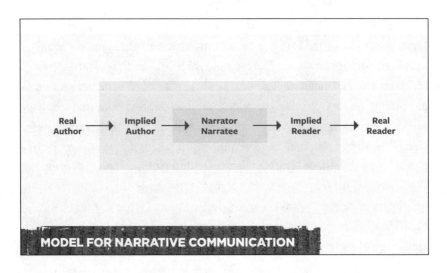

MODEL FOR NARRATIVE COMMUNICATION

This chart shows there is a teller (the *real author*) and a receiver (the *real reader*) outside the text.[75] Participants outside the text are exempted from consideration when using a method such as narratology within the text-focused approach. Text-focused approaches limit the brunt of their interpretation to what is within the text (and its participants, such as implied author, implied reader, narrator, and narratee).

1.3.8 INTERTEXTUALITY

With an increased interest in the texts themselves came an interest in how these texts related to other texts. In traditional, author-focused approaches to literary criticism, critics would attempt to understand and reconstruct the life and influences of the author in order to identify the outside influences that affected the text. An obvious example of this is when an author directly quotes, or makes a clear allusion to, another text or world event. With text-focused approaches that do not much consider the role of the author, there arose a need to examine the way texts relate to one another. Thus the complex relationship between a text and other texts was first identified as *intertextuality* by Julia Kristeva in 1967. Intertextuality takes place when, "in the space of a given text, several utterances, taken from

---

75. This chart is an adaption of the one first created and popularized by Seymour Chatman; see Seymour Chatman, *Story and Discourse: Narrative Structure in Fiction and Film* (Ithaca, NY: Cornell University Press, 1978), 151.

other texts, intersect and neutralize one another."[76] This should not surprise us, given that the word *text* originates from the idea of something woven together.[77] One result of the interest in intertextuality is the keen awareness that all texts are in some way interrelated. For biblical interpretation, intertextuality raises a number of questions, not just common questions such as how the NT uses the OT, but harder questions such as how the Bible uses echoes of noncanonical texts and in what way cultural "texts" feed into the biblical text.[78]

1.3.9 PLURALITY OF MEANING

Building on the idea of a text as an art form woven from many strands, a text's composite nature suggests that a text will possess a *plurality of meaning*. In making this claim, what this idea does *not* mean is that every text has several possible meanings.[79] Rather, the plurality of meaning that exists in a text exists in its most fundamental nature—it must have a plurality of meaning by its composite nature, and any attempt to see a singularity of meaning is really an interpretive illusion. Thus a critic cannot speak of a structure to a text, since a text's

> networks are many and interact, without any one of them being able to surpass the rest ... [a] text is a galaxy ... it has no beginning; it is reversible; we gain access to it by several entrances, none of which can be authoritatively declared to be the main one ... [its meanings] extend *as far as the eye can reach*.[80]

This plurality is not always obvious to the reader, as its intersection occurs in the subtle and uncertain process of reading a text for meaning.[81] In some ways this description is an ideal; many texts (such as nonfiction)

---

76. Julia Kristeva, *Desire in Language: A Semiotic Approach to Literature and Art*, ed. Leon Roudiez, trans. Thomas Gora, Alice Jardine, and Leon Roudiez (New York: Columbia University Press, 1980), 36.

77. Barthes, *Image, Music, Text*, 159.

78. For an example of intertextuality in the Bible, see Richard B. Hays, *Echoes of Scripture in the Letters of Paul* (New Haven, CT: Yale University Press, 1989).

79. Though this could be otherwise true; see Barthes, *Image, Music, Text*, 159.

80. Barthes, *S/Z*, 5–6.

81. Pierre Macherey, *A Theory of Literary Production*, trans. Geoffrey Wall (London: Routledge & Kegan Paul, 1978), 26.

subvert this by remaining closed to the reader, in order to encourage only one meaning or reading.[82] At the same time, the fundamental nature of a text as a plurality is what makes the text come alive for the reader—it is what makes it interesting, discussable, and dialogical.[83]

1.3.10 DECONSTRUCTION

In the 1970s, a new literary theory called *deconstruction* began to sweep Western culture as a result of the work of French philosopher Jacques Derrida. When we use the term "deconstruction," there is the popular meaning and the critical theory meaning.[84] The popular meaning—a caricature of the real meaning—refers to the act of taking apart something common and putting it back together again in a different (new, subversive) way (or tearing it apart completely). In contrast, the critical theory meaning is much more complex, in that it involves the questioning of norms accepted by Western metaphysics. It is less an answer than a means to an end. Even more so, the challenge is how to describe philosophical and literary deconstruction in a nutshell, in a short summary, as the whole purpose of deconstruction is to take apart short, easy summaries:

> The very meaning and mission of deconstruction is to show that things—texts, institutions, traditions, societies, beliefs, and practices of whatever size and sort you need—do not have definable meanings and determinable missions, that they are always more than any mission would impose, that they exceed the boundaries they currently occupy ... Whenever it runs up against a limit, deconstruction presses against it. Whenever deconstruction finds a nutshell—a secure axiom or a pithy maxim—the very idea is to crack it open and disturb this tranquility. Indeed, that is a good rule of thumb in deconstruction. *That* is what deconstruction is all about,

---

82. Raman Selden, Peter Widdowson, and Peter Brooker, *A Reader's Guide to Contemporary Literary Theory*, 5th ed. (Harlow, UK: Pearson, 2005), 151.

83. Steven Cohan and Linda M. Shires, *Telling Stories: A Theoretical Analysis of Narrative Fiction* (London: Routledge, 1988), 37.

84. David Mikics, *A New Handbook of Literary Terms* (New Haven, CT: Yale University Press, 2007), 80.

its very meaning and mission, if it has any. One might even say that cracking nutshells is what deconstruction is. In a nutshell.[85]

Thus, for the purposes of biblical interpretation, one of the roles of deconstructive interpretation is to undermine accepted interpretations that are felt to be determined (by history, consensus, group, or other).[86]

1.4 CONTRIBUTIONS OF THE LITERARY APPROACH

As biblical studies made the turn toward a literary approach in the late 1970s and early 1980s, early assessments predicted that the literary approach would be at best a small subsection within biblical studies or at worst a passing fad. What happened next was unexpected, as subsequent generations of biblical scholars began to embrace various methods within the literary approach. Early and influential books such as Kermode's *The Genesis of Secrecy* (1979), Alter's *The Art of Biblical Narrative* (1981), Frye's *The Great Code* (1982), Rhoads and Michie's *Mark as Story* (1982), and Culpepper's *The Anatomy of the Fourth Gospel* (1983) helped propel text-focused methods to the forefront of scholarly critical methods. This was followed soon after by more and more varieties of poststructuralist applications to biblical interpretation.

When a student engages the Bible through the postmodern literary approach, the student is cutting across two related traditions. First, the student is returning—albeit in a very twenty-first-century way—to more ancient concerns. Rather than using an empirical model for historical discovery that was so frequently applied to the Bible in the modern period, the literary approach to the Bible allows for a return-to-the-text approach that is quite supportive of rhetoric, aesthetics, and theology. The concerns of the earliest interpreters of Scripture seem in some ways more attuned to a postmodern literary approach than modern historical reductionism.[87]

---

85. John D. Caputo, ed., *Deconstruction in a Nutshell: A Conversation with Jacques Derrida* (New York: Fordham University Press, 1997), 31–32.

86. For examples of deconstruction in biblical studies, see Yvonne Sherwood, "Jacques Derrida and Biblical Studies," *SBL Forum*, http://sbl-site.org/Article.aspx?ArticleID=332.

87. Of course, some methods within the literary approach seem unrelated (and perhaps, incompatible) with ancient interpretive customs. A student may ask: "What has Marxist theory to do with Alexandrian exegesis?" In a sense, perhaps nothing. The contrast drawn,

Second, the student uses literary-critical tools that, while at first glance may seem to be unrelated to Scripture, are in some ways in the process of "returning home." The reason for this lies in the origin of literary criticism itself in the West. While there has always been interest in plumbing the depths of good and powerful writing, most attempts at interpreting a text in Western culture started in the Judeo-Christian tradition of biblical exegesis.[88] This is especially true with the turn from Romanticism; one of the first essays in Russian Formalism was Viktor Shklovsky's "The Resurrection of the Word," on the power of metaphorical meaning in words.[89] For students of the Bible, talk of "focusing on the text" and "reading closely" and "the response of the reader" are, generally speaking, more acceptable than not. It is something that is intensely relatable to the long-standing practice of biblical exegesis. Thus postmodern literary theory in some ways represents a (re)turn toward the *inspiration* of texts (in the nonreligious sense of the word).

As the literary approach to the Bible continues to grow and develop, two major contributions stand out so far. First, this approach renewed interest in the text itself within biblical scholarship. Instead of trying to look behind the text, scholars have turned to several influential methods within the literary approach and with those tools brought a new range of insights to the biblical text. This allows twenty-first-century students to engage the text without the (at times, artificial) history-narrative wedge created in the modern period up to the end of the twentieth century. Second, this approach has introduced a number of new strategies and methods that will make biblical interpretation more robust than ever. For example, the literary approach encourages the biblical interpreter to take the reader seriously, as well as to better understand the contextual impacts on reading Scripture in general. The Bible comes alive with its impact on audiences

---

however, is *not* between one *method* in the postmodern literary approach and one *method* in the modern historical or ancient approach, but rather between the postmodern literary approach (as a whole; its interest and values) and the modern historical and ancient approaches. Within each approach, there will always be useful and less useful tools (methods)—more important is the nature of the approach itself.

88. Wolfgang Iser, *The Range of Interpretation* (New York: Columbia University Press, 2000), 13; and also Gadamer, *Truth and Method*, 178.

89. Viktor Shklovsky, "The Resurrection of the Word," in *Russian Formalism: A Collection of Articles and Texts in Translation*, ed. Stephen Bann and John E. Bowlt (New York: Barnes & Noble, 1973), 41–47.

and situations, not just its original historical context, and this liveliness is now/once again a legitimate means of exploration within critical, biblical scholarship.

1.5 LIMITATIONS OF THE LITERARY APPROACH

While the literary approach is a promising development in biblical interpretation, there are several limitations that affect its usefulness as an interpretive approach. These limitations are exactly that; they are not flaws in the approach per se, but are factors that interpreters have to consider when using this approach. Every approach, whether historical, literary, or traditional, will have limitations.

The first major limitation of the literary approach is that it is a very *fragmented* approach. As there is no one, overarching method in the literary approach, or even agreement on what type of questions need to be asked or aspects of the texts need to be studied, there is not really any way to summarize the literary approach in a meaningful way (except by its history of development, which is what most theorists seem to do in literary introductions). Rather than having a few options, recent books that interpret the Bible may draw from a number of literary methods, many of which don't appear compatible. Even in reading this volume, Bible interpreters may be left to ask, "How can deconstruction and rhetoric work together? Are they compatible at all?"

The second major limitation is that the literary approach is far more *complex* than interpreters often assume. There is a temptation to think that literary features, and literary issues, are a little easier to tackle than historical issues—after all, historical issues require data on the past, whereas literary issues only require some creative thinking. This is not entirely the case. On the one hand, the literary theories and the philosophies that undergird them are often highly nuanced, built on centuries worth of philosophical reflection. The theories and philosophies generally require a great deal of time to understand and master. On the other hand, some of the methods in the literary approach (such as rhetorical criticism) require as much historical data as does any historical method. Therefore, in order to interpret the Bible through a literary approach, an interpreter must be prepared to spend as much time as with any of the other approaches.

The third major limitation is that the literary approach can some-times privilege *ideology* over objective interpretation. With a traditional historical-critical perspective, the text was said to be read from a detached, neutral perspective, with the goal of rendering the most precise interpre-tation possible. However, one of the catalysts for the literary turn was the realization that ideology often did creep in to so-called objective inter-pretations. The resulting shift was from a belief that an interpreter could avoid ideology (be truly neutral), to a recognition that an interpreter is always influenced by ideology, to (in some cases) a celebration of insert-ing ideology into the interpretation. While privileging ideology may have some benefit in reading literary texts, privileging ideology is much more problematic in biblical interpretation. It is easy to see how the pendulum can swing too far.

The fourth major limitation is that the literary approach is sometimes used as a *dodge* from important historical questions. At the end of the twentieth century, the breakup of the hegemony of the historical-critical method in biblical studies created an environment where biblical scholars could neatly ignore historical concerns if so desired. When this happens, it is unfortunate—a literary approach to the Bible may be ahistorical, but it should not be anti-historical. What this does *not* mean is that an effec-tive literary study of the Bible has to address historical issues. There will be times and places where the literary interpretation of the Bible does not interact with historical issues. What this does mean is that we should never use the literary interpretation so as to avoid hard historical issues. (We should never use the historical-critical method to avoid literary issues, either.) The aims of the student should be to address each text in the way that seems best in light of their interpretive goals.

1.6 RESOURCES FOR FURTHER STUDY

Agamben, Giorgio. *The Time That Remains: A Commentary on the Letter to the Romans.* Meridian: Crossing Aesthetics. Stanford, CA: Stanford University Press, 2005.

CONTEXT-FOCUSED APPROACHES: Given the enormous methodological diversity within context-focused approaches, there is perhaps not one work that is representative of all.

With that in mind, Giorgio Agamben's *The Time That Remains* reexamines Paul's letter to the Romans in light of a variant context. Other key thinkers who have affected context-focused approaches include Michel Foucault and Georg Lukács.

Aristotle. *Poetics*. Translated by Stephan Halliwell. Cambridge, MA: Harvard University Press, 1999.

ANCIENT: Though an ancient text, one of the most important works for understanding both ancient and postmodern literary theory is the *Poetics* of Aristotle. In this work, Aristotle sets the foundation for what a literary text is and how it can be apprehended and approached. In some ways, Aristotle foresaw many of the literary movements of the twentieth century. Other ancient thinkers who affect modern discussions include Dionysius of Halicarnassus and the various extant *progymnasmata* (rhetorical handbooks).

Eagleton, Terry. *Literary Theory: An Introduction*. Anniversary ed. Minneapolis: University of Minnesota Press, 2008.

INTRODUCTIONS: While introductions to literary theory abound, one of the most important of these overviews is Terry Eagleton's *Literary Theory: An Introduction*. Now in its third edition, this work introduces the reader to the idea of literature and moves through the various shifts in literary theory from the end of Romanticism to recent postmodern developments. Other important introductions to literary theory include those written by Raman Selden, M. A. R. Habib, and Mario Klarer.

Fish, Stanley. *Is There a Text in This Class? The Authority of Interpretive Communities*. Cambridge, MA: Harvard University Press, 1980.

READER-FOCUSED APPROACHES: One of the most important thinkers within the reader-focused approach is Stanley Fish. Fish's *Is There a Text in This Class?* develops the idea of interpretive communities (a group of like-minded readers) to explain what a text means. The community of readers fall between an unyielding text and a completely subjective reader. Other influential reader-focused theorists include Roland Barthes, Umberto Eco, and Wolfgang Iser.

Genette, Gérard. *Narrative Discourse: An Essay in Method*. Translated by Jane E. Lewin. Oxford: Basil Blackwell, 1980.

———. *Narrative Discourse Revisited*. Translated by Jane E. Lewin. Ithaca, NY: Cornell University Press, 1988.

TEXT-FOCUSED APPROACHES: Gérard Genette's two-volume discussion of the makeup of the narrative form is one of the most influential text-focused literary works written in the late twentieth century, coming at the end of structuralism and the beginning of poststructuralism. While Genette's method will seem a little dated to new students, its methodical role in the literary turn in biblical studies is unequaled among postmodern literary critics. Other critics with a similarly influential role include Mieke Bal, Gerald Prince, and Seymour Chatman.

Hirsch, E. D., Jr. *Validity in Interpretation*. New Haven, CT: Yale University Press, 1967.

AUTHOR-FOCUSED APPROACHES: Literary theorists of the twentieth century produced far fewer works subscribing to an author-focused approach, compared to the other three approaches. Perhaps the best known author-focused study is E. D. Hirsch Jr.'s *Validity in Interpretation*, a book that defends the idea that the meaning of a text must be determined by the intent of the author.

Kermode, Frank. *The Genesis of Secrecy: On the Interpretation of Narrative*. Cambridge, MA: Harvard University Press, 1979.

BIBLE AS LITERATURE: Frank Kermode, a famed literary critic, was one of a handful of critics from the literary world who helped launch the postmodern literary approach. Kermode became one of the major articulators of the Bible as literature approach to biblical interpretation. Other literary critics turned biblical interpreters with similar influence to Kermode include Robert Alter and Northrop Frye.

Propp, Vladimir. *Morphology of the Folktale.* Translated by Laurence Scott. Edited by Louis A. Wagner. 2nd ed. Austin: University of Texas Press, 1968.

EARLY TWENTIETH CENTURY: Of the early twentieth-century works that made great waves in later works, Vladimir Propp's *Morphology of the Folktale* (1928) is one of the most important. In this short book, Propp analyzes the structure of Russian folktales and discovers that many of the folktales contain similar narrative devices. Propp's work is groundbreaking in several ways, including his work in reading stories closely and precisely, plot movement, and characterization. Other influential theorists who broke new ground in the early twentieth century include John Crowe Ransom, Roman Jakobson, and Tzvetan Todorov.

2

CANONICAL CRITICISM

Ron Haydon and David Schreiner

C ritical study of the biblical texts includes a fair number of tools like textual criticism, historical criticism, and the variety of approaches within literary criticism. Still, the practice of *canonical* criticism tends to be marginalized within the scholarly guild, with many interpreters questioning its place within criticism altogether. Yet a canonical approach involves important, big-picture questions about the reception of biblical books in religious communities and about the impact the overall shape of the book and its place within a collection has on interpretation: Is it possible to read the books of Genesis or Revelation in any other location in the canon than their own? Could any reader interpret the Book of the Twelve (the Minor Prophets) without acknowledging its natural unity? How might one analyze the Torah apart from its five-part sequence? The importance of these questions—and the need to try to answer them—is one of the fruits that can be borne by canonical criticism. Canonical criticism takes these questions in a deeper, more intentional direction, but the baseline remains the same.[1]

---

1. Because there are various models of canonical interpretation promoted by a number of key scholars, we will take care to describe each scholar's unique contribution to canonical methodology rather than attempt a synthesis of canonical criticism as a whole. Since there are several important, but competing, methods within canonical criticism, we will mention all prominent models, as each one can speak meaningfully into the role of canon for interpretation, and their relationship to historical criticism.

This chapter covers various dimensions of canonical criticism, including major figures, tenets, and their reception throughout contemporary biblical interpretation. As with most forms of critical study, canonical methods branch out into many sub-disciplines. The majority of these iterations end in the same place—canonical criticism and its subsequent forms function as an interpretive tool and are as much theological approaches as they are literary approaches.

2.1 DEFINITION AND GOAL OF CANONICAL CRITICISM

Any reader of canonical interpretation studies will quickly find a series of terms common to this method. With reference to the Bible, the term *canon* refers to a closed list of sacred and authoritative books recognized as Scripture.[2] Likewise, *canonization* identifies the act of setting a biblical book within this final list so as to recognize its long-term authority for a specific faith community. However, canonical criticism and related canonical methods expand these definitions: *canon* becomes a framework for interpretation by future generations of believers, or simply another category for "Scripture." *Canonization*, therefore, can include the shaping, editing, and arranging of a biblical book to fit the finalized text into a collection of sacred writings. It is precisely within these shifts in scholarly understanding of canon and canonization that we encounter contemporary canonical methods.

2.1.1 VARIOUS CANONICAL METHODS

The various canonical methods all arose amid a sea change in the critical study of the Bible. Historical criticism in its modern form was waning while renewed interest in both the text and the reader was rising. Stephen Dempster notes that "the entire interpretive enterprise was being reconsidered."[3] During this change, scholars and interpreters began to see the

---

2. This is an augmented version of Timothy Stone's definition of canon: "Canon is a fixed list of scrolls (books) received and recognized as holy by a faith community" (*The Compilational History of the Megilloth* [Tübingen: Mohr Siebeck, 2013], 10–11).

3. Stephen G. Dempster, "The Canon and Theological Interpretation," in *A Manifesto for Theological Interpretation*, ed. Craig G. Bartholomew and Heath A. Thomas (Grand Rapids: Baker, 2016), 132–33.

canon as more than an ancient artifact or "literary deposit."[4] The canon was no longer regarded merely as one of "the victors in internecine theological struggles" or as a product of merely political moves. These canonical approaches constitute a "master narrative" that looks to the merits of the faith community to guide the interpretation of Scripture (to varying degrees).

2.1.1.a Sanders's Canonical Criticism

"Canonical criticism" as a technical term comes from James Sanders's 1972 work, *Torah and Canon*, where Sanders used the label to describe his method.[5] In the book, Sanders lays out a critical method that includes a brief history of the biblical canon's compilation, Israel's sociocultural context, and OT historical criticism—all brought together into a form of theological application for contemporary readers. Sanders's method illuminates "the clear identification of theological diversity within Scripture" and makes room for source, redaction, and tradition criticism.[6] Most notably, Sanders regards the canon, as well as its internal canonical processes, as an interchange between "stabilization" and "adaptability."[7] *Stabilization*, in this context, occurs when a scribal community agrees to delimit a text of Scripture, thereby considering that text a crystallized unit within the developing canon. The second category, *adaptability*, represents the pluralism of theological traditions and historical contexts (e.g., the exodus, the exile, the return). For example, the event of the exodus becomes a stream of theological emphases moving throughout the various texts of the OT canon (e.g., Isa 11:11–15). As these two dynamics begin to funnel into their ultimate shape, the reader is able to trace the movement and observe that presentation critically.

---

4. Dempster, "Canon," 132–33.

5. James Sanders, *Torah and Canon* (Philadelphia: Fortress, 1972), i–v.

6. Anthony C. Thiselton, "Introduction: Canon, Community and Theological Construction," in *Canon and Biblical Interpretation*, ed. Craig G. Bartholomew et al. (Grand Rapids: Zondervan, 2006), 4. For Christopher Seitz, canon criticism was a project that "took the form of hermeneutical suggestions, based upon text-critical and tradition-historical instincts" (*The Character of Christian Scripture: The Significance of a Two-Testament Bible* [Grand Rapids: Baker Academic, 2011], 28–29).

7. James A. Sanders, *From Sacred Story to Sacred Text: Canon as Paradigm* (Eugene, OR: Wipf & Stock, 1987), 11.

Sanders indeed claims readers ought to reflect upon the history of development within Israel's traditions, particularly through a canonical lens, but he also asserts that one must place the Bible "where it belongs in the believing community of today."[8] Given how he prioritizes Israel's own sacred testimony, Sanders's theology of canon appears as a phenomenology of religion (a study focused on religious experience). Although Israel, Yahweh's people, experiences its own development of theological traditions, it is through living them out in community that a theological bond is formed. All biblical communities—those that claim the witness of a Scriptural canon as authoritative—share in a mutual "search for identity in times of crisis."[9]

2.1.1.b Childs's Canonical Approach

Any introduction of canonical criticism must also include Brevard Childs. While Childs eschews the label canonical criticism, he does propose what he calls a canonical approach.[10] Childs summarizes his position:

> The authoritative Word gave the community its form and content in obedience to the divine imperative, yet, conversely the reception of the authoritative tradition by its hearers gave shape to the same writings through a historical and theological process of selecting, collecting, and ordering. The formation of the canon was not a late extrinsic validation of a corpus of writings, but involved a series of decisions deeply affecting the shape of the books.[11]

To call a text "canonical," according to Childs, is not to refer to a sacred book as part of a list or authoritative group of books but refer to canon as

---

8. Sanders, *Torah and Canon*, vii–viii.

9. Sanders, *Torah and Canon*, 1–7.

10. Brevard Childs, *Introduction to the Old Testament as Scripture* (Philadelphia: Fortress, 1979), 58–59. It is incorrect to label Childs's approach "canonical criticism," yet this error is sometimes repeated in secondary source discussion. Childs is on record saying, "I have always objected to the term 'canon(ical) criticism' as a suitable description of my approach ("An Interview with Brevard S. Childs [1923-2007]," http://www.philosophy-religion.org/bible/childs-interview.htm, February 1, 2014).

11. Childs, *Introduction*, 58–59.

a "cipher" that encircles and permeates "the various and diverse factors involved in the formation of the literature."[12]

Returning to the related categories of Scripture and canon, Childs does close the distance between these two terms in much the same way Sanders does. Childs, however, is quick to differentiate his view from Sanders: whereas Sanders's reason for a synonymous use of these terms stems from his model of *adaptability* and *stability* in Israel's sociopolitical shifts, Childs sees the canon as an interpretive device, an additional layer of textual meaning, and, finally, a mode of preservation. It is a guide for the stewards of God's Word and for matters of shaping and arrangement as well as a vehicle to amplify and forward God's message to subsequent generations.

2.1.1.c Sailhamer's Canonical Theology

John Sailhamer builds off Sanders's work. As with a number of authors of canonical models, Sailhamer dislikes the phrase "canonical criticism"; he prefers the phrase "canonical theology."[13] While Sailhamer identifies some surface similarities between his method and canonical criticism, he also notes fundamental differences. For Sailhamer, the primary difference is historicity. Canonical criticism, he argues, tends to invest in a number of historical-critical tools, and these tools are not often concerned with verifying the historical events of Scripture as actual moments in time and space.[14] This very point runs against the grain of Sailhamer's interpretive arc. Sailhamer goes further, pitting the concept of *canon* against *criticism*, as if they were opposite. *Criticism* becomes the mode in which one reads or interprets "behind" the text and focuses on the canon's developmental

---

12. Brevard Childs, *Biblical Theology of the Old and New Testaments: Theological Reflection on the Christian Bible* (Minneapolis: Fortress, 1992), 70.

13. John Sailhamer, *Introduction to Old Testament Theology: A Canonical Approach* (Grand Rapids: Zondervan, 1995), 198.

14. Sailhamer, however, does not seem to qualify how the events about which the biblical authors wrote pertain to the theological presentation of the text. He remains brief in his comparison between the two possibilities, but draws a bold line between the literary presentation of a biblical event and the event itself. This philosophical stance distances Sailhamer from most canonical critics.

stages. *Canon*, on the other hand, is a shorthand term for attention drawn toward a biblical text "at the time of the formation of the canon."[15]

2.1.1.d Seitz's Canonical Approach

As with the interchange between Sanders and Sailhamer, Christopher R. Seitz takes Childs's approach in a series of new directions. Seitz proposes five prominent characteristics for a canonical approach: first, a "critiqued and recalibrated use" of the historical-critical methodology; second, a final form of the biblical text that rejects "harmonization"—the claim that a final shape is an artificial network of references fueled by dogma and politics; third, a consideration of the complex relationship between Hebrew and Greek text-traditions; and fourth, a sensitivity to premodern interpretation with an eye to the "historical criticism season"[16] contemporary to Seitz; and fifth, a deep and expansive view of biblical theology, particularly how the two Testaments come together so as to reveal the Triune God through Christian Scripture. "The canonical approach," Seitz concludes, "with its capacity to listen to, appreciate, and penetrate to the abiding theological concerns of a long history of interpretation" stretches out over a "long horizon."[17]

2.1.2 RELATIONSHIP TO OTHER APPROACHES

Canonical criticism is not without a context—historically or methodologically. In this section, we attempt to set canonical criticism apart from other aspects of biblical criticism by explaining its relationship (or perceived relationship) with other exegetical approaches. At the same time, we must again stress that the label "canonical criticism" does not refer to a single, unified method. Rather, it is an umbrella term that encompasses various approaches that focus on canonical processes and their effect on biblical interpretation. In a strict sense, canonical criticism is Sanders's original method as noted above, but his approach and that of Brevard Childs have been developed into a number of models.

---

15. Sailhamer, *Introduction*, 222–23.

16. Christopher R. Seitz, "The Canonical Approach and Theological Interpretation," in *Canon and Biblical Interpretation*, ed. Craig G. Bartholomew et al. (Grand Rapids: Zondervan, 2006), 59.

17. Seitz, *Character of Christian Scripture*, 88.

2.1.2.a Canonical Criticism and Historical Criticism

Historically, this method was developed in response to the tendencies of historical criticism as exercised in the middle of the twentieth century. Consequently, some have characterized historical criticism as the necessary "foil" for canonical criticism.[18] This is not unwarranted, particularly since Childs and Sanders acknowledge a relationship between canonical criticism and historical criticism. In fact, both Childs and Sanders communicated positive feelings for historical criticism[19] even though they ultimately bemoaned its shortcomings and credited these as the impetus for the development of their ideas. Childs was convinced that the concerns of historical critical scholarship—namely its overwhelming concern for identifying and discussing the historical development of the biblical text—severely hindered, if not crippled, meaningful theological discourse. Historical criticism failed to consider the dynamics of the text as religious literature. Sanders asserted that historical criticism prevented meaningful results by fragmenting the text so that the "original" could be isolated from the later developments. The assumption required for such efforts: that the "original" text is authoritative, or at the very least more authoritative. The result was a sequestering of the Bible's relevance in antiquity. Interestingly, however, Sanders perceived canonical criticism to be an outgrowth, or next step, of historical-critical studies.[20]

A sense of irony often gravitates around the study of canonical criticism and its relationship with historical-critical scholarship. While canonical criticism was developed as a response to historical criticism, it is intimately

---

18. John Barton, "Canon and Old Testament Interpretation," in *In Search of True Wisdom: Essays in Old Testament Interpretation in Honour of Ronald E. Clements*, ed. Edward Ball, JSOTSupp 300 (Sheffield: Sheffield Academic Press, 1999), 46. Similarly, James Barr, "A Review Article on B. S. Childs, *Introduction to the Old Testament as Scripture*," in *Bible and Interpretation: The Collected Essays of James Barr*, ed. John Barton (Oxford: Oxford University Press, 2013), 2:335.

19. Childs states, "It seems impossible to deny the enormous gains which have been achieved in many areas of the study of the Old Testament. To compare the church fathers, or the Reformers for that matter, with modern scholarship in terms of philology, textual and literary criticism, or historical knowledge and exegetical precision should convince any reasonable person of the undeniable achievements of historical critical scholarship in respect to the Old Testament" (Childs, *Introduction to the Old Testament as Scripture*, 46). Sanders was fond of repeating the notion that historical criticism shed light on the history of the text, without which one's understanding of the compositional and developmental process would be severely lacking.

20. James A. Sanders, "Canonical Context and Canonical Criticism," *Horizons in Biblical Theology* 2 (1980): 192.

tied to it. The imprint of historical-critical scholarship upon biblical scholarship is deep. Yet the critics of the historical-critical method proved that
this method can only go so far. Indeed, the general importance of historical
issues (and their impact for understanding the text) are unquestionable,
leading to scholarly advances that would not have been possible otherwise. However, such an expressed interest in the past makes it difficult to
to accept or to understand the text's theological impact today. Both Childs
and Sanders offered canonical criticism as a suitable progression from
this method.

Consequently, the critical issue is to understand how canonical criticism and historical criticism interact. Unfortunately, Childs never offered
a robust explanation of method, only leaving his work to be analyzed by
his critics and students. While Sanders offered more thoughts, his idea
that canonical criticism represents the next logical step beyond historical criticism was still enigmatic. What is clear, however, is that a delicate
balance must be struck. Essentially, historical-critical endeavors should
be a means to an end.[21]

2.1.2.b Canonical Criticism and New Criticism

In addition to canonical criticism's relationship with historical criticism,
John Barton sees a link between canonical criticism and New Criticism, a
literary movement that started during the middle of the twentieth century.[22] However, the connection that Barton proposed was soon criticized.
Dickson Brown argued that Barton misunderstands New Criticism, calling
Barton's efforts an oversimplification and a case of comparing "apples to
oranges."[23] Yet Brown admits there are similarities, which could suggest

---

21. For example, one should use historical reconstruction selectively, critically, and with
an awareness that it must serve the purpose of understanding the theological implications of
the final form of the text; see Christopher Seitz, "Tribute to Brevard Childs at the International
SBL Meeting in Vienna, Austria," in *The Bible as Christian Scripture*, ed. Christopher R. Seitz
and Kent Harold Richards (Atlanta: Society of Biblical Literature, 2013), 4.

22. See John Barton, *Reading the Old Testament: Method in Biblical Study*, rev. and enl. ed.
(Louisville: Westminster John Knox, 1996), 145–53.

23. J. Dickson Brown, "Barton, Brooks, and Childs: A Comparison of the New Criticism
and Canonical Criticism," *JETS* 36 (1993): 481–84.

at least some influence.[24] Ultimately, though, assessing the impact of New Criticism on Childs's approach should begin with Childs himself:

> The canonical study of the Old Testament shares an interest in common with several of the newer literary critical methods in its concern to do justice to the integrity of the text itself apart from diachronic reconstruction. One thinks of the so-called "newer criticism" of English studies, of various forms of structural analysis and of rhetorical criticism. Yet the canonical approach differs from such a strictly literary approach by interpreting the biblical text in relation to a community of faith and practice for whom it served a particular theological role as possessing divine authority. ... The canonical approach is concerned to understand the nature of the theological shape of the text rather than to recover an original literary or aesthetic unity.[25]

From this quote, New Criticism was on Childs's radar. Yet, one also sees that Childs understood that the nature of Scripture—its authoritative and normative character—imports a critical variable into the entire discussion. Canonical criticism is, therefore, not merely the secular study of literature. While Childs admits the draw of these secular literary studies, namely their preference for studying the product over the process, the relationship is not as pronounced as Barton suggests.

2.1.2.c Canonical Criticism and Inner-biblical Exegesis

One final approach often associated with canonical criticism and its variations is inner-biblical exegesis.[26] An interpretive method originating with Michael Fishbane, inner-biblical exegesis shares a number of practices with canonical criticism, but it differs with regard to its goal and overall execution.[27] By definition, the method traces an "interbranching network of relationships that connects distant texts and binds them to one another."[28]

---

24. Brown, "Barton, Brooks, and Childs," 487–89.

25. Childs, *Introduction to the Old Testament as Scripture*, 74.

26. On inner-biblical interpretation, see chapter 4 of this volume.

27. Michael Fishbane, *Biblical Interpretation in Ancient Israel* (Oxford: Clarendon, 1985).

28. Yair Zakovitch, "Inner-Biblical Interpretation," in *A Companion to Biblical Interpretation in Early Judaism*, ed. Matthias Henze (Grand Rapids: Eerdmans, 2011), 27; compare Fishbane,

While most canonical models implement some form of intertextuality or textual networking, inner-biblical exegesis differs in that it pursues the corrected or updated presentation of the text and reconnects that update back to the earlier text prompting it. Take, for example, the promise outlined in Jeremiah 25 and 29: for Fishbane, Daniel 9:24 ("the seventy sevens") is an attempt made by late scribes to account for the apparent failing of God's promise (Jer 25:11; 29:19), in which Jeremiah the prophet proclaims "*seventy* years" before Israel's return. The later text of Daniel is intimately connected to these passages through preformed traditions and textual challenges. Formally, Fishbane labels the shaping activity *traditio* and the streams of tradition being redirected *traditum*.[29]

2.1.3 KEY CONCEPTS

There are multiple pillars that support a canonical methodology: the dynamics of canon, the relationship between historical criticism and canonical criticism, intertextuality, and the final form of Scripture.

2.1.3.a The Scope and Nature of the Canon

Canonical methods aim to interpret the Bible in a canonical context; such a claim assumes a *historical* dimension to canon as well as a contemporary one. First, we must understand the usage of the Greek word κανών (*canōn*) through time. *Canōn* is a broad term and exhibits a relatively complicated history of usage within Christian traditions. In Hellenistic Greek, it primarily meant "rule" or "standard," but by the fourth century, *canōn* came to refer to the "rule of faith" in the early church, a concept that explores interpretive and theological norms with respect to issues of faith and practice.[30] More concretely, *canōn* also came to refer to a list of authoritative documents that are united under God's providence and within his divine economy of the Word. Early church fathers put this reality into practice. Melito, the bishop of Sardis, received a question regarding the true scope of

---

Biblical Interpretation, 443–65.

29. Fishbane suggests that "inner-biblical exegesis starts with the received Scripture and moves forward to the interpretations based on it," speaking to his own version of the *final form* (Biblical Interpretation, 7).

30. John Webster, "Canon," in the Dictionary for Theological Interpretation of the Bible, ed. Kevin J. Vanhoozer (Grand Rapids: Baker, 2005), 97.

the OT, so he then went East to learn better "the books of the old covenant."[31] Inquiry into the proper list of OT books arose again with Athanasius's Festal Letter (AD 367), wherein he adds such books as Baruch, Judith, and Tobit. But in the latter half of the fourth century, Jerome confined the number of OT books to 39, a canon ultimately in agreement with the Protestant Reformers. The NT was constructed with the scaffolding of the OT canon in place, especially the four Gospels and the thirteen letters of Paul. As more and more books gravitated toward the NT, the heretic Marcion caused such figures as Irenaeus and Tertullian to return to the theology of canon and its ordained development.[32]

What is truly fascinating is how the hands that compiled the NT did so with reference to the OT, maintaining a sacred unity of Scripture. Seitz uses the analogy of an old bridge being replaced by a new bridge. While plans for the new bridge were designated—using points on the north and south side of the previous bridge as bearings—the old bridge was still doing its work, conveying cars from one side to the other. As the new bridge was finished, the old bridge was allowed to fall in to the river, but, Seitz explains, "anyone who recalls the old bridge knows how influential it was in forming the new bridge."[33] Such is the interpretive dynamic throughout the canonical presentation of the Old and New Testaments.

According to John Webster, the modern turn (eighteenth-nineteenth centuries) shows "the decline of theological and exegetical appeal" to the canon and is a major indicator of Scripture's changed status.[34] The work of Herbert F. Ryle in 1904 provides an example of this shift. Ryle began to focus on studying the OT in three distinct canonical groups: the Torah (closed c. 400 BC), the Prophets (closed c. 200 BC, the Maccabean

---

31. Stephen B. Chapman, "Collections, Canons, and Communities," in *The Cambridge Companion to the Hebrew Bible/Old Testament*, ed. Stephen B. Chapman and Marvin A. Sweeney (New York: Cambridge University Press, 2016), 28.

32. Chapman, "Collections," 28; see also Hans von Campenhausen, *The Formation of the Christian Bible* (Philadelphia: Fortress, 1972).

33. Christopher R. Seitz, *The Goodly Fellowship of the Prophets: The Achievement of Association in Canon Formation* (Grand Rapids: Baker Academic, 2009), 2-6.

34. Seitz, *Goodly Fellowship*, 97.

Era), and the Writings (closed AD 90 at the council of Jamnia).[35] Here, we see one of the first presentations taking a history-of-religions approach to the biblical canon, focusing on the compilational background rather than the theological makeup. The ripple effect emanating from Ryle's model of canonical composition was (and remains) significant—these ripples would form into the modern enterprise of canonical study.[36] Incidentally, this chapter in canonical interpretation projects the definition of "canon" and "canonical" back to the stark, minimalist definition of these terms, quite apart from any theological or confessional element. That recent discussions of canon overwhelmingly focused on the historical process that resulted in an accepted body of texts, which in turn silenced the normative and formative expectations traditionally associated with canon, is not surprising.

These nineteenth century developments encouraged the authors of canonical criticism to respond to such currents of thought when articulating their method. First, the idea must be broad enough to accommodate numerous connotations. Childs, Sanders, Seitz, and Carr all embrace the advances of historical critical scholarship with respect to understanding the process of canonization, but they agreed that the concept of canon must transcend merely a list of texts deemed authoritative. Contemporary models of canon development thus implore interpreters to consider the mutual interaction between the texts and the communities that preserved them.[37]

---

35. Herbert E. Ryle, *The Canon of the Old Testament: An Essay on the Gradual Growth and Formation of the Hebrew Canon of Scripture*, 2nd ed. (London: Macmillan, 1914).

36. See also Albert C. Sundberg, *The Old Testament of the Early Church* (Cambridge, MA: Harvard University Press, 1964); Frants Buhl, *Canon and Text of the Old Testament* (Edinburgh: T&T Clark, 1892); Gerrit Wildeboer, *The Origin of the Canon of the Old Testament: A Historico-Critical Enquiry* (London: Luzac, 1895). For more discussion surrounding the council of Jamnia (or Jabneh), see Shnayer Z. Leiman, *The Canonization of Hebrew Scripture: The Talmudic and Midrashic Evidence* (Hamden, CT: Archon Books, 1976), 126; Stephen B. Chapman, "The Old Testament Canon and Its Authority for the Christian Church," *Ex Auditu* 19 (2003): 125–48; E. Earle Ellis, *The Old Testament in Early Christianity: Canon and Interpretation in the Light of Modern Research* (Eugene, OR: Wipf and Stock, 2003).

37. According to both Childs and Sanders, the text and the community exist within a relationship. Childs states, "It is constitutive of Israel's history that the literature formed the identity of the religious community which in turn shaped the literature" (*Introduction*, 41). Similarly, Sanders asserts, "Canon owes its life to its dialogue with those believing communities, and the believing communities owe their life to their dialogue with it" ("Canonical Context and Canonical Criticism," 193).

2.1.3.b Historical Criticism and Canonical Criticism

Canonical criticism and other related methods do not discount historical critical tools. The catalyst for a new canonical method developed in response to the tendencies of historical criticism prominent in the middle of the twentieth century. Eventually, historical criticism grew to be recognized as the necessary foil for canonical criticism.[38] This shift was anticipated, particularly since fewer and fewer historical critics acknowledged a relationship between canonical criticism and historical critics. Scholars like James Barr view this brand of historical criticism as a half measure, imitating an authentic, critical tool for the sake of being *pan-biblical*.[39] Still, Childs, Sanders, and many other proponents utilize historical criticism even though they ultimately bemoan its shortcomings.[40] Childs was convinced that the concerns of historical critical scholarship—namely its dogged pursuit of the historical development of the biblical text—severely hindered, if not crippled, meaningful theological discourse. Sanders asserted that historical criticism prevented meaningful results by fragmenting the text so that the "original" could be isolated from the latter developments.

Historical criticism, to be sure, holds a position within canonical approaches, to varying degrees; however, most draw a bold line: canon as a vehicle for theological discourse versus canon as product of religious history.[41] The latter definition amplifies the historical-critical program beyond the boundaries of most canonical methods. Divine revelation remains at the center of a canonical approach, but history, in certain circles of

---

38. Barr, *Bible and Interpretation*, 2:335. See also Barton, "Canon and Old Testament Interpretation," 46.

39. James Barr, *The Concept of Biblical Theology* (Minneapolis: Fortress, 1999).

40. Childs states, "It seems impossible to deny the enormous gains which have been achieved in many areas of the study of the Old Testament. To compare the church fathers, or the Reformers for that matter, with modern scholarship in terms of philology, textual and literary criticism, or historical knowledge and exegetical precision should convince any reasonable person of the undeniable achievements of historical critical scholarship in respect to the Old Testament" (*Introduction*, 46). Sanders was fond of repeating the notion that historical criticism shed light on the history of the text, without which one's understanding of the compositional and developmental process would be severely lacking.

41. J. Gordon McConville, alongside Childs, names this a "trend as a type of history-of-religions approach" ("Old Testament Laws and Canonical Intentionality" in *Canon and Biblical Interpretation* [Grand Rapids: Zondervan, 2006], 271).

historical criticism, can be presented as a substitute for revelation.[42] As Gordon McConville phrases it, some interpreters see "the concept of canon as control," or a device that is part of an effort of "an elite group" within a community to understand "its identity in terms of its past."[43]

While canonical criticism was developed as a response to historical criticism, it is still tied to it. Narrative criticism, redaction criticism, and tradition criticism are only a few of the critical tools at the disposal of canonical methodology. One example is Childs's account of the "tent of meeting" tradition in Exodus 33-34 and its parallel in "the later priestly account."[44] Childs, in this example, has no problem tracing a theologically rich tradition through the book of Exodus while incorporating some historical- critical highlights. Consequently, the critical question here is to understand how canonical criticism and historical criticism interact. What is clear, however, is that a delicate balance must be struck. According to these scholars, the historical background of a biblical book is important, but it is not the locus of God's revelation in the text.[45]

2.1.3.c *Textual Association within Canon*

Proponents of canonical interpretation are also interested in analyzing textual associations throughout the Old and New Testaments, so that the unity of Scripture is established both theologically and textually. Allusions and quotations can indicate a connection between passages, chapters, or even books; naturally, these same literary qualities are a part of the canon's internal growth. Timothy Stone, in surveying the Megilloth (an OT collection that included the books of Ruth, Lamentations, Song of Solomon,

---

42. See Richard Burnett, "Historical Criticism," in the *Dictionary of Theological Interpretation*, ed. Kevin J. Vanhoozer (Grand Rapids: Baker), 291.

43. Burnett, "Historical Criticism," 270-71. This branch of historical criticism includes, but is not limited to, the following: Morton Smith, *Palestinian Parties and Politics That Shaped the Old Testament* (New York: Columbia University Press, 1971); Philip R. Davies, *In Search of "Ancient Israel": A Study in Biblical Origins* (Sheffield: Sheffield Academic Press, 1992); Joseph Blenkinsopp, *Prophecy and Canon: A Contribution to the Study of Jewish Origins* (Notre Dame, IN: University of Notre Dame Press, 1986).

44. Brevard S. Childs, *The Book of Exodus: A Critical, Theological Commentary* (Louisville: Westminster, 1974), 591.

45. For example, one should use historical reconstruction selectively, critically, and with an awareness that it must serve the purpose of understanding the theological implications of the final form of the text; see Seitz, "Tribute to Brevard Childs," 4.

Esther, and Ecclesiastes), comments on one example in particular: the picture of the "virtuous woman" (אֵשֶׁת־חַיִל; *eshet hayil*) in Proverbs 31:10–31 and its correlation with the woman Ruth (3:9–13; *eshet hayil*).[46] Ruth is an example of the proverbial woman, one who is wise and full of character. Canonically speaking, these associations together begin to connect biblical texts at the level of theme, book, and, ultimately, theological coherence.[47]

Some connect intertextuality and canonical methods so closely, they appear interchangeable. Sailhamer outlines a threefold canonical model for biblical theology, positioning "canonical shaping" at the second, intertextual stage, between "composition" of the text and "consolidation" within the community.[48] Interestingly, intertextuality occupies the same space as "canonical shaping," and it is configured between the writings of the original text and the canon's closure.

2.1.3.d The Final Form of the Text

To be sure, the majority of disagreement and debate surrounding canonical methods settles in one area: interpretation of the final form. Many interpret this concept simply as it is presented—namely, a mode of interpretation based solely on the privileging of Scripture's ultimate presentation. This picture of the final form implies a large-scale neglect of any earlier form of the biblical text or its nascent development as a canon. John Collins, for example, sees the final form as an "editorial process" that is meant "to take the edge off" of otherwise powerful oracles and statements in "the original words of the prophets."[49] Collins finishes by restating the

---

46. Stone, *Compilational History*, 134–35.

47. For a cross section of interpreters relating canon to textual association, see the following works: David M. Carr, "The Many Uses of Intertextuality in Biblical Studies: Actual and Potential," in *Congress Volume: Helsinki 2010*, ed. Martti Nissinen (Leiden: Brill, 2012), 505–36; Richard L. Schultz, "Intertextuality, Canon, and 'Undecidability': Understanding Isaiah's 'New Heavens and New Earth' (Isaiah 65:17–25)," *BBR* 20 (2010): 19–38; Craig C. Broyles, "Traditions, Intertextuality, and Canon," in *Interpreting the Old Testament: A Guide for Exegesis*, ed. Craig C. Broyles (Grand Rapids: Baker Academic, 2001), 157–75; Michael Fishbane, "Types of Biblical Intertextuality," in *Congress Volume: Oslo 1998*, ed. André Lemaire and Magne Sæbø (Leiden: Brill, 2000), 39–44.

48. John H. Sailhamer, "Biblical Theology and the Composition of the Hebrew Bible," in *Biblical Theology: Retrospect and Prospect*, ed. Scott J. Hafemann (Downers Grove, IL: IVP, 2002), 25–37.

49. John J. Collins, *Introduction to the Hebrew Bible: An Inductive Reading of the Old Testament* (Minneapolis: Fortress, 2004), 286.

importance of recognizing the "tension" between the earlier form and the final form.[50] It is not difficult to see how the final form takes the guise of an addition or, depending on degree of function, an appendage. In either respect, the addition is unnecessary. Seitz sums up opponents' characterizations well: "Frequently it sounds like this is a matter of examining a series of integers, all laid out in a row, and choosing the last ones over the first ones."[51]

Approaching the concept of a final form requires that we attend to its different construal within canonical approaches. For Sanders, the final form lies at the canon's closing, since "canon as *function* antedates canon as *shape*."[52] The text's earlier forms play a greater role in the interpretive process; each stage of textual development is as important as the final form. There is not a final shape, but a final decision to tie off the ongoing socioreligious function that the scriptural parts play for Israel as a faith community. The shaping of Israel's Scriptures lies in its fluid ability to renew traditions and recast historical circumstances in order to speak to ever-changing circumstances. Sailhamer, while sharing much with Sanders's understanding of canon, takes an alternate route with the final form: the final form of the text is unique in that it is defined apart from any critical underpinnings. The final shape of the text is then the ultimate literary product, according to Sailhamer, including word-choice, Masoretic marks, Hebrew vowels, and, most importantly, the network of intertextual markers throughout.[53] This model, in the end, locates canonical interpretation within the connections and intertexts woven throughout the biblical text, similar to the interpreters above who focus on canon and textual association.

---

50. Collins, *Hebrew Bible*, 286–87.

51. Seitz, *Character of Christian Scripture*, 51. Both Seitz and Childs write on the constant mischaracterization of the final form, starting with James Barr (*Holy Scripture: Canon, Authority, Criticism* [Philadelphia: Westminster, 1983]), to John Barton (*Reading the Old Testament: Method in Biblical Study*, rev. and enl. ed. [Louisville: Westminster John Knox, 1996]), and continuing through Julio Trebolle Barrera (*The Jewish Bible and the Christian Bible: An Introduction to the History of the Bible*, trans. Wilfred G.E. Watson [Leiden: Brill, 1998]).

52. James A. Sanders, "Canon: Hebrew Bible," in *AYBD* 1:843 (emphasis his).

53. Sailhamer, *Introduction*, 198–200.

The final form is not another way of saying the "only form" or the "only interpretation of text."[54] Rather, it is the "essential element" to a canonical approach, holding the interpreter to reading Scripture in "its own integrity."[55] The earlier forms of the biblical text are not dismissed but studied for the sake of the final form. Daniel 2:20–23, 44, for example, is a root theology threaded throughout the book, and the final form of Daniel—consisting of chapters 7–12—would not have any literary anchor in the text apart from these verses.[56] What is more, the exiled community living at the time of the rise of the Greek and Seleucid powers had authoritative scriptural examples (chs. 8–10) contemporary to their situation.[57]

Dempster likewise does not observe a systemic disregard for the textual pieces that make up the canonical whole. There are "signs," he acknowledges, within the documents themselves "and in their textual history."[58] But while this is the case, each biblical document in its unshaped, unfinalized form is still thought canonical in authority and in its innate ability to impart an additional "chapter" to God's textual self-revelation. In the OT, this very truth is borne out in the authoritative appeal and usage of the written Torah throughout Israel's prophetic oracles as well as in the commentary-like character of the Writings.

Canonical authority also undergirds each OT book (scroll) and continues through to the NT. Considering the OT canon as a structural blueprint for the arrangement of the NT is not a stretch in Dempster's thinking: "Thus, the early church was born with a canon in its hands."[59] Seitz, in like fashion, argues that "at a formal level, the OT has had a decisive influence"

---

54. See William John Lyons, *Canon and Exegesis: Canonical Praxis and the Sodom Narrative* (Sheffield: Sheffield Academic, 2002), 37. Even those unsympathetic to anything like a final form of the canon's shape realize that "canon implies the attempt to impose a definitive shape and meaning on the [biblical] tradition as it comes to expression in the texts" (Blenkinsopp, *Prophecy and Canon*, ix–xi).

55. Childs, *Introduction*, 59.

56. Ron Haydon, *"Seventy Sevens Are Decreed": A Canonical Approach to Daniel 9:24–27* (Winona Lake, IN: Eisenbrauns, 2016), 116–17.

57. Haydon, *"Seventy Sevens,"* 107–10.

58. Dempster, "Canon and Theological Interpretation," 137; see also Ched Spellman, *Toward Canon-Conscious Reading of the Bible: Exploring the History and Hermeneutics of the Canon* (Sheffield: Sheffield Phoenix, 2014).

59. Dempster, "Canon and Theological Interpretation," 137.

on the final, canonical shape of the New Testament.[60] Here, we locate at least one instance in which canonical interpretation is at odds with higher critical tools (tradition criticism).

Reading the final form of the text, therefore, welcomes such developments and demonstrates how the presentation of the text supports multiple voices while projecting them into the hearing range of future generations. The final form of the text uniquely bears witness to the full history of God's revelation. According to Seitz, the final form is the "aggregation" of the canonical process: "Only the final form bears the fullest witness to all that God has said and handed on with the historical community of faith."[61] How, then, do historical-critical considerations enter this conversation? While canonical critics do not have a problem incorporating redaction-critical and source-critical insights into their readings, it is another matter to claim these tools are able to account for the full unity of Scripture. It is this point that leads scholars like Childs to be skeptical of the aims and intentions of the critical endeavor—historical criticism is no substitute for the theological witness that runs through and binds the Old and New Testaments together. History, while qualified to take on theological tones, is a part of a canonical approach, as per Seitz and Dempster. Because the final form is the place where "normative history has revealed an end that the full effect of this revelatory history can be perceived,"[62] it must also be the place of interpretation. The final form provides the "critical norm" for the community, and constitutes the "critical theological judgment" on the entire canonization process.[63] As stated by Mark Gignilliat, "The final form functions as an authoritative commentary on the full scope of Israel's encounters with God."[64]

---

60. Seitz, *Character of Christian Scripture*, 165.

61. Seitz, "Canonical Approach," 102.

62. Childs, *Introduction*, 76.

63. Childs, *Introduction*, 76.

64. Mark S. Gignilliat, *A Brief History of Old Testament Criticism: From Benedict Spinoza to Brevard Childs* (Grand Rapids: Zondervan, 2012), 162.

2.2 APPLICATION OF CANONICAL CRITICISM
AND OTHER CANONICAL METHODS

In *Prophecy and Hermeneutics*, Seitz offers an introduction to the prophetic corpus that significantly diverges from the standard introduction.[65] Employing "figural interpretation" as the backbone of his canonical
approach,[66] Seitz begins with Christ as the central figure and attempts to
understand how the prophetical literature both relates to each other—
through utterances, form-critical observations, cross-references, etc.—
and carries divine revelation through specific eras to comprehend God
and God's work with Israel and Jesus Christ. In the second half he offers
some exegetical thoughts that emphasize the mutual interaction between
individual passages, or blocks of material.[67]

To illustrate what a canonical approach to the biblical text looks like,
Seitz surveys the Minor Prophets. His examples highlight four notable
ideas.[68] First, the canonical presentation intimately links the sociopolitical crises of the eighth century to the fifth century BC. The message of
the prophets echoes throughout Israel's exilic experience; from the fall of
Samaria to the rise of the Persian empire, the unified word of these twelve
messengers remains powerfully relevant. Second, the periodic emphasis
upon foreign nations throughout the corpus demonstrates that Israel's
place within God's ongoing work is special, but not unique. The twelve
Minor Prophets share these same themes, motifs, and theological instruc-
tion with the books of Isaiah, Jeremiah, and Ezekiel. Third, the prayers of
Jonah, Habakkuk, and Joel occur in strategic locations and embody "dis-
cernment necessary for comprehending the lessons of history."[69] A selection of these Minor Prophets offer a brief, narrative example of life as God's
servant, and a reader is able to learn from these episodes. Fourth, Seitz
maintains that prophetic formulas from Exodus ("Thus says YHWH") are
present throughout the Minor Prophets and provide "one of the strongest

---

65. Christopher R. Seitz, *Prophecy and Hermeneutics: Toward a New Introduction to the
Prophets* (Grand Rapids: Baker Academic, 2007). In the first part of this work, Seitz offers a
valuable "history of research" (*Forschungsgeschichte*) to explain how the standard introduction
developed to push aside theological questions for narrowly defined historical ones.

66. Seitz, *Prophecy and Hermeneutics*, 7–10.

67. Seitz, *Prophecy and Hermeneutics*, 204–19.

68. Seitz, *Prophecy and Hermeneutics*, 214–16.

69. Seitz, *Prophecy and Hermeneutics*, 215.

signs of a comprehensive editing of the Twelve."[70] The Book of the Twelve, therefore, is not a record of Israelite history but a canonical pattern of theological and textual thought that displays how YHWH's steadfast love emanates to all four corners of Israel's diaspora.

In this particular application, historical development is brought to the foreground in order to illuminate the final form of the text. Most importantly, Christ, in Seitz's estimation, is the hermeneutical lens for understanding how the Minor Prophets functioned as a critical phase on the historical continuum of God's revelation.

While Seitz's approach focuses on structural shifts (often book-wide) and the endurance of God's word through Israel's history, Sailhamer focuses largely on how words, phrases, and literary units associate with one another to produce a text-based theme. An example of this canonical approach is in the appendix of his OT theology.[71] He relates the role of the Mosaic law to the theological framework of the Pentateuch. Sailhamer reads the Pentateuch as juxtaposing Abraham and Moses as individuals who live by faith and the Law respectively. This juxtaposition forces the reader to see the contrast between the benefits of living by faith (Abraham) and the deficiencies of living by the Law.[72] Proceeding from these assumptions, Sailhamer cites Genesis 26:5, concluding that this phrase refers to the Mosaic Law and Abraham's trust in it. The reader is to realize that the text is intentionally presenting Abraham's faith as the catalyst for a life obedient to the law.[73] Sailhamer then proceeds to discuss Numbers 20:1–13—namely, the reason for Moses' punishment. Ultimately dissatisfied with the notion that Moses' inability to enter the promised land is linked to his striking of the rock or the harsh words to the people (Num 20:8–10), Sailhamer interprets the intentional silence within the text as encouraging the reader to ponder Moses' lack of faith.[74] All these associations constitute a "narrative strategy" that not only bears witness to the Pentateuch's

---

70. Seitz, *Prophecy and Hermeneutics*, 216.

71. Sailhamer, *Introduction*, 259–60.

72. The comparison, Sailhamer writes, "suggests that there has been a conscious effort to contrast the time before and leading up to the giving of the law with the time of Moses under the law" (*Introduction*, 259–60).

73. Sailhamer, *Introduction*, 265.

74. Sailhamer, *Introduction*, 269.

view of the Mosaic Law but also upholds Abraham as a model of faith and Moses as a model of faithlessness.[75]

2.3 LIMITATIONS OF CANONICAL CRITICISM

As with any interpretive approach or critical tool, there are noticeable difficulties with canonical criticism and its subsequent methods. These difficulties range from charges of ahistorical emphases and the import ing of dogmatic claims to an overemphasis on the text's authority. Here, we will address only a select few.

Since the final form of the canon is one of the hallmarks of a canonical approach, many judge the method to be historically deficient. Rather than attend to the sources that constitute the final text, scholars believe the approach glosses over the discordance inherent to the Bible's textual development. This was always a potential indictment, Childs thought, especially with the current feeling toward the "Yale School."[76] Intratextuality, or the association between passages and books, allegedly subsumes history.

It is within the sphere of compilation criticism that Eugene Ulrich remains one of the most audible voices in the argument over "canon" and "canonical processes."[77] For Ulrich, any biblical, canonical development is a "journey," but only one that ends in an "endorsement process" consisting of fixity and closure. No canonical process, according to Ulrich, holds any contemporary authority or long-stretching theological association. The very notion of a shaped, biblical canon is a Christian construct of standardization adopted from Judaism. Lee McDonald illustrates this argument in more detail, stating how fixity and closure function as indicators of authority, cultural popularity, textual sophistication, and connectivity throughout the literature of alternative cultures.[78]

---

75. Sailhamer, *Introduction*, 270–71.

76. Childs, "Appendix A," in *New Testament as Canon: An Introduction* (London: SCM Press, 1984), 551. By this, Childs refers to such figures as Hans Frei.

77. Eugene Ulrich, "The Notion and Definition of Canon," in *The Canon Debate: On the Origins and the Formation of the Bible*, ed. Lee M. McDonald and James A. Sanders (Peabody, MA: Hendrickson, 2002), 30. Ulrich provides his own interpretation of the canonical development of the Hebrew Bible ("The Evolutionary Composition of the Hebrew Bible," in *Editing the Bible: Assessing the Task Past and Present*, ed. John Kloppenborg and Judith H. Newman [Atlanta: Society of Biblical Literature, 2012], 23–40).

78. Lee Martin McDonald, *The Formation of the Christian Biblical Canon* (Peabody, MA: Hendrickson, 1995), 20.

David Carr, a student of Sanders, follows the lead of Ulrich and McDonald, observing the biblical canon to be more an *artifact* than an interpretive guide. Carr argues the Hasmonean monarchy (164–64 BC) is responsible for the formation of the Hebrew canon amid a storm of foreign oppression and political preservation.[79] Carr's thesis, therefore, does not leave room for a canonical hermeneutic or a final, literary shape: rather, detecting "canonical" evidence in the text entails finding "intentional shifts present in the Masoretic text that might link to interest and concerns of the Hasmoneans as surveyed in ... the profile of Hasmonean texts."[80] It is for the promotion of national identity that a royal class set to "initially defining the contours" of the OT text.[81] Carr's conclusion remains that most of these canonical methods ignore, at least, a tacit understanding of sociopolitical phases throughout biblical history.

James Barr, in his review of Childs's *Introduction to the Old Testament as Scripture*, labels Childs's approach as unsystematic, contradictory, unnecessarily repetitive, and, in concert with many critics, lacking in historical insight.[82] Furthermore, Barr laments over the irony of Childs's introduction. According to Barr, the areas in which Childs does well—such as offering historical critical insights and recounting the history of scholarship—are ultimately not valued, and the areas that are valued are done poorly. His position on canonical criticism is, put mildly, quite clear:

> In fact ... canonical criticism ... is simplistic. Basically it has only one idea: the controlling place of the canon. To others this may fall apart into several conflicting ideas but to the canonical critic himself it is all one idea. There is of course complexity even in the canon, but all that complexity can be dealt with by the one simple idea. ... The canonical principle leaves the believer at peace, alone with his Bible.[83]

---

79. David M. Carr, *The Formation of the Hebrew Bible: A New Reconstruction* (Oxford: Oxford University Press, 2011).

80. Carr, *Formation*, 167.

81. Carr, *Formation*, 156.

82. For example, "Brevard Childs is one of the great personalities of contemporary Old Testament study. ... One cannot but want to be on his side. His new and massive book presents, however, a strange set of puzzles and potential contradictions"; see Barr, *Bible and Interpretation*, 2:333.

83. Barr, *Holy Scripture*, 168.

Methodological criticisms arise as well. In particular, there are those who take issue with how many canonical scholars understand the dynamics of canon and what it means to interpret in a canonical context. Again, Barr is one of the more vocal critics. He criticizes Childs's understanding of canon as vague,[84] and he is quick to take aim at Sanders.[85] Barr believes Sanders's position is rooted in existential hermeneutics and the principles of the failed Biblical Theology movement of the mid-twentieth century. Moreover, Sanders's handling of the biblical evidence is "too speculative and too slight in substance to provide a solid framework for what is supposed to be a new movement in criticism."[86]

Evangelicals have also criticized canonical study, describing it as a slippery slope due to a close relationship to historical criticism and a broader sense of biblical inspiration.[87] John Oswalt observes an initial tendency for evangelicals to be receptive to canonical methods, which is linked to a preference for the final form of the text and the place of the community in interpretation. However, Oswalt cautions that the "gate-opening may be a bit premature."[88] For example, Sanders emphasizes how canonical criticism should build from the results of historical criticism and that inspiration should not lie with the author.[89] According to Oswalt, the Bible attests to the locus of inspiration being individuals and not communities.[90]

Oswalt is also skeptical of the method's seemingly ahistorical approach. For Oswalt, the truth of revelation is inextricably bound to the history about which it comments.[91] The biblical writers appeal to historical events

---

84. Barr, *Bible and Interpretation*, 2:334.

85. Barr, *Holy Scripture*, 156–57.

86. Barr, *Holy Scripture*, 157. Childs and Sanders have both responded to Barr's criticism. In both cases, they accuse Barr of fundamentally misunderstanding canonical criticism. See Brevard Childs, "Review of *Holy Scripture: Canon, Authority, Criticism* by James Barr," *Interpretation* 38 (1984): 66–70; James Sanders, "Review of *Holy Scripture: Canon, Authority, Criticism*, by James Barr," *JBL* 104 (1985): 501–2.

87. For example, John N. Oswalt, "Canonical Criticism: A Review from a Conservative," *JETS* 30 (1987): 317–25.

88. Oswalt, "Canonical Criticism," 319.

89. Oswalt, "Canonical Criticism," 319.

90. "The community, left to itself, is not a course of regeneration but of degeneration. Only when individuals are confronted by God and enter an obedient relationship with him does revelation come to the community"; see Oswalt, "Canonical Criticism," 322.

91. Oswalt, "Canonical Criticism," 320.

as a means of authenticating theological claims.[92] Oswalt, therefore, reads canonical interpreters as positing "a fictionalized account of that theology's origin."[93] Oswalt also pushes against a perceived tendency to emphasize the literary context as the critical context for interpretation. He contends a dichotomy between a literary and historical context cuts across the grain of biblical evidence.[94]

Lee McDonald also takes issue with this ahistorical posture. McDonald, for his part, asks the question "which canon" is the object of interpretation: Should canonical study assume the Masoretic, one of the versions of the Septuagint, or another reconstructed text?[95] According to McDonald, selecting a canon includes important criteria, such as a text's apostolicity and antiquity.[96] He also believes these considerations should play a role in establishing a canonical context over and against an uninformed commitment to a particular textual tradition. By ignoring the original form, McDonald believes that Childs, for example, comes close to uprooting Christianity from its origins.

Mark G. Brett echoes such criticisms but narrows them to a single point: canonical interpretation is too ambitious in scope. Champions of canonical methodology require a more modest perspective, according to Brett. These scholars should see canonical-interpretive approaches as one of many interpretive options.[97] Brett, in the end, wants to disassociate canonical interpretation from what is perceived to be absolutism. Canonical work in Scripture holds a seat at the table, offering but one possible level of biblical meaning to the interpretive task.[98]

Lastly, we note a criticism pertaining to the literary and theological aspects of canonical criticism, quite apart from the ahistorical concern.

92. Oswalt, "Canonical Criticism," 320.

93. Oswalt, "Canonical Criticism," 320–21.

94. Oswalt, "Canonical Criticism," 321.

95. For example, "Where is the evidence that the early church intended to read the Scriptures in the canonical context of the M[asoretic] T[ext] or *Textus Receptus* as opposed to the earliest form of the writing or the meaning intended by the original authors?" See Lee Martin McDonald, *The Biblical Canon: Its Origin, Transmission, and Authority*, 3rd ed. (Peabody, MA: Hendrickson, 2007), 470–71.

96. McDonald, *Biblical Canon*, 471.

97. Mark G. Brett, *Biblical Criticism in Crisis? The Impact of the Canonical Approach on Old Testament Studies* (Cambridge: Cambridge University Press, 1991).

98. Barton, *Reading the Old Testament*, 86.

John Barton apparently finds a link between canonical criticism and New Criticism, a literary movement that started during the middle of the twentieth century.[99] Following Barton's argument, Dickson Brown also sees a few similarities between the two interpretive movements, even if Barton's overall disagreement is an oversimplification ("apples and oranges").[100]

2.4 CONTEMPORARY INFLUENCE
OF CANONICAL CRITICISM

Since the development of canonical studies in 1970–1980, the field has broadened and continues to broaden in numerous directions, with some following closely in the footsteps of the original progenitors and others utilizing snippets of the formal models.[101] Some of these directions include the use of canonical interpretation in more systematic theological treatments as well as biblical theologies; the latter being where Childs, to cite an example, always envisioned his work moving.

Systematic theological treatments, as with Kevin Vanhoozer's work, identy a "canonical-linguistic" dimension in one's theological understanding and interpretation of the biblical text.[102] Kevin Vanhoozer's approach orients the role of the biblical canon around the normative role of "ecclesial

---

99. Barton, *Reading the Old Testament*, 145–53.

100. J. Dickson Brown, "Barton, Brooks, and Childs," 481–84, 487–89. Still, to assess the impact of New Criticism on Childs's approach, we might consider Childs's own voice as well: "The canonical study of the Old Testament shares an interest in common with several of the newer literary critical methods in its concern to do justice to the integrity of the text itself apart from diachronic reconstruction. One thinks of the so-called 'newer criticism' of English studies, of various forms of structural analysis and of rhetorical criticism. Yet the canonical approach differs from such a strictly literary approach by interpreting the biblical text in relation to a community of faith and practice for whom it served a particular theological role as possessing divine authority. ... The canonical approach is concerned to understand the nature of the theological shape of the text rather than to recover an original literary or aesthetic unity" (Childs, *Introduction*, 74).

101. Just within the last 15 years, we can see an increase in canonical proposals: Frank Thielman, *Theology of the New Testament: A Canonical and Synthetic Approach* (Grand Rapids: Zondervan, 2005); Charles J. Scalise, *Hermeneutics as Theological Prolegomena: A Canonical Approach* (Macon, GA: Mercer University Press, 1994); Bruce K. Waltke, *An Old Testament Theology: An Exegetical, Canonical, and Thematic Approach* (Grand Rapids: Zondervan, 2007); Scott W. Hahn, *Kinship by Covenant: A Canonical Approach to the Fulfillment of God's Saving Promises*, AYBRL (New Haven, CT: Yale University Press, 2009); Kevin J. Vanhoozer, *The Drama of Doctrine: A Canonical-Linguistic Approach to Christian Theology* (Louisville: Westminster John Knox, 2005).

102. Vanhoozer, *Drama of Doctrine*, 21–23.

culture."[103] Also, in this view, the canon displays a number of functions. It is the "church's authoritative script," in use throughout the divine theo-drama, working "as an authoritative and binding witness to the fact, and the terms, of the covenant relationship." It is a "playbook" that records "patterns of speech and action" as well as "a response to an evangelical exigence."[104] As for the nature of canon and the language Vanhoozer uses, the difference in nuance is simple enough to detect. We no longer encounter terms commonly associated with canon—shape, corpus, connection, editing, association, history—but instead find "covenant," "action," "communication," and "practice." This subtle distinction follows in light of Vanhoozer's differentiation between "a purely textual entity" and "a phenomenon of discourse."[105] Coupling textual unity with speech-act theory, some theologians take this same idea further, deeming the entire venture "canonical hermeneutics."[106]

Canonical biblical scholarship is exhibiting another shift. Methodological pluralism is *en vogue*, and encourages the growth of a theological interpretation of Scripture. This latest emphasis reminds the interpreter to be bold about his or her confessional positions and readings and to envision the text as the medium through which the reader encounters the Triune God. An emphasis such as this is to be expected given the aims and intentions of Childs, Seitz, Dempster, and Chapman—all scholars who value the ontological depth of the two-Testament canon.

While thinkers like Childs may not use the category "theological interpretation of Scripture," likeminded strides are being made. True canonical reading, for example, is not just a matter of comparing texts but encountering the "subject matter" of the text—namely, YHWH-who-is-Christ.[107] The Old and New Testament stand as a dual testimony disclosing the Triune God to his people; therefore, a faithful reader of canonical Scripture is interpreting a person, not a history. In this way, a robust canonical method—while

---

103. Vanhoozer, *Drama of Doctrine*, 16.

104. Vanhoozer, *Drama of Doctrine*, 125, 216.

105. Vanhoozer, *Drama of Doctrine*, 217.

106. See Kit Barker, "Speech Act Theory, Dual Authorship, and Canonical Hermeneutics: Making Sense of *Sensus Plenior*," *JTI* 3, no. 2 (2009): 227–39.

107. Brevard Childs, "The 'Sensus Literalis' of Scripture: An Ancient and Modern Problem," in *Beiträge zur Alttestamentlichen Theologie: Festschrift für Walther Zimmerli zum 70 Geburtstag*, ed. Herbert Donner, Robert Hanhart, and Rudolf Smend (Göttingen: Vandenhoek & Ruprecht, 1977), 90–92.

employing historical critical strategies—means to explore the Bible as God's Word and to see it for the theological disclosure it truly is. Therefore, canonical methods will gain popularity or diminish in appeal, depending on whichever model is referenced.

2.5 RESOURCES FOR FURTHER STUDY

Childs, Brevard. *Introduction to the Old Testament as Scripture.*
Philadelphia: Fortress, 1979.

> A must-read classic for anyone interested in Childs's canonical approach. As an introduction to the OT, Childs discusses the main content of each book along with the most important historical-critical issues and history of scholarship. Predictably, there is a concerted effort to discuss each book in a canonical context, considering its role as authoritative Scripture for the community. This is the result of many of Childs's methodological musings formulated during the 60s and 70s. For a similar treatment of the NT, see Childs's *The New Testament as Canon: An Introduction* (Philadelphia: Fortress, 1984).

———. *Biblical Theology of the Old and New Testaments: Theological Reflections on the Christian Bible.* Minneapolis: Fortress, 1992.

> In many ways, this work represents the culmination of Childs's canonical approach. It is extensive, covering the methodological and intellectual warrants for his approach as well as systematically arguing for trajectories that give the two testaments coherence. In this work, one can detect those methodological principles that have remained constant, as well as those that changed, throughout the decades of Childs's hermeneutical refinements—making the work critical for understanding Childs's method.

Noble, Paul. *The Canonical Approach: A Critical Reconstruction of the Hermeneutics of Brevard Childs.* Leiden: Brill, 1995.

> This work critically analyzes Childs's canonical approach from a methodological perspective. It is Noble's intention to "salvage" the method from the implications of the severe criticism it has attracted. Noble is bold and engaging, even offering a set of theses for canonical critics to adopt. Noble's is an important voice

among the critics of Childs's canonical approach and canonical criticism in general.

Sanders, James. *Torah and Canon*. Philadelphia: Fortress, 1972.

Arguably the most important work published by Sanders for understanding his method of canonical criticism, *Torah and Canon* investigates the first five books of the OT as canon. This work is exhaustive, discussing the diachronic realities of the Torah's formation and canonization as well as its function as Scripture for the community/communities. In this work, one can see Sanders's method in action, particularly his emphasis that the *process* of canonization is as important as the *result*. This is a must-read for students of Sanders's method or those who are fascinated by it. For a short introduction to his method of canonical criticism, see Sanders's *Canon and Community: A Guide to Canonical Criticism* (Philadelphia: Fortress, 1984). In this shorter guide, Sanders discusses somes of the differences that he perceives between himself and Childs.

Seitz, Christopher R. *The Character of Christian Scripture: The Significance of a Two Testament Bible*. Grand Rapids: Baker, 2011.

On one level, this work is a defense of Seitz's teacher, Brevard Childs. Seitz unashamedly defends Childs and his canonical approach against his most vocal critics. On another level, this work discusses how the OT functions with the NT as Christian Scripture. Seitz represents the "new school" of canonical criticism and is thus a critical voice for the method as it moves through the twenty-first century.

Seitz, Christopher R., and Kent Harold Richards, eds. *The Bible as Christian Scripture: The Work of Brevard S. Childs*. Atlanta: Society of Biblical Literature, 2013.

This collection of essays, written in honor of Brevard Childs in the wake of his premature death, consists of contributions by students of Childs and established scholars. The essays are inspired by the work of Childs or a particular theological concept emphasized by Childs. This insightful volume includes a comprehensive bibliography of Childs's publications.

3

OLD TESTAMENT RHETORICAL AND NARRATIVE CRITICISM

Suzanna Smith

T he methods of rhetorical and narrative criticism comprise a very broad portion of modern biblical criticism. Broadly defined, these are both text-oriented approaches to biblical interpretation that emphasize literary reading strategies attentive to a composition's style, structure, and communicative goals. The general approach is given many labels, including stylistics, poetics, literary artistry, aesthetics, or rhetoric.[1] This overview will provide an introduction to literary approaches to the Bible as a starting point for further study or specific applications.

3.1 DEFINITION AND GOALS OF OT RHETORICAL AND NARRATIVE CRITICISM

In general terms, rhetorical criticism or narrative criticism is an approach to biblical texts that uses a close reading strategy to read the text as a whole. The goal of the approach is to understand the author's communicative

---

1. The variety of labels is evident in the titles of different works that all deal in some way with the literary style of biblical texts: Robert Alter, *The Art of Biblical Narrative* (New York: Basic Books, 1981); *The Art of Biblical Poetry* (New York: Basic Books, 1985); Shimon Bar-Efrat, *Narrative Art in the Bible* (Sheffield: Almond, 1989); Adele Berlin, *Poetics and Interpretation of Biblical Narrative* (Winona Lake, IN: Eisenbrauns, 1994); Meir Sternberg, *The Poetics of Biblical Narrative: Ideological Literature and the Drama of Reading* (Bloomington: Indiana University Press, 1985); Phyllis Trible, *Rhetorical Criticism: Context, Method, and the Book of Jonah* (Minneapolis: Fortress, 1994).

goals and to realize how texts persuade readers by interpreting biblical passages according to general principles of literary convention.[2] Readers are interested in the literary texture of documents. They look for stylistic features—structure, repetition, key words, characterization, word choice, and discourse, for example.

To speak more precisely about this broad field is difficult because there are numerous exceptions to any generalization. The movement encompasses a wide range of scholars and struggles to define itself, even as it continues to evolve. The present description will begin with its historical aspect—how it has gone and where it is going—with a handful of examples with which the reader can engage the method.

To avoid confusion, it is necessary to discuss terminology at the outset. The separate labels of "rhetorical criticism" and "narrative criticism" could be understood as implying the existence of two distinct fields of biblical criticism. In practice, they often seem to be part of the same general approach, synonymous with such terms as literary criticism, synchronic criticism, poetics, style analysis, and aesthetic criticism. Martin Kessler notes that "'rhetoric' has proven to be a flexible term," and he sees such flexibility as an advantage for using it as a label to encompass both classical rhetoric and the newer literary approaches.[3] But Michael Fox counters that "a word loses value through inflation of its meaning," and he calls for a narrow understanding of rhetorical criticism: it is an endeavor to examine a text for the nature and quality of its persuasive force.[4] Fox's approach follows a traditional or classical understanding of rhetorical criticism. Since before the time of Aristotle, "rhetoric" denotes the art of persuasion.[5] In this sense, rhetorical criticism examines the interactions between writer ("rhetor") and audience to see the means through which a work achieves

---

2. This aspect of attempting to persuade readers is "rhetoric" in the more narrow sense of the word. This literary approach to the OT includes, but is not limited to, that aspect; see Meir Sternberg, "The Bible's Art of Persuasion: Ideology, Rhetoric, and Poetics in Saul's Fall," *HUCA* 54 (1983): 45–46.

3. Martin Kessler, "A Methodological Setting for Rhetorical Criticism," in *Art and Meaning: Rhetoric in Biblical Literature*, ed. David J. A. Clines, David M. Gunn, and Alan J. Hauser (Sheffield: JSOT Press, 1982), 14.

4. Michael V. Fox, "The Rhetoric of Ezekiel's Vision of the Valley of the Bones," *HUCA* 51 (1980): 1.

5. See Aristotle, *Rhet.* 1355b14.

a desired effect on a reader.[6] Thus, OT rhetorical analyses tend to fall into two types (though it is sometimes more of a placement along a spectrum): (1) those describing the art of composition, and (2) those interested in the art of persuasion. In the past decades, several OT scholars have called for reconsideration and clarification—namely, a return to the classical (or secular) understanding of rhetoric and a clear division between rhetorical and narrative criticism.[7] (Incidentally, this division is more distinct within NT criticism; critics typically employ the classical, and more restricted, understanding of rhetorical criticism.)[8] This introduction considers the method broadly. It is a method that is interested in the evaluation of a text's artful composition (literary style, aesthetic, etc.).

3.1.1 RELATIONSHIP TO OTHER APPROACHES

Narrative-critical approaches to the Bible have proliferated over the past fifty years. As such, it is helpful to understand this type of criticism in light of its historical development. It is also useful to compare the method with other approaches to the Bible in order to provide a picture of what rhetorical criticism is and is not.

From the eighteenth century until the mid-twentieth century, historical-critical methods were the predominant methods of interpreting the Bible in scholarly circles. These methods include source criticism, form criticism, tradition-historical criticism, and redaction criticism.[9] These are considered diachronic approaches: They are interested in how the texts of the Bible developed over time. They want to know the "backstory" of the stories in the Bible. They ask questions that are extrinsic to the text, such as: Who is the author? What are the author's characteristics? What is the background of the text? Rhetorical/narrative criticism, on the other hand, is interested in the biblical texts in their own right. Rhetorical/narrative critics pay less attention to outside (historical or authorial) contexts.

---

6. Fox, "Rhetoric of Ezekiel's Vision," 2–3; Mark Allen Powell, *What Is Narrative Criticism?* (Minneapolis: Fortress, 1990), 15.

7. These include Michael Fox, "Rhetoric of Ezekiel's Vision"; and David M. Howard Jr., "Rhetorical Criticism in Old Testament Studies," *BBR* 4 (1994): 87–104.

8. See chapter 6 of the present volume for a discussion of rhetorical criticism as used in NT studies.

9. On these approaches, see Douglas Mangum and Amy Balogh, eds., *Social and Historical Approaches to the Bible* (Bellingham, WA: Lexham Press, 2016).

Authorial intent and unity of texts are assumed in order to evaluate texts as they stand.[10]

Rhetorical criticism in OT studies developed when form criticism was the dominant method of study. Indeed, at its outset, James Muilenburg (often considered the father of OT rhetorical criticism) saw rhetorical criticism as a branch or outgrowth of form criticism. He understood the shortcomings of form criticism and sought to improve it by taking "full account of the features beyond the spectrum of the genre."[11] He argued that Hebrew literature did have aesthetic beauty and appreciated the nature of Hebrew literary composition *in addition to* form-critical analysis. Traditional form criticism looks for typical and representative patterns; rhetorical criticism seeks distinctive and unique features in the text. To Muilenburg, rhetorical criticism was not an alternative but a supplement to form criticism.[12]

In its current state, rhetorical/narrative criticism is not necessarily treated as a subset of form criticism. While form criticism seeks to separate texts into individual units based on genre and setting, rhetorical criticism studies texts in their entirety.[13]

As a text-centered method, rhetorical/narrative criticism can appear similar to redaction criticism. Both redaction and rhetorical/narrative criticism evaluate the final form of a text. But while redaction criticism asks about the historical development of the text by looking at the source components and intentions of the final compiler (the redactor), rhetorical criticism focuses on the text rather than the author. John Barton says that rhetorical criticism "welcomes the disappearance of the redactor" and instead concentrates on "the way a reader is pulled through a text."[14]

Another text-centered approach with which rhetorical criticism can be compared is structuralism. Structuralism is concerned with the text

---

10. John Barton, *Reading the Old Testament*, rev. and enl. ed. (Louisville, KY: Westminster John Knox, 1996), 201.

11. James Muilenburg, "Form Criticism and Beyond," *JBL* 88 (1969): 7.

12. Muilenburg, "Form Criticism," 8, 18.

13. However, form criticism has evolved since the 1970s into a more literary method under influence from OT rhetorical criticism and the self-consciously synchronic approaches of secular literary criticism and linguistics. On this development of form criticism, see Marvin A. Sweeney, "Form Criticism," in *To Each Its Own Meaning: An Introduction to Biblical Criticisms and Their Application*, ed. Steven L. McKenzie and Stephen R. Haynes, rev. and exp. ed. (Louisville, KY: Westminster John Knox, 1999), 65–68.

14. Barton, *Reading the Old Testament*, 23.

itself, to the complete exclusion of the author, whereas rhetorical/narrative criticism may acknowledge authorial intent. On a more literary level, structuralism looks for characteristic structures according to genre, but rhetorical criticism asks about the shape of arguments in the text.[15] While both approaches are synchronic, structuralists look for "deep structure" and relationships that comprise literary conventions, while rhetorical criticism concentrates on surface structures and particularities in texts.[16] The distinction between the two fields can appear philosophical; in practice, however, they can appear quite similar.

As rhetorical and narrative criticism are instances of literary criticism, the relationship between (secular) literary theory and biblical literary criticism is worth noting. Some secular theories have had a high impact on biblical scholarship (e.g., structuralism), while others have not (e.g., New Criticism).[17] Phyllis Trible uses secular literary theory to provide a background for biblical literary criticism: "As literary-critical theories have proliferated since the 1960s, so has their application to literary study of the Bible."[18] Biblical scholars often appropriate general literary theory, but they sometimes apply the theory and terminology in ways that "seem amateurish to literary critics," often due to biblical scholarship's traditional preoccupation with historical questions.[19] Moreover, literary critics have no exact counterpart for what is here labeled as rhetorical or narrative criticism.[20]

---

15. Barton, *Reading the Old Testament*, 199–200.

16. Trible, *Rhetorical Criticism*, 66.

17. Tremper Longman III, *Literary Approaches to Biblical Interpretation* (Grand Rapids: Academie, 1987), 33–38. However, again, this differs from the impact these approaches have made on NT criticism. See §3.1.2. for how the literary approach known as "New Criticism" has had some effect.

18. Trible, *Rhetorical Criticism*, 73.

19. Leland Ryken and Tremper Longman III, "Introduction," in *A Complete Literary Guide to the Bible*, ed. Leland Ryken and Tremper Longman III (Grand Rapids: Zondervan, 1993), 20.

20. This is especially true for narrative criticism as used in NT studies; see Powell, *What Is Narrative Criticism?*, 19. Biblical narrative criticism is loosely related to the field that secular literary critics would call "narratology"; see Adele Berlin, *Poetics and Interpretation of Biblical Narrative* (Winona Lake, IN: Eisenbrauns, 1994), 15. A synchronic, text-oriented approach to literary analysis is a common feature of literary criticism as broadly construed.

3.1.2 GUIDING ASSUMPTIONS

Rhetorical criticism and narrative criticism are text-centered approaches to the Bible that assume (and sometimes seek to demonstrate) integrity of texts, authorial intent, and deliberate compositional techniques. These principles underlie "textbook" rhetorical/narrative criticism, but individual critics demonstrate degrees of divergence from these assumptions, as can be seen in their analyses and exegesis. It is a broad field.

Rhetorical criticism works because it assumes that the texts studied maintain their textual integrity. As a method, it is built on the contention that biblical texts should be studied as whole entities. Thus, "persuasive unity" is the underlying assumption for this approach. This contrasts with other critical approaches that emphasize fragmentation of the text into constituent parts. The challenge with the rhetorical-critical perspective is not whether a text we have received is unified, but whether this unity is demonstrable from the text itself (since other methods claim to show fragmentation).[21] In response, rhetorical/narrative critics argue that they can make sense of a text as it stands by looking for narrative conventions. Consequently, rhetorical/narrative criticism is done on entire books and smaller pericopes within whole books. For example, Muilenburg's approach to rhetorical criticism specifies that readers should first delimit the passage under investigation using stylistic guides to determine boundaries.[22]

Persuasive argumentation assumes a deliberate author. Traditional literary criticism assumes and seeks authorial intent. Muilenburg's initial programmatic introduction of rhetorical criticism states, "[rhetorical criticism] will reveal to us the texture and fabric of the writer's thought, not only what it is that he thinks, but as he thinks it."[23] For example, Muilenburg's commentary on Isaiah 40-66 argues that the author arranged pericopes deliberately to persuade his audience of the imminent end of exile.[24]

---

21. Barton, *Reading the Old Testament*, 201, 208.

22. Text criticism may be part of this process. In fact, some analyses employ source criticism or form criticism before beginning a rhetorical analysis. "One can study the rhetoric of any stage of development he believes he can distinguish in the text"; see Fox, "Rhetoric of Ezekiel's Vision," 1.

23. Muilenburg, "Form Criticism," 7.

24. James Muilenburg, "The Book of Isaiah: Chapters 40-66," in *The Interpreter's Bible*, ed. George Arthur Buttrick (New York: Abingdon, 1956), 5:381-773.

But this assumption, too, operates on a sliding scale. Despite an underlying notion of authorial intent, some literary scholars place little emphasis on the author in their critical work. Especially recently, literary approaches tend to call themselves "work-centered." In fact, Gunn considers Muilenburg's group a part of the "new criticism" (a secular literary approach that emphasizes the text itself).[25]

Intertwined with and more prevalent than authorial intent is the assumption that texts have intentional form. "Rhetoric" implies artful composition: this means form is important for texts. Shimon Bar-Efrat writes, "It is through [the way the narrative material is organized and presented] that the meaning of the facts of the narrative is determined."[26] The narrative approach can be classified as "text-centered."[27] Although critics have interest in the author, their primary concern is with the text and its significance: meaning is determined from the text (like structuralism). Meir Sternberg's approach emphasizes this; he looks at the discourse of narrative rather than its genesis.[28] To quote Bar-Efrat again, "It makes no difference if the author used the techniques consciously or not, the crucial point is what formal methods are actually present in the work."[29] And it is not just the form of the text that is significant, but that the form enables and determines function. Meaning is based on the structure. How the author has built his arguments demonstrates what he wants his audience to understand. Muilenburg described this as "a proper articulation of form yields a proper articulation of meaning."[30]

---

25. David M. Gunn, "New Directions in the Study of Biblical Hebrew Narrative," in *Beyond Form Criticism: Essays in Old Testament Literary Criticism*, ed. Paul R. House (Winona Lake, IN: Eisenbrauns, 1992), 414.

26. Shimon Bar-Efrat, *Narrative Art in the Bible* (Sheffield: Almond, 1989), 10.

27. On the varying areas of focus in literary criticism, see §1.2 The Relationship of Author, Text, Reader, and Context.

28. Barton, *Reading the Old Testament*, 205.

29. Bar-Efrat, *Narrative Art*, 11.

30. Trible, *Rhetorical Criticism*, 27.

3.1.3 KEY CONCEPTS

3.1.3.a Conceptions of the Reader

In addition to describing the position of the author and the text, it is necessary to discuss the role of the reader within rhetorical/narrative criticism. Unlike the concept of reader-response criticism within biblical studies, which emphasizes the reader's role in creating meaning, rhetorical and narrative criticism focus on how the text influences the reader to respond in a certain way. Barton and Powell classify this position as "the reader in the text" (as opposed to "the text itself").[31] The reader is an agent of meaning. Meir Sternberg's work on biblical poetics illustrates this concept: there are "gaps" in the text, which invite and require the reader's participation in order to correctly understand a narrative. Thus, the reader discovers or creates meaning by solving puzzles and filling in gaps.[32] Sternberg argues that biblical narrative is created in such a way that it is "impossible to counterread," and the narrator controls reader response.[33]

Sternberg's work, and that of many others within this field of literary criticism, is interested in attentive readers. Narrative critics read with an eye for the type of reader the text presupposes. This type of reader is called the "implied reader."[34] The implied reader is not a real historical person but is revealed by the texts; a close reading of the text provides clues about what kind of reader is expected or implied by how the author chooses to create the text in anticipation of its future readership.[35] This implied reader is the person the writer addresses. (Rhetorical criticism, in its more narrow, classical sense, may ask about the way a writer is attempting to make the reader respond, or how a text persuades an audience. The focus is on the original reader to whom a work was first addressed, or the "intended audience" [also known as the "authorial audience"], and

---

31. Powell, *What Is Narrative Criticism?*, 18; Barton, *Reading the Old Testament*, 198, 210.

32. Meir Sternberg, *The Poetics of Biblical Narrative: Ideological Literature and the Drama of Reading* (Bloomington: Indiana University Press, 1985), 209.

33. Patricia K. Tull, "Rhetorical Criticism and Intertextuality," in *To Each Its Own Meaning*, 162.

34. See Wolfgang Iser, *The Implied Reader: Patterns of Communication in Prose Fiction from Bunyan to Beckett* (Baltimore: Johns Hopkins University Press, 1978).

35. Powell, *What Is Narrative Criticism?*, 19.

critics analyze a text's success in persuading this audience. This is more frequently seen in NT studies.[36])

But, increasingly, scholars do not assume there is an obedient audience that is willing to interpret according to the text's values: "No system of reading can ever guarantee the 'correct' interpretation of story."[37] Readers approach texts with a variety of assumptions or influences that instruct their reading.[38] Gunn and others see the field headed more and more toward reader-created meaning (such as reader-response criticism), with a focus shifted from the original reader to the modern reader.[39]

3.1.3.b Role of the Narrator

An integral part of narrative is the existence of the narrator within the narrative. The narrator is distinct from the author; background knowledge of the author or the author's context does not translate into a better understanding of the presentation of the story. The narrator stands between the reader and the events portrayed in the Bible, as it is the narrator who actually "tells" the story of the events to the reader. Everything the reader encounters is filtered through the narrator—"We see and hear only through the narrator's eyes and ears."[40] Close attention to the text reveals the nature of the narrator and aids the reader in understanding the intended argument of the story.

A narrator assumes a certain point of view. The narrator may take the perspective of an onlooker, relating action as if watching it from above or beside, without providing insight into characters' motives or thoughts. Or the narrator may assume an all-knowing position, able to see behind closed doors or into the minds of characters. In biblical narrative, the narrator usually takes an "omniscient" perspective, allowing the audience to go beyond the visual drama. The narrator may supply information regarding the emotions, intentions, and desires of characters. For example, "Jonah was exceedingly glad" (Jonah 4:6 ESV), "Eli perceived that the LORD was calling the boy" (1 Sam 3:8 ESV), and "The man and his wife were both naked

---

36. Powell, *What Is Narrative Criticism?*, 19.

37. David M. Gunn, "Narrative Criticism," in *To Each Its Own Meaning*, 201.

38. Tull, "Rhetorical Criticism and Intertextuality," 163–64.

39. Gunn, "New Directions," 416.

40. Bar-Efrat, *Narrative Art*, 13.

and were not ashamed" (Gen 2:25 ESV). The narrator also reports God's perspective. For instance, "The Lord was angry" (1 Kgs 11:9 ESV), or "The thing that David had done displeased the Lord" (2 Sam 11:27 ESV). However, the narrator does not reveal all unseen factors; the perspective is typically limited to that of an external observer. What the narrator does (and does not) relate is crucial to understanding the intent of the text.

It requires thoughtful reading to pinpoint the position of the narrator within a text. The biblical narrator tends to take an unobtrusive position. He almost never refers to himself. He shows up in phrases such as "to this day" or "in those days," making indirect reference to his own time. He can be seen when he offers explanations, interrupts action to supply background information ("Today's 'prophet' was formerly called a seer," 1 Samuel 9:9 ESV), or makes a judgment ("Solomon did what was evil in the sight of the Lord," 1 Kgs 11:6 ESV). Noticeable or not, the narrator is the one who leads the reader through biblical narrative: "The essence of the narrative world is entirely dependent on the narrator. ... The character of the narrators and the way in which they mediate is of supreme importance."[41]

3.1.3.c Analysis of Literary Features

Analysis of literary features comprises a large part of rhetorical/narrative criticism (sometimes to the disappointment of rhetorical critics, who complain that this is all literary critics do). This raises the question: What is the form of the narrative?

Critics examine the structure. In poetry, this means noticing details like parallelism, strophes and stichs, and coda. In narrative compositions, structure is often signaled by the use of repetitive words or keywords.[42] Rhetorical criticism in particular (in its classical sense) focuses on two devices that were used in the classical world and persist in modern theory: inclusio and chiasmus. Inclusio is type of repetition in which a key word or phrase is used at the beginning of a passage and repeated at the end. The

---

41. Bar-Efrat, *Narrative Art*, 13–14. As part of their understanding of the poetics of the Hebrew Bible, Bar-Efrat and Sternberg both provide thorough explanations of the importance and the presence of the narrator in the text.

42. Muilenburg, "Form Criticism," 17.

second instance serves to reinforce an idea and also signals a unity of the pericope by giving a conclusion.[43]

Chiasmus occurs when there is "an ordered set of inclusios."[44] It indicates a structure in which materials are arranged symmetrically, with certain components corresponding to others. In a four-part unit, we describe it as A—B—B′—A′ (the A sections corresponding to each other and the B sections to each other). The pattern can occur with the word order in a few lines of poetry or in larger portions of text, possibly even entire books.[45] Sometimes the pattern is disrupted by a single line in the middle that receives the emphasis.

Biblical scholars recognize other conventions as part of literary analysis. They refer to a "poetics" of the Bible or, put another way, "a theory of biblical narrative," which is an attempt to articulate the rules by which the biblical text works.[46] This is also within the arena of close reading. As a result, biblical literary critics strive to understand the compositional rules of texts. In Berlin's words, "If we know *how* texts mean, we are in a better position to discover *what* a particular text means."[47] Poetic interpretation can examine discourse, characterization, point of view, repetition, syntax, and plot. Examination of the details of a text according to these categories enables critics to make sense of units, to explain repetitions (previously considered "doublets" under source criticism and viewed as indicators of the redaction process), and to talk about narratives in light of their overall purpose.

3.2 DEVELOPMENT OF OT RHETORICAL AND NARRATIVE CRITICISM

One approach to explaining the development of rhetorical and narrative criticism of the OT is to consider the work of several key scholars at the beginning of the movement.

---

43. For example, the first two psalms may form an inclusio; see Jaime A. Grant, *The King as Exemplar: The Function of Deuteronomy's Kingship Law in the Shaping of the Book of Psalms* (Atlanta: Society of Biblical Literature, 2004), 60–65.

44. Barton, *Reading the Old Testament*, 202. Chiasmus is sometimes referred to as chiasm.

45. Trible, *Rhetorical Criticism*, 33.

46. Berlin, *Poetics and Interpretation*, 19.

47. Berlin, *Poetics and Interpretation*, 17.

3.2.1 MUILENBURG

James Muilenburg's 1968 presidential address at the annual meeting of the Society of Biblical Literature is considered the birth of modern rhetorical criticism in biblical studies, especially as applied to the OT.[48] Muilenburg was a form critic who became dissatisfied by the limitations of form criticism. He saw the details that diverged from formulaic genre and countered that they were valuable in analyzing texts. "Form criticism … is bound to generalize … [as] it applies an external measure to individual pericopes. It does not focus sufficient attention on what is unique and unrepeatable, upon the particularity of the formulation."[49] Muilenburg argued that biblical Hebrew texts did have aesthetic beauty and could be read as high quality literature.

Muilenburg proposed beginning an analysis with the methods of form criticism and then continuing with a careful inspection of the unique literary unit via three steps. First, delimit the passage under consideration, often using inclusio as a guide to isolating pericopes. Next, evaluate the composition or structure of the textual unit. Third, consider the stylistic phenomena of the passage. He intended this process to demonstrate the integrity of the text and the intentionality of the form, and also to provide a better understanding of the historical setting of the text. Muilenburg still considered himself a form critic. His method can be seen in his commentary on Isaiah 40–66 and his analysis of the Song of the Sea (Exod 15:1–18).[50]

Muilenburg himself introduced the term "rhetorical criticism," but some contend that he meant stylistic analysis, since he compared his approach to "stylistics or aesthetic criticism."[51] Thus, the overlap between literary criticism and "rhetorical criticism" still exists today.[52] But his employment of the term has also inspired many biblical scholars to turn to a classical understanding of rhetoric.

---

48. For example, see V. Steven Parrish, *A Story of the Psalms: Conversation, Canon, and Congregation* (Collegeville, MN: Liturgical Press, 2003). The address was later published as Muilenburg, "Form Criticism."

49. Muilenburg, "Form Criticism," 5.

50. See Muilenburg, "Book of Isaiah," 5:381–773; and Muilenburg, "A Liturgy on the Triumphs of Yahweh," in *Studia Biblica et Semitica*, ed. W. C. van Unnik and A. B. van der Woude (Wageningen: H. Veenman en Zonen, 1966), 233–51; respectively.

51. Muilenburg, "Form Criticism," 7.

52. Tull, "Rhetorical Criticism and Intertextuality," 159.

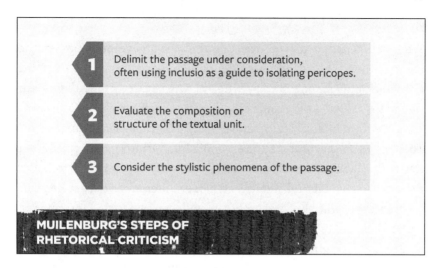

1 Delimit the passage under consideration, often using inclusio as a guide to isolating pericopes.

2 Evaluate the composition or structure of the textual unit.

3 Consider the stylistic phenomena of the passage.

MUILENBURG'S STEPS OF RHETORICAL CRITICISM

3.2.2 TRIBLE AND LUNDBOM

Two of Muilenburg's students clarified and extended his approach: Phyllis Trible and Jack Lundbom. Trible's work *Rhetorical Criticism: Context, Method, and the Book of Jonah* gives a thorough overview of the history of rhetorical criticism beginning with ancient times. Her guiding concept assumes the inseparability of form and content—in Muilenburg's words, "Proper articulation of form-content yields proper articulation of meaning."[53] Trible understands rhetorical criticism as a discipline that is practiced with two distinct concentrations: art of composition and art of persuasion. Her own exegesis of Jonah exhibits her method: a primary focus on "intrinsic reading" of the text, attention to details of construction, and poetic/stylistic analysis.

Lundbom's 1975 dissertation on Jeremiah followed Muilenburg's approach with a concentration on stylistic elements. He examined inclusio and chiasm as structural devices in Jeremiah. With a few considerations of Jeremiah's intended effects on audience, Lundbom's work anticipated a shift to audience-oriented reading. In 1997 Lundbom commented that the type of rhetorical criticism proposed by Muilenburg was basically close work on the biblical text, comprising "little more than an exercise in textual description." He contrasted the rhetorical criticism practiced in universities (outside biblical study) with its counterpart in biblical applications.[54]

---

53. Trible, *Rhetorical Criticism*, 91.
54. Tull, "Rhetorical Criticism and Intertextuality," 159–60.

While "rhetorical criticism" was taking shape and gaining momentum through Muilenburg and his students, a similar approach to the Bible was developing among literary scholars who began turning their attention to the Bible.[55] At the same time, various articles and books began to appear within biblical studies advocating a literary-critical approach.[56] Then in 1981, Robert Alter's *The Art of Biblical Narrative* drew great attention to this field and widely affected biblical studies. Alter seeks to bridge the gap between biblical studies and modern literary criticism. He reads the Hebrew narrative as a work of art, with complex characters and dramatic dialogue. In his view, the Bible uses "the most rigorous economy of means" to imaginatively portray God's relationship to humankind. He calls for "a literary perspective on the operations of narrative" to understand the Bible's rhetoric.[57] (Trible comments that "though he ignored rhetorical criticism, his analysis reflected the discipline."[58]) Alter studies the conventions of biblical narrative to see the Bible's literary artistry. These conventions include type-scenes (his designation for the historical critics' duplications), narration and dialogue, repetition, characterization, and the narrator.[59] Alter devotes an entire chapter to the issue of seemingly opposed accounts in the Bible, from which stemmed Julius Wellhausen's Documentary Hypothesis. Alter does not deny that there may have been multiple documents prior to their compilation in the Bible, but he contends that it is a biblical method to incorporate multiple perspectives into

---

55. In the 1980s and 1990s, literary critics such as Robert Alter, Meir Sternberg, Northrop Frye, and T. A. Perry all published books or articles applying their literary analysis to biblical texts. See Alter's *Art of Biblical Narrative* and *Art of Biblical Poetry*; Sternberg's *Poetics of Biblical Narrative*; Frye's *The Great Code: The Bible and Literature* (New York: Harvest, 1983); and T. A. Perry, "A Poetics of Absence: The Structure and Meaning of Genesis 1:2," *JSOT* 58 (1993): 3–11. See also Alter and Frank Kermode, eds., *The Literary Guide to the Bible* (Cambridge, MA: Belknap, 1987).

56. For example, Adele Berlin's *Poetics and Interpretation of Biblical Narrative*, first published in 1983; and J. P. Fokkelman's *Narrative Art in Genesis: Specimens of Stylistic and Structural Analysis* (Assen, Netherlands: Van Gorcum, 1975) and *Narrative Art and Poetry in the Books of Samuel*, 4 vols. (Assen, Netherlands: Van Gorcum, 1981, 1986, 1990, 1993).

57. Alter, *Art of Biblical Narrative*, 22.

58. Trible, *Rhetorical Criticism*, 76.

59. On Alter's starting point for study of the type-scene, see Walter Arend, *Die typischen Scenen bei Homer* (Berlin: Weidmann, 1933).

a "montage of viewpoints arranged in sequence," in order to communicate the biblical sense of an untidy, contradictory world.[60]

3.2.4 BAR-EFRAT

Shimon Bar-Efrat gave a lucid presentation of Hebrew narrative stylistics in 1979 (in Hebrew), and its translation to English in 1989 allowed a wider readership: *Narrative Art in the Bible*. Trible recommends this title as a more accessible introduction to biblical narrative than Sternberg's introduction.[61] Bar-Efrat's chapters on character, plot, narrator, time and space, and style demonstrate a literary approach to the text and contain many examples. The final chapter is a synthesis of these techniques applied to the story of Amnon and Tamar.

3.2.5 STERNBERG

Meir Sternberg, a professor in comparative literature at Tel Aviv University, published *The Poetics of Biblical Narrative* in 1985. His monumental book is a thorough approach to a poetics of biblical Hebrew narrative. Trible groups Sternberg's work under the (broad) label of rhetorical criticism, not because of his theoretical stance but because of the similarity of his exegesis with rhetorical criticism. Sternberg clearly states that he is not interested in only literary analysis of form, but in *how* texts function to communicate. He does not focus on the author or authorial intent, but on the text itself. He calls it discourse-oriented (as opposed to source-oriented) inquiry; he wants "to understand not the realities behind the text but the text itself as a pattern of meaning and effect."[62] Sternberg posits three principles by which biblical narrative functions: the historiographic, the ideological, and the aesthetic.[63] As part of the aesthetic, Sternberg discusses two narrative strategies of the Hebrew Bible: the use of gaps or discontinuities, and the use of repetition ("strategies of informational redundancy"). Sternberg emphasizes the role of the reader in navigating the gaps of narratives to resolve their ambiguity or incompatibility.

---

60. Alter, *Art of Biblical Narrative*, 154.
61. Trible, *Rhetorical Criticism*, 76.
62. Sternberg, *Poetics of Biblical Narrative*, 15.
63. Sternberg, *Poetics of Biblical Narrative*, 41.

He views the repetitions in the Hebrew Bible as a narrative style used by authors to cross-link texts and correct previous stories. Like Alter, Sternberg spends the bulk of his book explicating texts, doing "practical" literary analysis.[64]

3.2.6 BERLIN

Adele Berlin's 1983 book *Poetics and Interpretation of Biblical Narrative* presents the "mechanics" of narrative composition. Berlin's approach to the text is similar to Alter and Sternberg, yet in a more straightforward style. Berlin's explanation of poetics is finding the building blocks of literature— initially without attention to interpretation, contrary to Sternberg (she does spend a chapter discussing the interpretive implications of her poetic analysis). She calls it "the science of literature."[65] Whereas Muilenburg sought unique details and divergence from the norm, Berlin aims for generalized rules of composition to make conclusions about Hebrew narrative as a whole. This is her explanation of the difference between rhetorical criticism and poetics. Berlin's study focuses on character and point of view and uses many biblical texts to illustrate her theory of biblical poetics.

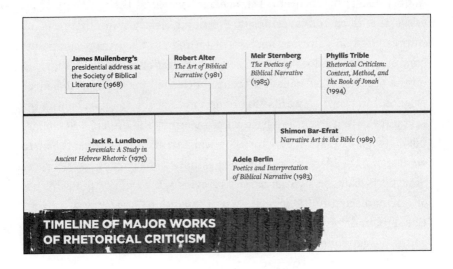

James Muilenberg's presidential address at the Society of Biblical Literature (1968)

Robert Alter
The Art of Biblical Narrative (1981)

Meir Sternberg
The Poetics of Biblical Narrative (1985)

Phyllis Trible
Rhetorical Criticism: Context, Method, and the Book of Jonah (1994)

Jack R. Lundbom
Jeremiah: A Study in Ancient Hebrew Rhetoric (1975)

Shimon Bar-Efrat
Narrative Art in the Bible (1989)

Adele Berlin
Poetics and Interpretation of Biblical Narrative (1983)

TIMELINE OF MAJOR WORKS OF RHETORICAL CRITICISM

64. Barton, *Reading the Old Testament*, 205.

65. Berlin, *Poetics and Interpretation*, 15.

3.3 APPLICATIONS OF OT RHETORICAL
AND NARRATIVE CRITICISM

The best introduction to rhetorical and narrative criticism comes through interaction with the textual studies undertaken by literary critics. Some of these are outlined here. Others are referenced in "Resources for Further Study" below. Scholars note the lack of methodological unity within this field.[66]

3.3.1 PENTATEUCH

Bernhard Anderson, in his tribute to James Muilenburg, states that Muilenburg never applied his method to the Pentateuch, which is traditionally the "testing-ground" for critical method.[67] Initial studies of the Pentateuch often approached texts on the basis of historical criticism. Kessler studied Genesis 7 with an eye toward source critics' traditional division of the verses. When analyzed, however, "convincing evidence is lacking that the two accounts are contradictory in any way." Kessler invokes the concept of *parallelismus membrorum* (a biblical poetic technique of stating the same thing twice in different ways) to explain the duplicate accounts within the flood story.[68]

Alter addresses the opposition between literary critics' approach to texts as unitary productions and historical scholarship's composite view of the Bible. Alter suggests that this "montage" effect can be understood as a distinct artistic medium used by biblical authors.[69] With this perception, the final redactor takes the role of artist. Alter does not claim to harmonize all contradictions within the Bible, but he makes the case for close, careful readings of literary segments to glimpse artistic unity. Rather than "editorial sloppiness," Alter points to careful and deliberate structuring, and

---

66. For example, Gunn, "Narrative Criticism," 212.

67. Bernhard W. Anderson, "The New Frontier of Rhetorical Criticism: A Tribute to James Muilenberg," in *Rhetorical Criticism: Essays in Honor of James Muilenburg*, ed. Jared J. Jackson and Martin Kessler (Pittsburgh: Pickwick, 1974), xiv.

68. Kessler, "Rhetorical Criticism of Genesis 7," in Jackson and Kessler, *Rhetorical Criticism*, 9.

69. Alter, *Art of Biblical Narrative*, 19. He references and credits an article by Joel Rosenberg here: "Meanings, Morals, and Mysteries: Literary Approaches to the Torah," *Response* 9 (1975): 67–94.

acknowledges that the sense of this opposes current notions of how a story should be structured.[70]

Narrative criticism in the Pentateuch (and elsewhere) thus assumes the task of demonstrating literary unity. For example, the story of Tamar and Judah, situated within the Joseph story, is frequently considered an interpolation with no connection to the surrounding historical narrative. Alter calls this assumption into question and goes on to demonstrate the intentional placement of the pericope. He points out vocabulary, thematic elements, and irony to conclude "careful splicing of sources by a brilliant literary artist."[71]

Likewise, narrative criticism demonstrates the artfulness of the creation story in Genesis 1–2. Instead of source criticism's fragmenting tendency,[72] it reveals the continuity of Exodus with Genesis and the role of the narrative voices in Deuteronomy as an introduction to the Deuteronomistic History.[73] Though the text of Leviticus and other law portions are minimally represented by literary critics, narrative criticism illustrates the thoughtful interspersion of law with narrative and views the placement of Leviticus "at the heart" of the Pentateuch as a sign of its centrality to the biblical text.[74]

Speaking of rhetoric in its persuasive sense, Alter understands the genre of biblical narrative as an argument in itself. The very fact that the Hebrew Scriptures are narrative—that Israel's sacred traditions are cast in prose—is significant. Whereas the pagan polytheistic cults used epic for their oral religious traditions, Hebrew authors deliberately employed another method. In Alter's words, "The Patriarchal narratives may be composite fictions based on national traditions, but in the writers' refusal to make them conform to the symmetries of expectation, in their contradictions and anomalies, they suggest the unfathomability of life in history

---

70. Alter, *Art of Biblical Narrative*, 136.

71. Alter, *Art of Biblical Narrative*, 10.

72. Barton, *Reading the Old Testament*, 203; J. P. Fokkelman, "Genesis," in *The Literary Guide to the Bible*, ed. Robert Alter and Frank Kermode (Cambridge, MA: Belknap, 1987), 40.

73. See Fokkelman, "Exodus," in Alter and Kermode, *Literary Guide to the Bible*, 59; and Polzin, "Deuteronomy," in Alter and Kermode, *Literary Guide to the Bible*, 92; respectively.

74. Damrosch, "Leviticus," in Alter and Kermode, *Literary Guide to the Bible*, 66.

under an inscrutable God."[75] We find psalms, proverbs, and oracles in other cultures, but we don't find a narrative history of one God in relationship with one people. The biblical narrative moves generally from creation, fall, exodus, and exile, with particular attention to Israel's disobedience and flawed leaders, such as Abraham, Jacob, Moses, and David. But it also addresses the unique God of Israel, Yahweh, who remains while everything else passes by like an assembly line.

3.3.2 HISTORICAL NARRATIVE

The large portions of narrative within the Hebrew Bible (Joshua–Kings) are fertile ground for narrative criticism. Scholars have undertaken sweeping overviews of the history as a whole, broad outlines of large portions within the historical narratives (e.g., "The Succession Narrative"), and detailed analyses of individual pericopes (e.g., David and Bathsheba, the Saul narrative, and the song of Hannah). Here we briefly survey several representative studies.

Anthony Ceresko applied Muilenburg-style rhetorical criticism to David's boast to Goliath (1 Sam 17:34–37). He shows the overall structure of the larger story, the intricate structure (including chiasm) of David's words, and the phonological patterns of the Hebrew words. Ceresko uses his analysis to counter textual critics' labels of corruption, to support source criticism, and to better understand the historical David.[76]

J. P. Fokkelman takes "a very short story" (the story of Elisha and the widow in 2 Kgs 4) and writes ten pages on it to exhibit the method and fruits of literary analysis. He first situates the text in its larger literary context, divides the text into lines or clauses, and undertakes a careful reading. He asks who the hero of the story is—at the outset, it appears to be Elisha. Fokkelman examines the action of the story, the spoken words, the vocabulary, and the movement. He describes a symmetrical, concentric structure for the story and also sees within it a parallel composition. All of these observations come together to support his conclusion that the widow, not Elisha, is the heroine of the story. Fokkelman warns that

---

75. Alter, *Art of Biblical Narrative*, 24.

76. Anthony R. Ceresko, "A Rhetorical Analysis of David's 'Boast' (1 Samuel 17:34–37): Some Reflections on Method," *CBQ* 47 (1985): 58–74. See overview in Trible, *Rhetorical Criticism*, 38–40.

narrative art is not initially transparent and that subtle discoveries are made via respectful, enthusiastic, open-minded reading.[77]

Adele Berlin uses Ruth to provide an example of the aspects of poetics along with interpretational insights. The book of Ruth is a frequent object of inquiry for literary analysts: its literary qualities are commonly recognized, and its boundaries are well defined. As far as characterization, Naomi is the main character, but Ruth appears to be the heroine; this is shown by point of view. All characters in the story are portrayed in relation to Naomi, but it is Ruth who consumes the reader's interest. The function of naming carries significance; Naomi stands independently, known only by her proper name, whereas Ruth is referenced in many telling ways, including "Moabitess," indicating the ongoing tension between Israel and foreigners. Berlin analyzes the use of *hinneh* (traditionally, "Behold!") in the story. *Hinneh* appears for three different reasons—first, "Look!"; second, to indicate point of view; and third, to introduce a new figure into ongoing action.[78] Plot, narrative structure, the narrator, and quotations are all presented, and then Berlin takes up the issue of the ending. The book of Ruth has three endings, and Berlin cogently shows that they can all be considered an integral part of the narrative (not later additions). The codas serve to connect the book to the time frame of the author's audience and to connect the Ruth narrative to the Bible's main narrative story in Genesis-Kings by the use of the word *toledot* ("generations"), thus elevating the story by association with King David.[79]

Shimon Bar-Efrat's explanation of plot in narrative uses Judges as an example. Judges is composed of a collection of narratives about the judges of Israel. Each of the judge units demonstrates literary cohesion (for example, Samson's personality ties together all of his exploits) in addition to comprising the entire book of Judges, whose unity is based on the cyclical chronology of the judges. Furthermore, the book of Judges finds its place within the larger biblical narrative by virtue of its worldview as well as its presentation of God—the one true God of history.[80]

---

77. J. P. Fokkelman, *Reading Biblical Narrative* (Louisville, KY: Westminster John Knox, 1999), 10–19.

78. Berlin, *Poetics and Interpretation*, 96.

79. Berlin, *Poetics and Interpretation*, 83–110.

80. Bar-Efrat, *Narrative Art*, 139–40.

3.3.3 PROPHETS

Rhetorical criticism, in its narrow and more literal sense, is frequently applied to the Prophets. Listing some critics who have undertaken the task, Howard notes, "These scholars have self-consciously studied the means of persuasion in biblical speeches. ... Their work clusters in the prophetic corpus, since the prophets tended to speak in discrete oracles, and a primary concern of theirs was persuasion."[81] Bar-Efrat similarly comments that in prophetic literature the narrator is overt and open about expressing his views.[82] Fox makes the same observation: "By any definition, prophecy is rhetoric."[83]

Fox applies this thinking to Ezekiel—specifically, Ezekiel's vision of the valley of the bones. He considers the rhetorical factors of the situation of the text—namely, that life for the exiles in Babylon was not too bad, and they were in danger of becoming either despairing or complacent, both of which could lead to their situation becoming permanent. Ezekiel's goal is thus to provide hope, encouragement, and a belief in national restoration someday, and his rhetorical strategy is to create irrational expectations to convince the exiles of the plausibility of the unlikely. Fox discusses the point of view, or role, of the speaker (he aligns himself with the audience as a spectator), the central image used in the argument (bones coming to life), and the strategy of the rhetor (imagery, argumentation, theme-word). The prophet uses these devices to demand a new receptiveness from the audience and a change in national perception.

Barton considers Hebrew prophecy a justification of the ways of God with the world and identifies the techniques of persuasion at work throughout the Hebrew Bible used to accomplish this. There are four: (1) rhetorical questions that legitimize divine punishment, (2) literary structures that produce rhetorical twists, (3) poetic justice, and (4) analogies to nature. Barton identifies these techniques throughout the Prophets to show their theologically persuasive skills.[84]

---

81. Howard, "Rhetorical Criticism," 100.

82. Bar-Efrat, *Narrative Art*, 16.

83. Fox, "Rhetoric of Ezekiel," 4.

84. John Barton, "History and Rhetoric in the Prophets," in *The Bible as Rhetoric: Studies in Biblical Persuasion and Credibility*, ed. Martin Warner, WSPL (London: Routledge, 1990), 51–64.

Yehoshua Gitay uses the categories of Aristotelian rhetoric to analyze Second Isaiah.[85] He explores the communication between Second Isaiah and the Jewish exiles in Babylon. The identified goal of Second Isaiah is to change the religious attitude of the exiles by identifying God's hand at work in the international scene. Gitay's method for each section of the book identifies rhetorical units and summarizes the content of each, considers the rhetorical methods Isaiah employed to reach his audience, commentates on the topics of each unit, and identifies stylistic/literary devices at work. Gitay relies heavily on both classical and modern rhetorical theory.[86]

Clifford too approaches Second Isaiah to examine the persuasive nature of the book.[87] His analysis does not involve Aristotelian categories or classical theory, but he understands Isaiah as an eloquent and persuasive rhetor. He considers the historical context of Second Isaiah and the literary techniques that are employed in each unit (e.g., parallelism, wordplay, and rhyme), and then offers a translation and commentary on the book to explicate the arguments of the rhetor, whose overall goal is "to persuade the people to return to Zion."[88]

Second Isaiah was also examined by Muilenburg. Though published before his 1968 SBL address, the commentary in the *Interpreter's Bible* is frequently cited as a prime example of rhetorical criticism.[89] Muilenburg's approach utilizes form criticism and aesthetic criticism with an eye toward Isaiah's overall argument. Muilenburg examines such features as form, parallelism, dramatic style, assonance, and meter. He divides the text into four pericopes and sees their deliberate arrangement as part of the author's argument that Israel is about to return from exile in triumph.[90]

Besides Muilenburg, other approaches to the Prophets also concentrate on stylistic analysis. Jack Lundbom, Muilenburg's student, wrote his dissertation on Jeremiah and later published a three-volume commentary

---

85. Yehoshua Gitay, *Prophecy and Persuasion: A Study of Isaiah 40–48* (Bonn: Linguistica Biblica, 1981).

86. Trible, *Rhetorical Criticism*, 41–42.

87. Richard J. Clifford, *Fair Spoken and Persuading: An Interpretation of Second Isaiah* (New York: Paulist, 1984).

88. Trible, *Rhetorical Criticism*, 43–44.

89. Muilenburg, "Book of Isaiah," 5:381–773. Referenced by Barton, *Reading the Old Testament*, 200; Trible, *Rhetorical Criticism*, 28.

90. Barton, *Reading the Old Testament*, 200–201.

on Jeremiah using rhetorical criticism.[91] His work looks at the structure of the book using inclusio and chiasm as controlling techniques; he finds these at the book level, in poems within the book, and in stanzas within poems. Keywords and speakers are the basis for his structural decisions. Using mainly structure and style, Lundbom demonstrates the argumentation in the discourse and points to a resistant audience.

The only narrative book within the Minor Prophets is Jonah. Trible analyzes Jonah, paying attention to details of construction: beginning and end, structure, plot, character, syntax, and particles.[92] In *The Literary Guide to the Bible*, Ackerman examines Jonah using narrative analysis. He looks at characterization, literary genre, and irony, and concludes that Jonah is intended to be satire.[93]

Fox points out that rhetorical criticism goes beyond the situation of the text, influencing its immediate audience; indeed, Hebrew prophecy constitutes an entire rhetorical movement that powerfully developed and influenced the national religion of Israel and Israel's own self-concept. It is a rhetorical movement distinct from the classical Aristotelian rhetoric, and it offers critics and scholars many promising avenues of study.

The many "rhetorical" studies of prophetic books of the OT highlight the variation and range of techniques employed by literary scholars. Although many scholars point to two "types" of rhetorical criticism, one focused on persuasive technique and one focused on stylistic technique, perhaps it is more accurate to talk about a spectrum along which the biblical literary critics fall. The readers who are more interested in persuasion often pay attention to style and structure, and the aesthetic critics often use their analysis to identify the point or purpose of the speaker of the text. Typically, rhetorical criticism looks at how the text/writer persuades, how one point flows to another, and what individual aspects of the text are particularly effective, whereas narrative criticism takes a "big picture" view, often providing rhetorical analysis in the way of concluding thoughts. This is to show the function of all the stylistic features of a document.

---

91. Jack R. Lundbom, *Jeremiah: A Study in Ancient Hebrew Rhetoric* (Missoula, MT: Scholars Press, 1975); *Jeremiah*, Anchor Yale Bible 21A–C (New York: Doubleday, 1999, 2004).

92. Trible, *Rhetorical Criticism*, 91–236.

93. Ackerman, "Jonah," in Alter and Kermode, *Literary Guide to the Bible*, 242.

3.3.4 POETRY

Narrative criticism is most frequently employed in narrative texts, which are found mostly from Genesis to Kings. Indeed, Alter comments that "the recent flowering of literary studies of the Bible has concentrated on narrative to the neglect of verse."[94] Berlin's *Poetics* mostly ignores these texts. It is here that the distinction between literary/stylistic criticism and rhetorical criticism (in its narrow sense) can be highlighted. Rhetorical criticism can easily turn from narrative to poetry, with the same goals and similar methods in each. This is demonstrated by the large number of rhetorical studies undertaken on prophetic poetry, several of which are noted above. The critic can ask about the speaker's goals and intended response from the audience just as easily with poetry as with prose. Similarly, the question of how a text persuades is valid with both narrative and verse, though the methods and mechanics of the two will exhibit some distinction.

David Clines' essay on Job is a deconstructionist reading that Trible classifies under "rhetoric as the art of persuasion."[95] Clines argues that the book undermines itself; the contradictions between the dogma throughout and the conclusions in the epilogue seem disharmonious. Yet the book is sustained by its power to persuade and its eloquent ability to identify with many readers. Clines' reading of Job is not a close, literary study but an examination of its general effect.[96]

Dale Patrick and Allen Scult composed a rhetorical study of Job with a tribute to Muilenburg. They sought to "move beyond the mere identification of forms and genres towards reconstituting the text as a piece of living discourse."[97] Somewhat similar to Clines' approach, Patrick and Scult's method was a rhetorical overview (rather than verse-by-verse analysis). For them, the book of Job persuades by engaging the reader to make connections and supply meaning between the narrative frame and central speeches. Patrick and Scult were interested in reader-response rather than

---

94. Alter, *Art of Biblical Poetry*, x.

95. Trible, *Rhetorical Criticism*, 41–48.

96. Clines, "Deconstructing the Book of Job," in Warner, *Bible as Rhetoric*, 65–80. See also Trible, *Rhetorical Criticism*, 45.

97. Quoted in Trible, *Rhetorical Criticism*, 46.

authorial intent. To them, rhetoric must involve "the way a text manages its relationship with its audiences."[98]

Now the real meaning of narrative criticism is brought to bear and needs delineation. For narrative criticism really does apply only to narrative texts—those sections that relate a series of events, string together clauses with "and then," "he said," etc., and have a strong focus on plot.[99] (The Hebrew Bible does not contain epic poetry.) The works by Alter, Sternberg, Fokkelman, and Berlin fit here. But aesthetic or stylistic or literary criticism is applicable to Hebrew poetry: scholars ask about the artful devices used in poetry to make it meaningful and effective. Indeed, this is practiced widely throughout biblical scholarship and falls nicely under the heading "literary criticism." And so, in the tradition of James Muilenburg, there are many analyses of versified text.

in 1966 Muilenburg himself wrote a critical study on the Song of the Sea (Exod 15:1–18), a lyrical text embedded in prose narrative.[100] Muilenburg first evaluated the poem form-critically to discuss setting and genre, then he turned to an in-depth analysis of structure and style. He identified motifs and refrains that serve as structural markers. He looked at key words, meter, parallelism, imagery, and assonance to comment on the content and how it creates meaning. Also, he used his analysis to argue for the textual coherence of the song, despite previous scholars noting its composite nature. Trible comments, "His exegesis disclosed the integrity of the text."[101]

Like the Song of the Sea, small poems are scattered throughout narrative texts, such as Lamech's song, Deborah's song, and Balaam's oracles. In his book on reading Hebrew narrative, Fokkelman includes a chapter on poetry, which focuses mainly on the short poems embedded in prose. He holds that the poetic lines function to enliven or intensify the prose (and occasionally vice versa).[102] A critical analysis of the Song of Hannah

---

98. Dale Patrick and Allen Scult, *Rhetoric and Biblical Interpretation* (Sheffield: Almond, 1990), 8.

99. See Douglas Estes, "Biblical Narrative," in *Lexham Bible Dictionary*, ed. John D. Barry (Bellingham, WA: Lexham Press, 2016).

100. Muilenburg, "Liturgy," 233–51.

101. Trible, *Rhetorical Criticism*, 32.

102. Fokkelman, *Reading Biblical Narrative*, 178.

by David Ritterspach, who uses Muilenburg's principles, supports similar conclusions.[103] After emending the text several times and establishing its genre and original context, Ritterspach evaluates the strophic structure based on thematic elements and key words. These stylistic elements enable him to explicate the high thanksgiving and praise for a mighty God alongside the quiet concepts of barrenness, birth, and motherhood.

In the *Literary Guide to the Bible*, Alter's chapter on the book of Psalms presents an approach that is reminiscent of Muilenburg's.[104] First he discusses Psalms from a form-critical standpoint, mentioning the various genres of psalm. But rather than just labeling and interpreting each psalm according to its type, the valuable insights come in finding where the writers deviated from the formula. The traditional forms are mere departure points. Alter moves on to style, demonstrating that tradition and imagery are the main characteristics of the Psalms. As for psalmic structure, Alter argues that the most prominent device is called "envelope structure," where a psalm emphatically indicates its beginning and end by use of the same significant terms at both points.[105] Alter's work is a reminder that analysis of large sections of a text is valuable; often the "atomistic habits" of critics miss the larger principles of organization within the longer psalms. He concludes with a discussion of themes, many of which are recurrent throughout the book of Psalms. In this, Alter highlights death and rebirth, as well as the power of language.

Incidentally, biblical poetry has also found itself the focus of specific poetry-oriented analysis, what we may call the *poetics* of poetry. Robert Alter followed up his initial work on Hebrew narrative with a companion devoted to Hebrew poetry, *The Art of Biblical Poetry* (1985). He contrasts the recent influx of incisive works on biblical narrative with the historical investigation of poetry, which is vast and chronologically deep (and extremely varied in their conception of how poetry works). Robert Lowth first identified biblical parallelism in *The Lectures on the Sacred Poetry of*

---

103. Ritterspach, "Rhetorical Criticism and the Song of Hannah," in Jackson and Kessler, *Rhetorical Criticism*.

104. Robert Alter, "Psalms," in Alter and Kermode, *Literary Guide to the Bible*, 244–62.

105. For example, Psa 8 begins and ends with the same phrase: "O LORD, our Lord, how majestic is your name in all the earth!" (Psa 8:1, 9 ESV).

the Hebrews,[106] and many studies in this vein have since been published—Kugel's *The Idea of Biblical Poetry* and O'Connor's *Hebrew Verse Structure* being two recent examples.[107] Fokkelman's chapter on reading poetry in *Reading Biblical Narrative* is a concise introduction to the field of biblical poetry and its various aspects. The theories and studies regarding biblical poetry are often at odds with one another; clearly there is still much to learn regarding biblical poetry.

3.4 LIMITATIONS OF OT RHETORICAL AND NARRATIVE CRITICISM

Some traditional historical critics perceived the appearance and flourishing of rhetorical/narrative criticism in the field of biblical studies as slightly naïve or as a detour from more important research. Traditional critics had been at the forefront of biblical studies for over two hundred years, and a historical approach to the Bible was considered "foundational" in many departments of biblical study. This assumption was called into question by a text-centered approach, despite the provenance of Muilenburg's proposal. Gunn notes that historical critics want to insist that literary criticism builds on their achievements in historical study.[108] To an extent, this demand has value, and it also illustrates a limitation of rhetorical/narrative criticism: it cannot provide the historical story of the text. But literary critics counter that this is not the goal of their reading. Indeed, literary criticism can be in direct contradiction to historical criticism (and vice versa). Herein some see another weakness of the movement: its relationship with historical criticism is unclear and sometimes competitive or antagonistic. To reject the question "Where did this text come from?" can be to neglect a valuable observation.[109]

Another limitation of narrative criticism is thought to be its potential for subjectivity and ideology to enter into a reading of the text. That is,

---

106. Robert Lowth, *Lectures on the Sacred Poetry of the Hebrews*, trans. G. Gregory, 3rd ed. (London: Thomas Tegg & Son, 1835).

107. James L. Kugel, *The Idea of Biblical Poetry: Parallelism and Its History* (New Haven, CT: Yale University Press, 1981); and M. O'Connor, *Hebrew Verse Structure* (Winona Lake, IN: Eisenbrauns, 1980).

108. Gunn, "Narrative Criticism," 227.

109. Gunn, "Narrative Criticism," 226–28. Note also Gunn's comment that despite many years of historical probing, the provenance of much of the Bible is still speculative.

the reader reads in a text exactly what the reader *wants* or *intends* to read in the text. For example, literary critics seem to be able to detect a chiasm wherever they want. While this potential exists in all methods—subjectivity and ideology are present in all types of criticism—literary criticism is considered more susceptible to this charge than historical criticism. As a result, it is important to identify the presuppositions a scholar brings to his or her reading of the text. The relationship of style to meaning is difficult to fully explicate, and rhetorical/narrative critics can substantiate their interpretation with textual observations that may seem unrelated to other scholars.[110] A related criticism is that rhetorical analysis of biblical texts often amounts to nothing more than a catalogue of literary features without exegesis. This is because some studies in this field we should probably designate as an "aesthetic analysis" rather than more formal literary criticism.[111] Moreover, some scholars demand greater acquaintance between biblical and secular critical theory, and this is often lacking.[112]

Patricia Tull states that "as with other forms of criticism, [rhetorical criticism's] chief limitations lie with the imagination, analytical faculties, and intellectual honesty of the exegete."[113] This is an apt statement. Literary criticism of the Bible is valuable and worthwhile. It strives to understand the text as it stands and to make logical inferences in a way that is sensitive to the details and peculiarities of the writing. But it is an endeavor that, like all approaches to texts (especially one as ideologically and emotionally laden as the Bible), is susceptible to the reading skills, worldview, and degree of care possessed by the scholarly reader.

3.5 CONTEMPORARY INFLUENCE OF OT
RHETORICAL AND NARRATIVE CRITICISM

This field of biblical criticism is difficult to nail down. Its boundaries are ragged; its center is moving. While this can represent a difficult learning curve for students, it also indicates its breadth. It can be approached from different perspectives and engaged in by scholars of various backgrounds.

110. Gunn, "Narrative Criticism," 228; also see Gunn, "New Directions."

111. E.g., Fox, Gitay, Wuellner, and Black. See also Trible, *Rhetorical Criticism*, 48–49; Howard, "Rhetorical Criticism," 101.

112. Barton, *Reading the Old Testament*, 208; Gunn, "Narrative Criticism," 227.

113. Tull, "Rhetorical Criticism and Intertextuality," 178.

In spite of its resistance to labels or categories (and perhaps because of it), biblical literary criticism flourishes. It is broad and many-peopled.

The many people participating in it caused it to stretch, grow, and assume new territory. Gunn discusses this movement in his essay on the direction of literary studies.[114] Whereas Sternberg and others focused on text and how "manipulations of text manipulate readers," literary criticism has grown to be more reader-oriented, emphasizing "that meaning is also and always the manipulation of the text by the reader."[115] Gunn's impression is that the literary approach to Hebrew Bible is part of the issue of *how* one reads the text ("the question of normative reading"), and this movement is headed toward the ideology of whatever person is reading it. In Gunn's words, "Reader-oriented theory legitimizes the relativity of different readings."[116] Some of this new territory comprises fields such as feminism, deconstructionism, and Marxism.

Finally, one result of the rise of narrative and rhetorical criticism has been the "dethroning" of historical criticism as the primary method for study of the OT.[117] The value of these literary approaches lies in their ability to help critics see a text as it now stands, no matter its historical journey to get there.

3.6 RESOURCES FOR FURTHER STUDY

Alter, Robert. *The Art of Biblical Narrative.* New York: Basic Books, 1981; *The Art of Biblical Poetry.* New York: Basic Books, 1985.

> Alter's books were extremely influential in drawing the attention of biblical scholars to the insights gained from reading biblical texts as deliberately crafted, artistic literary works. For the study of narrative, he demonstrated the literary function of type-scenes and other forms of repetition that had traditionally

---

114. Gunn, "New Directions," 414–17.

115. Gunn, "New Directions," 416. On the increasing role of the reader in literary interpretation, see Roland Barthes, *Image, Music, Text*, trans. Stephen Heath (New York: Hill and Wang, 1977), 142–48. On the different areas of focus in literary theory, see §1.2 The Relationship of Author, Text, Reader, and Context.

116. Gunn, "New Directions," 416.

117. Gunn, "New Directions," 414. See also Berlin, *Poetics and Interpretation*, chap. 5, on the relationship of poetics to historical criticism.

been used by historical criticism to mark the breaks between discrete sources.

Alter, Robert, and Frank Kermode, eds. *The Literary Guide to the Bible.* Cambridge, MA: Belknap, 1987.

> This collection offers a great introduction to the main literary features of specific biblical texts, providing a brief chapter on every book in the Bible.

Bar-Efrat, Shimon. *Narrative Art in the Bible.* Sheffield: Almond, 1989.

> This text offers a straightforward and accessible introduction to the key elements of stories—narrator, characters, plot, time, space, and style—and shows how those elements work in biblical narrative.

Berlin, Adele. *Poetics and Interpretation of Biblical Narrative.* Winona Lake, IN: Eisenbrauns, 1994.

> Berlin's short book is also an excellent introduction to reading biblical narratives closely and attending to how aspects like characterization and point of view are used in biblical narrative. She also offers a helpful chapter discussing how a literary approach relates to the traditional historical-critical methods of source and form criticism.

Fokkelman, J. P. *Reading Biblical Narrative: An Introductory Guide.* Louisville: Westminster John Knox, 1999.

> This book is an introduction to the method with a "how-to-do-it-yourself" approach and includes specific "hints" for further study of biblical stories.

Trible, Phyllis. *Rhetorical Criticism: Context, Method, and the Book of Jonah.* Minneapolis: Fortress, 1994.

> Trible was a student of James Muilenburg, the founder of OT rhetorical criticism. Her book provides a thorough discussion of the methodology of rhetorical criticism that also relates its development to the concurrent movements in the literary study of the Bible (such as the studies of Alter and Sternberg). Since Trible explicitly includes classical rhetoric, literary criticism,

and the evolution of form criticism in her discussion of the background of rhetorical criticism, her account is quite helpful for understanding the similarities in these approaches, despite differences in labeling.

4

INNER-BIBLICAL INTERPRETATION AND INTERTEXTUALITY

Jeffery Leonard

After twenty-three years of calling for Judah's repentance, met with only continued rebellion, the prophet Jeremiah finally pronounces the divine verdict against the nation: Yahweh will raise up the peoples of the north, led by "my servant" Nebuchadnezzar, king of Babylon (r. 605–562 BC), and destroy the nation (Jer 25:8–9). Jeremiah then goes on to announce the length of the sentence declared against the nation: "'All this land shall be a desolation and an object of horror, and these nations shall serve the king of Babylon for seventy years. And when the seventy years are fulfilled, I will punish the king of Babylon and that nation and the land of the Chaldeans,' declares YHWH, 'and make it a place of everlasting devastation'" (Jer 25:11–12).[1] In time, the Babylonian onslaught will come, Jerusalem will be destroyed, and many of the nation's leading lights will be carried away into captivity. But when the disaster of exile had passed, various biblical authors writing in later settings would return to Jeremiah's prophecy of seventy years, finding in it a message of continuing relevance.

Zechariah refers to Jeremiah's seventy-year decree twice. In Zechariah 1:12, the prophet looks for the restoration of Jerusalem now that the end of the punishment is at hand. Zechariah relays a vision in which the angel of

---

1. Unless otherwise noted, biblical quotations are the author's own translation.—Eds.

Yahweh asks, "How long will you withhold mercy from Jerusalem and the towns of Judah, with which you have been angry these seventy years?" Yahweh's response is that Jerusalem will be restored and his house will be rebuilt in it. Later, in 7:5, Zechariah again refers to the seventy years of punishment, harking back to "the message of the earlier prophets" who had called for the people to act justly but whose message had been ignored.

Jer 25:11 (LEB)	All this land will become a site of ruins, a desolation, and these nations will serve the king of Babylon seventy years.
Zech 1:12 (LEB)	O Yahweh of hosts, how long will you have no compassion on Jerusalem and the cities of Judah, with which you showed fury these seventy years?
Zech 7:5 (LEB)	Say to all the people of the land and to the priests: 'When you fasted and lamented in the fifth and seventh months for these seventy years, did you really fast for me?
2 Chr 26:20–21 (LEB)	... to fulfill the word of Yahweh by the mouth of Jeremiah, until the land has enjoyed its Sabbaths. All the days of desolation it kept Sabbath, to fulfill seventy years.
Dan 9:2 (LEB)	I, Daniel, observed in the scrolls the number of the years that it was that were to be fulfilled according to the word of Yahweh to Jeremiah the prophet for the devastation of Jerusalem—seventy years.

JEREMIAH'S PROPHECY FOR SEVENTY YEARS

As the Chronicler recalls the destruction of Jerusalem, the exile in Babylon, and the proclamation of return issued by King Cyrus of Persia, he specifies that these events took place "when the word of YHWH spoken by Jeremiah was fulfilled" (2 Chr 36:22). He adds that the people were exiled "in fulfillment of the word of YHWH spoken by Jeremiah" until "the land had enjoyed its Sabbaths; all the days of its desolation, it kept Sabbath, till seventy years were completed" (2 Chr 36:21). Here Jeremiah's prophecy is interpreted in light of Lev 26:32–35, a legal text warning that failure to observe the Sabbath years God had decreed would lead to exile so the land could make up for the Sabbaths it had missed.

Many years later, Jeremiah's seventy years would again be recalled in the book of Daniel. As the book recounts the story, Daniel "consulted the books concerning the number of years that, according to the word of YHWH to Jeremiah the prophet, must be fulfilled for the destruction of Jerusalem: seventy years" (Dan 9:2). When Daniel offers a penitential prayer on behalf of the nation, the angel Gabriel appears to relay the divine response. Gabriel's message informs Daniel that Jeremiah's seventy years actually signify seventy weeks of years that must pass before the nation is fully restored. Seventy years are now interpreted to be 490 years.

Similar patterns are evident in the NT. In Romans 4, for example, the Apostle Paul lays out a case for the efficacy of faith alone as the means of salvation. As supporting evidence for his case, Paul turns to the life of Abraham. Paul demands of his interlocutor, "What does the Scripture say?" (Rom 4:3), a question he goes on to answer by quoting Genesis 15:6: "Abraham believed God, and it was reckoned to him as righteousness." The apostle then presses his case, asking, "How then was it reckoned to him? Was it before or after he had been circumcised?" (Rom 4:10). Here Paul focuses on the chronology of Abraham's life as it is recounted in Genesis. The declaration that Abraham was righteous was made in what is now Genesis 15. But Abraham's circumcision did not take place until Genesis 17. Thus, Paul insists, Abraham was righteous while he was still uncircumcised. In the apostle's words, circumcision was merely "the seal of the righteousness that he had by faith while he was still uncircumcised" (Rom 4:11).

Rom 4:11 (LEB)	Jas 2:20–21 (LEB)
And he received the sign of circumcision as a seal of the righteousness by faith which he had while uncircumcised, so that he could be the father of all who believe although they are uncircumcised, so that righteousness could be credited to them.	Do you want to know, O foolish person, that faith apart from works is useless? Was not Abraham our father justified by works when he offered up his son Isaac on the altar?

ABRAHAM'S FAITH IN THE NEW TESTAMENT

A nearly identical interpretive method is employed in the second chapter of James. Focusing, as did Paul, on the chronology of Abraham's life in the book of Genesis, James arrives at essentially the opposite conclusion concerning the relationship of faith and works. James asks, "What good is it, my brothers and sisters, if you say you have faith but do not have works?

Can faith save you?" (Jas 2:14). But what of Paul's argument that Abraham was righteous before he was circumcised? James counters, "Do you want to be shown, you senseless person, that faith apart from works is barren? Was not our ancestor Abraham justified by works when he offered his son Isaac on the altar?" (Jas 2:20–21). James' observation rests on how, while Abraham may have been declared righteous in Genesis 15, it was not until he had passed the divine test in Genesis 22 that it could be said, "Now I know that you fear God" (Gen 22:12). James concludes: "You see that faith was active along with his works, and faith was brought to completion by the works. Thus the scripture was fulfilled that says, 'Abraham believed God, and it was reckoned to him as righteousness,' and he was called the friend of God. You see that a person is justified by works and not by faith alone" (Jas 2:22–24).

The preceding examples—the use and reuse of Jeremiah's prophecy of seventy years and the reliance on the chronology of Abraham's life from Genesis in the writings of Paul and James—attest to a phenomenon scholars have found to be increasingly evident in both the Hebrew Bible[2] and the NT. Throughout the Scriptures, later biblical authors refer to, rely on, and reinterpret the works of their biblical antecedents. This process of reliance and reinterpretation is known as inner-biblical interpretation.

4.1 DEFINITION AND GOAL OF INNER-BIBLICAL INTERPRETATION

Inner-biblical interpretation can be defined as the interpretation of earlier biblical texts by later biblical authors. This relatively simple definition masks an important and complex issue: Which texts and authors count as *biblical* texts and authors? Because the boundaries of the biblical corpus are drawn differently within Judaism and Christianity (and indeed within one segment of Christianity versus another), the term "biblical" is apt to be misunderstood. Scholars have generally distinguished between

---

2. "Hebrew Bible" is a designation for the OT in Hebrew, also known as the Tanakh. The label is more specific than "Old Testament" since different writings were considered part of the OT by different religious groups. For example, the Septuagint includes Greek compositions that are not considered part of the Hebrew Bible or Tanakh.—Eds.

the interpretation of biblical texts by tradents[3] within the Hebrew Bible/ Tanakh and the interpretation of these same texts by the authors outside this corpus. In this article, we consider inner-biblical interpretation within both the Hebrew Bible and the NT. This focus on the Tanakh and NT should not obscure the broad continuities that exist between the interpretive strategies evident in these works and the similar patterns evident in other early Jewish corpora such as the Dead Sea Scrolls, the deuterocanonical books, the Pseudepigrapha, and rabbinic literature.

4.1.1 RELATIONSHIP TO OTHER APPROACHES

We can further define the nature of inner-biblical interpretation by comparing it to other, similar interpretive methods. Three such methods—intertextuality, tradition history, and redaction criticism—are particularly significant for understanding inner-biblical interpretation.

4.1.1.a Intertextuality

Interpreters often treat the relationship between biblical texts under the heading of intertextuality. For literary critics such as Julia Kristeva and Roland Barthes, however, intertextuality refers not to specific linkages between texts but to the larger web of inherited cultural knowledge that makes discourse intelligible. As Jonathan Culler clarifies, "Intertextuality thus becomes less a name for a work's relation to prior texts than a designation of its participation in the discursive space of a culture."[4] While this approach may have value for biblical studies, it is rightly distinguished from the more narrow focus of inner-biblical interpretation described

---

3. The term "tradent" refers to someone involved in preserving and passing on traditional teachings or beliefs. Tradents often rework the tradition for a contemporary audience in some way as they pass it on. For example, a Septuagint translator was a tradent, reworking passages of the Hebrew Bible in the process of translating them into Greek.—Eds.

4. Jonathan Culler, *The Pursuit of Signs: Semiotics, Literature, Deconstruction* (Ithaca, NY: Cornell University Press, 1981), 103. Introductions to the study of intertextuality defined in this fashion are available in Richard B. Hays, *Echoes of Scripture in the Letters of Paul* (New Haven, CT: Yale University Press, 1989), 14–21; Benjamin D. Sommer, *A Prophet Reads Scripture: Allusion in Isaiah 40–66* (Stanford: Stanford University Press, 1998), 6–10; and especially Beth LaNeel Tanner, *The Book of Psalms through the Lens of Intertextuality*, Studies in Biblical Literature 26 (New York: Peter Lang, 2001), 26.

here.[5] The specific concern of the study of inner-biblical interpretation is the allusion of one biblical text to another. Benjamin Sommer summarizes:

> Intertextuality is interested in a very wide range of correspondences among texts, influence and allusion with a more narrow set. Intertextuality examines the relations among many texts, while influence and allusion look for specific connections between a limited number of texts.[6]

Because identifying specific allusions from one text to another features so prominently in this approach, scholars often refer to the phenomenon as inner-biblical allusion rather than inner-biblical interpretation.

4.1.1.b Tradition History

Inner-biblical interpretation/allusion is distinct from tradition history. With the publication of *Schöpfung und Chaos* in 1895, Hermann Gunkel broke new ground in the study of the "history of the traditions" (*Überlieferungsgeschichte*) that came to form the Hebrew Bible.[7] Gunkel demonstrated that the traditions of Israel underwent significant development *prior to* their attaining more fixed forms as literary texts. Thus traditions were inherited and reshaped in a variety of ways before they came to be written down.

The trajectory marked by Gunkel reached its apex in the studies of Gerhard von Rad and Martin Noth. Von Rad considered the composition of the Pentateuch (or, more accurately, the Hexateuch) as a whole from a form-critical perspective. He argued that certain texts that he identified as ancient creedal statements (Deut 26:5–9; 6:20–24; Josh 24:2–13) formed the basic structure of Israel's sacred history. The Hexateuchal authors (and most notably the Yahwist) were essentially collectors of ancient traditions

---

5. This distinction does not always hold up in practice; within biblical scholarship, scholars will often use "intertextuality" to include both specific linkages between texts as well as inner-biblical interpretation and inner-biblical allusion.—Eds.

6. Sommer, *Prophet Reads Scripture*, 8.

7. Hermann Gunkel and Heinrich Zimmern, *Schöpfung und Chaos in Urzeit und Endzeit: Eine religionsgeschichtliche Untersuchung über Gen 1 und Ap Joh 12* (Göttingen: Vandenhoeck und Ruprecht, 1895). English translation: Hermann Gunkel, *Creation and Chaos in the Primeval Era and the Eschaton: A Religio-Historical Study of Genesis 1 and Revelation 12*, with contributions by Heinrich Zimmern, trans. K. William Whitney Jr. (Grand Rapids: Eerdmans, 2006).

who organized their materials along the lines already established by these creeds.[8] Extending and, in some cases, challenging von Rad's work, Noth focused especially on the pre-Yahwistic, and thus pre-literary, stage of the Pentateuchal traditions. Less concerned with specific creedal statements than von Rad, Noth traced the development of a number of key themes from tradition to literary composition. He maintained that these themes were joined at a very early stage into a common source document (or *Grundlage*) that both J and E relied on. He then proceeded to analyze the development of the individual traditions that were assembled to fill out these themes.[9]

Key for both von Rad and Noth was the emphasis they placed on the evolution of Israel's traditions before they were captured in the literary product that is the Pentateuch/Hexateuch. Various Scandinavian scholars, such as Johannes Pedersen and Ivan Engnell, took this emphasis on oral traditions even further, reacting strongly against the literary model for the development of the Pentateuch proposed by Julius Wellhausen.[10] While most traditio-historical studies have stopped short of Pedersen and Engnell's conclusions, it is nevertheless the case that a focus on orality is key to tradition history. Indeed, it is this focus on the oral phase of the tradition that distinguishes tradition history from inner-biblical interpretation. In his introduction to the discipline of tradition history, Douglas Knight insists that "*a tradition ceases to be such at that point at which it is removed* (by an individual or by a subgroup of its usual traditionists) *from its normal context in life and is entered into a written composition, thereby losing its ability to develop and adapt*" (emphasis his).[11] For inner-biblical interpretation, however, it is the written compositions, not the pre-literary traditions, that are most important. As Michael Fishbane observes, "Whereas the study of tradition-history moves back from the written sources to the oral

---

8. Gerhard von Rad, *The Problem of the Hexateuch and Other Essays* (Edinburgh: Oliver and Boyd, 1966).

9. Martin Noth, *A History of Pentateuchal Traditions*, trans. Bernhard W. Anderson, SPRT (Atlanta: Scholars Press, 1981).

10. Ivan Engnell, *Gamla Testamentet: En traditionshistorisk inledning*, vol. 1 (Stockholm: Svenska Kyrkans Diakonistyrelses Bokförlag, 1945).

11. Douglas A. Knight, *Rediscovering the Traditions of Israel*, 3rd ed., SBLStBL 16 (Atlanta: Society of Biblical Literature, 2006), 22.

traditions which make them up, inner-biblical exegesis starts with the received Scripture and moves forward to the interpretations based on it."[12]

4.1.1.c Redaction Criticism

Somewhat closer to inner-biblical interpretation is redaction criticism. Key to the notion that the Pentateuch, and indeed much of the rest of the Bible, was composed through editing together earlier documentary sources is the attendant notion that an editor or editors must have worked to accomplish this process. For reasons discussed more fully below (see "Development of Inner-biblical Interpretation"), early source critics were often reluctant to allow the voice of these redactors to be heard at full volume. More recently, though, and again especially through the influence of von Rad and Noth, the unique contribution of the redactor to the redactional process has received greater emphasis. In his commentary on Genesis, von Rad goes so far as to lend a measure of support to Franz Rosenzweig's comment that the siglum "R" (for "Redactor") ought really to stand for *Rabbenu* ("our Master") since it is through him that we receive the Torah.[13]

Redaction criticism and inner-biblical interpretation overlap in some respects and diverge in others. They are most alike in their sensitivity to the presence of interpretive and explanatory comments from later tradents. Indeed, many of the examples of inner-biblical exegesis grouped by Fishbane under the heading of "scribal comments and corrections" could just as readily be treated as redactional activity.[14] Where redaction criticism and inner-biblical interpretation tend to part company is in the role each casts for the interpreter. In redaction criticism, the interpreter serves as editor. In this role, he may arrange and rearrange, comment and expand on the traditions that he has inherited. Ultimately, though, the weight of the composition remains on the shoulders of the earlier tradents who passed the materials down to the redactor. By contrast, in inner-biblical interpretation, the interpreter serves as author. Like the redactor,

---

12. Michael A. Fishbane, *Biblical Interpretation in Ancient Israel* (Oxford: Clarendon, 1985), 7.

13. Gerhard von Rad, *Genesis: A Commentary*, trans. John H. Marks, OTL (Philadelphia: Westminster, 1961, 1972), 42. See also Franz Rosenzweig, "Die Einheit der Bibel: Eine Auseinandersetzung mit Orthodoxie und Liberalismus," in *Die Schrift und ihre Verdeutschung*, ed. Martin Buber and Franz Rosenzweig (Berlin: Schocken, 1936), 47.

14. Fishbane, *Biblical Interpretation*, 23–88.

the inner-biblical exegete draws on earlier materials. He does so, however, through echo, allusion, and quotation, activating the older text in *his own* composition rather than injecting his interpretive work into another author's composition.

4.1.2 THE GOAL OF INNER-BIBLICAL INTERPRETATION

The overarching goal of inner-biblical interpretation is to use the light shed by the reuse and reinterpretation of texts in the Bible to trace the development of religious thought and practice in the biblical period. Examining the ways in which later communities deployed earlier biblical texts allows scholars to address two crucial questions:

1. *How does the later community's* Sitz im Leben *("life setting") differ from that of the community that originally produced the text?* The composition of the Hebrew Bible was such that only a few books provide a definite historical context for examining the kinds of inner-biblical interpretation employed by their author(s). In the case of Ezra and Nehemiah, for example, the details of the books' postexilic setting are sufficiently abundant as to shed light on the social and historical factors at play in their reinterpretation of earlier texts. A similar situation exists in the case of Chronicles. Elsewhere, though, such historical specificity is often lacking. In such cases, the manner in which earlier texts are reused can help to shed light on the historical setting of the author.

   An example of this process is in the description of Joseph's sojourn in Egypt in Psalm 105:16–22. While the psalm shares sufficient verbal overlap with the narrative in Genesis to suggest it is dependent on Genesis, the psalm differs in several respects from this underlying narrative. Whereas Genesis describes Joseph's imprisonment in relatively benign terms, casting him as someone akin to a privileged prison trustee, the psalmist tells a much harsher tale: "His feet were subjected to fetters; an iron collar was put on his neck" (Psa 105:18). Then, in Psalm 105:19, the psalmist suggests Joseph's time of travail "purged him." The Genesis account, of course, offers very little evidence that Joseph was in need of moral or spiritual refining. Even the description of the ruler of Egypt as "ruler of nations" (Psa 105:20) rather than Pharaoh strikes an odd note. Taken together, these differences stand as clues pointing toward the historical setting of the psalm's composition. While fetters and iron collars have no place in the Genesis narrative, they are prominent features of exilic humiliation (Deut 28:48; Pss 107:16; 149:8; Isa 45:2). Similarly, the language of refinement through suffering is a regular feature of the prophetic descriptions of exile (Isa 1:25; 48:10; Jer 6:29; 9:6; Zech 13:9). And the reference to the "ruler of nations" sounds very much like the Hebrew Bible's descriptions of the kings of Assyria, Babylon, and Persia (Isa 10:13; Jer 34:1; Ezra 1:2). The shaping of the materials borrowed from Genesis suggests that Psalm 105 was addressed to an exilic audience, an audience that might find in the courageous example of Joseph a source of confidence for facing their own exile.

2. *How has the community's religious thought and practice developed over time?* The texts that came to form the Hebrew Bible emerged over the course of centuries. At least a millennium separates early poetic works like the Song of the Sea (Exod 15) and the Song of Deborah (Judg 5) from the apocalyptic book of Daniel. Almost inevitably, the nation's experience of God changed as it experienced the exodus, the rise and fall of the northern and southern monarchies, the exile under Babylon, and the return under Persia. These changes, some smaller, some larger, can be elucidated by considering the way later communities reinterpreted the texts they inherited.

Michael Fishbane notes an example of theological development made evident by inner-biblical interpretation in his examination of Nehemiah's actions to safeguard the Sabbath in Nehemiah 13:15–22. In this text, Nehemiah recounts his efforts to proscribe practices such as treading grapes and transporting goods to Jerusalem on the Sabbath. Fishbane argues Nehemiah's condemnation is based on Jeremiah 17:19–27, both because this Jeremianic text is the only other passage in the Bible that condemns the transport of goods to Jerusalem on the Sabbath (Jer 17:21) and because it, like Nehemiah, links the punishment of exile to Sabbath violation (Neh 13:18; Jer 17:27). Nehemiah expands on Jeremiah's prohibition against transporting goods to Jerusalem on the Sabbath by also condemning the sale of goods on this day (Neh 13:15–16), a violation Jeremiah never mentions. But Fishbane notes that Nehemiah's lemma in Jeremiah is itself an interpretive expansion of Deuteronomy 5:12–14. The link between the texts is made clear by Jeremiah's repetition of both Deuteronomy's "keep the Sabbath" (Exod 20:8 has "remember") and its reference to the command having been given to ancestors. Jeremiah adds to the command, though, prohibitions against bringing a burden into the gates of Jerusalem and taking burdens from one's home on the Sabbath. And though neither of these prohibitions is mentioned in the Torah, Jeremiah circumscribes them with the divine utterance "as I commanded your ancestors" (Jer 17:22). In Jeremiah's interpretive expansion of the Deuteronomic command and in Nehemiah's expansion of Jeremiah, a clear indication of the increasing importance of Sabbath observance is evident.

1 How does the later community's *Sitz im Leben* ("life setting") differ from that of the community that originally produced the text?

2 How has the community's religious thought and practice developed over time?

THE QUESTIONS OF INNER-BIBLICAL INTERPRETATION

The examples cited here are only small samples of a larger pattern evident in the Hebrew Bible. As later communities faced new social and historical circumstances, they responded by taking up earlier literary traditions and redeploying them in these new settings. In so doing, these tradents allowed texts that had achieved a level of authority in the community to continue to speak with authority to later situations. This process of reusing and reinterpreting earlier texts, widely evident in the Hebrew Bible itself, provided a matrix from which the similar interpretive techniques of Qumran, the NT, and the Tannaim[15] would emerge.

4.1.3 GUIDING ASSUMPTIONS

The study of inner-biblical interpretation proceeds from a number of guiding assumptions: First, the reinterpretation of texts evident in the postbiblical period is also evident within the Hebrew Bible itself. Second, criteria can be established for determining *when* a textual allusion has taken place. Third, criteria can be established for determining *the direction* of textual allusions. Fourth, the interpretive methods used by tradents who allude to earlier texts can be analyzed.

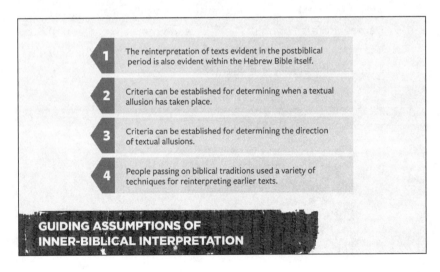

1 The reinterpretation of texts evident in the postbiblical period is also evident within the Hebrew Bible itself.

2 Criteria can be established for determining when a textual allusion has taken place.

3 Criteria can be established for determining the direction of textual allusions.

4 People passing on biblical traditions used a variety of techniques for reinterpreting earlier texts.

GUIDING ASSUMPTIONS OF INNER-BIBLICAL INTERPRETATION

---

15. The Tannaim were rabbis of the formative period of rabbinic Judaism, roughly the first and second centuries AD. Their teachings are preserved in the earliest rabbinic texts such as the Mishnah and the Tosefta.—Eds.

4.1.3.a Reinterpretation Is Evident

Scholars have given substantial attention to the ways in which later communities of faith continued to reinterpret and reapply texts from the Hebrew Bible in their own religious works. Whether for guidance, inspiration, authority, or legitimation, the Dead Sea Scrolls, the deuterocanonical books, the Jewish Pseudepigrapha, the NT, and rabbinic literature constantly connect their own writings to the writings of the Hebrew Bible. At times, these connections take the form of direct quotations; elsewhere, they consist of little more than subtle allusions. The existence of these connections and their usefulness for understanding these early religious groups, however, is taken as a given.

Less commonly recognized is that the pattern so evident in the postbiblical period of reusing and reinterpreting earlier biblical texts has its antecedents in the Hebrew Bible itself. Already within the biblical period, authors were fully engaged in the process of reusing earlier biblical texts. As Fishbane observes:

> One may say that the entire corpus of Scripture remains open to these invasive procedures and strategic reworkings up to the close of the canon in the early rabbinic period, and so the received text is complexly compacted of teachings and their subversion, of rules and their extension, of topoi and their revision. Revelation and Tradition were thickly interwoven and interdependent, and the received Hebrew Bible is itself, therefore, the product of an interpretive tradition.[16]

It has long been recognized that the literature of the Hebrew Bible was composed not as large, discrete blocks but as a succession of layers built one on another. What Fishbane and others have made apparent is that these strata become interwoven as later biblical authors allude to and then reconfigure earlier layers of tradition.

---

16. Michael A. Fishbane, "Inner Biblical Exegesis: Types and Strategies of Interpretation in Ancient Israel," in *Midrash and Literature*, ed. Geoffrey H. Hartman and Sanford Budick (New Haven, CT: Yale University Press, 1986), 36.

4.1.3.b Textual Allusions Can Be Determined

If the notion that some biblical texts allude to others is accepted, it remains to determine when an actual allusion has taken place. Cynthia Edenburg has outlined a range of literary phenomena that tend to trigger textual associations in the mind of the reader:

1. common formal structure—structural similarities that result from shared genres, type-scenes, and narrative patterns

2. common motifs—recurrent motifs such as the destruction of Sodom or the faithful youth in the court of a foreign king

3. doublets—parallel accounts of a single event

4. variant accounts—differing versions of a circumstance such as the manner of David's entry into Saul's service (1 Sam 15:14–23 vs. 17:55–18:2)

5. text commenting on text—such as inner-biblical exegesis in which one text comments on, explains, or actualizes another text

6. allusion—achieving a "covert level of significance" by indirectly referring to another text

7. quotation—using a direct quotation, whether marked or unmarked, in a new literary context[17]

While these "textual triggers" can help to identify associations between texts, Edenburg notes that most of these triggers also have the potential to suggest literary connections where none exists. Thus, for example, two business letters will share a common formal structure even when no direct textual connection exists between the two.

When evidence emerges for one text's dependence on another, some standard is needed for gauging the strength of that evidence. Edenburg proposes five markers helpful for "establishing author devised interrelations":

---

17. Cynthia Edenburg, "How (Not) to Murder a King: Variations on a Theme in 1 Sam 24; 26," *SJOT* 12 (1998): 65–70.

1. unique recurrence of peculiar formations—Are the texts connected by otherwise unattested forms or by common forms used in a unique way?

2. similarity of context and/or structure—Is the connection strengthened through use in a similar context or structure?

3. transformation and reactualization of a common element—Is the form or function of an element common to both texts intentionally changed in the borrowing text?

4. "ungrammatical" actualization of a common element—Is the common element highlighted by being grammatically set apart from its context as a foreign element?

5. interaction between texts—Does one text respond to the other through "interpretation, supplementation, or polemic"?[18]

In his study of Paul's use of Scripture, Richard Hays offers an expanded list of criteria:

1. availability—Was the proposed source of the textual echo available to Paul?

2. volume—How explicit is the repetition of words and syntactical patterns from the source text, and how prominently do these words feature in the borrowing text?

3. recurrence—How often does Paul rely on the same passage?

4. thematic coherence—How well does the proposed echo fit into Paul's argument?

5. historical plausibility—Could the author and the readers (Paul and his first-century audience, in this case) have intended and understood the alleged meaning?

6. history of interpretation—Have other readers heard the same echoes before?

---

18. Edenburg, "How (Not) to Murder a King," 72–73.

7. satisfaction—Does the proposed meaning make sense?[19]

At the heart of Edenburg's and Hays's suggestions is a recognition that not all textual allusions are created equal. To use an obvious example, a paragraph-long quotation, complete with citation, would naturally present a stronger claim for a textual connection than would a single, subtle wordplay offered without citation. Although this example is so clear cut that it may seem unnecessary, we could formulate certain principles for evaluating the claims of the two potential connections. For example, we could stipulate that a quotation constitutes stronger evidence for a connection than a wordplay, that a passage with a citation presents a stronger candidate for allusion than a passage without, and so forth. These principles are fairly straightforward. For cases that are less clear cut, the following eight principles may serve as methodological guidelines:

1. *Shared language is the single most important factor in establishing textual connections.* Textual allusions may occur on both thematic and lexical levels. As Risto Nurmela has pointed out, though, many "themes" appear across broad sections of the Hebrew Scriptures. As a result, there is often little basis for narrowing a thematic connection to one section of the Tanakh as opposed to another. As a result, while it may be the case that not all textual allusions contain shared language, Nurmela is surely correct in insisting that verbal parallels provide the most objective and verifiable criteria for identifying these allusions.[20] Fishbane makes a similar point in his treatment of textual allusions that lack explicit citation formulae, arguing, "The identification of aggadic exegesis where external objective criteria are lacking is proportionately increased to the

---

19. Hays, *Echoes of Scripture*, 29–32.

20. Risto Nurmela, "The Growth of the Book of Isaiah Illustrated by Allusions in Zechariah," in *Bringing Out the Treasure: Inner Biblical Allusion in Zechariah 9–14*, ed. Mark J. Boda and Michael H. Floyd, with Rex Mason, JSOTSup 370 (London: T&T Clark, 2003), 246–47. See further Risto Nurmela, *Prophets in Dialogue: Inner-Biblical Allusions in Zechariah 1–8 and 9–14* (Åbo: Åbo Akademi University Press, 1996), 21–27; and Nicholas H. F. Tai, *Prophetie als Schriftauslegung in Sacharja 9–14: Traditions- und kompositionsgeschichtliche Studien* (Stuttgart: Calwer, 1996), 7–8.

extent that multiple and sustained lexical linkages between two texts can be recognized."[21]

2. *Shared language is more important than non-shared language in a potential textual connection.* The presence of shared language may indicate a connection between texts. Just as importantly, though, that a text may contain additional language that is idiosyncratic or not shared *in no way* undermines the possibility of such a connection. Unique or idiosyncratic language may be a reflection of an author's creativity or writing style. It may even point to an author's use of multiple sources. It tells us very little, however, about the existence or nonexistence of allusions in the language that is shared with other texts. By way of example, the verbal correspondences between Psalm 106:31 ("and it was reckoned to him as righteousness") and Genesis 15:6 ("and he reckoned it to him as righteousness") raise the possibility of an allusion from one text to the other. It is possible that no allusion exists between the two. That the psalmist uses the phrase in reference to Pinchas and the tradent in Genesis to Abram, however, in no way undermines the likelihood of the allusion.[22] To deny outright the possibility of a textual connection, one must show either that the texts do not share significant lexical links or that the borrowing text must have drawn its shared language from another source. Anything short of this leaves open the possibility, at least, of a connection.

3. *Shared language that is rare or distinctive suggests a stronger textual connection than does language that is widely used.*[23] Shared

---

21. Fishbane, *Biblical Interpretation*, 285. Adapting terms from Douglas Knight, Fishbane uses *traditum* to refer to the "content of tradition" and *traditio* to signify the "long and varied process of transmission" (see Knight, *Recovering the Traditions of Israel*, 5).

22. Paul Noble adopts essentially the opposite view to the one expressed here, arguing those searching for textual connections are obliged to give equal weight to both similarities and dissimilarities between the texts in question (Paul Noble, "Esau, Tamar, and Joseph: Criteria for Identifying Inner-Biblical Allusions," *VT* 52 [2002]: 224–25).

23. This principle is similar to Hays's "volume" and Edenburg's "unique recurrence of peculiar formulations" criteria (see Hays, *Echoes of Scripture*, 30; Edenburg, "How [Not] to Murder a King," 72).

vocabulary opens the possibility that one text alludes to another. Proving that such an allusion exists, though, depends in part on the kinds of lexical connections the texts share. A textual overlap consisting solely of common terms would not negate the possibility of a connection, but it would make it quite difficult to *prove* that one text alludes to the other.[24] On the other hand, if the language shared by two texts is relatively rare or is used in a manner that is distinctive, it can lend support to the possibility of a connection.[25]

4. *Shared phrases suggest a stronger textual connection than do individual shared terms.* Individual terms are often sufficient to establish an allusive connection between texts. The sharing of longer phrases, however, serves to strengthen such a connection. In the case of Psalm 106:31 cited above, the psalmist could well have alluded to Genesis 15 using only the word "righteousness." Were this the case, though, readers would be hard pressed to prove the allusion (or perhaps even to identify it in the first place). That the psalmist replicates a longer phrase from Genesis makes the allusion more likely.

5. *The accumulation of shared language suggests a stronger textual connection than does a single shared term or phrase.* The presence of an isolated shared term or phrase could well suggest one text has alluded to another. The likelihood of a connection increases, though, with the accumulation of other shared terms. Thus Sommer concedes that a textual connection based on just one or two allusions could be dismissed but insists, "If I find scores of such borrowings, and if they display consistent patterns in their reuse of older material, then the notion that

---

24. A similar point is made in Sommer, "Allusions and Illusions: The Unity of the Book of Isaiah in Light of Deutero-Isaiah's Use of Prophetic Tradition," in *New Visions of Isaiah*, ed. Roy F. Melugin and Marvin A. Sweeney, JSOTSup 214 (Sheffield, UK: Sheffield Academic Press, 1996), 159.

25. A contrary view is again offered by Noble, who argues even inherently improbable resemblances between texts are to be expected, provided the texts in question are sufficiently long (Noble, "Esau, Tamar, and Joseph," 249–51).

all these cases result from happenstance becomes untenable."[26] Similarly, Edenburg introduces her criteria for establishing textual dependence by arguing, "Since each individual criterion is subjective to some degree, the weight of accumulative evidence will strengthen the claim of interrelatedness."[27]

An important corollary to this principle is that strong evidence for allusions in some cases can lend support to less certain allusions elsewhere. With each additional connection, the supporting evidence for affirming less obvious allusions grows stronger. As Rex Mason argues in his analysis of parallels between Zechariah 9–14 and the rest of the Twelve:

> While great caution has to be shown in too quickly assuming that a certain verse or reference has been inspired by this particular text or that, there is a cumulative weight to a great number of probabilities which in the end proves decisive.[28]

6. *Shared language in similar contexts suggests a stronger textual connection than does shared language alone.*[29] As noted above, common terms are less conclusive than distinctive terms for establishing a textual allusion. Even common terms can support a connection, though, when they occur in similar contexts. To cite just one example, terms such as "fire" and "hear" would normally provide a slender base for positing a textual connection. But when both Psalm 78 and Numbers 11 use these terms in the same context, namely to describe the divine response to the Taberah incident, the likelihood of a connection goes up.

7. *Shared language need not be accompanied by shared ideology to establish a textual connection.* There is no reason to expect that a writer who draws on the language of an earlier tradition

---

26. Sommer, *Prophet Reads Scripture*, 5; see also page 72.

27. Edenburg, "How (Not) to Murder a King," 72.

28. Rex Mason, "The Use of Earlier Biblical Material in Zechariah 9–14: A Study in Inner Biblical Exegesis," in Boda and Floyd, *Bringing Out the Treasure*, 201. Hays pursues a similar idea under his "recurrence" test (Hays, *Echoes of Scripture*, 30).

29. Noted also by Edenburg, "How (Not) to Murder a King," 72.

would understand or feel compelled to duplicate the theological or ideological concerns of the earlier tradent. As Sommer observes, new texts often "present an innovative variation of the older text's ideas," noting they sometimes even argue against the text to which they allude.[30] Many of the most obvious examples of this tendency are found in the literature of early Christianity and Rabbinic Judaism. Authors from these faith communities allude *constantly* to earlier texts and traditions, yet they apparently felt liberty to push those allusions in new and unexpected directions that could hardly have been anticipated by the original authors. But that these later writers advanced different ideologies from the original authors *has no bearing* on the question of whether they allude to their writings.[31]

8. *Shared language need not be accompanied by shared form to establish a textual connection.* Just as there is little reason to expect writers from later generations to duplicate the ideology of the texts on which they relied, there is little reason to expect they would share the literary form of these texts. As Fishbane notes:

> Materials are always moving from one setting to another, being joined to different genres, and resulting in new redactional units for instruction. Indeed, we must take note of the fact that traditions were always being integrated and moved from one sphere of instruction—be that oral, written, priestly, sapiential, or whatever—to another.[32]

---

30. Sommer, *Prophet Reads Scripture*, 27–28.

31. Fishbane identifies an example of this process in Isa 58's use of terminology from the Yom Kippur legislation in Lev 16 (Michael A. Fishbane, "The Hebrew Bible and Exegetical Tradition," in *Intertextuality in Ugarit and Israel*, ed. Johannes C. de Moor [Leiden: Brill, 1998], 26). He argues Isa 58 uses several "punning allusions" as a "deliberate attempt to invert false piety by turning the terms of one tradition—the ritual theme of affliction or fasting—towards other values."

32. Fishbane, "Hebrew Bible and Exegetical Tradition," 18.

Texts tend to share genres when they reflect a shared setting. Once that life context has changed, there is no reason for
the later tradent to borrow the form of an earlier text when
alluding to it. On the contrary, it seems more likely that the
different life settings these later authors faced would have
prompted them to use the elements of the earlier traditions in quite different ways. Ironically, common form, as in
Edenburg's example of business letters noted above, may actually point away from an allusion by raising the possibility that
commonalities between texts are the result of parallel rather
than dependent development.

4.1.3.c The Direction of Textual Allusion Can Be Determined

Once one identifies a textual allusion, it remains to determine the direction of the allusion. Edenburg lists two primary tests for determining this
direction:

1. Does an element of one text motivate the "shape, formulation or topic" of the other? Edenburg places heavy emphasis
   on the "ungrammaticality" of the borrowed element in the
   dependent text.

2. Does the comprehension of the one text depend on knowledge
   of the other?

Here the emphasis is on the way in which the borrowing text makes use
of elements from the antecedent text.[33] Elements of Hays's tests for identifying allusion, particularly his *availability* and *recurrence* tests, touch on
the matter as well.

At issue is that establishing textual priority is not always a straightforward affair. When one text is obviously later than another, as for example in NT or Tannaitic allusions to passages from the Hebrew Bible, the
direction of allusion is easily determined. For passages within the Tanakh,
though, the priority of texts can be much more difficult to determine. This

---

33. Edenburg, "How (Not) to Murder a King," 73–74.

is especially so since texts often exhibit diverse compositional strata, and even demonstrably early texts often contain later, secondary elements.

Some scholars have found the difficulties in assigning dates to texts so great as to warrant the abandonment of the diachronic approach altogether. Lyle Eslinger has expressed tremendous pessimism concerning "the diachronic assumptions of historical-critical literary history," arguing the only legitimate approach to inner-biblical allusion is a "self-consciously literary analysis" that reads texts "atemporally and without assumptions about vectors of dependence."[34] He is sharply critical of Fishbane's tendency to identify interpretive glosses in texts, going so far as to suggest his method shares in the "literary naiveté" of historical criticism.[35] Eslinger's position is born out of a skepticism over the Bible's value as a historical resource. The history of the biblical text, he argues, presupposes a plot of ancient Israel's history, which is in turn derived from the Bible. He maintains this is an enormous bit of circular reasoning, concluding, "There is little basis for consensus about Israel's history, once we set aside the plot of the Bible itself, and even less for a dependent scheme of biblical literary history."[36] The phenomenon of inner-biblical allusion is one that ought to raise questions about the minimalist approach to begin with, however. In that some texts manifestly do allude to others (direct quotations stand as obvious proof), it is clear that there is at least some diachronic element at work in the biblical text. The task remains to work out methods for charting this process of development. Here a series of fundamental questions can guide the search.

1. *Does one text claim to draw on another?* Various texts in the Hebrew Bible explicitly claim to draw on earlier texts. Nehemiah 8:14–15, for example, cites the instructions for celebrating Sukkoth from Leviticus 23:40 using the citation marker "as it is written." As noted above, a variety of biblical texts

---

34. Lyle Eslinger, "Inner-Biblical Exegesis and Inner-Biblical Allusion: The Question of Category," VT 42 (1992): 52, 56–58. Eslinger's arguments are ably addressed by Sommer in his article "Exegesis, Allusion and Intertextuality in the Hebrew Bible: A Response to Lyle Eslinger," VT 46 (1996): 479–89.

35. Eslinger, "Inner-Biblical Exegesis and Inner-Biblical Allusion," 49.

36. Eslinger, "Inner-Biblical Exegesis and Inner-Biblical Allusion," 52.

refer specifically to Jeremiah when drawing on his prophecy of seventy years of desolation for the nation (e.g., Zech 1:12; 7:5; 2 Chr 36:22; Dan 9:2). And numerous texts refer to some variation of "the Book of the Law of Moses" (e.g., Josh 8:31, 34; 23:6; 2 Kgs 14:6 // 2 Chr 25:4; Ezra 6:18). Other texts that fall short of identifying a particular text as their source do admit to their reliance on earlier traditions. The introduction to Psalm 78, for example, announces the author's intention to "pour forth riddles from of old, which we have heard and known, which our fathers have told us" (Psa 78:2–3). This sort of acknowledgement of reliance on earlier sources suggests there is some warrant for searching out the underlying historical traditions the psalm may have used.

2. *Are there elements in the texts that help to fix their dates?* Most biblical texts are marked by features that can help at least to narrow the range of dates available for their composition. Orthography, morphology, syntax, vocabulary, and content all work to paint a general picture of the Hebrew Bible's composition. Thus, for example, Jacob Milgrom has argued for the pre-exilic origins of the priestly literature by contrasting the terminology and institutions described in the priestly material in Numbers with the priestly practices of the post-exilic period.[37] Other scholars, such as David Robertson and especially Avi Hurvitz, have produced studies charting the linguistic development of biblical Hebrew and its implications for dating biblical texts.[38] Naturally, each of these features is subject to debate, as evidenced by how reputable scholars manage to settle on divergent dates for a wide variety of

---

37. Jacob Milgrom, *Numbers*, JPS Torah Commentary (Philadelphia: Jewish Publication Society, 1990), xxxii–xxxv.

38. Avi Hurvitz, "Can Biblical Texts Be Dated Linguistically? Chronological Perspectives in the Historical Study of Biblical Hebrew," in *Congress Volume: Oslo, 1998*, ed. André Lemaire and Magne Sæbø (Leiden: Brill, 2000), 143–60; and David A. Robertson, *Linguistic Evidence in Dating Early Hebrew Poetry* (Missoula: Society of Biblical Literature, 1972), 154.

biblical texts. Despite the debates that attend these issues, however, these lines of evidence remain a fruitful area for research.[39]

3. *Is one text capable of producing the other?* When considering texts that share an allusive connection, it is important to consider whether one text has sufficient breadth and depth to produce the other. It has long been observed that numerous poetic passages in the Bible share imagery and terminology with Babylonian and Canaanite accounts of creation. Psalm 74:12-14, for example, describes the God of Israel as a king who "divided the sea," "broke the heads of the dragons," and "crushed the heads of Leviathan" (see also Psa 89:5-12 [Heb. 6-13]; Job 7:11-12; 9:4-14; 26:12-13; Isa 27:1; 51:9-10). While it seems quite possible that this psalm and other passages like it in the Bible might have borrowed imagery from the lengthy epics of their neighbors, it is difficult to imagine how the reverse could be true. The scant allusions here and there in Israel's poetic literature are insufficiently broad to produce the expansive stories found in Mesopotamia and the Levant.

Within the Bible itself, similar examples are available. One Pentateuchal text describes a famine that strikes the land of Canaan, forcing God's people to go down to Egypt. While there, Pharaoh threatens the survival of the people, relenting only when God strikes his house with plagues. In the aftermath of the plagues, Pharaoh drives the people out of Egypt, though not before they have amassed great wealth. At first blush, this account reads obviously as the story of the exodus. In fact, though, it is the account of Abram and Sarai's ill-fated sojourn in Egypt, found in Genesis 12:10-20. The parallels between this story and the exodus narrative are so striking that the two must obviously be connected. In considering the direction of the connection, it seems quite plausible that a skillful tradent recounted Abram and Sarai's journey in such a way as

---

39. See Bob Becking, "No More Grapes from the Vineyard? A Plea for a Historical Critical Approach in the Study of the Old Testament," in Lemaire and Sæbø, *Congress Volume*, 123-41.

to foreshadow the exodus from Egypt. It is difficult to imagine how the reverse could be true, though. This episode in the life of Abram seems too brief to have produced the great complex of traditions that form the exodus story.[40]

4. *Does one text assume the other?* In medieval Jewish commentaries, partial citations are often used to represent more extensive cross-references. Though the commentator may cite only a few words from a text, the reader knows to bear in mind the larger passage when considering the interpretation. Biblical authors likewise allude to other passages in ways that indicate the reader's knowledge of the earlier text is assumed. When, as Edenburg suggests, "comprehension of the one text is dependent upon knowledge of the other text," there is ground for considering the possibility of literary dependence.[41] An example of this phenomenon is in Psalm 106:14–15:

> They craved a craving in the wilderness.
> They tested God in the desert.
> He gave them what they asked for,
> Then he sent a wasting disease against them.

Here the psalmist refers to the events of the Kibroth Hattaavah incident found in Numbers 11. He does so, however, in such a way that the audience's familiarity with the Numbers text is clearly assumed. The psalmist never mentions the people's disdain for manna, their longing for meat, or even God's provision of quail. That these details must be supplied by the reader alerts us that the psalmist is alluding to and dependent on an earlier text that the reader already knows.

5. *Does one text show a general pattern of dependence on other texts?* When an author is found to be in the habit of borrowing from other texts, some precedent is set for deciding the case of an

---

40. Additional examples are detailed in Yair Zakovitch, *"And You Shall Tell Your Son ...": The Concept of Exodus in the Bible* (Jerusalem: Magnes, 1991), 46–98.

41. Edenburg, "How (Not) to Murder a King," 73–74.

uncertain textual connection. This is especially true when only one of the texts marked by literary overlap shares this tendency. In a study of Joel 2:1–17 and Jonah 3:1–4:11, Thomas Dozeman highlights numerous intertextual connections between the two passages. Rather than argue for a particular direction of dependence, though, Dozeman opts instead to read Jonah first as an inner-biblical interpretation of Joel and then Joel as an inner-biblical interpretation of Jonah. Dozeman's case for Jonah as a satire of Joel's oracle is particularly strong. His treatment of Joel as an interpretation of Jonah, however, is much weaker. Rather than read these two synchronically, it appears Dozeman would have been on firmer ground in simply arguing Jonah followed and relied on Joel.[42] Here Dozeman would have found support in the numerous studies that highlight Jonah's penchant for satirizing earlier material, a feature not equally evident in Joel.[43]

6. *Are there rhetorical patterns in the texts that suggest one text has used the other in an exegetically significant way?* In his analysis of Deutero-Isaiah, Sommer focuses heavily on stylistic and rhetorical features as a means of determining the direction of inner-biblical allusions. He notes that Deutero-Isaiah uses terminology drawn from other biblical texts in various recurring patterns. These patterns, among which he includes the "split-up" pattern, sound play, wordplay, and identical word order, are "common enough and distinctive enough to serve as a sort of stylistic signature of Deutero-Isaiah, a flag that points to the presence of an allusion or echo."[44] He adds, "A stylistic pattern recurrently displayed by borrowed vocabulary

---

42. Thomas B. Dozeman, "Inner-Biblical Interpretation of Yahweh's Gracious and Compassionate Character," *JBL* 108 (1989): 207–23. Dozeman's approach is not strictly synchronic in the sense that Eslinger advocates, since he does, for example, argue that both Joel and Jonah draw on Exod 32–34.

43. Dozeman is, of course, aware of the literature on this subject and draws on it in his reading of Jonah (see his helpful list of works on 213n17). He does not take advantage of this tendency in Jonah, however, to draw conclusions about a particular direction of influence in Jonah and Joel.

44. Sommer, *Prophet Reads Scripture*, 71.

can help a reader identify genuine cases of allusion. Such a pattern highlights and emphasizes the dependence on the older text."[45] When these markers are found in places where Deutero-Isaiah reshapes the connected text, reversing its meaning, announcing its fulfillment, or redirecting its focus through "repredictions," their value as indicators of allusion is underscored.

4.1.3.d The Methods of Reinterpretation Can Be Analyzed

Addressing the topic of allusion, Robert Alter offers the following:

> Allusion occurs when a writer, recognizing the general necessity of making a literary work by building on the foundations of anteced-ent literature, deliberately exploits this predicament in explicitly activating an earlier text as part of the new system of meaning and aesthetic value of his own text.[46]

Essential to the process of inner-biblical interpretation is an examina-tion of the techniques later biblical authors used to "activate" these earlier texts. Fishbane suggests these techniques can be grouped under four main headings: scribal, legal, aggadic, and mantological exegesis.[47]

1. *Scribal exegesis.* Scribal exegesis refers to the varied ways in which scribes corrected and commented on the traditions they passed along to future generations. At one end of the spectrum, this sort of exegesis includes brief explanatory insertions such as updating place names for later audiences (e.g., "that is, Beth-El" alongside "Luz" in Josh 18:13). At the other end are pious corrections of traditions thought to be theologically prob-lematic. Here, for example, would fall texts such as 1 Sam 3:13,

---

45. Sommer, *Prophet Reads Scripture,* 67.

46. Robert Alter, *The Pleasures of Reading: In an Ideological Age* (New York: Simon and Schuster, 1989), 116.

47. The term "mantological" refers to interpretation related to prophetic oracles. The term "aggadic" labels a broader category that generally involves moral, ethical, or theological interpretation.—Eds.

in which a scribe has likely changed "God" (אלהים; *'lhym*) to "themselves" (להם; *lhm*) to avoid the notion that members of the priestly family of Eli might have cursed the deity. Another example would be the scribal (over)correction of "sons of God/El" (בני אל; *bny 'l*) to "sons of Israel" (בני ישראל; *bny yśr'l*) to eliminate any suggestion of the existence of multiple gods (e.g., Deut 32:8).

2. *Legal exegesis.* Fishbane includes in this category the numerous examples of legislative updating found in the Bible. Some examples of this sort of exegesis are found in the Torah itself. In the two cases involving Zelophehad's daughters (Num 27:1–11; 36:1–13), for example, Fishbane argues historical traditions have been redeployed to provide an opportunity for the laws of inheritance to be updated to accommodate families whose ancestral property would be lost because they lacked sons. Legal exegesis is also found regularly outside the Torah, and especially in late texts such as Ezra, Nehemiah, and Chronicles, as earlier legal traditions are broadened to address a post-exilic setting. The example noted above of Nehemiah's (and Jeremiah's) expansion of the Sabbath laws fits into this category.

3. *Aggadic exegesis.* The term *aggadah* derives from ancient rabbinic interpretation and includes a wide range of moral, theological, and ethical interpretation and application. The sorts of inner-biblical exegesis Fishbane includes in this category are equally wide-ranging and, indeed, too broad in scope to address adequately here. He notes that legal traditions, historical narratives, liturgical traditions, cultic materials, and prophetic oracles are all subject to later aggadic reinterpretation. Thus, for example, Jeremiah applies laws concerning a thief caught in the act of breaking into a house (Exod 22:2) to the sinful conduct of the nation as a whole (Jer 2:26, 34). Haggai draws on the laws concerning ritual impurity to cast the entire nation as defiled (Hag 2:11–14). Deutero-Isaiah alludes to the priestly creation account in Genesis 1:1–2:4 but

does so in such a way that several features of the account are challenged and reinterpreted (e.g., Isa 45:7, 18; 40:18, 25; 46:5). Chronicles repeatedly reshapes traditions from Samuel-Kings. Even psalms can be reinterpreted, as, for example, in the case of Job's ironic reworking in Job 7:17–18 of Psalm 8:5–7.

4. *Mantological exegesis.* Under the heading of mantological exegesis, Fishbane includes "the study of material which is ominous or oracular in scope and content."[48] An example of this sort of exegesis is found in Ezekiel's reuse of a basic prophetic form from Zephaniah 3:3–4. In Ezekiel 22:25–28, each line of Zephaniah's oracle is paraphrased, but with Ezekiel's "clear homiletical embellishments designed to clarify and specify the imagery and general condemnations."[49] Another example is evident in the Chronicler's clarification of an oracle first given to David in 2 Samuel. In 2 Samuel 7:11–15, David is promised that a son would succeed him and build a temple to Yahweh. Though this son would eventually prove to be Solomon, Solomon is not named in the oracle, and future allusions to this oracle in the book of Kings refused the chance to direct the reference to Solomon, even once Solomon had assumed the throne (1 Kgs 5:5 [Heb. 5:19]; 8:19). When Chronicles repeats the same oracle in 1 Chronicles 28, however, the text specifies twice that Solomon was the son promised as David's successor (1 Chr 28:5–6).

Although no other standard has emerged to replace them, the categories suggested by Fishbane for classifying textual allusions have not been widely accepted. In a review that broadly praises Fishbane and his work, James Kugel nevertheless criticizes him for employing an overly synchronic approach that imposes on the biblical material categories too slavishly derived from the techniques of rabbinic exegesis. Kugel also questions whether every textual allusion in the Bible ought to be regarded as an

---

48. Fishbane, *Biblical Interpretation*, 443.
49. Fishbane, *Biblical Interpretation*, 462–63.

example of exegesis, wondering whether some authors might not evoke earlier texts in ways that fall short of that description.[50]

Drawing on the work of Ziva Ben-Porat, Sommer divides textual connections into three categories: *explicit citation*, in which "the later text uses some formula to make manifest that it is referring to, depending on, disagreeing with, or explaining an older text"; *implicit reference*, in which markers such as borrowed vocabulary point to the older text; and *inclusion*, in which whole sections of an older text are borrowed word for word. He then considers six purposes for which an author might rely on an older text: exegesis, influence, revision, polemic, allusion, and echo.[51]

1. *Exegesis.* By exegesis, Sommer refers specifically to one text's attempt "to explain the meaning of a specific older text." In this regard, he moves in a direction contrary to Fishbane, noting that most of the examples Fishbane labels as inner-biblical exegesis are not, in fact, exegetical and should instead be labeled as allusions.

2. *Influence.* Under the heading of influence, Sommer includes texts that are shaped by and reflect the ideology and viewpoint of an earlier text. Thus, for example, he notes that Deuteronomy influenced Joshua, Judges, Samuel, and Kings, and Samuel-Kings influenced Chronicles. Sommer observes that the later text will often allude back to texts from its predecessor but need not do so.

3. *Revision.* In the category of revision, Sommer includes examples in which one text draws on another but alters the meaning of the older text as it does so. Unlike exegesis, the later text does not purport to explain the earlier text; and unlike the following category, polemic, it does not directly challenge

---

50. James L. Kugel, "The Bible's Earliest Interpreters," review of Michael Fishbane, *Biblical Interpretation in Ancient Israel. Prooftexts* 7 (1987): 274–76, 280. Similar criticisms are lodged by William M. Schniedewind, "'Are We His People or Not': Biblical Interpretation During Crisis," *Biblica* 76 (1995): 541; and Michael H. Floyd, "Deutero-Zechariah and Types of Intertextuality," in Boda and Floyd, *Bringing Out the Treasure*, 225.

51. Sommer, *Prophet Reads Scripture*, 20–31. See also Ziva Ben-Porat, "Intertextuality," *Ha-Sifrut* 34 (1985): 170–78.

the text. Instead, it maintains a connection with the older tradition while at the same time reapplying it or even subtly subverting its original meaning.

4. *Polemic*. Under this heading, Sommer treats biblical texts that argue directly against other biblical texts. He notes, for example, that numerous later texts disavow the notion found in Exodus 34:6–7 that God punishes descendants for the transgressions of their ancestors (e.g., Deut 7:9–10; Psa 103:8–9; Jonah 4:2; Joel 2:12).

5. *Allusion*. In an allusion, a later text redeploys some portion of an older text in order to bolster some claim of the later author, to make his message more easily understood, or to create analogy. Sommer includes in this category textual connections that draw on an earlier text but not for any obvious exegetical or explanatory purpose. The alluding author's intention is to illuminate his own text, "not to suggest a particular understanding of the old one."

6. *Echo*. Echo resembles allusion in that it also borrows vocabulary and imagery from the older text. Sommer clarifies that in an allusion, the source text is intended to affect the meaning of the alluding text; in an echo, language and imagery from an earlier text may be reused, but this reuse is not intended to shape the meaning of either the older or the newer text.

The range of inner-biblical textual connections is such that no one taxonomy may be able to fully account for the phenomenon as a whole. With Fishbane, it is helpful to consider how inner-biblical allusion differs from one genre of biblical material to another. Sommer's insistence that textual connections can take many forms beyond exegesis is vital, however.[52]

---

52. See further James D. Nogalski, "Intertextuality and the Twelve," in *Forming Prophetic Literature: Essays on Isaiah and the Twelve in Honor of John D. W. Watts*, ed. James W. Watts and Paul R. House (Sheffield: Sheffield Academic, 1996), 102–24; and David L. Petersen, "Zechariah 9-14: Methodological Reflections," in Boda and Floyd, *Bringing Out the Treasure*, 210–24.

EXPLICIT CITATION

The later text uses a formula to make clear that is referring to an older text.

IMPLICIT CITATION

The later text uses markers such as borrowed vocabulary to point to an older text.

INCLUSION

The later text borrows whole sections of an older text word-for-word.

THREE CATEGORIES OF TEXTUAL CONNECTIONS

4.1.4 KEY CONCEPTS

Traditum The traditional material, whether it be law, legend, historical account, oracle, song, or other content, transmitted from one generation to another.[53]

Traditio The process by which the *traditum* is transmitted, including the way in which a *traditum* is shaped, whether deliberately or inadvertently, as it is passed to the next generation.[54]

Allusion The phenomenon whereby elements of an earlier text—vocabulary, imagery, structure, etc.—are reproduced by a later text. The purposes for which one text alludes to another are varied, though it is taken as a given that an allusion is made to enhance the meaning of the later text, whether that enhancement be one of aesthetic, explanatory, or authoritative value.

Synchronic and diachronic readings In a synchronic reading, the intersecting relationships among texts are explored without reference to their chronological priority or actual dependence on one another. In a diachronic reading, an effort is made to determine the order in which texts

---

53. Knight, *Recovering the Traditions of Israel*, 5.
54. Knight, *Recovering the Traditions of Israel*, 5.

were composed and whether one text relied directly on another. In general, synchronic readings are associated with the study of intertextuality and diachronic readings with the study of inner-biblical interpretation.

Intertextuality The branch of study that treats all texts as reliant on a larger web of inherited cultural knowledge that makes their discourse intelligible. Intertextuality, as the term is often used outside biblical studies, is not concerned with a given text's reliance on another particular text, but, as Culler clarifies, with its "participation in the discursive space of a culture."[55]

Tradition history The study of the development of biblical traditions prior to their becoming fixed as literary compositions. Known in German as *Überlieferungsgeschichte*.

Redaction criticism The branch of critical biblical study focused on the role of the redactor in selecting, arranging, and supplementing earlier literary traditions. Distinguished from tradition history by its focus on literary as opposed to oral traditions. Distinguished from inner-biblical interpretation by the redactor's role as editor of existing traditions rather than author of new compositions.

4.2 DEVELOPMENT OF INNER-BIBLICAL INTERPRETATION

The study of inner-biblical interpretation may be said to have its earliest origins in the *Wissenschaft des Judentums* movement of the nineteenth century. As this movement began to study Judaism from a critical and scientific stance rather than a religious one, scholars directed their attention to the discovery of the earliest strata of post-biblical Jewish exegesis. It soon became obvious that the same hermeneutical patterns evident in this post-biblical exegesis could also be discerned within the Hebrew Bible itself. By 1832, Leopold Zunz argued that Chronicles was a reworking of

---

55. Culler, "Presupposition and Intertextuality," 103. As noted above, within biblical studies, "intertextuality" is often used with reference to a relationship between two particular texts (see §4.1.1.a Intertextuality).

Kings.[56] Two and a half decades later, Abraham Geiger contended that the same exegetical reworkings evident in the Septuagint and Samaritan Pentateuch are also evident in the Hebrew text.[57] As Nahum Sarna observes concerning Geiger's main contribution to biblical studies, *Urschrift und Übersetzungen der Bibel*:

> At the root of that great work lies the basic presupposition that the history of the biblical text is interwoven with the history of the people, that the text itself, being a response to life, constantly adapted itself to the needs of the people so that it is possible to reconstruct the inner history of Israel's faith from the external history of the biblical text. In other words, Geiger believed that what the process of midrash and exegesis accomplished in a later age, was achieved through textual manipulation in the period before the final stabilization of the biblical text.[58]

Despite this early recognition of exegetical development within the Bible, it was more than a century before the first systematic treatment of inner-biblical exegesis emerged in the form of Michael Fishbane's *Biblical Interpretation in Ancient Israel*. In a review of Fishbane's work, James Kugel traces this extraordinary delay to the largely Protestant origins of critical biblical scholarship.[59] Because Protestant biblical interpretation was keenly interested in stripping away what it considered to be centuries of "Church-sponsored misinterpretation or willful obfuscation," it set up "a general opposition between the 'biblical' (good) and anything that was 'postbiblical' (bad, because a corruption of the biblical)." This tendency was eventually extended into the Bible itself, with early materials treated as better than late, the work of the prophets as of a more noble spirit than that of the later priests, the *ipsissima verba* of the prophets as more authentic than the later reports of their messages. Casting redactors as analogous in the

56. Leopold Zunz, *Die gottesdienstliche Vorträge der Juden: Historisch entwickelt* (Berlin: A. Asher, 1832).

57. Abraham Geiger, *Urschrift und Uebersetzungen der Bibel in ihrer Abhängigkeit von der innern Entwickelung des Judenthums* (Breslau: Julius Hainauer, 1857, 1928).

58. Nahum Sarna, "Abraham Geiger and Biblical Scholarship," in *New Perspectives on Abraham Geiger: An HUC-JIR Symposium*, ed. Jakob Josef Petuchowski (Cincinnati: Hebrew Union College-Jewish Institute of Religion, 1975), 25.

59. Kugel, "Bible's Earliest Interpreters," 269–70.

Protestant view to the pope in their tendency to stand between the reader and the true Word of God, Kugel observes:

> And so the Protestant task (and consequently that of modern biblical scholarship) has always been to cast such interlopers out, to recover the authentic (or "most authentic") text, oracle, event, and throw the rest away. Little wonder, then, that the biblical text that seeks to interpret or elaborate upon an earlier biblical text has been viewed ipso facto as of secondary importance, and that the processes of interpretation and assimilation that underlie such acts were for some time generally judged unworthy of scrutiny.[60]

Kugel notes that this pattern began to change, inevitably in one respect, as the Protestant search for the authentic words of the prophets required an ever more attentive consideration of the redactors "even if only to separate chaff from wheat." At the same time, the entry of greater numbers of Jewish interpreters into critical biblical scholarship brought new sensitivities to the hermeneutical value of what would previously have been seen only as evidence of redaction.

Single examples of inner-biblical exegesis, such as Sarna's treatment of Psalm 89 published in 1963, continued to appear piecemeal through the twentieth century.[61] It was only with the 1985 publication of Fishbane's magnum opus on the subject, however, that the study of inner-biblical exegesis reached its critical mass. The sheer breadth of Fishbane's work and its relentless roster of example after example of inner-biblical allusion demonstrated the pervasiveness of this sort of exegesis within the Bible. At the same time, it laid out a convincing case for the biblical origins of the interpretive methods that came to characterize post-biblical religious communities including Qumran, early Christianity, and especially early rabbinic Judaism. While aspects of his approach were challenged, as for example in the aforementioned review by Kugel, there can be little question that Fishbane's work set the stage for a tremendous outpouring of studies on the subject.

---

60. Kugel, "Bible's Earliest Interpreters," 270.

61. Nahum M. Sarna, "Psalm 89: A Study in Inner Biblical Exegesis," in *Biblical and Other Studies*, ed. Alexander Altmann (Cambridge, MA: Harvard University Press, 1963).

Two scholars, Bernard Levinson and Benjamin Sommer, have been particularly effective in advancing the study of inner-biblical allusion and interpretation in the areas of biblical law (Levinson) and prophecy (Sommer). In *Deuteronomy and the Hermeneutics of Legal Innovation*, Levinson argues that the legal corpus of Deuteronomy 12–26 represents a "radical revision of the Covenant Code" (Exod 20:22–23:33):[62]

> The authors of Deuteronomy sought to implement a far-reaching transformation of religion, law, and social structure that was essentially without cultural precedent. They therefore turned to the earlier code in order to anchor their departure from legal convention in the very textual heritage from which they cut themselves free in substantive terms. They deliberately presented their new vision of the Judaean polity as continuous with the abrogated past and used the earlier textual material, carefully transformed, to sanction their own independent agenda.[63]

From this beginning, Levinson moves on to demonstrate how the Deuteronomic law code worked both to borrow from earlier legal traditions and to revise those traditions to support its innovative agenda of cultic centralization. Inner-biblical interpretation in Israel's legal traditions also lies at the heart of Levinson's book *Legal Revision and Religious Renewal in Ancient Israel*. Here Levinson addresses a variety of legal topics, charting the underlying principles for legal innovation in the Bible and providing a lengthy survey of key scholarly developments in the area of inner-biblical exegesis.[64]

Levinson's attention to inner-biblical exegesis in Israel's legal traditions is paralleled by Sommer's examination of the same phenomenon in the prophets. In a lengthy treatment of Deutero-Isaiah's use of inner-biblical allusion, Sommer demonstrates that this latter half of Isaiah alludes constantly to earlier biblical texts, sometimes reversing earlier prophetic messages and sometimes extending their reach by "repredicting"

---

62. Bernard M. Levinson, *Deuteronomy and the Hermeneutics of Legal Innovation* (New York: Oxford University Press, 1997), 3.

63. Levinson, *Deuteronomy and the Hermeneutics of Legal Innovation*, 3.

64. Bernard M. Levinson, *Legal Revision and Religious Renewal in Ancient Israel* (New York: Cambridge University Press, 2008).

them. To cite just one example of Sommer's findings, he notes that Deutero-Isaiah draws repeatedly on Jeremiah 30–33, calling this section of Jeremiah "the richest mine for Deutero-Isaiah as he restates positive prophecies."[65] A noteworthy difference between Deutero-Isaiah and the underlying text in Jeremiah has to do with their description of the covenantal relationship between God and Israel. Sommer observes that Jeremiah's view of the covenant was quite radical: "He claimed that God renounced His eternal covenant with Israel, as the destruction of the temple and dethronement of the Davidic monarchy indicated."[66] For Jeremiah, a new covenant would have to be made after the return from exile. Deutero-Isaiah relies heavily on Jeremiah's covenantal language. The author does so, however, in a way that reshapes the former prophet's message. For Deutero-Isaiah, the covenant remains inviolable. As Sommer argues:

> Here Deutero-Isaiah does not merely allude but alters or interprets. He suggests that we should not take Jeremiah's words too literally, for they imply that YHWH's covenant could be broken (even if only to be renewed). On the contrary, Deutero-Isaiah insists, the covenant is eternal and unshakable.[67]

Deutero-Isaiah preserves a basic continuity between himself and Jeremiah by alluding to and paraphrasing the earlier prophet's message. Sommer demonstrates, though, that the refining experience of exile has caused Deutero-Isaiah to reshape Jeremiah's message and thus redefine the nature of God's covenant with the nation.

As the study of inner-biblical interpretation has garnered greater interest among biblical scholars, the literature devoted to the subject has grown apace, with the result that nearly every corner of the Hebrew Bible has been examined through this important methodological lens.

---

65. Sommer, *Prophet Reads Scripture*, 46.
66. Sommer, *Prophet Reads Scripture*, 48.
67. Sommer, *Prophet Reads Scripture*, 50.

4.3 APPLICATIONS OF
INNER-BIBLICAL INTERPRETATION

Every interpreter will have his or her own unique approach to identifying and exploring examples of inner-biblical interpretation. Here, one possible approach is outlined using Psalm 78's recitation of the plagues that struck Egypt as a proving ground.

4.3.1 STEP ONE: FINDING POTENTIAL TEXTUAL CONNECTIONS

In the search for allusions between texts, there is no substitute for a deeply rooted familiarity with the biblical text. Just as a well-read individual will hear echoes of Shakespeare or Milton or Tennyson in the works of other writers, a person with an intimate knowledge of the Bible will hear unlooked-for echoes of one text while reading another. Facility in the original languages of the Bible can be equally helpful, since an echo present in the underlying Hebrew (or Aramaic or Greek) will often be obscured in translation. Thus, the echo of Genesis 1 in Exodus 2:2, "and she saw that he was good," will be missed in a translation such as "and when she saw that he was a fine child" (NRSV).

When potentially allusive texts do not automatically spring to mind, consulting commentaries, concordances, and even digests of cross-references can aid in the search. In some cases, a commentary will demonstrate that a textual connection is well-known and has been extensively researched. In other cases, however, a potential connection may only be hinted at and remain open for further exploration. In the case of the plagues found in Psalm 78:42–51, the search for a potential textual connection is made easier by how well-known the plague narrative in Exodus 7–12 is. Even here, though, further research will reveal that the plagues are also recited in Psalm 105:26–36, providing another candidate for a connection.

4.3.2 STEP TWO: TESTING POTENTIAL TEXTUAL CONNECTIONS

Once one identifies a potential textual connection, the next step is to test that connection to determine whether it is genuine. In the case of Psalm 78's plagues, one must determine whether the psalm and the Exodus account are directly connected or whether the two have merely provided independent versions of a familiar event from the nation's past. The guidelines outlined earlier can help to establish or rule out such a connection.

Here the emphasis is on determining whether the two texts share significant lexical links. An examination of Psalm 78 and Exodus 7–12 suggests this is in fact the case. Many of the terms used to describe the plagues— blood (דָּם; *dām*), swarms of flies (עָרֹב; *'ārōb*), frogs (צְפַרְדֵּעַ; *ṣepardēa'*), locusts (אַרְבֶּה; *'arbe*), hail (בָּרָד; *bārād*), pestilence (דֶּבֶר; *deber*), and the striking of the firstborn (בְּכוֹר; *bekôr*)—are shared by these two passages. Just as importantly, some of the terms the passages share in common are exceedingly rare in biblical Hebrew. The terms used for the swarms of flies (*'ārōb*) and the frogs (*ṣepardēa'*), for example, occur solely in the descriptions of the plagues in Psalms 78 and 105 and in Exodus 7–12. This sort of lexical overlap suggests these texts are connected directly to one another.

4.3.3 STEP THREE: DETERMINING THE DIRECTION OF INFLUENCE

When seeking to determine whether Psalm 78 has relied on the Exodus account or Exodus has relied on Psalm 78, the guidelines outlined above can again provide assistance. That the psalmist admits freely to his goal of expounding lessons and riddles inherited from his ancestors (Psa 78:2–3) should, at the outset, alert us to the possibility that it is the psalmist who has relied on earlier traditions. More important, though, is that it is quite difficult to imagine how the tradent in Exodus might have constructed his account of the plagues from the exceedingly brief roster of plagues in Psalm 78. For the psalmist, the task would have lain solely in picking out plagues and abbreviating their description. The author of the Exodus account, though, would have gleaned little information working in the opposite direction. Psalm 78's blood plague, for example, is recounted in only six words, its frogs plague in only two (one of which likely belongs to the swarms, not the frogs). It seems unlikely that Psalm 78 could have produced the Exodus account.

The likelihood that Psalm 78 relied on the Exodus account is underscored by how the psalm appears to have exegetically reshaped the Exodus materials. A variety of such features can be noted, but one will suffice. Psalm 78 presents the plagues in a different order from the Exodus account. Exodus, for example, describes the dreadful hail that strikes the land as being followed by the onslaught of the locusts. This ordering presents a problem, though. After the hail wiped out Egypt's vegetation, what would be left for the locusts to devour? Psalm 78 resolves this problem by presenting the plagues in a different order. In the psalm, the locusts come first, applying their more discriminating palates to the tender shoots of the Egyptians' crops and produce. Only then does the hail come, wiping out the hardier vines and sycamores that have survived. Not only this, but a clear pattern of escalation can be seen in Psalm 78, as the plagues move from attacks on vegetation (locusts and hail) to attacks on the animals and people (pestilence) and then finally to the attack on firstborn sons.

4.3.4 STEP FOUR: DRAWING IMPLICATIONS FROM THE REUSE

When one has identified a textual connection and determined its direction of dependence, it remains to consider whether the connection can shed light on larger questions related to the nation's religious and cultural development. In a broad sense, the psalm's rehearsal of the plagues stands as witness to their continuing significance for the nation as a sign of God's judgment (on Egypt) and mercy (toward Israel). Close examination of the psalm's dependence on the Exodus account reveals another significant finding, however.

While the psalm clearly relies on the plagues found in Exodus, it does not rely on all of them. The gnats (כִּנִּים; kinnîm), boils (שְׁחִין; šeḥîn), and darkness (חֹשֶׁךְ; ḥōšek) plagues are entirely absent from Psalm 78. What is noteworthy about these plagues is that each belongs to the priestly strata of the plague narrative. When Psalm 78 draws on the plagues in Exodus, it relies solely on the plagues found in the non-priestly, or JE, materials. When two versions of a plague are present, such as gnats and swarms or pestilence and boils, Psalm 78 only connects with the JE plagues (swarms and pestilence), not with the P plagues (gnats and boils). This fact, combined with other more detailed pieces of evidence from the psalm, suggests Psalm 78 had access solely to the JE exodus traditions at a time before they were joined literarily to P.

4.4 LIMITATIONS OF INNER-BIBLICAL INTERPRETATION

Although inner-biblical interpretation can provide a valuable critical lens through which to approach the biblical text, it, like all such approaches, has its own limitations. Two such limitations loom especially large: (1) establishing a methodologically sound process for certifying allusions and their direction of dependence; and (2) determining the thought process behind an allusion.

4.4.1 ESTABLISHING A METHODOLOGICALLY SOUND PROCESS

At the heart of inner-biblical interpretation/exegesis lies the identification of direct connections between texts. Distinguishing between intentional allusions from one text to another and the inevitable overlap that results from authors sharing a common culture and language is an ever-present challenge. Responding to an example of inner-biblical allusion that he finds lacking, H. G. M. Williamson observes:

> In conclusion, in the case of inner-biblical allusions, as opposed to full citations, it will never be possible finally to prove that a writer was consciously dependent on one source rather than another, especially when much of the vocabulary to which appeal is made is relatively common, as in the present example. In such cases, it is more than ever important to attend to such matters of method, referred to above, as the close juxtaposition in the parent text of the items alluded to and the desirability of tracing grammatical and syntactical as well as just lexical similarities in the determination of the most likely antecedent.[68]

Williamson does not deny the existence of inner-biblical allusion in the Bible. He does sound a cautionary note about the importance of methodology, however. The guidelines offered above are intended to lay the foundation for just such a methodology. But that there is an element of art as well as science involved in the process is undeniable.

4.4.2 DETERMINING THE THOUGHT PROCESS

When one has established one text's reliance on another, the reason for the invocation of the earlier text may still not be readily apparent. Fishbane's division of allusions into four exegetical categories—scribal, legal, aggadic, and mantological—is an attempt at such an explanation. As Kugel has argued, though, these categories are more at home in post-biblical rabbinic

---

68. H. G. M. Williamson, "Isaiah 62:4 and the Problem of Inner-Biblical Allusions," *JBL* 119 (2000): 734–39.

exegesis and often prove unwieldy when addressing biblical materials. Further, as both Kugel and Sommer have noted, not every allusion from one text to another rightly belongs in the category of exegesis. Sommer especially notes a wide range of ways in which one text can redeploy another. Even when an allusion is transparently exegetical, the logic behind the allusive author's exegesis may remain opaque. Without conceding to the literary critics the impossibility of capturing an author's intention, it is nevertheless true that all such attempts remain provisional.

4.5 CONTEMPORARY INFLUENCE OF INNER-BIBLICAL INTERPRETATION

Among the most important beneficiaries of the attention given to inner-biblical interpretation in the Hebrew Bible has been the field of NT studies.[69] Because allusions to the Hebrew Bible feature so prominently in the NT, charting the connections between the Testaments has always formed an important component of NT research. The complexities and nuances of NT authors' allusions to the Hebrew Bible have not always been appreciated, though. This is doubtless due in part to the awkward fashion in which some NT authors reinterpret earlier texts christologically (e.g., Matt 2:15; 1 Cor 10:4). When one sees enough such reinterpretations, it becomes tempting to label the NT's use of the OT as christological and leave it at that.

Further contributing to the oversimplification of the NT's interpretive techniques is that the NT books have rarely been situated as squarely in the matrix of other early Jewish biblical interpretation as they should be.[70] Because the study of inner-biblical interpretation emerged largely from the work of Jewish biblical scholars, it brought to the Hebrew Bible a profound sensitivity to the exegetical methods evident in early rabbinic Judaism (not to mention the extensive exegetical works of the medieval Jewish

---

69. The benefits for the study of extrabiblical literature are also readily apparent. See, for example, James H. Charlesworth, "The Pseudepigrapha as Biblical Exegesis," in *Early Jewish and Christian Exegesis: Studies in Memory of William Hugh Brownlee*, ed. Craig A. Evans and William F. Stinespring (Atlanta: Scholars Press, 1987), 139–52; Steven Weitzman, "Allusion, Artifice, and Exile in the Hymn of Tobit," *JBL* 115 (1996): 49–61; and George W. E. Nickelsburg, "Tobit, Genesis, and the Odyssey: A Complex Web of Intertextuality," in *Mimesis and Intertextuality in Antiquity and Christianity*, ed. Dennis R. MacDonald (Harrisburg, PA: Trinity Press International, 2001), 41–55.

70. Note, for example, Hays's frustration with the too-frequent labeling of NT interpretation simply as "midrash" (Hays, *Echoes of Scripture*, 10–14).

commentators). When inner-biblical interpretation was subsequently applied to the NT's use of the Hebrew Bible, it brought with it, albeit by a circuitous route, these same sensitivities.

One of the most notable works in the study of the NT's interpretation of Scripture is Richard Hays's study *Echoes of Scripture in the Letters of Paul*. Hays's approach stands out for its methodological continuity with the advances made by scholars such as Fishbane. His analysis of Paul's use of Scripture in Romans is particularly illuminating. Here he challenges the notion that Paul's interpretation is christocentric, arguing it is instead primarily "ecclesiocentric." That is, Paul methodically uses the Scriptures he inherited from his spiritual forebears to show that the ingathering of Gentiles into the people of God was a feature of God's covenant with Israel from the very start. While Hays admits that elements of Paul's treatment of the Hebrew Bible will remain a bridge too far for modern, critical interpreters of the Bible, he also demonstrates that, in the main, Paul's interpretive moves have a greater logic and consistency to them than has previously been recognized.

4.6 RESOURCES FOR FURTHER STUDY

Boda, Mark J., and Michael H. Floyd, eds. *Bringing Out the Treasure: Inner Biblical Allusion in Zechariah 9–14*. With Rex Mason. London: T&T Clark, 2003.

> This book offers a helpful collection of essays on inner-biblical allusion in Zechariah, including several with important methodological insights.

Dozeman, Thomas B. "Inner-Biblical Interpretation of Yahweh's Gracious and Compassionate Character." *JBL* 108 (1989): 207–23.

> Dozeman's article models an intertextual reading of passages in Joel and Jonah exploring how reading one in light of the other can reveal new insights. His discussion of how Jonah can be read as a satirical reworking of Joel is particularly strong.

Edenburg, Cynthia. "How (Not) to Murder a King: Variations on a Theme in 1 Sam 24; 26." *SJOT* 12 (1998): 64–85.

Edenberg presents valuable methodological insights for identifying allusions and determining their direction of dependence. Her approach offers a good beginning for how to study inner-biblical interpretation.

Eslinger, Lyle. "Inner-Biblical Exegesis and Inner-Biblical Allusion: The Question of Category." *VT* 42 (1992): 47–58.

Eslinger offers a sharp critique of the diachronic approach common in inner-biblical interpretation.

Fishbane, Michael A. *Biblical Interpretation in Ancient Israel*. Oxford: Clarendon, 1985.

This is a seminal volume on inner-biblical exegesis, responsible for the increased attention scholars have given to the phenomenon in the past thirty years. The book is filled with excellent examples and novel insights, but it is a difficult read for those new to the subject.

Hays, Richard B. *Echoes of Scripture in the Letters of Paul*. New Haven, CT: Yale University Press, 1989.

Hays's work is an important study of Paul's use of Scripture that extends the insights of inner-biblical interpretation into the NT. Hays also provides an excellent method for studying the NT's use of the OT.

Kugel, James R. "The Bible's Earliest Interpreters." Review of Michael Fishbane, *Biblical Interpretation in Ancient Israel*. *Prooftexts: A Journal of Jewish Literary History* 7 (1987): 269–83.

Kugel gives a broadly positive review of Fishbane's book that also provides a helpful critique of Fishbane's method.

Levinson, Bernard M. *Deuteronomy and the Hermeneutics of Legal Innovation*. New York: Oxford University Press, 1997.

Levinson applies the methods of inner-biblical interpretation to Deuteronomy, arguing that Deuteronomy is a reinterpretation of the covenant code from Exodus 20–24.

———. *Legal Revision and Religious Renewal in Ancient Israel*. Cambridge: Cambridge University Press, 2008.

This brief book consists of several case studies exploring how a legal principle could be reworked in later texts. The last chapter surveying recent developments in inner-biblical interpretation is most helpful for further study of the subject.

Noble, Paul R. "Esau, Tamar, and Joseph: Criteria for Identifying Inner-Biblical Allusions." *VT* 52 (2002): 219–52.

Noble calls for stronger methodological controls in the identification of inner-biblical allusions.

Sarna, Nahum M. "Psalm 89: A Study in Inner Biblical Exegesis." In *Biblical and Other Studies*, edited by Alexander Altmann, 29–46. Cambridge, MA: Harvard University Press, 1963.

Sarna's essay is an important early study of the phenomenon of inner-biblical exegesis.

Sommer, Benjamin D. "Exegesis, Allusion and Intertextuality in the Hebrew Bible: A Response to Lyle Eslinger." *VT* 46 (1996): 479–89.

Sommer provides a detailed response to Eslinger's criticisms of the diachronic assumptions inherent in inner-biblical interpretation.

———. *A Prophet Reads Scripture: Allusion in Isaiah 40–66*. Stanford: Stanford University Press, 1998.

This important study of inner-biblical interpretation in Deutero-Isaiah explores the relationship between Isaiah 40–66 and other biblical texts, especially Jeremiah and Isaiah 1–39. It is particularly valuable for its attention to methodology.

Williamson, H. G. M. "Isaiah 62:4 and the Problem of Inner-Biblical Allusions." *JBL* 119 (2000): 734–39.

Williamson offers some helpful methodological comments concerning the identification of inner-biblical allusions.

5

NARRATIVE CRITICISM OF THE NEW TESTAMENT

Daniel Brendsel

> If we know *how* texts mean, we are in a better position to discover *what* a particular text means.
> —Adele Berlin, *Poetics and Interpretation of Biblical Narrative*[1]

> To me it is now clear that the subject of the rhetoric of narration is in principle universal to all telling of stories ... people meeting people *through* story, people offering and receiving gifts *as* story.
> —Wayne C. Booth, *The Rhetoric of Fiction*[2]

A s the essays in this volume indicate, the late twentieth and early twenty-first centuries have seen an explosion of new approaches to reading the Bible. One approach, while new in terms of its critical development and appropriation in the scholarly guild, is founded on a very old observation: The Bible tells stories. Narrative criticism has focused its attention especially on the formal implications of this observation as it relates to the narrative literature of the NT.

---

1. Adele Berlin, *Poetics and Interpretation of Biblical Narrative* (Winona Lake, IN: Eisenbrauns, 1994), 17, emphasis original.

2. Wayne C. Booth, *The Rhetoric of Fiction*, 2nd ed. (Chicago: University of Chicago Press, 1983), 408, emphasis original.

5.1 DEFINITION AND GOAL OF NEW
TESTAMENT NARRATIVE CRITICISM

Defining the method is no easy task. Confusion easily arises, as terminology varies across disciplines, and sometimes differing terminology is
employed by different individuals within what is ostensibly a single discipline. Secular criticism of narrative knows no "narrative criticism" but only
"literary criticism." In biblical studies, various historical-critical methods have typically been referred to as "literary criticism,"[3] but narrative
criticism (especially in its early years) was often intentionally positioned
over against traditional historical-critical methods. Narrative criticism
sometimes deals with matters of rhetoric, but "rhetorical criticism" is a
distinct approach; so also structural criticism is to be distinguished from
narrative criticism, though the latter shares great interest in the formal
characteristics and structures of narratives and has been influenced by
structuralism.[4] To complicate matters further, narrative-critical practitioners and theorists have spilt much ink debating what constitutes "*genuine* narrative criticism."[5]

   If we keep to the realm of the descriptive, we may say that narrative
criticism is a distinct type of *biblical*, and particularly NT, criticism.[6] David
Rhoads is often credited as the first to name narrative criticism as a distinct approach to NT interpretation, identifying it, in his 1980 SBL Markan

---

3. Thus David Clines and Cheryl Exum refer to historical critical approaches as *Literarkritik*
in order to distinguish them from "the new literary criticism" (see David J. A. Clines and J.
Cheryl Exum, "The New Literary Criticism," in *The New Literary Criticism and the Hebrew Bible*
[Valley Forge, PA: Trinity Press International, 1993], 11–25, at 11–12; see also David E. Aune,
"Literary Criticism," in *The Blackwell Companion to the New Testament*, ed. D. E. Aune [West
Sussex, UK: Wiley-Blackwell, 2010], 116–39, at 116–17).

4. See the chapters in the present volume on rhetorical criticism and structural criticism.
See also Dennis L. Stamps, "Rhetorical and Narratological Criticism," in *Handbook to Exegesis
of the New Testament*, ed. S. E. Porter (Leiden: Brill, 1997), 219–39; Mark Allan Powell, *What Is
Narrative Criticism?* (Minneapolis: Fortress, 1990), 11–21.

5. Mark Allan Powell, "Narrative Criticism: The Emergence of a Prominent Reading
Strategy," in *Mark as Story: Retrospect and Prospect*, ed. K. R. Iverson and C. W. Skinner (Atlanta:
Society of Biblical Literature, 2011), 19–43, at 22, emphasis original.

6. Stephen D. Moore, *Literary Criticism and the Gospels: The Theoretical Challenge* (New
Haven, CT: Yale University Press, 1989), xxii; see also David M. Gunn, "Narrative Criticism,"
in *To Each Its Own Meaning: An Introduction to Biblical Criticisms and Their Application*, ed. S. L.
McKenzie and S. R. Haynes, rev. and exp. ed. [Louisville, KY: Westminster John Knox, 1999],
201–29, at 201). As Moore also notes, narrative criticism is peculiarly North American in its
origin and practice (see *Literary Criticism and the Gospels*, xiv–xv).

Seminar paper, as the investigation of "the formal features of narrative in the texts of the Gospels, features which include aspects of the story-world of the narrative and the rhetorical techniques employed to tell the story."[7] Operating with the assumption that the story-world and rhetoric of a narrative are (autonomous) objects of study in their own right, narrative critics focus on matters of narrative form (and the final form of the text). They aim especially to understand what it means for the NT narrative literature to be *narrative*, and to articulate how it works or, as Berlin puts it in the epigraph above, how it *means* as a narrative.[8]

Thus narrative criticism is chiefly an approach to reading the Gospels and Acts.[9] Concern about historical/real authors and readers "behind the text" recedes or is often bracketed in favor of attending to the implied author and implied readers "in the text" or to responses of readers "in front of the text." Formal narrative elements such as point of view, characterization, setting, and the use of literary devices such as metaphor, irony, and symbolism dominate attention. By focusing on textual form, narrative critics tend to view themselves as attempting to "discover and disclose the narrative's own intrinsic points of emphasis, thereby facilitating its interpretation and consequently helping to discriminate among various possible interpretations."[10]

---

7. Rhoads's paper was published in 1982 as "Narrative Criticism and the Gospel of Mark," *JAAR* 50 (1982): 411–34, quotation at 412–13.

8. See R. Alan Culpepper, *Anatomy of the Fourth Gospel: A Study in Literary Design* (Philadelphia: Fortress, 1983), 5–6. As Powell comments, "A *narrative* may be defined as any work of literature that tells a story" (*What Is Narrative Criticism?*, 23, emphasis original; for extended discussion on what "narrative" is, see Joel B. Green, "Narrative Criticism," in *Methods for Luke*, ed. J. B. Green [Cambridge: Cambridge University Press, 2010], 74–112, at 92–95).

9. Narrative-critical approaches to Revelation have also appeared; see, e.g., David Barr, *Tales of the End: A Narrative Commentary on the Book of Revelation* (Santa Rosa, CA: Polebridge, 1998); James L. Resseguie, *Revelation Unsealed: A Narrative Critical Approach to John's Apocalypse* (Leiden: Brill, 1998). Additionally worth noting is Norman Petersen's innovative approach to an epistle in *Rediscovering Paul: Philemon and the Sociology of Paul's Narrative World* (Philadelphia: Fortress, 1985).

10. Richard G. Bowman, "Narrative Criticism: Human Purpose in Conflict with Divine Presence," in *Judges and Method: New Approaches in Biblical Studies*, 2nd ed., ed. G. A. Yee (Minneapolis: Fortress, 2007), 19–45, at 19.

5.1.1 RELATIONSHIP TO OTHER APPROACHES

As Petri Merenlahti points out, beginning in the late 1970s narrative criticism sought inclusion "as a new member in the family of exegetical methods" for interpreting the NT narratives.[11] But the relationship of the "new member" to the reigning "family of exegetical methods"—namely, to *traditional historical-critical methods*—is open to debate.

Some scholars portray narrative criticism as a logical development or extension of historical-critical approaches. *Form-critical analyses* of scenes, structure, characters, and conventions may provide early forerunners of narrative-critical pursuits.[12] More strikingly, one may discern much affinity between certain *redaction-critical* work and the aims of narrative criticism. Redaction critics and narrative critics alike ask after the "why" of the final form of the text and the message that a writer/redactor has sought to communicate in the arrangement of the story. Powell comments that the rise of redaction criticism "partially met" the need "for greater attention to the larger form of the Gospel itself."[13] Where redaction criticism has recognized the creativity and artistry of the evangelists in appropriating their sources, "many New Testament narrative critics have made redaction criticism a valuable partner in literary studies."[14] Aiding in this partnership is *composition criticism*, which, in its focus on the overall compositional form of the NT narratives (and not simply divergences from purported sources), has served as something of a midpoint between redaction criticism (or what Powell has called "emendation analysis"[15]) and narrative criticism.[16]

---

11. Petri Merenlahti, *Poetics for the Gospels? Rethinking Narrative Criticism* (London: T&T Clark, 2002), 17.

12. Powell, *What Is Narrative Criticism?*, 6–7. In OT studies, Hermann Gunkel's form-critical work has been noted "as a possible foundation for narrative criticism" (Christopher T. Paris, *Narrative Obtrusion in the Hebrew Bible* [Minneapolis: Fortress, 2014], 7; see also 10; see Shimon Bar-Efrat, *Narrative Art in the Bible* [Sheffield, UK: Almond, 1989], 9; Leland Ryken, "The Bible as Literature: A Brief History," in *A Complete Literary Guide to the Bible*, ed. L. Ryken and T. Longman III [Grand Rapids: Zondervan, 1993], 49–68, at 59).

13. Powell, *What Is Narrative Criticism?*, 3; see also Bowman, "Narrative Criticsm," 620; Mary Ann Tolbert, *Sowing the Gospel: Mark's World in Literary-Historical Perspective* (Minneapolis: Fortress, 1989), 23.

14. Paris, *Narrative Obtrusion*, 19.

15. Powell, "Narrative Criticism: The Emergence of a Prominent Reading Strategy," 32.

16. See Moore, *Literary Criticism and the Gospels*, 4–13, for helpful discussion.

While it is possible to see narrative criticism as a kind of development of and a needful partner to traditional historical-critical approaches, at the same time narrative criticism has not infrequently been advanced with strong polemic against traditional approaches. Robert Alter criticizes an "excavative" scholarship that is satisfied with simply uncovering meanings of obscure words, historical backgrounds and influences, original life situations, and compositional histories and sources.[17] Adele Berlin sharply distinguishes the concerns of *source criticism*, with its "thrust ... toward the fragmenting of the narrative," from the concern to understand biblical narrative in its own right.[18] Narrative critics agree with historical critics that the NT writers used and redacted sources, but they spend little or no time laboring to identify possible sources, sometimes expressly out of skepticism that such sources can be confidently uncovered.[19] Whereas *redaction critics* tend to focus on where/how redaction (i.e., additions, subtractions, changes to purported sources) appears as the key to determining a theological outlook, and thus they are concerned to identify sources and a historical redactor's theology "behind the text," narrative criticism begins with the assumption that the final form of the text as a whole, as a carefully structured and worded unity, is a proper object of critical inquiry. *Composition criticism* retains the redaction-critical concern to recover a writer's theology, viewing the narrative form chiefly as a vehicle for the transfer of theology/ideas, while narrative criticism emphasizes that meaning cannot be reduced beyond form, for form *is* meaning or is inseparable from it.[20]

Thus, in relation to traditional historical-critical approaches, narrative criticism involves a shift in *activity*: from fragmenting biblical narrative texts into forms and sources and layers, to analyzing the unity of the final form of the text. Narrative criticism also involves a shift in *attention*:

---

17. Robert Alter, *The Art of Biblical Narrative*, rev. and updated ed. (New York: Basic, 2011), 55–56, 61. However, as M. C. de Boer points out, "Historical criticism ... does not *require* an evolutionary view of a Gospel or any other biblical document" ("Narrative Criticism, Historical Criticism, and the Gospel of John," *JSNT* 47 [1992]: 35–48, at 39n24, emphasis original).

18. Berlin, *Poetics and Interpretation of Biblical Narrative*, 121. Source criticism has never fared well in the estimation of narrative critics.

19. With regard to OT narrative, Berlin comments that since the final forms of the narratives before us often prove to display artistic sophistication, creativity, and beauty, a synchronic approach "is more than just a matter of convenience or ignorance" (*Poetics and Interpretation of Biblical Narrative*, 121).

20. See Moore, *Literary Criticism and the Gospels*, 4–13.

from attentiveness to the history behind the text, to attentiveness to the story-world in/of the text and/or responses to the story-world by different readers in front of the text.[21] Indeed, Kenneth R. R. Gros Louis, an early proponent of a literary approach to biblical narrative, expressly commends "the study of the Bible as literature, *without regard to* its textual and histor- ical background, its religious and cultural foundations."[22] Likewise, Powell suggests that narrative criticism in its purest form does not so much deny the concerns/findings of historical criticism as it simply ignores them in practice.[23]

Most of the differences between narrative criticism and traditional historical-critical approaches can be summed up as the difference between diachronic and synchronic concerns.[24] There is also a further crucial differ- ence in origin: while we cannot rightly appreciate narrative criticism's rise apart from its associations with traditional historical-critical approaches (especially redaction and composition criticism), the fact is that its

---

21. Another way to state this second shift is as a shift in the postulated location of mean- ing: from the author's theology/intentions (or the compositional history of the text, or the communities that produced or first received the text) to the form of the narrative itself or to what readers enact in their readings of the narrative. See James L. Resseguie, *Narrative Criticism of the New Testament: An Introduction* (Grand Rapids: Baker, 2005), 19.

22. Kenneth R. R. Gros Louis, introduction to *Literary Interpretations of Biblical Narratives*, ed. K. R. R. Gros Louis, J. S. Ackerman, and T. S. Warshaw (Nashville: Abingdon, 1974), 10–15, at 12, emphasis added. If read charitably, Gros Louis' words are of an (over)corrective nature, since he longs for the kind of "balance ... between historical reality and literary reality" that is enjoyed in, e.g., Shakespearian study to be characteristic of biblical study.

23. Powell, *What Is Narrative Criticism?*, 7. However, Powell admits an important *preliminary* role that historical insight plays for narrative criticism (see *What Is Narrative Criticism?*, 86). In this he is representative of most narrative critics. But some, such as Jack Dean Kingsbury, view narrative critical work as coming properly *first* as preparation for historical recon- structive work (see "Reflections on the 'Reader' of Matthew's Gospel," NTS 34 [1988]: 442–60, at 459; see also de Boer, "Narrative Criticism," 48). For pushback against the notion that one approach enjoys a principled temporal priority, see Meir Sternberg, *The Poetics of Biblical Narrative: Ideological Literature and the Drama of Reading* (Bloomington: Indiana University Press, 1985), 18–19.

24. However, as Berlin well notes, the two approaches, historical critical (diachronic) and literary (synchronic), are not independent of each other. Furthermore, she suggests that it is possible and necessary to pursue "diachronic poetics." See Berlin, *Poetics and Interpretation of Biblical Narrative*, 111–12, 128–29; see also David Rhoads, "Narrative Criticism: Practices and Prospects," in *Characterization in the Gospels: Reconceiving Narrative Criticism*, ed. D. Rhoads and K. Syreeni (Sheffield: Sheffield Academic, 1999), 264–85, at 274–75; and Merenlahti, *Poetics for the Gospels?*, 5–7, who speaks of "historical, not objective poetics" (quotation at 6; see also 118).

theoretical and practical genesis was in (early to mid-) twentieth-century secular literary criticism (on which see below under "Development of the Method").[25]

In addition to traditional historical-critical methods, narrative criticism has important relationships with newer *literary approaches* to the study of the NT. Our comments here can be briefer.[26]

Structuralism is, like narrative criticism, a text-centered approach, in that its concerns center on the formal characteristics of narrative, but it differs from narrative criticism in its focus on deep structures that transcend any particular narrative; narrative criticism, in general, revels in the particularity of each narrative. *Rhetorical criticism* shares with narrative criticism interest in the effects of a narrative on readers, or how those effects are brought about by the language and structure/sequencing of the text, but narrative criticism draws not on the "rhetoric of persuasion" (Aristotelian) but on the "rhetoric of narrative/fiction" (narratology; the Chicago School of criticism).[27] *Reader-response criticism* focuses on readers in front of the text (like rhetorical criticism), who construct (or deconstruct) meaning or critique ideology, and is less occupied with the characteristic narrative-critical concern with how the text determines or guides the responses of (implied) readers. But both reader-response criticism and narrative criticism are interested in the dynamics of reading.[28]

The relationship of narrative criticism to one further approach is worth mentioning—namely, *canonical criticism*. Canonical criticism may be indebted to New Criticism, the latter of which played a major formative role on narrative criticism, but the relationship is debated.[29] In any

---

25. Moore, *Literary Criticism and the Gospels*, 8–9.

26. The following paragraph is heavily indebted to Powell, *What Is Narrative Criticism?*, 11–21.

27. See Powell, *What Is Narrative Criticism?*, 15. For the formalist concerns of the "Chicago school of criticism" (the chief figure of which was Wayne Booth) and the influence of the Chicago school on narrative criticism, see Aune, "Literary Criticism," 122–23.

28. Moore sees reader-response approaches to be "largely an extension of (or variation on) narrative criticism" (*Literary Criticism and the Gospels*, xxii). See also Resseguie, *Narrative Criticism of the New Testament*, 32–33; Aune, "Literary Criticism," 125.

29. For the proposed relationship, see John Barton, *Reading the Old Testament: Method in Biblical Study*, rev. and enlarged ed. (Louisville: Westminster John Knox, 1996), 141–45. For demurral, see Mary C. Callaway, "Canonical Criticism," in McKenzie and Haynes, *To Each Its Own Meaning*, 142–55, at 152.

case, in their assumption that the unity of the text is interpretatively significant and meaningful, narrative critics share the concerns of canonical criticism, which (in certain forms) emphasizes the theological and literary meaningfulness of the final form and sequencing of the canonical text. Indeed, Stephen Dempster asserts, "The biblical books, by virtue of their canonical unity and by virtue of their genre as literature, require a literary perspective," and he seeks to draw narrative conclusions from the sequencing of the Hebrew canon.[30] The attempt is fraught with difficulty, however, and most narrative critics claim that rendering an account of canonical unity is beyond the limits of narrative criticism proper.[31]

5.1.2 GUIDING ASSUMPTIONS

There is no universal agreement concerning what constitutes and drives narrative criticism. Nevertheless, for our present purposes, we may identify the following seven assumptions with which narrative criticism (typically) operates.

1. *The final forms of the NT narrative literature are proper objects of critical analysis and not only or chiefly a means to some other object of study.* For narrative critics, the text is "not primarily a source to recover the events and persons associated with the original writing and reception of the text, but an event in itself."[32] Narrative criticism seeks to understand this "event in itself."

2. *The story-worlds of the NT narratives have their own autonomous integrity.* This assumption is closely related to (or even a different facet of) the preceding one. If the NT narrative books have an autonomous literary integrity, then their meaning is not dependent on (or at least is truly, if not comprehensively, accessible apart from) knowledge of historical matters outside the story-world and discourse of the narrative.[33] We need not

---

30. Stephen G. Dempster, *Dominion and Dynasty: A Theology of the Hebrew Bible*, NSBT 15 (Downers Grove, IL: InterVarsity, 2003), 24; see further 15–43.

31. See Powell, *What Is Narrative Criticism?*, 101; also Richard B. Hays, "Can Narrative Criticism Recover the Theological Unity of Scripture?," *JTI* 2 (2008): 193–211.

32. Stamps, "Rhetorical and Narratological Criticism," 229.

33. Rhoads, "Narrative Criticism and the Gospel of Mark," 413; see also Bowman, "Narrative Criticism," 19; Moore, *Literary Criticism and the Gospels*, 8–9.

know about the compositional history of the text, or the socio-cultural-historical contexts out of which it was written and to which it was originally addressed, or any possible extra-textual realities to which the narrative refers, in order to enter, understand, and meaningfully engage with the story.[34] Similarly, narrative critics tend to assume that interpretive agendas *brought* to the text are not determinative of the text's meaning and do not infringe on its autonomous integrity.[35]

3. *The unity of the text as an object before us (the unity of the final form) is taken as an invitation to articulate or determine the unity and coherence of the story/ meaning of the text as a whole.* Narrative critics typically assume that there is unity or coherence to the meaning of narrative as a whole, or at least many see their task as one of seeking to offer persuasive formulations of a narrative's unity and coherence.[36] Often emphasized along with the important assumptions of unity and coherence is that the narrative as a whole is what is unified and coheres, and the narrative as a whole is the proper context for understanding.

4. *A sequential reading of the story with an understanding of how the whole leads to its end is crucial to narrative understanding.* As Powell has asserted with respect to the Gospels, they "are stories about Jesus ... intended to be read from beginning to end, not dissected and examined to determine the relative value of individual passages."[37] Though less frequently commented on than the preceding points, the assumption that a narrative develops meaningfully all the way to its conclusion, and that readers must follow this development, is of crucial importance to narrative criticism (at the same time, the present point, together with the following point, helps to underline that narrative-critical concerns and inquiries into literary form

---

34. Elizabeth Struthers Malbon, "Narrative Criticism: How Does the Story Mean?," in *Mark and Method: New Approaches in Biblical Studies*, ed. J. C. Anderson and S. D. Moore (Minneapolis: Fortress, 1992), 23–49, at 24.

35. Bowman, "Narrative Criticism," 19.

36. Moore, *Literary Criticism and the Gospels*, 7–8; Aune "Literary Criticism," 132; Paris, *Narrative Obtrusion*, 8.

37. Powell, *What Is Narrative Criticism?*, 2, emphasis added. The "relative value" Powell speaks of is the value of the Gospels as historical testimony.

stretch back as far as Aristotle's Poetics).[38] The aim or telos toward which a narrative builds "guides the selection and organization of the elements of story," thus the meaning of the story is only fully comprehended (revealed) at the story's denouement.[39]

5. *The narrative literature of the NT can be usefully divided up into content (or story, "what") and form (or discourse, "how").* Narrative critics, particularly under the influence of Seymour Chatman, have distinguished between "story" and "discourse." As Malbon explains,

> Story is the *what* of a narrative; discourse is the *how*. Story indicates the content of the narrative, including events, characters, and settings, and their interaction as the plot. Discourse indicates the rhetoric of the narrative, how the story is told. ... The story is where the characters interact; the discourse is where the implied author and implied reader interact.[40]

Malbon rightly adds, "Story and discourse are not really separable. What we have, in Chatman's words, is the story-as-discoursed."[41] However, narrative critics assume that the distinction has value in examining the text. For example, working with the distinction when reading Luke 7:36–50 enables readers to recognize the narrative artistry at work: while the host's failure to wash his guest's feet would have occurred near the beginning of the *story* (as Jesus arrived at the dinner party), nevertheless in the *discourse* we are not told this important point until the end of the scene (at 7:44–46). The story-discourse distinction is a useful tool that sheds light on compositional artistry and raises or clarifies key interpretative questions: Why has the story in Luke 7 been told in *this way*?[42]

---

38. See especially Aristotle's discussion of matters such as plot and action, and structure and sequence, in *Poetics* 6–12.

39. Green, "Narrative Criticism," 94. For theological hermeneutical reflections on this point, see Peter J. Leithart, *Deep Exegesis: The Mystery of Reading Scripture* (Waco, TX: Baylor University Press, 2009), 35–74.

40. Malbon, "Narrative Criticism," 26–27. Moore, *Literary Criticism and the Gospels*, 58–68, problematizes the story-discourse (form-content) binary.

41. Malbon, "Narrative Criticism," 27. See also Resseguie, *Narrative Criticism of the New Testament*, 18–19.

42. For the example from Luke 7, see Resseguie, *Narrative Criticism of the New Testament*, 208–9, who appeals at this point not to Chatman's "story" and "discourse" but to a similar

6. A close reading of the literary features of the text—the "what" and the "how" of the text, and their interplay—will clarify the narrative meaning of the text. The kind of question just raised about Luke 7 comes about by paying careful, disciplined attention to the literary features and form of the narrative, its content, and how it is expressed. What Alter calls "minutely discriminating attention to the artful use of language, to the shifting play of ideas, conventions, tone, sound, imagery, syntax, narrative viewpoint, compositional units, and much else" is the bread and butter of narrative criticism.[43] Narrative critics frequently speak of this as "close reading" (following the lead of early twentieth-century New Criticism). While close reading may be put in the service of exposing indeterminacy or ambiguity in the narrative,[44] it is more often an attempt to understand the interaction of, or the transactions that take place between, the (implied) author and (implied) reader—that is, it is believed to be a means of understanding the meaning/ message which is the story.[45] An important prior assumption at this point that has not yet been expressly named is that the biblical narratives work as literature: "Biblical narrative literature exhibits literary characteristics that are also apparent in literature in general."[46] Attentive, close reading of the biblical stories is a reading disciplined to ask after the elements that characterize "literature [or narrative] in general," such as plot, narrator, setting, and point of view.

7. The narrative is the meeting point between author and reader, with the result that narrative meaning is best understood as a communicative event. A biblical narrative work is a complex speech-act. As a result, "One of the tasks of narrative criticism ... is to deal with these questions: What are

---

distinction made by the Russian Formalists between *fabula* (story) and *sjužet* (plot).

43. Alter, *Art of Biblical Narrative*, 13.

44. See Resseguie, *Narrative Criticism of the New Testament*, 24.

45. See Malbon, "Narrative Criticism," 26–27, quoted in the preceding point. For a methodological questioning of "close reading," together with a perceptive contrasting of literary (aesthetic) close reading with spiritual/allegorical reading, see Merenlahti, *Poetics for the Gospels?*, 45–58.

46. Resseguie, *Narrative Criticism of the New Testament*, 19, emphasis added. See also Merenlahti, *Poetics for the Gospels?*, 19–20.

the New Testament narratives doing? And, literarily, how do they do it?"[47] Frequently, narrative criticism assumes that the biblical narratives are labors in persuasion. For example, Resseguie asks specifically, "What point of view does the narrative want the reader to adopt or reject?"[48] Narrative literature tends to pursue this purpose of persuasion in indirect ways. Bar-Efrat offers a basic contrast: "Whereas the Prophetic and Wisdom literature express their views directly, openly urging that they be accepted, the narrative operates in an oblique and unobtrusive way."[49] This is a matter of degree or scale, since sometimes biblical narrators directly state their views and agendas (e.g., John 20:30–31; Luke 1:1–4). Perhaps the best statement of the aims and intended effects of the NT narrative literature is offered by Joel Green, best because it rightly acknowledges the complex narrative, historical, and ideological character of the NT writings:

> To shape the identity of their audiences, to legitimize a movement, and to demonstrate continuity with the past—such aims as these characterize these texts, whose character then must be understood in rhetorical terms, as acts of persuasion, and not simply with regard to literary artistry.[50]

The NT narratives have agendas, purposes, and intended effects on *readers*. But it is not only readers that are within the purview of narrative criticism; to speak in terms of agendas, purposes, and intended effects is to speak in terms of agency—indeed, it is to speak in terms that require an *author*.[51] New Testament narrative is a meeting place between (implied) authors and (implied) readers, and its meaning is best understood in terms of transactions or communicative activity. Unpacking this final guiding assumption is one way of tying the more text-centered approach of narrative criticism to more traditional author-centered approaches of historical

---

47. Rhoads, "Narrative Criticism: Practices and Prospects," 273; also 274. See Powell, *What Is Narrative Criticism?*, 8–10, drawing expressly on Roman Jakobson's communication model.

48. Resseguie, *Narrative Criticism of the New Testament*, 40.

49. Bar-Efrat, *Narrative Art in the Bible*, 16. Bar-Efrat is well aware that narratives can and do take the direct route of explanation or comment, thus "enabling clear and unequivocal messages to be conveyed to readers" (*Narrative Art in the Bible*, 26).

50. Green, "Narrative Criticism," 91.

51. To remain formally text-centered, narrative critics typically appeal to the category of the *implied* author (see below under key concepts for discussion).

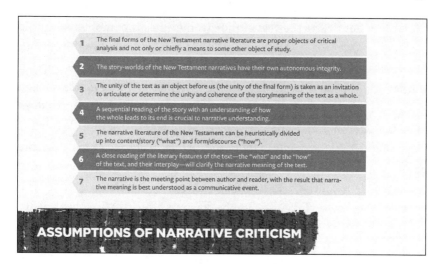

The final forms of the New Testament narrative literature are proper objects of critical analysis and not only or chiefly a means to some other object of study. **[1]**

The story-worlds of the New Testament narratives have their own autonomous integrity. **[2]**

The unity of the text as an object before us (the unity of the final form) is taken as an invitation to articulate or determine the unity and coherence of the story/meaning of the text as a whole. **[3]**

A sequential reading of the story with an understanding of how the whole leads to its end is crucial to narrative understanding. **[4]**

The narrative literature of the New Testament can be heuristically divided up into content/story ("what") and form/discourse ("how"). **[5]**

A close reading of the literary features of the text—the "what" and the "how" of the text, and their interplay—will clarify the narrative meaning of the text. **[6]**

The narrative is the meeting point between author and reader, with the result that narrative meaning is best understood as a communicative event. **[7]**

ASSUMPTIONS OF NARRATIVE CRITICISM

criticism and newer reader-centered approaches, thus opening the door wider for interdisciplinary partnership.

5.1.3 KEY CONCEPTS

Two key concepts enable narrative critics to focus their attention chiefly on the world "in the text" and not primarily on matters "behind the text" or "in front of the text"[52]—the implied author and the implied reader.

The concept of the *implied author* has been of great importance to narrative critics, since the authors of the NT narrative literature are typically unidentified, and, in any case, we have no direct access to the "real" or "empirical" authors. What we do have direct access to is the author's self-projection that is developed by the narrative before us. This projection is the implied author. Better, as we read we construct an image of the author that is implied by the narrative—by the perspective of the overall narrative, by the values and beliefs reflected and advanced therein, by the decisions that must have been made that account, for example, for the narrative's sequencing and setting and rhetoric.[53] The implied author provides narrative critics with a basis for interpretation in the absence of confidence

---

52. However, as our comments above (and also in the sections to follow) indicate, this does not necessarily mean narrative critics can or should completely ignore those foci.

53. See Culpepper, *Anatomy of the Fourth Gospel*, 6–7; Malbon, "Narrative Criticism," 27–28; Mark Allan Powell, "Narrative Criticism," in *Hearing the New Testament: Strategies for Interpretation*, 2nd ed., ed. J. B. Green (Grand Rapids: Eerdmans, 2010), 240–58, at 241–42.

about the identity of the real author (sometimes the implied author is invoked precisely as a reason why we do not *need* to know anything about the real author).[54] Narrative critics also at times appeal to the implied author as a way of steering clear of the "intentional fallacy." It is open to debate whether and to what degree, in function, reading indications of the implied author of the narrative differs from more traditional attempts to gather "internal evidence" about the historical author. Regardless, the implied-author concept enables narrative critics to maintain that they focus on the narrative text itself, allowing it to "speak for itself": "The interpretive key no longer lies in background information, but within the text itself."[55] Powell's comment is particularly significant, indicating that the findings and complex labors of behind-the-text historical-critical work are not necessary to meaningfully engage the NT narratives. It is not an accident that some commend narrative criticism as a way of empowering nonspecialists to read Scripture.[56]

Like the implied author, the *implied reader* is a heuristic fiction, one useful for learning. As the implied author is to be conceptually distinguished from the real author, so also the implied reader must be distinguished from real readers (either the original audiences to which the NT books were addressed or any real readers in the history of interpretation and today). There are competing accounts of the implied reader, and the concept has performed differing functions in narrative-critical practice. For some, the implied reader may also be called the "ideal reader"—that imaginary reader who responds "to the text at every point with whatever emotion, understanding, or knowledge the text ideally calls for."[57] For

---

54. The implied author has also been invoked as important in light of the *composite* nature of the NT narrative literature (and the Gospels, in particular). It does not matter that a text is a composite of differing sources arising from differing hands, for the final form of the text "will always evince particular values, beliefs, and perceptions that can be described as representative of its implied author" (Powell, "Narrative Criticism," 242). It is arguable that this move does not take adequately into account the reality of agency as discussed in point 7 above in §5.1.2 Guiding Assumptions.

55. Powell, *What Is Narrative Criticism?*, 5.

56. See Leland Ryken and Tremper Longman III, introduction to Ryken and Longman, eds., *Complete Literary Guide to the Bible*, 15–39, at 22; see also Culpepper, *Anatomy of the Fourth Gospel*, 4; and Moore, *Literary Criticism and the Gospels*, xvi–xvii, with appropriate critical questions posed to the turn to accessibility.

57. Jack Dean Kingsbury, *Matthew as Story*, 2nd ed. (Philadelphia: Fortress, 1988), 38.

others (under the influence of Wolfgang Iser), the implied reader is to be found "at the intersection of a text and its empirical readers," since "actual readers necessarily contribute to the meaning of the text by filling in its inherent gaps. By doing so, they give shape to the implied reader as the one who actualizes the intentions of the narrative."[58] We have, on the one hand, the ideal reader as "an unchanging property of the text," and, on the other hand, the ideal reader as "neither wholly actual nor wholly ideal ... in part a creation of the text and in part a real individual."[59] In either case, the concept of the implied reader allows narrative critics to assert their (at least temporary) independence from historical-critical pursuits to reconstruct the original audience. We might view identification of the implied readers as a kind of chastened historical-critical pursuit, inasmuch as it provides a textually constructed index of an originally intended (or "imagined") audience.[60] But identification of the implied reader may serve a still more important function for exegesis: it can provide a standard to which responsive readers can seek to conform. As Malbon has suggested, if narrative-critical study "can help us align ourselves with the implied reader, our own role as real readers—and re-readers—of Mark will surely be enriched."[61]

---

58. Jeannine K. Brown, "Narrative Criticism," in *Dictionary of Jesus and the Gospels*, 2nd ed., ed. J. B. Green, J. K. Brown, and N. Perrin (Downers Grove, IL: InterVarsity, 2013), 619–24, at 621. Resseguie, *Narrative Criticism of the New Testament*, 32, cites Mark Allan Powell as an exponent of the position represented above by Kingsbury, but he cites Powell's 1990 *What Is Narrative Criticism?* By 1995, Powell began sounding more like an Iserian, as he speaks of the implied reader as "one who actualizes the potential for meaning in a text, who responds to it in ways consistent with the expectations that we may ascribe to its implied author" (see Powell, "Narrative Criticism," 242, which reproduces the first-edition statement from 1995).

59. Moore, *Literary Criticism and the Gospels*, 99–101. In Resseguie's estimation, there is little difference in practice between the two differing accounts of implied readers (see *Narrative Criticism of the New Testament*, 32).

60. See, e.g., W. J. Kurz, "Narrative Models for Imitation in Luke-Acts," in *Greeks, Romans, and Christians: Essays in Honor of Abraham J. Malherbe*, ed. D. L. Balch, E. Ferguson, and W. A. Meeks (Minneapolis: Fortress, 1990), 171–89, who speaks of implied readers as "the kinds of readers who are imagined or expected by the writers" (173–74). Described in this way, the implied reader can provide an index of the originally intended audience (the language of "index" comes from Kingsbury, *Matthew as Story*, 147).

61. Malbon, "Narrative Criticism," 47. See also Brown, "Narrative Criticism," 621; and Powell's early articulation of the matter in *What Is Narrative Criticism?*, 20–21.

5.2 DEVELOPMENT OF NEW TESTAMENT
NARRATIVE CRITICISM

There are very early precedents for narrative-critical study of the NT.[62] But for our purposes, we can begin the story in the twentieth century. Already in 1946, Erich Auerbach drew attention to the poetic strategy of biblical narration, and his reflections have been quoted many times over in biblical studies.[63] Menakhem Perry and Meir Sternberg undertook concerted investigation of the poetics of OT narrative literature in the late 1960s,[64] and in the 1980s appreciation of the narrative artistry of OT literature began to soar with publications by Robert Alter (*The Art of Biblical Narrative* [1981]), Adele Berlin (*Poetics and Interpretation of Biblical Narrative* [1983]), and Shimon Bar-Efrat (*Narrative Art in the Bible* [1989]).[65] In NT studies, William Beardslee produced a guide to literary criticism of the NT in 1970,[66] in 1974 Hans Frei's *The Eclipse of Biblical Narrative* sought to draw attention to "the narrative shape" of the Gospels,[67] and in 1978 Norman Peterson labored in literary-critical theory for NT studies.[68]

---

62. As noted above, narrative criticism can claim a genealogy going all the way back to Aristotle (see also William A. Beardslee, *Literary Criticism of the New Testament*, GBS [Philadelphia: Fortress, 1970], 4–5; Merenlahti, *Poetics for the Gospels?*, 18).

63. Erich Auerbach, *Mimesis: The Representation of Reality in Western Literature*, trans. W. R. Trask (Princeton: Princeton University Press, 1953); see especially 7–16 and 40–49.

64. See Menakhem Perry and Meir Sternberg, "The King through Ironic Eyes: The Narrator's Devices in the Story of David and Bathsheba and Two Excurses on the Theory of the Narrative Text," *Ha-sifrut* 1 (1968): 263–93; this Hebrew original was published in English as "The King through Ironic Eyes: Biblical Narrative and the Literary Reading Process," *Poetics Today* 7 (1986): 275–322.

65. For surveys of the modern development of narrative (or literary) approaches to OT literature, in addition to the earlier essay in the present volume, see Gunn, "Narrative Criticism," 202–12; R. Christopher Heard, "Narrative Criticism and the Hebrew Scriptures: A Review and Assessment," *ResQ* 38 (1996): 29–43. For suggestions why the development of literary criticism of the OT has developed along a slightly different trajectory and pace from NT narrative criticism, see Gunn, "Narrative Criticism," 202; Brook W. R. Pearson, "New Testament Literary Criticism," in *Handbook to Exegesis of the New Testament*, ed. S. E. Porter (Leiden: Brill, 1997), 241–66, at 241–42.

66. Beardslee, *Literary Criticism of the New Testament*.

67. Hans W. Frei, *The Eclipse of Biblical Narrative: A Study in Eighteenth and Nineteenth Century Hermeneutics* (New Haven, CT: Yale University Press, 1974), 13. As Moore has noted, Frei's influence on narrative criticism is, at best, "indirect" (see Moore, *Literary Criticism and the Gospels*, 60n4).

68. Norman R. Petersen, *Literary Criticism for New Testament Critics*, GBS (Philadelphia: Fortress, 1978). Though having a genealogy distinct from that of narrative criticism, the "Bible as literature" movement is also of relevance in understanding the diverse factors leading to the rise of narrative criticism (see Aune, "Literary Criticism," 119–20).

But convention and convenience allow us to mark 1980 as the birth-date of narrative criticism as a distinct approach to the study of NT narrative literature; in that year David Rhoads coined the term in his seminal SBL Markan Seminar paper, later published as "Narrative Criticism and the Gospel of Mark."[69] From that point on, a steady stream of narrative-critical works began appearing. In 1982 Rhoads, together with his Carthage College colleague (and literature professor) Donald Michie, published *Mark as Story: An Introduction to the Narrative of a Gospel*, which was massively influential.[70] Soon after came R. Alan Culpepper's *Anatomy of the Fourth Gospel: A Study in Literary Design* (1983), Jack Dean Kingsbury's *Matthew as Story* (1986), and volume 1 of Robert Tannehill's *The Narrative Unity of Luke-Acts: A Literary Interpretation* (1986).[71] Other important narrative-critical studies appeared in this same period, but these stand out as some of the most often cited.

The aforementioned studies are also significant because they represent thoroughgoing narrative-critical analyses of the whole of each of the four Gospels (and Acts). Particularly the Gospel of Mark has been a particularly important field of experimentation and demonstration for narrative criticism. The decade-long SBL Markan Seminar (1971–80) involved many of the brightest lights of early narrative criticism. And the influence of *Mark as Story* far extends what one might expect from its slim size. The connection of the rise of narrative criticism with the study of the Gospel of Mark may be explained, in part, as the intersection of a long-standing critical debate in Markan scholarship and rising dissatisfaction with many of the results of traditional historical criticism. With Markan priority as the dominant starting point in historical-critical scholarship, debates raged over whether this first Gospel writer was a creative artist or a clumsy scissors-and-paste

---

69. Rhoads, "Narrative Criticism and the Gospel of Mark."

70. David Rhoads and Donald Michie, *Mark as Story: An Introduction to the Narrative of a Gospel* (Philadelphia: Fortress, 1982). A second edition of *Mark as Story*, adding Joanna Dewey to the authorial team, appeared in 1999, and a third edition was published in 2012. The influence of this slim volume was, no doubt, in large part owing to how it is "concise, elegantly written, and easy to read" (Merenlahti, *Poetics for the Gospels?*, 21).

71. Culpepper, *Anatomy of the Fourth Gospel*; Jack Dean Kingsbury, *Matthew as Story* (Philadelphia: Fortress, 1986); Robert C. Tannehill, *The Narrative Unity of Luke-Acts: A Literary Interpretation*, 2 vols. (Philadelphia: Fortress, 1986–90).

editor.[72] At the same time, frustration at the dissection of the Gospels into various sources, compositional strata, and forms as evidence of various originating life settings led to a reactionary "shift from fragmentation to wholeness"[73]—the wholeness, that is, of the final forms of the books before us. We may attribute narrative criticism's rise to its effectiveness in addressing both matters. On the one hand, it was a strategic way to answer affirmatively with respect to Mark's literary artistry and sophistication;[74] on the other hand, it suggested a way to reclaim the forest that was felt to be lost for attention to the trees (and perhaps, some may have suspected, to trees that were part of a *different* forest).[75] Narrative critics felt they had found a viable alternative to the reigning historical-critical method, or a needful complement that addressed the literary features of the biblical text that had long been neglected.

The early labors in narrative criticism were about interpretive praxis through and through. They offered narrative *criticism* (or descriptive poetics) rather than labors in narrative *theory*. For theory, narrative critics turned to the work of secular literary criticism.[76] In general, narrative criticism is the fruit of Gospels scholars appropriating the categories and inquiries used by literary critics in reading modern (and sometimes ancient) fiction: "Literary criticism examines biblical narratives using the same methods and techniques that critics use to study the short stories of Kate Chopin and Ernest Hemingway, or the novels of Toni Morrison and the plays of William Shakespeare."[77] To say it this broadly, however, may be misleading. Narrative criticism does not, as Moore points out, reflect "the

---

72. There was, after all, no objective point of reference and comparison on the assumption of Markan priority. The question is, of course, a question bound up with the development of redaction criticism as well.

73. Rhoads, "Narrative Criticism and the Gospel of Mark," 412.

74. See, e.g., Malbon, "Narrative Criticism," 24; also Tolbert, *Sowing the Gospel*, 21–23. See also the discussion in Merenlahti, *Poetics for the Gospels?*, 20–21.

75. See, e.g., Werner Kelber's quip in 1979: "Because we have focused on the individual stories *in* Mark we have not really come to know the story *of* Mark" (*Mark's Story of Jesus* [Philadelphia: Fortress, 1979], 11, emphasis original). See further Hays, "Can Narrative Criticism Recover the Theological Unity of Scripture?," 197.

76. Moore, *Literary Criticism and the Gospels*, 7–13, 41, 55.

77. Resseguie, *Narrative Criticism of the New Testament*, 19. As John W. Sider has noted, "Consciously or not, Christians have always been indebted to secular literary theories in their reading of the Bible" ("Nurturing Our Nurse: Literary Scholars and Biblical Exegesis," *ChrLit* 32 [1982]: 15–21, at 16).

whole of [secular] literary criticism or its definitive concerns," but only "a particular movement whose golden age is now long past."[78] The "particular movement" to which Moore refers is New Criticism, which arose and came to considerable prominence in the inter- and postwar years of the twentieth century. New Criticism emphatically defended the text's unity and coherence. It argued that historical background information is unnecessary to the proper interpretation of texts (i.e., we need not concern ourselves with authors or readers, but must only focus on the text before us and understand it "on its own terms"), and it developed a strategy of "close reading" of literary texts. These moves had an early and very deep influence on NT narrative criticism.[79]

In addition to New Criticism, the theoretical work of Seymour Chatman, particularly his binary of "story" and "discourse," is necessary to note.[80] Chatman's 1978 *Story and Discourse: Narrative Structure in Fiction and Film* has exerted such tremendous influence on NT narrative criticism that Aune calls Chatman "the foster-father of narrative criticism,"[81] and Merenlahti identifies him as "perhaps the most important single source of inspiration for narrative critics of the New Testament."[82] Wayne Booth has also provided narrative criticism with a toolbox of concepts (e.g., that of the implied author) and inquiries for analyzing the "rhetoric of fiction."[83] While New Criticism, Chatman's variety of structuralism, and Booth's

---

78. Moore, *Literary Criticism and the Gospels*, 11; see also Powell, *What Is Narrative Criticism?*, 19; Stamps, "Rhetorical and Narratological Criticism," 229; Johannes C. de Klerk, "Situating Biblical Narrative Studies in Literary Theory and Literary Approaches," *R&T* 4 (1997): 190–207, at 203–4.

79. See Powell, *What Is Narrative Criticism?*, 4–5; Malbon, "Narrative Criticism," 24–25; Resseguie, *Narrative Criticism of the New Testament*, 21–25; see also Aune, "Literary Criticism," 121–22. Moore especially emphasizes the indebtedness to New Criticism (see *Literary Criticism and the Gospels*, 9–12). Early narrative critics typically left unstated the theoretical and methodological genealogy of their approach (in addition to Moore, see Merenlahti, *Poetics for the Gospels?*, 19).

80. Seymour Chatman, *Story and Discourse: Narrative Structure in Fiction and Film* (Ithaca, NY: Cornell University Press, 1978). The Russian Formalists' distinction between *fabula* (story) and *sjužet* (plot) has also been drawn on by a number of narrative critics.

81. Aune, "Literary Criticism," 125.

82. Merenlahti, *Poetics for the Gospels?*, 18–19. See further Moore, *Literary Criticism and the Gospels*, 43–52. Chatman has also influenced OT literary-critical approaches (e.g., Berlin).

83. See Booth, *Rhetoric of Fiction*. On the more general influence of the "Chicago school of criticism," the "second generation" of which Booth was a part, see Aune, "Literary Criticism," 122–23.

literary toolbox all contributed a decidedly formalist shaping force on narrative criticism, in more recent years varieties of reader-response criticism have turned narrative-critical attention to such matters as the responses of the implied readers aimed at by the implied author, the dynamics of reading (what happens as real readers read NT narrative), the responsibility of ethical and ideological criticism, and the production (or deconstruction) of meaning by readers.[84]

We cannot, of course, do full justice here to the complex development of narrative criticism. Several other important secular literary theorists and critics whom we have not addressed above have in various ways exerted considerable influence on the practice of NT narrative criticism (e.g., Mieke Bal, Gerald Prince, Gérard Genette, Wolfgang Iser, and Russian Formalists such as Vladimir Propp and Roman Jakobson). In any case, it is plain that narrative criticism is an eclectic discipline, arising from and partnering with diverse (and sometimes paradoxically conjoined) approaches.[85]

5.3 APPLICATIONS OF NEW TESTAMENT NARRATIVE CRITICISM

Green comments,

> One kind of reader experiences the text under the tutelage of the narrator generally without realizing what is in the foreground, midground, or background. Another kind of reader, the narrative critic, is interested not only in the mere "that" of the text's emphases but also in "how" the text serves to generate particular readerly experiences.[86]

Narrative criticism seeks to analyze the "how" of NT narratives by paying careful attention to and explicating the way in which several key narrative elements appear in the stories: narrator, character, setting, point

---

84. Resseguie credits reader-response criticism as helping to recover the reader excluded by New Criticism (see *Narrative Criticism of the New Testament*, 32–33).

85. Aune, "Literary Criticism," 125–33; see also Pearson, "New Testament Literary Criticism," 243.

86. Green, "Narrative Criticism," 95.

of view, plot, and rhetoric.[87] Through narrative-critically disciplined observation (noting how narrative elements appear) and inquiry (asking why the narrative elements appear in the manner they do),[88] narrative criticism seeks to enhance our *reading/interpretation* of the NT stories to better appreciate and receive the "what" of the narratives, or to identify the kinds of responses to which the narrative may lead the (implied) reader. In demonstrating the approach, we will briefly consider two portions of NT narrative, highlighting how narrative-critical observations and inquiries fuel interpretation.[89]

5.3.1 THE PARABLE OF THE GOOD SAMARITAN

We can begin with the well-known parable of the Good Samaritan (Luke 10:25-37).[90] Though the parable itself is embedded within a dialogue between Jesus and an anonymous lawyer, we can focus our attention for the time being on the parable proper in 10:30-35. In this story, we can note at least nine different events/stages (the sequence of events in the *story* seems to be more or less identical with the sequence of the *discourse*):

---

87. The "elements of narrative" are surveyed in diverse ways, with differing categorizations, subdivisions, and at times terminology. For helpful surveys (helpful both in terms of their content and in terms of comparison and contrast of approaches), see Powell, *What Is Narrative Criticism?*, 23-83 (as well as his more recent and brief introductory survey in "Narrative Criticism," 245-49); Malbon, "Narrative Criticism," 26-36; Resseguie, *Narrative Criticism of the New Testament*, 242-44; Green, "Narrative Criticism," 95-98. See also the influential approaches of Culpepper, *Anatomy of the Fourth Gospel*; and Rhoads, Dewey, and Michie, *Mark as Story*.

88. Several have spoken of narrative critical reading as posing certain kinds of *questions* to NT narratives; see, e.g., Resseguie, *Narrative Criticism of the New Testament*, 19; Malbon, "Narrative Criticism," 23; Beardslee, *Literary Criticism of the New Testament*, 3; see also Alter, *Art of Biblical Narrative*, 222-23. Helpful lists of narrative critical questions are provided by Powell, *What Is Narrative Criticism?*, 103-5; Resseguie, *Narrative Criticism of the New Testament*, 242-44.

89. For practical purposes, we are considering scenes/sections. It is important to note, however, that "narrative criticism focuses on understanding the Gospels as entire books" (Powell, *What Is Narrative Criticism?*, 103).

90. Much in this section follows Resseguie, *Narrative Criticism of the New Testament*, 192-96, though we will speak in broader terms than Resseguie, who makes all his points under the banner of *point of view* (using Boris Uspensky's categories: spatial, temporal, psychological, phraseological, ideological). In a sense, *everything* about a narrative could be situated under point of view since we cannot approach a narrative in any way other than as a mediated (narrated) reality, as a matter of "rhetoric" (or "discourse") through and through (see Moore, *Literary Criticism and the Gospels*, 40, 58-63).

1. A "certain man" is on a journey from Jerusalem to Jericho (v. 30).

2. He falls among robbers (v. 30).

3. The robbers do what robbers do to him (v. 30).[91]

4. A priest comes along, sees (ἰδών) the man, and passes by (ἀντιπαρῆλθεν) (v. 31).

5. A Levite comes along, sees (ἰδών) the man, and passes by (ἀντιπαρῆλθεν) (v. 32).

6. A Samaritan comes along, sees (ἰδών) the man, and feels compassion (v. 33).

7. The Samaritan approaches (προσελθών) the man, bandages the man up, and pours oil and wine on the man's wounds (v. 34).

8. The Samaritan sets the man on his own beast and brings the man to an inn, where he continues to tend to the man's needs (v. 34).

9. The following day, the Samaritan pays the innkeeper to tend to the man in his absence (v. 35).

We can begin by noting the *pacing* of the story. By far, the largest amount of time is spent narrating the activity of the Samaritan. Whereas in the space of the initial three verses (or stages 1–5) of the story we encounter innumerable acting subjects (literally, in that the number of "robbers" is left unclarified), in the latter three verses (10:33–35, or stages 6–9 of the story), which account for nearly sixty percent of the words in the story, we meet only one acting subject—the Samaritan. The narrator[92] has the other characters in verses 30–32 performing their duties in a couple or a few verbs and participles each; the Samaritan is the subject of more verbs,

---

91. The piling up of participles (ἐκδύσαντες, ἐπιθέντες, ἀφέντες) adds vividness to the scene.

92. Most seem to agree that, in NT narrative literature, there is little to no practical difference between the narrator and the implied author (see Culpepper, *Anatomy of the Fourth Gospel*, 7, 16; see also Berlin, *Poetics and Interpretation of Biblical Narrative*, 148n24).

and the conceptual subject of as many adverbial participles,[93] than all the other characters combined. As Resseguie comments, "A narrator can accent what is important by slowing down the temporal pace of the narrative or can gloss over narrative events by speeding up the pace."[94] In this parable, the speed of the narration clearly slows down when talking about the Samaritan, so that we can focus on the Samaritan's activities in detail.

In terms of *characterization*, a few things stand out.[95] A number of characters serve more or less as props or "agents."[96] The robbers and the innkeeper simply fill a function in the narrative; nothing about their persons besides the actions necessary to keep the plot moving (and in the innkeeper's case, no activity at all apart from being the recipient of the Samaritan's money and instructions) is allowed into the story. Similarly, the anonymous man is also a mere functionary, a point highlighted by the fact of his anonymity, as well as by how after verse 30 he is never again the subject of a verb but always an object on which others act (or fail to act). Already in verse 30, as he "falls among robbers," he is losing his identity as an acting subject.[97] He is important to the story only in his passivity.

In contrast to the robbers, the innkeeper, and the "certain man"—whose importance lies not in their persons but in their roles, which keep the plot moving—the person or character of the priest and of the Levite is significant for the plot. We might call them flat characters or "types." They represent a single quality or trait. In their case, it is the lack of a trait, for their

---

93. The precise number depends on text-critical decisions on variants in verses 30, 32, and 35.

94. Resseguie, *Narrative Criticism of the New Testament*, 193. The slowing down of narrative time can also perform other narrative functions. In Acts 13–14 a disproportionate amount of discourse time is spent on Paul and Barnabas' time in Pisidian Antioch (13:14–52); none of the other five stops on the first missionary journey receives more than thirteen verses (and most far less). In this instance, we may read Paul and Barnabas' experience in Pisidian Antioch as *paradigmatic* for the rest of the first missionary journey (and the rest of Acts). Narrative time slows down in Acts 13:14–52, because the passage is representative of Paul and Barnabas' ministry in each new place they went to and of the responses they encountered.

95. On characterization in Luke-Acts more generally, see Frank Dicken and Julia Snyder, eds., *Characters and Characterization in Luke-Acts* (London: Bloomsbury, forthcoming).

96. See Berlin, *Poetics and Interpretation of Biblical Narrative*, 23–24, who offers a helpful threefold taxonomy of character types: full-fledged characters (i.e., round characters), types (i.e., flat characters), and agents (i.e., functionaries).

97. Joel B. Green, *The Gospel of Luke*, NICNT (Grand Rapids: Eerdmans, 1997), 429, notes that the anonymity of the man makes the classifying of him "as either friend or foe" impossible and thus subverts the whole basis of the question posed to Jesus by the lawyer in verse 29.

inaction is what raises eyebrows, and their inaction *alone* (the narrator completely ignores their motive[s]).[98] Or better, their inaction raises eyebrows when contrasted with the multiplicity of actions that the Samaritan undertakes.

VERSE	ACTOR	ACTION 1	ACTION 2
31	Priest	saw	passed by
32	Levite	saw	passed by
33	Samaritan	saw	had compassion

THE REPEATED SEQUENCE IN THE
PARABLE OF THE GOOD SAMARITAN

The priest and the Levite prove to be foils for the Samaritan, who stands out as the only truly round or "full-fledged" character. The Samaritan performs an abundance of actions, in contrast to the few actions of all the other characters. The Samaritan alone has an emotional (inner) life, or his is the only one the narrator allows us to see (note the compassion of verse 33). The Samaritan is the only one who speaks, the only one with a voice (10:35), a point of particular *irony* given that the priest and Levite, *not* the Samaritan, would have been the ones with "a voice in Israelite society."[99]

Both pacing and characterization focus attention on the Samaritan, revealing differing kinds of emphases concerning him. So, too, a *repeated sequence* highlights the Samaritan's role and helps us as readers to zero in on the narrative meaning of this parable.[100] Sequencing and patterning may be

---

98. This is confirmed by the centrality of *praxis* and active *doing* (note the verb ποιέω in verses 25, 28, 37) in the larger discussion in which the parable is embedded (see Green, *Gospel of Luke*, 425).

99. Resseguie, *Narrative Criticism of the New Testament*, 192–93.

100. Repeated sequences or patterns can also be used as structuring devices. For example, a repetition of a word/phrase/motif/sequence may frame a section of narrative, signaling that it is to be read as a unit (consider, e.g., the twin healings of the blind in Mark 8:22–26

considered under the broad heading of *narrative rhetoric*, which Merenlahti describes as "the variety of choices and techniques of storytelling that the gospel applies to condition and control the ways its readers read it."[101] The verbs in 10:31–33 are patterned to condition readers for a surprise. In verses 31–32, both the priest and the Levite are said to *come along*, to *see* (ἰδών), and to *pass by* (ἀντιπαρῆλθεν).[102] A clear pattern is established,[103] which leads readers to expect its recurrence when a Samaritan *comes along* and *sees* (ἰδών)—but here the expected pattern is broken.[104] Where we would expect, based on the preceding pattern, a *passing by*, we have a *pitying*, and a *coming up to*,[105] and a bandaging, and a pouring of oil and wine, and on and on—a plethora of contrary actions. The repeated sequence is broken at the moment of the Samaritan's *compassion*.[106]

Finally, we may notice the shape of the parable's *plot*. Clearly, what we have here is a U-shaped plot for the "certain man." His story starts well as he sets out on his journey, then a great difficulty develops, and finally it concludes (we are led to expect) with a happy ending. And the turning point in the plot (indeed, the structural midpoint of the parable) proves to be precisely what the other narrative elements we have considered draw our attention as readers to: the appearing of the Samaritan and, in particular, his compassion.

Inquiring into the way in which various narrative elements in the story appear fixes our attention on the Samaritan's compassion in verse 33 as

---

and 10:46–52, framing the material in between, which includes all three passion predictions). Repetitions can also serve to structure a work as a whole (e.g., it has long been suggested that the repeated phrase "When Jesus had finished ..." is a structuring device in the narrative of Matthew's Gospel).

101. Merenlahti, *Poetics for the Gospels?*, 68. As Green comments, "Narrative order is a form of persuasion" ("Narrative Criticism," 95).

102. Both Green and Resseguie speak of a "cadence" (see Green, *Gospel of Luke*, 430; Resseguie, *Narrative Criticism of the New Testament*, 193).

103. Perhaps not clear enough for some early scribes, who sought to make the parallelism more precise by adding αὐτόν as the object of ἰδών in verses 32 and 33.

104. As Resseguie notes, the pattern is already broken at the beginning of verse 33, with Σαμαρίτης put in emphatic initial position (see *Narrative Criticism of the New Testament*, 194).

105. A repeated root (ἀντιπαρῆλθεν, προσελθών) highlights that the Samaritan's action is the directional opposite of that of the priest and the Levite (see also Resseguie, *Narrative Criticism of the New Testament*, 195).

106. Or differently, we might say that his "seeing" was different from that of the priest and Levite. The Samaritan is the only one who truly *saw* his neighbor, the one right before him and not the one he decided for himself.

the central point of the story. But the story is part of a larger dialogue. The working out of that dialogue not only suggests that there is a *right reading* of the story, but also confirms that narrative-critical analysis has helped us to attain it. For the dialogue concludes with the lawyer, who first asked, "Who is my neighbor?" getting the point: the story is about the doing of mercy (verse 37). And, as if to make sure we readers do not miss the point, Jesus affirms the lawyer's assessment. The parable exposes the bankruptcy of the initial question posed to Jesus, "Who is my neighbor?" (verse 29), a question that views other people not as real people made for relationships of love but as abstractions to categorize.[107] It is also a question that, as the *narrator's aside* in verse 29 clarifies for us, stems from a self-justifying heart.[108] "Who is my neighbor?" ("Do they deserve my love?") objectifies people, treats them not as persons to love but as objects we can evaluate in the abstract, as so many commodities to choose among, as tools to wield for our own self-justification. All such objectifying makes true love-of-neighbor impossible, and, by implication, makes love of God impossible (see verse 27). Jesus asks a different question—not "Who is my neighbor?" but "Who proved to be a neighbor?"—thus revealing his differing "ideological point of view."[109] It is the compassionate who are neighbors. It is compassion (both the feeling of it and the *doing* of it [note the lawyer's assessment in verse 37]) that fulfills the law, which is to say that the Samaritan fulfills the law.[110] The lawyer (and the implied reader) are called to "Go and do the same" (verse 37).

---

107. See the perceptive essay by Paul Ricoeur, "The *Socius* and the Neighbor," in *History and Truth*, trans. C. A. Kelbley (Evanston, IL: Northwestern University Press, 1965), 98–109.

108. When the narrator steps out of the background to make an express comment on the story, it is almost always freighted with great significance for right understanding of the narrative (see Paris, *Narrative Obtrusion*, 1; as Paris notes, biblical scholarship has typically attended to narrative obtrusions in the analysis of redaction [see 14]). For example, when the narrator in John's Gospel offers the precise chronological marker "on the first day of the week" in John 20:1, 19 (in the second instance, adding it apparently *unnecessarily*), we have very good reason to believe that the fact that it was the "first day," or a day one, is literarily and/or theologically significant for the story.

109. Resseguie, *Narrative Criticism of the New Testament*, 195–96.

110. That a *Samaritan* fulfills the law may be a Lukan signal concerning whom the law identifies as true Israelites (see Green, *Gospel of Luke*, 426–27).

5.3.2 THE CHARACTERIZATION OF JESUS IN JOHN 2–4

As we have seen in the parable of the Good Samaritan, attending to characterization (the way a narrator makes the characters in the story distinctive, known, understood) is of great importance for a narrative-critical understanding of texts. A number of things contribute to the development of characters in the narrative: direct and indirect speech, actions, gestures/postures, clothing, narrative description (by the narrator or other characters in the narrative), whether and how characters are named or how they are referred to, environment/setting, social location, and history. A number of features in John 2–4 combine to characterize Jesus in a striking manner.[111]

Jesus' first major splash on the public scene, his first manifestation of his true glory, takes place at a wedding (2:1–11). This *setting* is especially significant, contributing to a specific way in which the narrative seems to develop Jesus as a character. Jesus' actions at the wedding are telling. Specifically, he provides wine (verse 7), a task that would, in that culture, have been the bridegroom's responsibility.[112] Narrative critics might point not to the background culture but to the continuation of the narrative itself. In verses 9–10, the surprised headwaiter goes to the (anonymous) bridegroom as the person he assumes is responsible for the unorthodox provision of superior wine at the end of the party. But Jesus is the one who really had provided the wine. Jesus was acting the part of the bridegroom.[113]

---

111. Compare much of what follows with Jocelyn McWhirter, *The Bridegroom Messiah and the People of God: Marriage in the Fourth Gospel* (Cambridge: Cambridge University Press, 2006), 47–76. Scholarly attention to characterization in John's Gospel has exploded in recent years; see, e.g., Christopher W. Skinner, "Characterization," in *How John Works: Storytelling in the Fourth Gospel*, ed. Douglas Estes and Ruth Sheridan (Atlanta: SBL Press, 2016), 115–32; Cornelis Bennema, *Encountering Jesus: Character Studies in the Gospel of John*, 2nd ed. (Minneapolis: Fortress, 2014); Steven A. Hunt, D. Francois Tolmie, and Ruben Zimmermann, eds., *Character Studies in the Fourth Gospel: Narrative Approaches to Seventy Figures in John* (Tübingen: Mohr Siebeck, 2013); Christopher W. Skinner, ed., *Characters and Characterization in the Gospel of John*, LNTS 461 (London: Bloomsbury, 2013); see also Alicia D. Myers, *Characterizing Jesus: A Rhetorical Analysis on the Fourth Gospel's Use of Scripture in Its Presentation of Jesus* (London: T&T Clark, 2012).

112. See, e.g., D. A. Carson, *The Gospel according to John*, PNTC (Grand Rapids: Eerdmans, 1991), 174; see 172–73 on the possible identification here of Jesus as the true Bridegroom.

113. See Edward W. Klink III, "The Bridegroom at Cana: Ignorance Is Bliss," in Hunt, Tolmie, and Zimmerman, eds., *Character Studies in the Fourth Gospel*, 233–37, at 235–36; Mary L. Coloe, "The Woman of Samaria: Her Characterization, Narrative, and Theological Significance," in Skinner, ed., *Characters and Characterization in the Gospel of John*, 182–96, at 185.

In case we miss such literary subtleties in chapter 2, the narrator states the matter expressly in chapter 3—or rather, the narrative states the matter directly in the speech of one of the characters in the story. In 3:22–36, the disciples of John the Baptist are concerned about Jesus' rising popularity. The Baptist responds by comparing himself to a friend or attendant of the Bridegroom, the Bridegroom being the "Christ" (verses 28–29).[114]

These scenes in John 2–3 seem calculated to characterize Jesus as a bridegroom. In this light, what occurs next in chapter 4 is significant: Jesus meets a woman at a well. In Robert Alter's influential terminology, what we have to do with here is a "type-scene."[115] A well is an archetypal setting for the beginnings of love stories—or at least in biblical literature,[116] meetings at wells are the stuff of romantic love (see Gen 24; 29; Exod 2).[117] A betrothal is the expected sequel to a meeting between a man and woman at a well. Here the implied author is employing a well-known literary convention or type-scene, and one of the effects is to cast Jesus, yet again, as a bridegroom, or (in this instance) one in search of a bride.[118]

The characterization of Jesus in John 2–4 would lead readers to expect a betrothal and a wedding. It is remarkable, then, that when Jesus meets the Samaritan woman at the well, their encounter does *not* end in a marriage (though they do address marriage; see 4:16–18[119]). In fact, for the most part, the bridegroom/wedding motif and connotations fade in the rest of the Gospel. It is possible that the resurrection appearance in a garden contains

---

114. See further Coloe, "Woman of Samaria," 185. Coloe notes the additionally relevant point that earlier in the narrative, the Baptist (i.e., the "friend of the bridegroom") had already directed the attention of two disciples to Jesus at "about the tenth hour" (1:35–39), the traditional hour at which weddings would have been held.

115. See Alter, *Art of Biblical Narrative*, 55–78.

116. Based on nothing further than the abundance of scriptural quotation formulas in the Fourth Gospel, it is clear that the implied author knows and draws heavily on biblical literature. For this reason, Green rightly includes "intertextuality" as a crucial field of narrative-critical attention (see "Narrative Criticism," 98).

117. "Well" imagery also appears in connection with sexual love (see Prov 5:15; Song 4:15; also Prov 23:27).

118. See Bennema, *Encountering Jesus*, 162–63; Coloe, "Woman of Samaria," 186; Thomas L. Brodie, *The Gospel according to John: A Literary and Theological Commentary* (New York: Oxford University Press, 1993), 217–19.

119. Coloe, "Woman of Samaria," 190–91, thinks this point is directly tied to the bridegroom/betrothal motif.

Text	Characterization
Chapter 2	Jesus provides wine at a wedding, which was usually the bridegroom's responsibility.
Chapter 3	John the Baptist compares himself to a friend of the bridegroom, with Jesus as the bridegroom.
Chapter 4	Jesus meets a woman at a well, the archetypal setting for the beginning of love stories, but this encounter does not end in a betrothal.

THE CHARACTERIZATION OF JESUS AS A BRIDEGROOM IN JOHN

many allusions to the Song of Songs, as some have argued,[120] but the fact of the matter is that the story ends without a wedding.

At this point, a number of different options (not all of which are mutually exclusive) are open to the narrative critic who is convinced that John 2–4 does, in fact, characterize Jesus as a bridegroom. The narrative critic might seek a literary-theological explanation. McWhirter, for example, recognizing the anomaly of no betrothal at the conclusion of the well type-scene in John 4, explains the omission as a purposeful development beyond Genesis 29: whereas Jacob and Rachel's meeting at a well resulted in the birth of the twelve patriarchs, the meeting of Jesus and the Samaritan woman at the well results in the birth of a new "family of faith" (see 4:39–42).[121] Differently, we might suggest that John's Gospel does mean for us to anticipate a union in marriage, just not within the pages of this Gospel. That is to say, it may be that John's Gospel is written in a purposefully open-ended manner, as a kind of love story in search of a sequel.[122] The

---

120. See, e.g., Ann Roberts Winsor, *A King Is Bound in the Tresses: Allusions to the Song of Songs in the Fourth Gospel*, StuBibLit 6 (New York: Lang, 1999), especially ch. 3; and McWhirter, *Bridegroom Messiah*, especially ch. 4.

121. McWhirter, *Bridegroom Messiah*, 65. Bennema is representative of those who think that the Samaritan woman's confession of faith "symbolizes a spiritual betrothal" (*Encountering Jesus*, 171).

122. We could note, for example, that the plot line implicit in Gen 2:24 (a man [1] leaves his father and mother [2] to be united to his bride) is reflected in the very opening of the Fourth Gospel: (1) The Logos has left his Father's side (John 1:1, 18) to come into the world (1:9), (2) in order that he might be united to a bride. It is the second part that is left unfulfilled in the Gospel.

narrative critic might turn, here, to her *historical-critical* colleagues, who, in their concern with historical authors and provenances, have much to say about the relationship between John's Gospel and Revelation. Could it be that Revelation, which concludes with the Bridegroom's marriage feast and union to his Bride, serves as a kind of sequel to John? The narrative critic will, of course, want to refrain from commenting, unless and until the findings of historical criticism persuade her that John and Revelation (like Luke and Acts) are from the same hand (or at least the same school, or community and tradition).[123] Or, if she prefers, the narrative critic might turn to her *canonical critical* colleagues, who might want to reflect on the theological significance of a Gospel that leaves us wanting a wedding and a concluding canonical work that gives us one.

5.4 LIMITATIONS OF NEW TESTAMENT NARRATIVE CRITICISM

In the three-plus decades of its development and practice, narrative criticism has faced a number of recurring critiques,[124] which have helped to refine the approach and to identify its boundaries and limits. We can address three such limits here.

First, so long as narrative criticism assumes literary unity and coherence as a starting point for discovery, it cannot by itself really defend unity and coherence as an apologetic endpoint in debates about a text's history of composition. In his important 1980 address, Rhoads fittingly encapsulates the tenor of nearly all early commendations of narrative-critical approaches:

> Literary questions about narrative features tend to reveal Mark's Gospel as whole cloth ... One can discover the unity of this Gospel in terms of the remarkable integrity of the "story" which it tells,

---

123. It is possible, as well, that the historical critic will take a different track altogether, arguing that the Cana-to-Cana section of John (chapters 2–4) derives largely from a pre-Johannine signs-source. After all, the express numbering of "signs" that frames this section (2:11; 4:54) is also abandoned in the rest of the Gospel. The bridegroom/wedding motif may be a remnant of a pre-final form literary source, and its presence in John is largely accidental. We should not expect it to appear in a thoroughgoing way elsewhere in the Gospel.

124. See the helpful and concise summary of the most significant critiques in Brown, "Narrative Criticism," 621–23. Two of the most sustained and important critiques of narrative criticism are Moore, *Literary Criticism and the Gospels*, and Merenlahti, *Poetics for the Gospels?*.

and come to trust that many apparent enigmas and discrepancies may be satisfactorily solved within the larger whole of the story.[125]

This is an agenda to "reveal" and "discover" the unity of the Gospels *through* narrative criticism. At the same time, however, Rhoads assumes from the outset that the Gospel narratives have "autonomous integrity,"[126] and Powell claims that "narrative unity is not something that must be proved from an analysis of the material. Rather it is something that can be assumed." In fact, "the presence of inconsistencies in no way undermines the unity of a narrative but simply becomes one of the facets to be interpreted."[127] Apparently, what is assumed by narrative criticism is the very thing that is discovered through narrative criticism.[128] In 1999, Rhoads explained that unity and coherence is only "a *working hypothesis, a heuristic device*," which enables narrative critics to explore what kinds of interpretations arise *on such an assumption*.[129] This may be the most appropriate starting point and acknowledgment. Some scholars may find that narrative criticism produces viable ways of reading the NT narratives as whole cloths, with the result that "it will be difficult now for scholars to distinguish tradition from redaction."[130] But it seems reasonable to call for further argumentation drawn from approaches other than narrative criticism from those who wish to *defend* the unity and coherence of the NT narratives.[131]

---

125. Rhoads, "Narrative Criticism and the Gospel of Mark," 412–13.

126. Rhoads, "Narrative Criticism and the Gospel of Mark," 413.

127. Powell, *What Is Narrative Criticism?*, 92.

128. Merenlahti has pointed out the circularity most forcefully (see *Poetics for the Gospels?*, 23–24, 30). Additionally, Moore has directly called to account the assumption that literary readings of the NT texts *must* assume from the outset the text's unity; this is no necessary assumption in contemporary secular literary theory and readings, which NT narrative critics so often cite in support for their own readings. Indeed, "In appropriating literary theory, narrative critics regularly defuse it" (Moore, *Literary Criticism and the Gospels*, 54; see further 51–55; see also Pearson, "New Testament Literary Criticism," 243).

129. Rhoads, "Narrative Criticism: Practices and Prospects," 267, emphasis original. See Brown, "Narrative Criticism," 622, for further discussion. Brown adds that we may do well to distinguish literary coherence from "coherence of purpose and meaning," with the latter being an even better "working assumption." See also Hays, "Can Narrative Criticism Recover the Theological Unity of Scripture?," 202; and Alter, *Art of Biblical Narrative*, 11–12.

130. Rhoads, "Narrative Criticism: Practices and Prospects," 267.

131. For example, Merenlahti has suggested that the notion of coherence as a poetic desideratum was available to the (real) authors of the Gospels (via, e.g., Aristotle, Horace),

In narrative criticism, assumptions about unity extend only to single books. The approach refrains in a principled manner from speaking into the matter of unity and coherence at a whole-canon level. This marks a second limitation of narrative criticism. Ironically, for all its deploring of the fragmentation of biblical *narratives*, narrative-critical work has contributed to fragmentation of another kind—of any sense of an overall biblical *narrative*. Narrative criticism has made the challenge of rendering an account of the unity and coherence of the canonical Scripture all the more difficult by its focus on the autonomous integrity and individuality of each NT narrative work.[132] We can consider, for example, the way in which narrative criticism in the past few decades has helped us better appreciate the literary distinctiveness and unique message of each of the four Gospels. In doing so, narrative critics have done a great service. But as Powell noted early on, "Because narrative criticism attempts to understand each Gospel on its own terms, the interpreter will finally be left with four different stories of Jesus ... Is it possible to speak of a 'story of Jesus,' in the singular?"[133] As a lone discipline, narrative criticism cannot answer the question. Thus, "*the practice of narrative criticism—understood as close reading—is necessary, though not in itself sufficient, to articulate the elusive unity of the biblical witness.*"[134] To take on that task, we must look elsewhere—for example, to canonical criticism, or to early Christian reflections on the fourfold Gospel of Jesus Christ. As Martin Hengel has noted, it is "a near-miracle that the early church resisted the temptation to replace the four Gospels, which in parts are so different, with a unitary Gospel Harmony."[135] The early church wrestled long and hard with the embarrassment of four narrative accounts of Jesus. Yet their wrestling produced great insight concerning the *fourfold*

---

combining this historical insight with the observations that what each of the Gospels do offer is "a linear, sequentially ordered narrative," and that one Gospel writer expressly claims to have written "an orderly account [καθεξῆς]" (Luke 1:3). An interdisciplinary argument for coherence (but coherence "only up to a certain point") can be made for the Gospels (see *Poetics for the Gospels?*, 30-31).

132. Hays, "Can Narrative Criticism Recover the Theological Unity of Scripture?," 199.

133. Powell, *What Is Narrative Criticism?*, 101.

134. Hays, "Can Narrative Criticism Recover the Theological Unity of Scripture?," 205, emphasis original.

135. Martin Hengel, *The Four Gospels and the One Gospel of Jesus Christ: An Investigation of the Collection and Origin of the Canonical Gospels*, trans. J. Bowden (Harrisburg, PA: Trinity Press International, 2000), 24.

form (diversity) of the *one gospel of Jesus Christ* (unity). A reconsideration of their labors may prove to be of profound help in facing similar challenges to unity in diversity today,[136] especially in light of the focalizing of diversity in narrative-critical work.

Third and finally, while Powell has recently suggested that narrative criticism affirms "polyvalence within perimeters," nevertheless it is an open question where and how such perimeters are established. For Powell, the perimeters are "set by what would accord with expected responses attributable to the narrative's implied reader."[137] But since the implied reader is a *textual* construct, this seems little different from saying that the perimeters are established by the brute fact of the text before us. This will not provide much of a perimeter to those for whom "there are no texts, only readings."[138] "Insofar as interpretation is what we do," says Merenlahti, "there is, basically, no limit to the meaningful connections we can make in a given text."[139] Narrative critics, by and large, seek perimeters not just defining a definite object *of* interpretation but also perimeters *on* interpretation. While acknowledging the polyvalency of biblical narrative, Rhoads still speaks of "faithful interpretations."[140] In other words, narrative criticism pursues some way, however tenuous and fraught with difficulty, of measuring *validity in interpretation*. But to attain such, it will need help from outside its own approach. The specter of Hirsch may be appropriate to raise here, inasmuch as critical methodologies that help us better understand the "author" (and, more generally, "behind the text" matters) are necessary to check the findings of narrative criticism.[141] Likewise, properly reader-centered approaches ("in front of the text" approaches) may help to expose some fissures in narrative-critical readings that render them invalid or insufficient. Even as these other methodologies can offer accountability to narrative-critical labor, narrative-critical work is (has

---

136. See, e.g., Francis Watson, "The Fourfold Gospel," in *The Cambridge Companion to the Gospels*, ed. S. C. Barton (Cambridge: Cambridge University Press, 2006), 34–52.

137. Powell, "Narrative Criticism: The Emergence of a Prominent Reading Strategy," 24.

138. Merenlahti, *Poetics for the Gospels?*, 5, 29n36, alluding in both places to Harold Bloom's claim that "there are not texts, but only interpretations."

139. Merenlahti, *Poetics for the Gospels?*, 29–30.

140. Rhoads, "Narrative Criticism: Practices and Prospects," 283–84.

141. E. D. Hirsch Jr., *Validity in Interpretation* (New Haven, CT: Yale University Press, 1967).

often shown itself to be) a useful strategy for checking and refining the labors of other methods. All this is to say that narrative criticism cannot be its own critic and must not work in isolation. At its best, it will work in dialogue with other critical (and pre-critical) approaches for a fully responsible engagement with the biblical narrative literature.[142]

5.5 CONTEMPORARY INFLUENCE OF NEW TESTAMENT NARRATIVE CRITICISM

It may be that the way forward for narrative criticism was signaled before it ever arose by Wayne Booth, one of the most influential figures on the development and practice of narrative criticism. For Booth, the real subject of interest, which examining the "rhetoric of fiction" and "rhetoric in fiction" is a means to entering and investigating, is a communicative event: "people meeting people *through* story, people offering and receiving gifts *as* story."[143] Critical study that focalizes the author, or the text, or the reader is needful, helpful, and stimulating, but what ties all such foci together in a common pursuit of criticism "is the transactions among them."[144]

Narrative criticism has helped to elucidate the crucial middle member of the transaction or communicative event (i.e., the text), arising at a time when doubts about the effectiveness of traditional pursuits after the first part (i.e., the author) were growing in strength. As a predominantly text-centered approach, it bracketed out other concerns in an effort to show that meaningful engagement with the text before us is possible. It sought to apply questions after what John Sider has called "old-fashioned critical concepts of plot, character, setting, point of view, and diction," directly to the NT narratives to understand how they mean.[145] By offering a disciplined way of slowing down to ask certain kinds of questions of these

---

142. The need for interdisciplinary work is a common, and welcome, refrain among those discussing the merits of narrative criticism. For example, Rhoads, "Narrative Criticism: Practices and Prospects," can be viewed as a sustained attempt to show that and how narrative criticism can "play well" with other methods or, in Merenlahti's helpful phrase, "modes of investigation" (*Poetics for the Gospels?*, 118). Merenlahti cautions that narrative criticism cannot simply aim for methodological inclusiveness without also and especially engaging in "hermeneutic reflection and reconsideration of the entire framework of biblical interpretation as a whole" (*Poetics for the Gospels?*, 115–16).

143. Booth, *Rhetoric of Fiction*, 408, emphasis original.

144. Booth, *Rhetoric of Fiction*, 442.

145. Sider, "Nurturing Our Nurse," 19–20.

stories,[146] narrative criticism has illuminated them in numerous ways. In particular, it has shed light on their complex and vibrant story-worlds so that readers may more ably and eagerly *enter* those worlds (and have their perceptions of their own worlds transformed by them[147]). It has thus shown itself to be a viable reading strategy[148] and has, together with other newer approaches, contributed to an increasing "methodological eclecticism" in biblical studies.[149]

But viable is not the same as sufficient. Narrative criticism will prove most effective as it comes out of its provisional "brackets"[150] and engages in dialogue with other approaches and methods in a collegial effort to develop skill in "receiving gifts *as* story."

5.6 RESOURCES FOR FURTHER STUDY

Berlin, Adele. *Poetics and Interpretation of Biblical Narrative*. Winona Lake, IN: Eisenbrauns, 1994.

While Berlin's work is focused on OT narratives, her book provides a readable introduction to an approach to biblical literature that is attentive to literary style and structure.

Merenlahti, Petri. *Poetics for the Gospels? Rethinking Narrative Criticism*. Studies of the New Testament and Its World. London: T&T Clark, 2002.

Merenlahti argues for the importance of studying the Gospels as literature, but he also offers a helpful evaluation of narrative criticism as a theory of interpretation and suggests ways that narrative criticism could develop into an even more integrated approach to biblical interpretation.

---

146. Green, "Narrative Criticism," 98.

147. See J. Todd Billings, *The Word of God for the People of God: An Entryway to the Theological Interpretation of Scripture* (Grand Rapids: Eerdmans, 2010), 43–45.

148. Powell prefers to speak of narrative criticism as a "reading strategy" rather than a "method" ("Narrative Criticism: The Emergence of a Prominent Reading Strategy," 22).

149. Brown, "Narrative Criticism," 623.

150. The language of "bracketing" appears in both Powell, *What Is Narrative Criticism?*, 8; and Rhoads, "Narrative Criticism and the Gospel of Mark," 413.

Powell, Mark Allan. *What Is Narrative Criticism?* Minneapolis: Fortress, 1990.

> Powell provides an accessible introduction to narrative criticism as one of the leading practitioners of the method. In approximately 100 pages, Powell explains the major aspects of narrative analysis (including characterization and setting) and demonstrates how to use the method for biblical exegesis.

Rhoads, David, Joanna Dewey, and Donald Michie. *Mark as Story: An Introduction to the Narrative of a Gospel.* 3rd ed. Minneapolis: Fortress, 2012.

> David Rhoads was influential in the development of narrative criticism for the study of the NT. The first edition of this book, published in 1982 and co-authored with Donald Michie, is widely considered to be the work that introduced the discipline of narrative criticism to NT studies. The second edition was published in 1999 with the addition of Joanna Dewey as co-author. That edition was a substantial revision reflecting the advances in narrative criticism in the intervening years. Their analysis of the Gospel of Mark demonstrates the narrative-critical concern for "the formal features of narrative such as tone, style, narrator, setting, plot, character, and rhetoric" (xi). The third edition brings this standard introduction of narrative criticism up to date with the latest advances in research on Mark.

Rhoads, David M., and Kari Syreeni, eds. *Characterization in the Gospels: Reconceiving Narrative Criticism.* London: T & T Clark, 1999.

> This volume presents a collection of essays both applying and evaluating narrative criticism. The contributors demonstrate narrative criticism's continuing usefulness as a literary method, but they also discuss important new directions for users of narrative criticism to consider in future research.

6

RHETORICAL CRITICISM OF THE NEW TESTAMENT

Douglas Estes

6.1 DEFINITION AND GOAL OF NEW TESTAMENT RHETORICAL CRITICISM

Rhetorical criticism stands out from other modern critical methods used to interpret the Bible because of its historical origins. In fact, rhetorical criticism is anything but modern—it was a method for understanding texts long before the NT was even written. Nonetheless, recent turns in scholarly interests toward rhetorical criticism have led to a renaissance in the use of this critical method to better understand and interpret the NT.

Rhetorical criticism is a critical method of interpretation that identifies and examines various language devices within communication that are designed to persuade an audience. As a critical method, it is based on the use of rhetoric—the technique of creating persuasive oral (and written) communication. The history of rhetoric begins in the fifth century BC on the Greek peninsula.[1] It was here that newfound democratic

---

1. It is often pointed out that Western scholars too quickly equate "rhetoric" with Graeco-Roman rhetoric and ignore other examples of rhetoric in other cultures, such as Hebrew, Egyptian, and Chinese. However, except for Hebrew (i.e., biblical) rhetoric and new rhetoric, addressed below, these other uses of rhetoric either tend to be too tangential to the study of the NT (as in the case of ancient Chinese rhetoric), or the particulars of their use are long lost to history (as in the case of ancient Egyptian rhetoric). Of course, since the NT is written in Greek, the persuasive devices of that language are the most important in interpretation.

sentiments, especially in and around Athens, propelled interest in a more refined approach to public speaking—an approach that could sway the legal and political battles waged in the assembly and the courts. Ancient rhetoricians credit Corax and Tisias of Sicily with discovering the art of rhetoric (sometime after 466 BC),[2] and sophists—so-called skilled men often without allegiance to any party—were the earliest promoters of the craft.[3] To promote the high ideal of democratic discourse and civic action, Isocrates (436–338 BC) founded the first school of the rhetorical arts in about 393 BC. Isocrates' school, though soon overshadowed by the creation of the philosophical academies, was known for producing great leaders in the Greek world.[4]

6.1.1 KEY TERMS

The first extant use of the term "rhetoric" (ῥητορική) to describe this discourse technique occurs in Plato's *Gorgias* (circa early 380s BC).[5] There, Plato has Socrates distinguish rhetoric from dialectic (διαλεκτική, dialogical argumentation).[6] Socrates scorned rhetoric, and the distinction between the two is akin to the distinction between politics (influencing to win) and philosophy (discussing to learn). Socrates' concern with rhetoric—and its sophistic practitioners—was that truth was overlooked in favor of flamboyant and flattering words spoken merely to win the argument without regard to truth.[7] This emphasis is exemplified by how some rhetoricians trained their students to argue both sides of a dispute. Since rhetoric came out of

---

2. Cicero, *On the Orator* 1.20.91; and Cicero, *Brutus* 12. See below on the "discovery" of rhetoric in that its origin was one of pragmatism and observation, based on noticing what worked well and what did not; see Quintilian, *Institutes of Oratory* 3.2.3, 5.10.120; and Cicero, *On the Orator* 3.51.197.

3. Ancient writers believed there was a generation or two of orators before Corax and Tisias who used rhetoric but without the benefit of a formal method; these orators included Empedocles, and their impact on the first recorded sophists is evident. Eventually, these two strains would become fully interwoven and improved on to become what today falls under the category of Graeco-Roman rhetoric; see George A. Kennedy, *A New History of Classical Rhetoric* (Princeton, NJ: Princeton University Press, 1994), 17–19.

4. Brian Vickers, *In Defence of Rhetoric* (Oxford: Clarendon, 1988), 9; and see Cicero, *On the Orator* 2.22.94.

5. Plato, *Gorgias* 448d.

6. Although compare Aristotle's view that the two are fundamentally related; see Aristotle, *Rhetoric* 1356a25–26.

7. Plato, *Gorgias* 459b.

the growth of civic discourse in new, democratic, and political applications, much of this history is beyond the scope of this chapter—but necessary reading for any student wishing to get a real sense for applying rhetorical criticism to the Bible.[8]

It is important to distinguish between the use of rhetoric and persuasion in the ancient world. Before the fifth century and the dawn of the Classical Age, a key goal of public discourse was persuasion.[9] To the Greeks, persuasion was a talent of great worth, but at first it was not thought of as a skill (τέχνη) that could be codified and taught.[10] As the stakes for persuasive speech grew, so did the need to create a skill set; and from this comes the classic definition of rhetoric as "the art of persuasion by words."[11] The route of persuasion was through well-crafted speech, which points us to one of the more famous definitions of rhetoric in the ancient world: "the art of good speech" (bene dicendi scientia).[12] For the sake of clarity, though, persuasion (any word or style that influences) can be distinguished from rhetoric (specifically identifiable devices and strategies that promote a desired outcome).[13] In light of these definitions, the NT can be regarded as *intentionally persuasive* because it is not (nor pretends to be) neutral about what it communicates to its readers. Thus, the NT is in at least one sense undeniably rhetorical.

It is also important to distinguish the term "rhetoric" in modern English usage from what scholars really mean when they talk about the art of persuasion. Current parlance associates negative and sometimes pejorative stereotypes with the term "rhetoric."[14] In modern culture, rhetoric is often used to mean "bloviating speech devoid of substance." In light

---

8. For a more detailed treatment of the history of rhetoric, please see George Kennedy's leading work, *New History of Classical Rhetoric*.

9. Kennedy, *New History of Classical Rhetoric*, 12.

10. The Greeks even deified persuasion into a god; for example, Hesiod, *Works and Days* 73.

11. Kennedy, *New History of Classical Rhetoric*, xi; Aristotle, *Rhetoric* 1355b2.

12. Quintilian, *Institutes of Oratory* 2.15.38.

13. Of course, we cannot draw sharp lines around ideas from the ancient world; not only are those days long past and our knowledge of them far from perfect, but also ancient writers regularly disagreed over definitions and usage of words and skills (no different from today).

14. Wayne Booth, a well-known modern rhetorician, shares many examples of the way "rhetoric" is often-used—incorrectly—to mean a style of speaking with ornamentation and without substance; see Wayne C. Booth, *The Rhetoric of Rhetoric: The Quest for Effective Communication*, Blackwell Manifestos (Oxford: Blackwell, 2004), viii–xii.

of this, George Kennedy notes that modern people are too quick to side with Socrates (philosophy, truth) over Gorgias (rhetoric, aesthetics), not realizing that ancient rhetoric was not always about tricky speech, just as ancient philosophy was not always about high ideals.[15] In order to give rhetorical criticism a fair evaluation, those studying the NT must understand rhetoric as a tool that can be used in many different ways, including to persuade people of the truth of the gospel.

6.1.2 THE PURPOSE OF RHETORICAL CRITICISM

Rhetorical criticism, broadly defined, provides students of the NT with a way to understand some of the deeper structures of its books, which leads to a better working knowledge of the best interpretative practices. In some cases, failing to understand the rhetorical design of a section of the NT would be no different from missing an important piece of archeological, linguistic, or symbolic information—such as the cultural meaning of "angel" (ἄγγελος) or the symbolic meaning of sheep (πρόβατον). By understanding the rhetorical force of a NT passage, the interpreter is able to better appreciate what argument the passage intends, how the passage would have influenced earliest audiences, what the rationale was for any complexity in the passage, and why the passage was constructed in the way that it was. When used correctly, as any tool, rhetorical criticism can be a powerful one in the interpreter's toolbox in exegeting the NT.[16]

6.1.3 RELATIONSHIP TO OTHER APPROACHES

One of the primary challenges facing the diversity of critical methods applied to the NT is compatibility: How can different methods—often resulting in different interpretations—all be correct? Is there one "super" method, or do all of these methods lead to no better than partial understandings of

---

15. Kennedy, *New History of Classical Rhetoric*, 9.

16. It can also be a powerful tool in the proclamation of the NT. For example: When a pastor *teaches* from a letter of Paul, is the purpose of that speaking to educate or to persuade? And if it is not solely to educate, and if the *teacher* knows not just Paul's theology but also his rhetoric, that pastor can convey something significant that is not possible without a good foundational knowledge of rhetoric. That pastor may also have thought a great deal about how persuasion works and thus will be better equipped to exhort the audience to believe in and adhere to whatever theological principle is taught.

any given passage? Like most critical methods, rhetorical criticism struggles to answer these questions.

As a method, scholars can use rhetorical criticism in a primary or secondary role. In a primary role, the scholar uses rhetorical criticism as the overarching interpretive key to a passage. In a secondary role, the scholar uses rhetorical criticism alongside other critical methods, creating a syncretistic system of interpretation. This distinction is sometimes described as the difference between macro-rhetoric and micro-rhetoric, a topic mentioned above. At the same time, rhetorical criticism has one advantage in that it can frequently be used not to give answers but to provide tools for further solutions. Thus, when properly considered, rhetorical criticism can work quite well with certain other types of modern critical methods.

6.1.3.a Rhetorical Criticism and Form Criticism

Form criticism, a critical method that interprets the NT in light of what we can discover about preliterary, often oral forms that contributed to the development of the NT's final form, relates to rhetorical criticism only tangentially. In the study of the NT, scholars have applied form criticism mostly to the Synoptic Gospels, whereas scholars have applied rhetorical criticism mostly to the letters of Paul. Though both raise questions as to how other "forms" of communication contributed to an author's creation of his work, rhetorical criticism probably stands on a more solid foundation in that its forms are more evidential. The two places where the two methods work more closely together are (1) in the area of genre, especially in attempts to understand the macro-rhetorical scheme of a few of the letters; and (2) in the area of recognition of a preliterary tradition that probably stood behind the written forms of argumentation (even in Paul's letters).

6.1.3.b Rhetorical Criticism and Source Criticism

Source criticism, a critical method that interprets the NT according to discoverable sources that stand behind and are interwoven into the texts, relates less to rhetorical criticism than most other modern critical methods. In some ways its relationship to rhetorical criticism is akin to that of form criticism, only weaker. Like form criticism, source criticism tends to focus on the Gospels and less on the Letters. Unlike source criticism, rhetorical criticism views the work of the orator (and in the case of the NT, the book writer) as an invention of persuasive ideas that further the message. While the process of invention can rely on prior sources, the arrangement process used in the development of rhetoric is different from the compilation process posited to be at work within source criticism.

6.1.3.c Rhetorical Criticism and Narrative Criticism

Narrative criticism, a critical method that interprets the NT according to the way stories are created, formed, and told, integrates very well with rhetorical criticism for two reasons. First, narrative criticism is a type of literary criticism, which is a critical method that shares almost as meaningful a provenance as rhetorical criticism. Therefore, unlike other modern critical methods, some of the concerns over anachronistic interpretations can be mitigated by either of these two methods. Second, since narrative and persuasion are both major features of the NT and work hand-in-hand, these methods help us understand why stories work the way they do and are very useful interpretive tools. After all, the Gospels record the *stories* that Jesus tells so as to *persuade* readers of who Jesus is. Unfortunately, where these theories don't work well together is in the highly rhetorical parts of the NT, especially the nonnarrative Letters—narrative criticism only works with narrative, which is primarily limited to the Gospels, Acts, and Revelation.

6.1.3.d Rhetorical Criticism and Social-Scientific Criticism

Social-scientific criticism, which interprets the NT in light of the social worlds and structures that lie behind the writings of the NT, touches on rhetorical criticism of the NT in several areas. First, both social-scientific criticism and rhetorical criticism can help us to understand the world of the author and audience, especially as it relates to the social uses of persuasion in religious discourse. Second, whereas rhetorical criticism can pinpoint the argument at play, social-scientific criticism can help explain why that argument would work with ancient audiences (a prime example being the effects of honor and shame in the Letters). Social-scientific and rhetorical criticism, in different ways, give insight into the culture surrounding the earliest church.

6.2 DEVELOPMENT OF NEW TESTAMENT RHETORICAL CRITICISM

The NT was written during a time when rhetoric played a key role in virtually all forms of communication. Koine Greek, the language of the NT, differs from the Greek that was used in rhetorical and philosophical discourse during the Classical Age; rather, it was the language of the common people in the Hellenistic Age. Nevertheless, during these centuries the classical forms of rhetoric filtered down from the most elite schools in Syracuse, Sicily, and Athens to the more widely read forms of literature, to the simple handbooks of schoolchildren (*progymnasmata*); in some cases, it even began to permeate other languages (e.g., Latin, Mishnaic Hebrew, and Aramaic). While the extent to which rhetoric influenced the language of the NT is debatable, there is no question that the writings of the NT use some of the rhetorical methods developed by and employed in Graeco-Roman literature.[17]

GRECO-ROMAN RHETORIC	HEBRAIC (BIBLICAL) RHETORIC	NEW RHETORIC
A distinct system of rhetoric that was discovered, codified, and taught in much of Greco-Roman society.	Hebrew forms of persuasion and argumentation that were not found in Greco-Roman rhetoric, such as parataxis and binarity.	A term used to describe the use of insights gained from modern fields like linguistics, psychology, literary studies, and others.

THREE TYPES OF RHETORIC IN NEW TESTAMENT STUDIES

As noted above, the term "rhetoric" has several different meanings, but when scholars speak of applying rhetoric to the NT, they are likely referring to one of three major possibilities: Graeco-Roman rhetoric, Jewish (biblical)

---

17. Ben Witherington III, *New Testament Rhetoric: An Introductory Guide to the Art of Persuasion in and of the New Testament* (Eugene, OR: Cascade, 2009), 7.

rhetoric, and new rhetoric.[18] Of the three types, the Graeco-Roman one is the most prevalent in use today by NT interpreters. In fact, when most scholars speak of rhetorical criticism, what they mean is the application of Graeco-Roman forms of rhetoric to unlock the meaning of the text. The other two types, however, are growing in popularity and work very well to complement insights from the Graeco-Roman type.

6.2.1 GRAECO-ROMAN RHETORIC

Graeco-Roman rhetoric involves more than the way Greeks and Romans used language to persuade an audience. Instead, it refers to a very distinct system of rhetoric that was discovered, codified, and taught in much of the Graeco-Roman world. From near the beginning of the study of rhetoric, Greek (and later, Roman) rhetoricians created guidebooks that describe how rhetoric works. While many of these are lost, six major works are still in existence: *Rhetoric* (c. 330 BC) by Aristotle (384-322 BC); *Rhetoric, to Alexander* (c. 335 BC) by, in all likelihood, Anaximenes of Lampsacus (c. 380-320 BC); *Rhetoric, to Herennius* (c. 86-82 BC), by an unknown scholar; *On the Orator* (c. 55 BC) and *On Invention* (c. 87-81 BC) by Cicero (106-43 BC); and *Institutes of Oratory* (c. AD 92-96) by Quintilian (c. AD 35-100). Beyond these references, there are many extant examples of speeches, letters, and literature that use rhetoric.[19] In looking at these works, Graeco-Roman rhetoric is not particularly understandable to the modern reader; some parts seem cliché, and other parts seem unnecessarily convoluted by today's standards. Further, there was at times disagreement between the various rhetorical theories, and therefore the present discussion of rhetoric is eclectic, taking into account all of the different theories.[20] However, Graeco-Roman rhetoric was particularly effective in much of Graeco-Roman

---

18. Scholars sometimes identify a fourth type of rhetorical method: socio-rhetorical criticism. This method, pioneered by Vernon Robbins, tends to be a distinct hybrid of literary and rhetorical criticism, and therefore it fits best as a distinct subset of new rhetoric. For more details, see Vernon K. Robbins, *Jesus the Teacher: A Socio-Rhetorical Interpretation of Mark* (Minneapolis: Fortress, 1992). For a more exhaustive explanation of why socio-rhetorical criticism is a hybrid, see Peter Lampe, "Rhetorical Analysis of Pauline Texts—Quo Vadit? Methodological Reflections," in *Paul and Rhetoric*, ed. J. Paul Sampley and Peter Lampe (New York: T & T Clark, 2010), 8-10.

19. A great example is the speeches of Demosthenes (384-322 BC).

20. Robert N. Gaines, "Roman Rhetorical Handbooks," in *A Companion to Roman Rhetoric*, ed. William Dominik and Jon Hall (Oxford: Blackwell, 2007), 166.

society during the time of the NT, and the importance of its thought forms for understanding the NT cannot be overstated. Thus, it is worth the time to examine despite the innate difficulties.

6.2.1.a Classical Rhetorical Categories

According to the organization of ancient rhetorical reference books, rhetoricians considered rhetoric to have several defining aspects as well as many different devices that could be used to create persuasive speech. All of these aspects and devices are important for ancient rhetoric, but they were not always grouped in an easily comprehensible way to modern people.[21] They tended to be topical, working from the big picture to the smallest details. Rhetorical theories also tended to be elaborate in their division, often creating subdivisions within subdivisions within subdivisions, making them less accessible to beginners. Since each major ancient reference work had a different agenda and gave priority to different uses of rhetoric, the aspects below are culled from the most popular and universal aspects under discussion throughout these books.

The first significant aspect is the *category* of rhetoric in use. Aristotle points out that of the three human elements in oratory (speaker, judge, and crowd), the way the crowd perceived the speech was the best determinant of the type of speech.[22] Therefore, from the audience's point of view, there are three categories of rhetoric: judicial, deliberative, and epideictic.

1. Judicial rhetoric, sometimes called legal or forensic rhetoric, persuades an audience as to what has happened (in the past). This type of rhetoric often depends on an attack and a defense—two contrastive sides the orators debate in order to persuade the audience of the truth of their position (over

---

21. These aspects and devices were not always organized with a consistent nomenclature, so attempts at taxonomy are merely approximations. Several modern authors have written outlines of rhetoric that attach bullet points to the most notable features of classical rhetoric; for example, see Thomas Habinek, *Ancient Rhetoric and Oratory* (Oxford: Blackwell, 2005), 101–07; or Richard A. Lanham, *A Handlist of Rhetorical Terms*, 2nd ed. (Berkeley: University of California Press, 1991), 163–80.

22. Aristotle, *Rhetoric* 1358a36–38. Note, however, that Aristotle's influence on the world of rhetoric appears to be limited in the centuries that immediately followed, as the Roman rhetoricians likely follow the work of others instead of Aristotle; see Sara Rubinelli, *Ars Topica: The Classical Technique of Constructing Arguments from Aristotle to Cicero* (Dordrecht: Springer, 2009), 95.

against the competing position of the other orator). Everyday examples of epideictic rhetoric include prosecutors or defense attorneys arguing their cases in a court of law. In the ancient world, judicial rhetoric was the rhetoric of the courts. In some ways, little has changed between ancient-world and modern-world usage, and judicial rhetoric is often easy to spot.

2. Deliberative rhetoric, sometimes called political rhetoric, persuades an audience to take a course of action—either against another course of action or in lieu of no action. This type of rhetoric depends on the orator's ability to sway an audience through argumentation to act (or refrain from acting) in some capacity. Everyday examples of deliberative rhetoric include senators and members of parliament who have as a goal action on legislation, or candidates for political office who want votes. In the ancient world, deliberative rhetoric was the rhetoric of the civic assembly. Like judicial rhetoric, little has changed between ancient-world and modern-world usage of deliberative rhetoric, again referring to the broad scope, not the specific devices in use.

3. Epideictic rhetoric, sometimes called ceremonial rhetoric, persuades an audience to accept an idea or truth. This type of rhetoric connects the audience to the good or bad of something and is meant to engender belief in the orator's claims. It often influences morality by extolling virtue and discouraging vice. Everyday examples of epideictic rhetoric include eulogies delivered at funerals, awards given at civic events, and, in some cases, sermons delivered in a religious context. In the ancient world, epideictic rhetoric was the rhetoric of the poet. It was also the type of rhetoric most often associated with written works, even as early as the fourth century BC.[23] In some ways, epideictic rhetoric is the category of rhetoric that has changed the most since ancient times. Epideictic rhetoric is also the most important category for the study of the

---

23. Aristotle, *Rhetoric* 1414a6.

NT, as it is arguably the most common type of rhetoric used in biblical context.

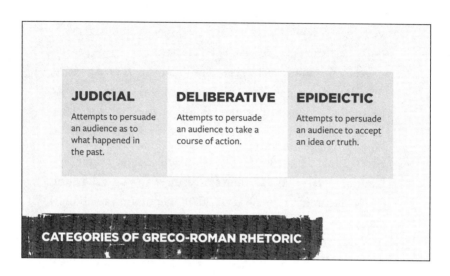

JUDICIAL

Attempts to persuade an audience as to what happened in the past.

DELIBERATIVE

Attempts to persuade an audience to take a course of action.

EPIDEICTIC

Attempts to persuade an audience to accept an idea or truth.

CATEGORIES OF GRECO-ROMAN RHETORIC

Another way to distinguish these types of rhetoric is to identify the time signature of the persuasive speech, whether past, present, or future.[24] Judicial rhetoric focuses on the *past*, as it looks to persuade an audience to what happened. Epideictic rhetoric focuses on the *present*, as it wants to persuade an audience to believe something. Deliberative rhetoric focuses on the *future*, as it hopes to persuade an audience to act in a certain way going forward.

The second significant aspect is the mode of rhetoric in use. The mode of a rhetorical oration or letter describes the *feel* that it has in its impact on the audience or reader. Unlike the three categories of rhetoric—all of which are popular and in use today—the three modes of rhetoric are less evenly utilized today.[25] In Graeco-Roman rhetoric, there are three modes for persuasion (πίστις), identified as *logos*, *ēthos*, and *pathos*.[26]

---

24. Vickers, *In Defence of Rhetoric*, 21.

25. In *Rhetoric, to Alexander*, the focus is on seven species of rhetoric: exhortation, dissuasion, eulogy, vituperation, accusation, defense, and investigation; see, *Rhetoric, to Alexander* 1421b10–11.

26. Aristotle introduced these modes as part of *invented* argumentation, in contrast to argumentation based solely on demonstrable facts; this distinction became less formal over time. See Aristotle, *Rhetoric* 1356a7.

- *Logos* (λόγος) is the simplest of the three modes; it involves an appeal to proof or evidence provided in the oration. Classical rhetoric understood *logos* as a reasoned probability based on available evidences, and not any evidence in and of itself.[27] Today people expect the *logos* to be the basis for any argument, generally finding speeches based on *ēthos* or *pathos* to be trite, clichéd, and at times manipulative. This was not the case in the ancient world. Still, some famous rhetoricians, such as Aristotle, tried to push the needle in the direction of *logos*.[28]

- *Ēthos* (ἦθος) is the mode of persuasion wherein the orator proclaims his trustworthiness and as a result shows the validity of his argument. In the ancient world, the reputation and honor of a speaker was of paramount importance, and a superior *ēthos* was often enough to sway the verdict. Today it would be like a politician showing up to a debate over taxation with their main argument being, "Vote for me, as I am a better person" without ever actually addressing the issue at hand. While this strategy seems wily or duplicitous to modern ears, ancient audiences considered it an acceptable strategy for winning in the court or assembly.

- *Pathos* (πάθος) is the mode of persuasion wherein the orator attempts to appeal to the emotional state of the crowd or audience in order to sway them to accept the validity of his argument. Like *ēthos*, *pathos* was considered an effective, winning strategy that an orator could employ in the ancient world, even as modern people would hear and feel something very different (heavy-handed manipulation). Using pathos would be like a politician showing up to a debate over taxation with their main argument being, "Taxes really stink! Aren't you mad with all you have to pay?" without ever addressing the issue itself.

---

27. George A. Kennedy, *New Testament Interpretation through Rhetorical Criticism* (Chapel Hill: University of North Carolina Press, 1984), 16.

28. Vickers, *In Defence of Rhetoric*, 20.

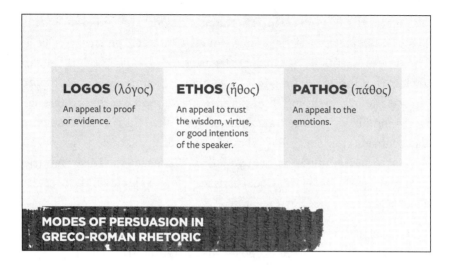

In addition to these major aspects of rhetoric, various rhetoricians addressed a number of other issues (before moving on to more detailed concerns). Some of these include *res* (λόγος) and *verba* (λέξις), which addressed the distinction between the substance of an argument and the expression of the argument; and lifelikeness, which emphasized the need for persuasion to be grounded in as natural a manner as possible. These were broad, influential ideas interwoven throughout the study of rhetoric.[29] Perhaps the most important of these issues included *stasis theory*, a complicated and variegated idea that received varying degrees of attention in different rhetorical works.

Stasis (στάσις/*status*), or the question at hand, is the differentiation of the base issue or concern of a rhetorical discourse. In rhetorical criticism it is usually translated as "issue,"[30] but an alternative and perhaps superior translation for *status* is "stance," meaning that the stasis theory in classical rhetoric identified the stand or position on which the argument rested.[31] Both nuances of the word were in play in ancient rhetoric. Stasis theory held to three or four major types (and more minor types), but the complicated and debated nature of the theory limits its use in most modern evaluations.[32]

---

29. On *res* and *verba*, see for example Quintilian, *Institutes of Oratory* 8.Pr.18; on lifelikeness, see for example Aristotle, *Rhetoric* 1355a12; and compare Vickers, *In Defence of Rhetoric*, 41–44.

30. Vickers, *In Defence of Rhetoric*, 26.

31. Habinek, *Ancient Rhetoric and Oratory*, 104.

32. Kennedy, *New Testament Interpretation through Rhetorical Criticism*, 36.

Reference works on rhetoric in the ancient world tended to shift focus to the individual devices that orators could use to create persuasive speech. There were essentially two major categories of individual devices used in ancient rhetoric: topics (*loci*/τόπος) and figures (*figurae*/σχῆμα). So important was rhetoric in the minds of the ancients that some of these reference works contained seemingly exhaustive lists of all of the rhetorical devices that could enter into play. Even though the reading is laborious to modern students, these minutiae had a huge cultural impact on the Western world up into the early modern period. Below are a few examples of the possible rhetorical devices used in ancient works:

- *Enthymeme* (*enthymēma*/ἐνθύμημα) is a type of logical proof wherein one of the propositions is omitted from the argument and assumed. This term is roughly synonymous with the modern use of the term "syllogism," with the exception that one of the propositions in an enthymeme is assumed (whereas both of the propositions are explicit in a syllogism). Thus, it can be referred to as a "rhetorical syllogism." This type of proof is a more informal method of debate, not intending to be exacting or exhaustive; further, there was not always full agreement on its meaning or use in the ancient world.[33]

- *Ekphrasis* (*descriptio*/ἔκφρᾰσις) is the use of vivid description in the pursuit of persuasion. Speakers and writers used this figure to make the audience "feel there," with a strong, detailed, and colorful painting of the thing under discussion. The difference between the use of this device and a general description of something is the degree of vividness—in this case, the English word "description" is a weak translation of *descriptio*. *Ekphrasis* increased in importance to the degree that it usually held its own category in the *progymnasmata*.[34]

- *Prosōpopoiia* (*prosōpopoiia*/προσωποποιία) is the act of personifying, either impersonating another person in a rhetorical

---

33. See for example, Lanham, *Handlist of Rhetorical Terms*, 65–66.

34. See for example the different uses in *Progymnasmata: Greek Textbooks of Prose Composition and Rhetoric*, trans. George A. Kennedy (Atlanta: Society of Biblical Literature, 2003).

argument or giving human speech and emotions to an animal or inanimate object. Quintilian saw *prosopopoiia* as a figure of ornamentation, giving the orator the power to speak as if someone else in order to imbue the speech with greater liveliness.[35]

6.2.1.b *The Five-Stage Process of Rhetoric*

Ancient rhetorical handbooks also include discussions of how to create persuasive discourse. This part of the creation of rhetoric became streamlined and codified much as the other parts did. The result was the use of a five-stage process to move the orator or writer through the creation of rhetoric. These five stages are often referred to as invention, arrangement, style, memory, and delivery. This process is summarized well by Cicero in his work *On Invention*:

> And these are the divisions of it, as numerous writers have laid them down: Invention; Arrangement; Elocution; Memory; Delivery. Invention, is the conceiving of topics either true or probable, which may make one's cause appear probable. Arrangement, is the distribution of the topics which have been thus conceived with regular order. Elocution, is the adaptation of suitable words and sentences to the topics so conceived. Memory, is the lasting sense in the mind of the matters and words corresponding to the reception of these topics. Delivery, is a regulating of the voice and body in a manner suitable to the dignity of the subjects spoken of and of the language employed.[36]

Not every rhetorician broke the oratorical process into five stages. Many discussions of rhetoric in the ancient reference works shortchange the reader in the areas of memory and delivery. The five functions of the orator (and the five stages of rhetorical creation) are:

- *Invention* (*inventio*/εὕρεσις) is the first step, in which the orator identifies the stuff from which the argument may be

---

35. Joy Connolly, "Virile Tongues: Rhetoric and Masculinity," in *A Companion to Roman Rhetoric*, ed. William Dominik and Jon Hall (Oxford: Blackwell, 2007), 93–94.

36. Cicero, *On Invention* 7, in *The Orations of Marcus Tullius Cicero*, trans. C. D. Yonge (London: Henry G. Bohn, 1853).

made—what is true or probable and can be cogently argued.[37]
"Invention" is a misnomer for this step when used in English;
this stage does not imply that the orator is creating something
new or unique. Instead, the orator must discern all of the evidences (such as eyewitnesses) and probabilities (such as the
ēthos of the arguer) that can support the point of the argument.
The writers of the NT use a variety of arguments to make their
case, including appeals to eyewitnesses, OT proofs, evidence
of miracles, proof found in the natural world, and probabilities based on human experience.[38] Identifying the point of the
argument was extremely important; rhetoricians called this
the "question at hand" (the *stasis*) and felt it was necessary to
create the arguments that would answer it. The raw form of
each idea was called a topic (*loci*/τόπος), and these topics could
be used in a variety of ways to strengthen the argument.

- *Arrangement* (*dispositio*/τάξις) is the second step, in which the
  different parts "invented" by the orator are assembled into a
  meaningful and cogent whole. The importance of this step
  cannot be overstated; if the orator has great material but poor
  organization, the argument will fail. Thus, arrangement is
  likened to a sculptor who, taking the parts of clay, can either
  assemble a statue of a person (with good arrangement) or that
  of a monster (with poor arrangement).[39] As students, orators
  were taught a standard arrangement of four to six divisions in
  a rhetorical scheme (much the way students today are taught
  schemes such as the five-paragraph essay), but in practice
  other factors (such as evidences and audience) often drove

---

37. In modern culture, an argument (especially a legal one) is expected to be made on
what is true versus what is false. However, in the ancient world, truth was often second to
probability. Many cases seem to have been decided not based on external evidence (such as
appeals to eyewitness testimony), but to arguments of likelihood. These kinds of "evidences"
in arguments seem illogical to modern people, but they were widely accepted in Greek courts.

38. Kennedy mentions only three, but there are more; see Kennedy, *New Testament
Interpretation through Rhetorical Criticism*, 14.

39. Quintilian, *Institutes of Oratory* 7.Pr.2.

the needs of the arrangement. Arrangement was as much an art as it was a science.

- *Style* (*elocutio*/λέξις) is the third step, in which the orator shapes the feel of the material based on the argument and the audience. It is as intentional a process as any of the other steps. Ancient rhetoric taught that there were three major styles: a simple or low style, a temperate or medium style, and a grandiose or high style. The low style was plain, unadorned, and readily transparent to even the most uneducated of audiences. In contrast, the high style was very ornate, cumbersome, and at times hard to penetrate, even for the most informed of audiences. The middle style was just that—in the middle.

- *Memory* (*memoria*/μνήμη) is the fourth step in oratorical development and deals exclusively with the technique of remembering the speech for delivery. There were two kinds of memory: natural and artificial. Artificial memory describes the use of visual images to trigger the memory. Because of the need for mnemonic devices in a predominantly oral society, the use of memory had the effect of altering an argument (such as in brevity or rhythm, an issue that is often irrelevant in the modern world).

- *Delivery* (*pronuntiatio*/ὑποκρῖσις) is the final step in the development of an oration. Like memory, it was sometimes omitted from discussion, but unlike memory, it carried weight in the need for development. Ancient rhetoricians held that there were two parts to delivery: the role of the voice and the role of the body.[40] With the voice, one consideration was the forcefulness of the speech, and so the speaker had to decide between normal voice (*sermo*), argumentative voice (*contentio*), or an emotional voice (*amplificatio*).[41] With the body, rhetoricians cataloged an extensive list of movements, some of which were borrowed from the world of drama and the theater.

---

40. Quintilian, *Institutes of Oratory* 3.11.19.
41. *Rhetoric, to Herennius* 3.13.23.

INVENTION	The orator identifies the material to be shaped into an argument.
ARRANGEMENT	The orator assembles the material into a meaningful and cogent whole.
STYLE	The orator shapes the feel of the material based on the argument and the audience.
MEMORY	The orator commits the speech to memory.
DELIVERY	The orator delivers the speech, paying attention to the modulation of the voice and the position of the body.

THE FIVE STAGES OF GRAECO-ROMAN RHETORIC

6.2.1.c The Six Parts of a Rhetorical Work

When it came time for an orator to persuade an audience, the orator needed to organize the material for maximum effectiveness. In essence, there were two immediate parts for the orator to identify: (1) the scope of the subject under consideration, and (2) the way of demonstrating the arguments that support the subject.[42] The argument was broken down into parts for greater effect. While rhetoricians had differing views on the number of parts, typically ranging from four to seven, most of the areas covered were the same. One prominent system held by Aristotle divides the argument into just four parts: proem (προοίμιον), narration (πρόθεσις), proof (πίστις), and epilogue (ἐπιλόγος).[43] More prominent in later resource books was the sixfold division, which included: opening, narration, partition, confirmation, refutation, and conclusion (or peroration).[44] Each of these parts played a crucial role in the overall development of the argument. The author of the rhetorical reference book to Herennius summarizes the sixfold division as:

> The Introduction is the beginning of the discourse, and by it the hearer's mind is prepared for attention. The Narration or Statement of Facts sets forth the events that have occurred or might have

---

42. Aristotle, *Rhetoric* 1414a30–31.

43. Aristotle, *Rhetoric* 1414b8–9.

44. See Gaines, "Roman Rhetorical Handbooks," 168. Quintilian preferred five, not six, feeling the partition to be redundant; see Quintilian, *Institutes of Oratory* 3.9.1.

occurred. By means of the Division we make clear what matters are agreed upon and what are contested, and announce what points we intend to take up. Proof is the presentation of our arguments, together with their corroboration. Refutation is the destruction of our adversaries' arguments. The Conclusion is the end of the discourse, formed in accordance with the principles of the art.[45]

From this, we can make the following additions to the role of each division in the creation of a rhetorical argument:

- The opening (exordium) is where the orator makes the subject known and introduces the audience to the direction of the argument. The orator can open the argument with either a direct (principium) or indirect (insinuatio) approach.[46] Either way, it was acceptable for the orator to use clichéd techniques to grab the attention of the audience. Since the goal was to grab the audience's attention, having some knowledge of the audience was important.[47]

- The narration (narratio) is where the orator tells the story that bolsters the argument. In forensic rhetoric, the narratio recounted is the orator's version of the events, and there was no problem with an orator who could "set forth the facts and turn every detail to our advantage."[48] In the ancient world, plausibility was less important than probability (though realism was still important). Depending on the need of persuasion, the narration could be developed as realistic (argumentum), historical (historiam), or legendary (fabulam), yet for modern people, none of these (including realistic) are necessarily true. Included in this section was often a retelling of the key facts of the issue, and in some cases a summary statement for the audience.

---

45. *Rhetoric, to Herennius* 1.3.4, in *Rhetorica ad Herennium*, trans. Harry Caplan (Cambridge, MA: Harvard University Press, 1954).

46. *Rhetoric, to Herennius* 1.4.6; and cf. Quintilian, *Institutes of Oratory* 4.1.42.

47. Cicero, *On Invention* 1.15.20; and *Rhetoric, to Herennius* 1.3.4.

48. *Rhetoric, to Herennius* 1.7.12.

- The partition (*partitio* or *divisio*) is where the orator divides the subject matter up into what is agreed on or established and what is in dispute. The orator will next turn to these disputed issues. The goal for this section of the speech is brevity and clarity, in order that what is at stake is clearly established for the audience.[49] Some rhetoricians, such as Quintilian, felt that the *divisio* was not a formal part of the speech, but rather an element that an orator must interweave throughout.[50]

- The confirmation (*confirmatio*) is where the orator makes points in order to prove the case. This, along with the refutation, was considered the proof part of the rhetorical scheme. Its nature is to be a constructive aspect of the argument.[51] Rhetoricians often considered this to be the heart of the speech, and much time could be spent on developing the details.[52]

- The refutation (*confutatio*) is where the orator works to undermine the confirmations of the opposing side. This part was the second half of the proof. Its nature is to be the destructive aspect of the argument.[53]

- The conclusion (*conclusio*) is where the orator brings his argument to a close. The *conclusio* generally could include three parts: a summarization of the argument, a chance to denigrate the argument of the opponent (or the opponent himself), and an attempt at swaying the audience's sympathy toward his side of the case.

6.2.1.d First Exercises: The Progymnasmata

The proliferation of rhetoric in the ancient world meant that it was used not only among elite quarters (e.g., the senate or assembly), the courts of

---

49. Vickers, *In Defence of Rhetoric*, 70.

50. Quintilian, *Institutes of Oratory* 3.9.2.

51. Quintilian, *Institutes of Oratory* 3.9.5.

52. M. L. Clarke, *Rhetoric at Rome: A Historical Survey*, rev. D. H. Berry (London: Routledge, 1996), 26.

53. Quintilian, *Institutes of Oratory* 3.9.5.

OPENING (exordium)	The orator introduces the subject and the direction of the argument.
NARRATION (narratio)	The orator tells a story that bolsters the argument.
PARTITION (partitio or divisio)	The orator divides the subject matter into what is established and what is disputed.
CONFIRMATION (confirmatio)	The orator makes points to prove the case.
REFUTATION (refutatio)	The orator undermines the confirmations of the opposing side.
CONCLUSION (conclusio)	The orator brings the argument to a close.

THE SIX PARTS OF A RHETORICAL WORK

law, and the houses of epic literature, but also within common spheres of Graeco-Roman society, such as commerce, religion, and education.[54] Of these, it was education that was perhaps most affected; rhetoric became central to the curriculum taught in much of the Mediterranean world at the time of the NT. As rhetoric permeated more common levels of the educational system, it became more and more a part of the greater culture. It may even be possible to see traces of this development in the NT—books that may originate in (or be addressed to) more Graeco-Roman influenced areas arguably have more Graeco-Roman rhetorical influence.[55] The advent of these textbooks also coincided with the increased focus on written rhetoric and the development of style in written discourse.

With rhetoric beginning to dominate the educational system of the Greek world, introductory handbooks on the use of rhetoric, called *progymnasmata* (προγυμνάσματα), or "preliminary exercises," began to appear. Of all of these handbooks, a useful number are still extant today. While most date to the Roman era, the concept has a favorable pedigree and dates to at least the mid-fourth century BC, as they are first mentioned

---

54. For example, as it relates to Greek religion, *Rhetoric, to Alexander* 1423a30–1424a8.

55. While this statement may at first appear somewhat commonsense, it is actually quite debatable once we get into the heart of what rhetoric was and how it shaped the ancient world. For example, it is impossible to know whether some writers in the ancient world who do not appear to use much rhetoric, rather than being ignorant of it, intentionally chose not to use it. The result is that the study of rhetoric and its impact on the NT is a wide-open field even two millennia later.

in *Rhetoric to Alexander*. The three most popular of the surviving *progymnasmata* are those of Aelius Theon (circa first century AD), Hermogenes (circa second century AD), and Aphthonius (circa fourth century AD). These handbooks were composed of step-by-step exercises that increased in difficulty, designed to grow the beginning student in greater rhetorical competence. The most common exercises included: fable (*mythos/ἀπολογος*), *chreia* (*chria/χρεία*), narrative (*narratio/διήγησις*), description (*ekphrasis/ ἔκφρᾰσις*), personification (*ēthopoiia/ἠθοποιία* or *prosōpopoiia/προσωποποιία*), comparison (*comparatio/σύγκρῐσις*), and thesis (*thesis/θέσις*).

6.2.2 HEBRAIC (BIBLICAL) RHETORIC

The second type of rhetoric that can be applied to the interpretation of the NT is Hebraic (biblical) rhetoric. While the NT was written in Greek, every book shows a mixture of Hebraic and Greek thought, with different degrees in different books. This begs the question: What is the relationship between the Hebraic elements and Graeco-Roman rhetoric? What is the relationship between the Hebraic way of thinking and persuasive discourse in general? The recent interest in rhetoric has resulted in some scholars asking whether Hebrew forms or expectations about persuasion and argumentation affected the development of the NT. If so, what impact would they have on early Christian discourse? This question is a defining one for biblical rhetoric in that biblical rhetoric is descriptive, looking at past examples, rather than prescriptive, offering a process to follow (as in Graeco-Roman rhetoric).[56] The process for applying biblical rhetoric takes place as readers discern the logic of the texts at hand. As an example, two of the most notable features of biblical rhetoric are *parataxis* (groupings by juxtaposition, not development) and *binarity* (speaking in doubles).[57] As a result, this method tends to lean toward areas often covered by literary criticism (though the goals of the methods are different). If there is a weakness to the study of Hebraic or biblical rhetoric, it is that it so far has not had the interpretive power or value that other methods have mustered.

---

56. Roland Meynet, *Treatise on Biblical Rhetoric*, trans. Leo Arnold (Leiden: Brill, 2012), 3.

57. Meynet, *Treatise on Biblical Rhetoric*, 429.

6.2.3 NEW RHETORIC

The third type of rhetoric that can profitably be applied to the study of the NT is often referred to as "new rhetoric," largely because it is an ongoing modern theory and does not have as distinct boundaries as, say, Graeco-Roman rhetoric. In essence, "new rhetoric" is the term used by biblical scholars to describe the use of insights gained from modern fields of study such as linguistics, psychology, literary studies, and many more fields that offer explanations for the way speech and text persuade their audiences. Scholars typically trace its origins (and its name) to the work of Chaïm Perelman and Lucie Olbrechts-Tyteca.[58] This new rhetoric does not stand in contrast to Graeco-Roman or biblical rhetoric, but it would include those tools alongside modern ones. In a sense, it is both descriptive and prescriptive, both eclectic and pragmatic in attitude. As a result, new rhetoric has promising potential to explain significant issues in the work of persuasion in the NT. As with any new approach to NT interpretation, one concern with new rhetoric is that it can be guilty of anachronism, especially if the interpreter does not fully take into account cultural and historical considerations. But the interpreter can balance this concern against the original Greek concern for rhetoric, as espoused by Aristotle, which itself was not thought of as a complex system of language use for special situations, but rather a general acknowledgement of the power of language to influence through human universals.[59] In fact, new rhetoric is very much eclectic, much in the same way that the average Graeco-Roman rhetorician would most likely have conceived his practices. And it is not actually that new—the Reformer Philip Melanchthon (1497–1560) approached the letters of Paul through a new rhetoric scheme, starting with Graeco-Roman rhetoric and creating new categories and devices from Paul's unique words.[60]

---

58. Chaïm Perelman and Lucie Olbrechts-Tyteca, *The New Rhetoric: A Treatise on Argumentation* (Notre Dame, IN: University of Notre Dame Press, 1969).

59. Kennedy, *New Testament Interpretation through Rhetorical Criticism*, 10; and see also Douglas Estes, *The Questions of Jesus in John: Logic, Rhetoric and Persuasive Discourse* (Leiden: Brill, 2013), 11–12.

60. Carl Joachim Classen, *Rhetorical Criticism of the New Testament* (Tübingen: Mohr Siebeck, 2000), 10–14.

6.3 APPLICATIONS OF NEW TESTAMENT
RHETORICAL CRITICISM

Applying rhetorical criticism to the NT can be a very fruitful critical method for both biblical interpretation and preaching. Developing skills in rhetorical criticism is valuable regardless of the specific method of interpretation: "That all biblical texts are in some measure persuasive in character means that some knowledge of rhetoric should be part of the normal scholarly equipment of all exegetes."[61] Understanding the way in which the Bible can and does persuade its readers is an integral part of any reading of Scripture—a part that modern readers tend to be unaware of in favor of reading the NT for data rather than persuasion. Rhetorical criticism, when applied well to the NT, can be a healthy (and historic) antidote for overly modernistic approaches.

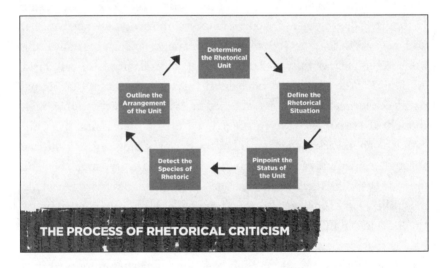

THE PROCESS OF RHETORICAL CRITICISM

How does one do rhetorical criticism on the NT? This is actually a more difficult question than it first seems. Most critical methods involve—or seem to involve—going to the text and looking for forms/sources/literary motifs/literary devices/theological concepts/cultural ideas/etc., and then creating commentary around what is discovered in the text. But there is a

---

61. Pontifical Biblical Commission, "The Interpretation of the Bible in the Church." The text is available from the Vatican in several languages at http://www.vatican.va/roman_curia/congregations/cfaith/pcb_doc_index.htm. See also http://catholic-resources.org/ChurchDocs/PBC_Interp-FullText.htm.

better way. While fully exploring this question is beyond the scope of an introductory chapter, we can identify the main parts of attempting Graeco-Roman rhetorical criticism on the NT. To begin with, George Kennedy lists five steps to performing this type of criticism.[62] They are meant less as a linear path and more as a circle of development:

In Kennedy's approach, a reader follows these steps:

- Step 1: The reader *determines the rhetorical unit* by delimiting the text at hand into a complete but manageable whole. To do this, the reader must identify where the rhetorical unit begins and ends. An obvious example of this is a speech; generally, one would not want to perform rhetorical criticism on a part of a speech rather than the whole. In the NT it is unlikely that a single verse or two will make up a rhetorical unit—unlike as in other methods of criticism, rhetorical units are by design and necessity larger units (in some cases, possibly whole NT books).

- Step 2: The reader *detects the rhetorical situation* of the argument by examining the circumstances that caused and affect the need for argumentation. Like the idea of *Sitz im Leben* in other forms of NT criticism, the rhetorical situation is helpful in order for the interpreter to better grasp the nuances of the argument. As an example, an epideictic speech made at a funeral will come from a different rhetorical situation than an epideictic speech made during a triumph, and knowing the difference between the two can provide a stronger interpretation for the reader. In the NT, the challenge is to avoid a circular hermeneutic, wherein the persuasion alters the interpreter's view of the situation, which in turn alters the view of the persuasion, and so forth.

- Step 3: The reader *pinpoints the stasis of the unit* by trying to answer the questions: "What is the point of the rhetoric?" and "What is the approach of the rhetor?" For the sake of beginning rhetorical criticism, a rough approximation is sufficient. As

---

62. The following information, including steps and chart information, is adapted from Kennedy, *New Testament Interpretation through Rhetorical Criticism*, 33–38.

Kennedy warns, this particular step is difficult to do in detail by any but the experienced scholar. For now, simply being able to restate the primary argument is enough to move to the next step.

- Step 4: The reader *defines the species of rhetoric* in use by figuring out whether the address is intended as judicial, deliberative, or epideictic. Remember: if the argument means to persuade its audience to commit to do an action in the future, it is deliberative; if the argument means to persuade its audience to pass judgment on some action or activity in the past, it is judicial; and if the argument means to persuade its audience of the good or bad of something now, it is epideictic. While there is some debate, deliberative rhetoric often is the easiest to identify, and therefore readers may want to start there. Epideictic, which is widely used, tends to be the least distinct.

- Step 5: The reader *outlines the arrangement of the unit* by distinguishing the different parts of the rhetorical unit. This includes, on the one hand, recognizing the divisions (such as *exordium, narration*, etc.) within the unit; and on the other hand, spotting the various topics and figures that fill out the persuasive devices within the unit. This is normally not something accomplished in one attempt; most "natural" rhetoric tends to avoid formal categorization, and thus the more familiar a reader is with the rhetorical unit, the more likely they will be able to better qualify its arrangement.

As above, once the reader has completed these steps, better rhetorical criticism encourages the reader to repeat the steps as necessary in order to continue to flesh out the argumentation strategy. Unlike modern methods, with goals that imply exactness, rhetorical criticism is not a method based on modern, scientific precision—readers may think of it more profitably as an "art" of the ancient world. In supplement to what Kennedy has written, I add the following additional steps that will help the reader successfully integrate Graeco-Roman rhetorical criticism into the toolbox of NT interpretation. They are:

- *Develop an appreciation for the classics.* Many today who read the NT are unfamiliar with the majority of Graeco-Roman writings—writings that were the cultural norms for the educated classes for more than two millennia, right up into the mid-modern period. As a result of the move away from Western classics, readers can gain a great deal of understanding about the way persuasion worked in the ancient world if they take time to familiarize themselves more in the way ancients argued their points and developed their stories. If nothing else, it will provide a newfound appreciation for Paul's writings.[63]

- *Start from the big and work to the small.* In many cases, readers of the NT start at the verse level, hunting and pecking for little examples that support the larger method. While this approach in general has its weaknesses, it is especially untenable for applying rhetorical criticism. Since rhetorical criticism involves an appreciation of the art of persuasion, the reader must read the larger whole (be it book or passage or argument) to best understand the point of the argument before proceeding to the individual parts.

- *Reapply the five-stage process of rhetorical design.* Since the five-stage process is not limited to one form of rhetoric, but ties in with verbal argumentation strategies in general, speakers and writers in the ancient world would have been familiar with the general ideas behind the process, even if they may not have known about the theory. Such is true with much of the NT; some writers may have known nothing about the theory, but they still understood that they needed to gather possible proofs, have some type of outline, identify a style for making

---

63. I was fortunate enough to have been exposed to the classics (in a small degree) at a young age. At the 2012 Institute for Biblical Research address, Ben Witherington asked the crowd of biblical scholars to evaluate (1) whether they had spent time in the classics, and (2) whether they believed in the value of rhetoric for interpreting the NT. Not many raised their hands on the classics, but those who did seemed to be very convinced of the value of rhetoric for NT interpretation.

their point, have a way to remember their points, and have a good delivery. As with outlining the argument scheme and pinpointing the stasis, reapplying the five-stage process is not particularly easy, nor is it going to be precise on the first attempt. However, getting some sense of the way the author developed the material can be very helpful in understanding the reason behind the argument. Even a philosopher like Plato took note of this very thing.[64]

Remember that what moderns call Graeco-Roman rhetoric was not called this by people living in and around the NT time period. For them, it was just the art of persuasive speech. Thus, any attempt to overly codify their art into a modern science will always meet with failure. Of course, this assumes good practices are followed at the outset of the application. One of the dangers with any critical method is that the text can become slave to the method, and this is no less true with rhetorical criticism.

6.3.1 MACRO-RHETORIC AND MICRO-RHETORIC

One concern in the application of Graeco-Roman rhetoric that scholars raise is whether macro-rhetoric exists as such in the NT. In the field of rhetorical criticism, scholars use the term "macro-rhetoric" to describe a work that fully conforms to a rhetorical scheme (for example, a deliberative speech with obvious fivefold division and rhetorical figures and devices woven throughout), and "micro-rhetoric" to describe a work (or parts of a work) that contains elements of rhetoric argumentation (such as figures and devices), but does not appear to conform to an overall formal rhetorical scheme. In the study of the NT, a battle line is often drawn between these two camps: For example, the macro-rhetoric camp thinks that some of Paul's letters can be defined by their overall rhetorical organization, whereas the micro-rhetoric camp thinks that while Paul used some rhetorical devices and figures in his letters (such as enthymemes), his letters are still merely letters with some occasional argumentation added for good measure. This debate continues, and the actual answer may be less clear-cut than either camp will sometimes admit.

---

64. See Plato, *Phaedrus* 236a.

For the macro-rhetoric camp, one of the most troubling arguments is that not only do the books of the NT not contain a clear-to-many rhetorical scheme, but proposed rhetorical schemes are often contrastive rather than complementary. For example, in their studies of 1 Peter, Barth Campbell and Ben Witherington come away with two different macro-rhetorical structures for the letter.

When this type of disagreement occurs, it can provide ammunition for those disinclined to the use of rhetorical criticism. However, such disagreement does not mean that macro-rhetoric is not valid; rather, it means that the books of the NT have other narrative intersections and goals in addition to persuasion. In fact, the schemes suggested by Campbell and Witherington are not radically different. And while we may not be able to say with certainty that macro-rhetoric exists, the scope, logic, and intent of parts of the NT lead many to believe that there is a persuasive scheme at work.

6.3.2 "FORCED" RHETORIC

This leads to the second concern: the challenge of "forced" rhetoric. This refers to the temptation of scholars and readers to force parts of the NT into a Graeco-Roman rhetorical scheme, even though the fit is inexact. This concern is hardly unique to Graeco-Roman rhetorical criticism, since it is a concern that touches on using any particular method to interpret biblical books. However, rhetorical criticism is highly susceptible to this problem because the method comes to us from the ancient world in a highly prescriptive manner (unlike most of the other types of modern biblical criticism). To overcome this, modern readers of the NT must be able to understand the organic proclamation process that went into the development of persuasion in the ancient world (and the same that occurs today). Ancient orators outside the NT who spoke as adults in public did not slavishly follow the outlines provided for them to practice on in the education of their youth.[65] The result is the normal proclamation process, which can be simply described in three parts: invention, daily use, and written form (see illustration on the next page).

---

65. Clarke, *Rhetoric at Rome*, 46.

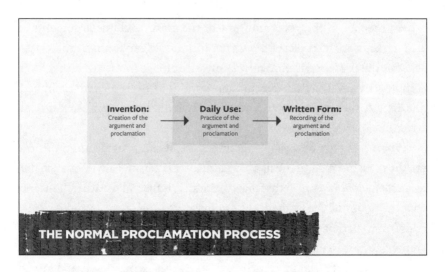

THE NORMAL PROCLAMATION PROCESS

Understanding this process is quite simple: A religious orator (such as Paul) *invents* the arguments (rhetorical, theological, historical) and then *arranges* these arguments—not just once for the one big speech in the assembly, as a Greek political orator might, but for the first sermon in a synagogue, and then rehashes for the next sermon, and the next, throughout his apostolic journeys. Over time, this continual *arrangement* of his proclamation becomes stronger but continues to move further away from any student reference book. When the orator's words were recorded, *memory* and *delivery* were omitted (as with other Graeco-Roman orators with recorded speeches), and the *invention* and evolved *arrangement* stand, but the *style* is now adjusted for the intended recipients of the letter (for example, more Asiatic, as in 2 Peter). The end result of this process is books in the NT that are highly rhetorical, but in the natural proclamation process as they were written, which makes it difficult for us to put them neatly into boxes.

6.4 LIMITATIONS OF NEW TESTAMENT RHETORICAL CRITICISM

As with any method of interpretation, it is important to identify the limitations of rhetorical criticism for analyzing the writings of the NT :

- Rhetorical criticism only works on rhetorical sections of the NT. Because rhetorical criticism is the study of persuasion, it may not be useful in interpreting sections, or even whole books, of the NT. Much depends here on how the reader understands and applies rhetorical criticism; if this term is synonymous with Graeco-Roman rhetorical criticism, then the limitation is more severe—much of the Gospels, Acts, and Revelation, plus a few parts of the Letters, may not be very applicable. Of course, if rhetoric played as great a role as scholars believe in the educational system of Greek writers, then Graeco-Roman rhetoric could in some way affect all of the NT. However, if the interpreter defines rhetorical criticism more along the lines of Hebraic/biblical literary criticism, then most of the NT books become available (though it seems to lose the explanatory power of Graeco-Roman rhetorical criticism). Likewise, if the reader defines rhetorical criticism along the lines of new rhetoric, then the entire NT opens up (though it may lose most of its historical ties).

- Rhetorical criticism does not, by design, factor in key historical information. The exclusion of historical information occurs in two main ways. First, the ancients used rhetoric mostly in a different setting from the religious contexts of the early church. There is no doubt that, while persuasion is universal, the needs of the assembly and law courts were different from the needs of the early church. In addition, there is the very real possibility that the socioeconomic differences between the rhetoricians and orators and the NT authors were significant enough to affect the ways they appropriated persuasion. Second, on the reverse, rhetorical criticism speaks little to the Hebraic qualities that permeate the NT.[66] Therefore, while rhetorical criticism can tell readers a great deal about how the NT writers may have constructed some of their works, it does not provide much light on the religious, historical, and theological factors that influenced the writing.

---

66. Ben Witherington disagrees in part, suggesting that Graeco-Roman rhetoric touches on every part of the NT, including the "most Jewish of materials"; see Witherington, *New Testament Rhetoric*, 235. While Witherington's argument for the relevance of Graeco-Roman rhetoric to the entire NT is compelling, it is hard not to see it as a little uneven given the wide variety of genres, writers, goals, and approaches contained within the NT.

- Rhetorical criticism possesses a rigidity that the NT does not. As we mentioned above, one of the challenges of rhetorical criticism (especially Graeco-Roman rhetorical criticism) is that it is a highly prescriptive theory. This is an interpretation challenge, as the rhetorical schemes found in the NT do not follow from the rhetorical exercises of students (nor should we expect them to do so). However, this is also a limitation, in that most of the NT falls outside rhetorical prescription, giving the interpreter a less clear view on the meaning of the texts. As an example, many scholars who are skeptical of the use of rhetorical criticism argue that Paul's Letters, for example, are letters, and thus interpreters should consider epistolary theory ahead of rhetorical theory.[67] While this argument has its own weaknesses, critics have used it quite successfully to limit the impact rhetorical criticism has had on NT interpretation.

6.5 CONTEMPORARY INFLUENCE OF NEW TESTAMENT RHETORICAL CRITICISM

As far as modern methods go, the influence of rhetorical criticism on the interpretation of the NT is small but increasing. It is fair to say that the issue generates more discussion of method than actual interpretation. From the time of the writing of the NT, there has been a consistent trickle of scholars who interpret the NT through rhetorical criticism. In the last century, the work of Hans Betz—who wrote a major commentary on Galatians based on the application of Graeco-Roman rhetoric—and

---

67. To this Philip Tite writes, "Although the rhetorical handbooks are concerned with ancient speeches, rather than letters, this does not mean that rhetorical arrangement is useless for early Christian epistolary analysis. These letters, including the internal letter bodies, are not ancient speeches. They are letters—written to maintain an ongoing discursive engagement between writer and recipient(s) by means of an asynchronic mode of communication. Thus, we should not be looking for specific parts of speech, such as the *exordium, narratio, propositio, probatio,* and *peroratio.* Rather than identifying specific organizational components, and thus forcing epistolary content into formal speech structures, we can look at the discursive function of arrangement, a function that nicely applies to diverse communicative contexts." See Philip L. Tite, *The Apocryphal Epistle to the Laodiceans: An Epistolary and Rhetorical Analysis* (Leiden: Brill, 2012).

James Muilenberg—who in a major address called for (among other things) the rediscovery of biblical rhetoric—are probably the two most influential scholars in spurring on a renewed interest in the method of rhetorical criticism.[68] Shortly afterward, George Kennedy wrote an influential introduction to rhetorical criticism that is still regularly used by biblical scholars.[69] Since that time, an increasing number of research publications has appeared, giving the beginning reader many more options for learning about rhetorical criticism: Ben Witherington has written numerous NT commentaries containing rhetorical criticism; Paul Sampley and Peter Lampe produced a book covering a variety of rhetorical critical issues in Paul's Letters; Philip Tite and others approached early Christian books outside the NT through rhetorical analysis; Carl Classen developed a brief history of the approach; Stanley Porter edited an encyclopedia on rhetorical practices; and all this is not to mention a growing number of monographs, articles, translations of ancient rhetorical exercises, bibliographies, and new forays into other forms of rhetoric.

Rhetorical criticism has made major inroads into the study of the letters in the NT and is starting to gain traction in the study of the remaining parts of the NT. While rhetorical criticism will continue to play a major role in biblical interpretation in the future, it is likely to be a method whose future is consistent with its past: it will ebb and flow as new methods become popular and old ones die out, but, because of historical underpinnings, should never be ignored.

6.6 RESOURCES FOR FURTHER STUDY

As noted above, rhetorical criticism of the NT underwent a renaissance in the late twentieth century; hence, compared to other critical methods, this subfield of NT studies does not yet have such a voluminous amount of works that can discourage new participants in the field. As a result, there are a number of easily manageable resources to provide a great snapshot of the study of rhetorical criticism, as well as ideas for further study and research. Some of the most significant of these include:

---

68. See Hans Dieter Betz, *Galatians: A Commentary on Paul's Letter to the Churches in Galatia*, Hermeneia (Philadelphia: Fortress, 1979); and James Muilenberg, "Form Criticism and Beyond," *JBL* 88 (1969): 1–18.

69. Kennedy, *New Testament Interpretation through Rhetorical Criticism*.

Kennedy, George A. *A New History of Classical Rhetoric: An Extensive Revision and Abridgement of the Art of Persuasion in Greece, the Art of Rhetoric in the Roman World, and Greek Rhetoric under Christian Emperors, with Additional Discussion of Late Latin Rhetoric.* Princeton, NJ: Princeton University Press, 1994.

Kennedy's *A New History of Classical Rhetoric* is perhaps the best-known introduction of classical rhetoric in print, covering more than a millennia of rhetorical practice in the ancient world. It is a must read for students who are serious about understanding the scope of rhetoric.

———. *New Testament Interpretation through Rhetorical Criticism.* Studies in Religion. Chapel Hill: University of North Carolina Press, 1984.

A groundbreaking work that helped reignite the current wave of rhetorical studies, Kennedy's work provides an introduction to identifying the rhetorical devices in the NT and their meaning and importance for interpretation today. To some degree, recent scholarship has surpassed his work in this volume, but almost none has commanded as much attention.

Sampley, J. Paul, and Peter Lampe, eds. *Paul and Rhetoric.* New York: T&T Clark, 2010.

Sampley and Lampe's *Paul and Rhetoric* offers a partial history of the recent interest in rhetoric in Paul's writings, plus a much more detailed overview of various types of rhetorical devices found in the letters of Paul. This book provides the reader with examples of how to accomplish rhetorical criticism, while at the same time provoking thought toward new areas of study in Paul.

Witherington, Ben, III. *New Testament Rhetoric: An Introductory Guide to the Art of Persuasion in and of the New Testament.* Eugene, OR: Cascade, 2009.

Perhaps the most accessible introduction to NT rhetoric, Witherington's book tackles not only formal rhetorical patterns but also aspects of persuasion that went into the creation of much of the NT. Witherington's introduction also makes a strong case for the value of rhetorical criticism, alongside (and in some cases, superior to) other types of critical NT studies.

7

STRUCTURAL CRITICISM

Gretchen Ellis

7.1 DEFINITION AND GOAL OF
STRUCTURAL CRITICISM

Structuralism approaches meaning in human communication as emerging from a system of relations or common structures that make understanding possible. Although broadly a philosophy of knowledge and a theory of human consciousness, structuralism entered biblical criticism primarily as an exegetical method that promised relief from some problems perceived with the historical-critical method. Tired of the excessive fixation with sources and diachronic development of the text, biblical structuralists sought a holistic, synchronic approach to the text that focused on the meaning of the present text rather than the proposed meaning of an ideal historical text and how it developed over time. While the practice of structuralism was never fully embraced in biblical scholarship—likely due to an overabundance of technical terminology and the structuralist predilection for complex charts and diagrams—many of its insights continue to this day in other methodologies, such as canonical criticism and rhetorical criticism.[1]

---

1. John Barton, *Reading the Old Testament: Method in Biblical Study*, rev. and enl. ed. (Louisville, KY: Westminster John Knox, 1996), 124, 133–36.

Structuralism arose as a reaction to the historical approach to language that had dominated the nineteenth century.[2] Frustrated with the seemingly atomistic approach of historical linguistics, linguistic structuralism studies language as a system in which words have meaning not in isolation but as part of a system of relations.[3] Literary structuralism applies this same way of thinking to texts—namely, that texts have meaning as a part of a literary system shared by all human beings. The belief in a shared system of literary meaning allowed scholars to be able to read certain genres of literature (such as myths, folktales, and legends) with more insight than historical criticism had afforded.[4] Those genres that lacked a singular author and had a high degree of shared symbolism cross-culturally were now understood as participating in a system of meaning that explained why such authorless texts could still be meaningful to contemporary audiences. Thus, reading individual texts such as myths provided insight into the shared literary structures of the human brain that produced meaning, and elucidating these structures became the professed goal of literary structuralism.

7.1.1 RELATIONSHIP TO OTHER APPROACHES

Structuralism may seem a strange theory to adopt in biblical scholarship because, on the face of it, structuralism is less interested in *what* texts mean than it is in developing a theory of *how* and *why* texts mean. Nevertheless, Barton proposes that biblical scholars gravitated toward structuralism in the mid-twentieth century partly because they were disillusioned by

---

2. As an approach to language, structuralism developed in the first half of the twentieth century. It was applied to the social sciences and literary criticism, and it experienced its period of greatest influence on those disciplines in the 1960s, 1970s, and early 1980s. For further details, see §7.2 Development of Structural Criticism.

3. For the sake of clarity, when referring to the broad swath of scholars engaged in the discipline (both religious and secular), we will use the term "structuralists" rather than listing every influential structuralist scholar. At times, however, it is necessary to distinguish between secular and biblical structuralist scholars, due to their differences with respect to the philosophy of structuralism more broadly. When this is necessary, we will use the terms "secular structuralists" and "biblical structuralists." When we use the term "biblical structuralists," we are referring to those biblical scholars who practice the distinct form of structuralism that came to exist in biblical scholarship—namely, a form that adopts some of the analytical techniques of structuralism without embracing its philosophical presuppositions (see Elizabeth Struthers Malbon, "Structuralism, Hermeneutics, and Contextual Meaning," *JAAR* 51, no. 2 [1983]: 209–10).

4. Barton, *Reading the Old Testament*, 105.

the traditional historical-critical methodology.[5] This methodology, so they thought, was missing the forest for the trees. Such methods had not led to a satisfactory ability to read the biblical text as it stood. Since its inception, biblical criticism has gravitated toward places in the text that appear incoherent or inconsistent (this is in contrast to the church fathers and rabbis, who presumed the reliability of Scripture).[6] Source critics posited multiple sources were edited together. Form critics sought a hypothetical ideal "form" for the text that might explain both the origin of and developmental process that created the present text. Tradition-historical criticism highlighted the interweaving of religious traditions that may have created these tensions. The literary structure of the text was destabilized, and any attempt to discern meaning in what resulted from these procedures was tentative at best. Structuralism swept all that away.

According to literary structuralist theory, the perception of incoherence is just that: a perception. Rather than seeking to explain perceived incoherence by means of historical development, structuralism asks the question: "What is the point of view that one must adopt in order to perceive [the text's] continuity, its unfolding, and its connectedness?"[7] In this way, structuralists sought to better understand the meaning of the text, bringing it in line with the goals of all other forms of biblical criticism. Historical-critical methods focused on historical meaning—that is, the meaning the text had for the author in the author's own time and context. For structuralists, meaning is a product of the text itself. Meaning resides in the relationship among words and concepts within the text, not the author's mental state coupled with a historical *Sitz im Leben* (or "life setting"). Structuralism thus allowed biblical scholars to focus on a synchronic reading of the Bible and to sidestep any ideological qualms they might have had with traditional historical-critical methods.

Structuralism also connected biblical scholars with current trends in the broader field of literary criticism from the 1960s to the early 1980s.

---

5. Barton, *Reading the Old Testament*, 105.

6. For example, Augustine defends the trustworthiness of Scripture by claiming apparent errors are the result of faulty manuscripts, translation, or interpretation (*Reply to Faustus the Manichaean* 11.5).

7. J. Jean Calloud, "Toward a Structural Analysis of the Gospel of Mark," *Semeia* 16 (1979): 135.

While the discomfort with historical-critical methods evinces a conscious movement *away* from the trajectory biblical criticism had been on, this latter observation reflects a self-conscious movement *toward* something else—namely, literary criticism. There may have been an element of the reactionary in the jump to structuralism, but it also reflects a growing awareness in biblical criticism that the Bible is both literature and a sacred text. The influence of structuralism on biblical studies was part of a general shift toward methodologies with roots in literary criticism. Rhetorical criticism, narrative criticism, poststructuralist criticism, and canonical criticism all, in some sense, can be traced back to the same shift in thinking that is reflected in the move to structuralism.[8]

Biblical structuralism must also be read against the background of existential theology that was dominant in the post-WWII years. Also reacting to the emphasis on historical meaning, theologians such as Rudolf Bultmann argued that the biblical text was a code to a deeper, existential meaning. Bultmann famously distinguished between the "Jesus of history" and the "Christ of faith," emphasizing that the latter was more important than the former. History doesn't matter so much as what its implications are for present existence. In other words, the symbolic reference of Jesus (i.e., Christ, the risen savior) mattered more than the personal history of the man Jesus. Texts were read for their symbolic inferences and "demythologized" into a symbolic code that could be meaningful for contemporary audiences.[9] Structuralists argued that this method created a text outside the text that, in turn, decoded the meaning of the text, which—according to structuralism—was absurd. Rather than read the text as meaningful based on the way the words and concepts interacted with one another *in the text*, existential theology created meaning based on a symbolic/existential code that existed *outside the text*. The process was convoluted and resulted in textual meaning that was created by something other than the text itself. Thus, biblical structuralism sought to avoid both of these pitfalls: a purely historical meaning located in authorial psychology and religious history, and a purely existential meaning located in a symbolic code outside the text.

---

8. On these different literary approaches, see chapters 2, 3, 5, and 8 of the present volume.

9. See Rudolf Bultmann, *Jesus Christ and Mythology* (New York: Scribner, 1958).

7.1.2 GUIDING ASSUMPTIONS

While it may appear to be merely another way to say that texts have genres that determine setting, plot, and how characters interact, literary structuralism was more than that. As it was originally conceived, structuralism was not so much an exegetical tool as it was an epistemology (theory of knowledge) and a philosophy of human language, science, and culture.

As an epistemology, it claimed to be the precondition for *any* kind of scientific knowing. Structuralism argued that human consciousness has a structure that exists prior to any kind of knowing and, in fact, shapes both how something is known and what can be known. Put another way, consciousness doesn't create structure; it *is* a structure—and a universal one at that. This universal structure, in turn, shapes human knowledge and all that human knowledge creates, such as languages.[10]

Linguistics is the heart of structuralist theory, and most of the assumptions of the philosophy of structuralism were originally formulated as theories about language.[11] For example, one of the core assumptions of structural analysis is that texts, like language, have meanings that stem from generative, or "deep," structures.[12] In linguistics, this refers to the idea that the sentences "She kicked the dog" and "The dog was kicked by her" have the same conceptual framework underlying them—namely, the concept of a female ("she/her") striking a dog with her foot ("kicked the dog/the dog was kicked"). The arrangement of individual words may be different, but the concept is the same. This distinction was applied to texts. It is assumed that underneath every text is a conceptual universe/system/structure that creates, or generates, the surface structure (i.e., the

---

10. Immanuel Kant (1724-1804), in reaction to the overconfidence of some Enlightenment thinkers to grasp reality, argues in *Critique of Pure Reason* that we cannot gain direct knowledge of the external world—"things in themselves"—because our minds form the matter of our sensory input. We construct meaning even before our interpretations. What is perceived, then, is not reality but a map of the terrain. Reality cannot be known in the raw. Further discussion of the philosophical development of structuralist theory is beyond the scope of this chapter; for more information, see Brian Watson Kovacs, "Philosophical Foundations for Structuralism," *Semeia* 10 (1978): 85-105.

11. Linguistic structuralism is associated with Ferdinand de Saussure (1857-1914), whose lectures were published after his death as the *Cours de linguistique général* (Paris: Payot, 1916). For more on Saussure, see the section on the §7.2 Development of Structural Criticism.

12. For a definition of deep and surface structures, see §7.1.3 Key Concepts.

series of words, sentences, and paragraphs that make up the literal text).[13] This carries with it the attendant assumption that, as in linguistics, a deep structure is capable of producing a near-infinite array of surface structures. The same story can be told in many ways without violating the underlying conceptual framework. Structuralism argues that the distinction between deep and surface structures explains the proliferation of different versions of the same story, as is the case with fairy tales such as Cinderella or Snow White.[14]

In turn, deep structures, whether linguistic or literary, are assumed to reflect the universal structures of human consciousness. As a product of the structure of consciousness mentioned above, textual deep structures are a reflection of it. By analyzing texts one can gain greater insight into the universal structure of human consciousness—it is the professed goal of secular structuralism to do just that. Think of the game of chess. If you watched two people play a game, you would learn something about the rules that govern how chess is played. True, you could read a manual, but suppose you didn't have a manual; all you had was the game. The more games of chess you watched, the more you would learn about it: what the best strategies are for different playing styles, how to read your opponent to learn what he will do, and what moves are the best or worst to make in specific situations. In other words, you could learn the "structure" of chess by watching it. Substitute the game of chess with texts and the rules of chess with the structure of human consciousness, and there is literary structuralism.

But how is one supposed to discern the structure from the text? Reading a text to learn its structure is more complicated than learning the rules of chess by watching a game. Linguistic structuralism had posited that the heart of language was a system of conceptual binary oppositions, and the relationship between these oppositions created meaning. We know what

---

13. Structural discussions use these three words—"system," "universe," and "structure"—almost interchangeably. Therefore, if you see "deep structure" in one discussion and "system of deep values" or "semantic universe" in another, you should understand them as referring to the same thing.

14. The classic work on the structural similarities found in folklore is Vladimir Propp, *Morphology of the Folktale*, 2nd ed., trans. Laurence Scott, rev. and ed. Louis A. Wagner (Austin: University of Texas Press, 1968).

"good" means because we also have the concept of "bad." These oppositions allow one to discern linguistic systems. Literary structuralists believe that textual structure may also be accessed through the system of conceptual binary oppositions and their relations. It is not the opposition of words per se, but the concepts that underlie them—e.g., male/female, life/death, divine/human, wholeness/incompleteness—that create meaning.

In this system, meanings are either unmarked (the normal state of affairs) or marked (the unusual or opposite state of affairs), which is a function of the author's cultural worldview. Put more simply, cultures—which are also a product of the universal system of human consciousness—define what the "normal" state of affairs should be, and concepts opposing that are considered "marked." In a culture that valued nature, for example, the opposing concept of technology would be marked, and whenever it showed up in literature, how it was portrayed as well as the relationship between nature and technology would be significant for interpreting the meaning of the text. It should be noted that rarely, if ever, does a single binary pair control the meaning of the text. For most structuralists, both biblical and secular, the meaning of the text is a product of an entire system of binary opposites and how they interweave together in the story.

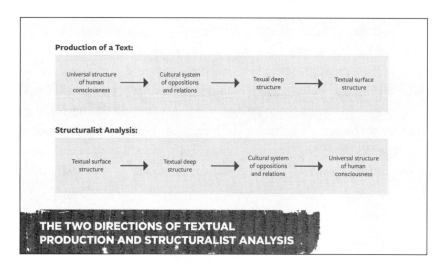

Production of a Text:

Universal structure of human consciousness → Cultural system of oppositions and relations → Texual deep structure → Textual surface structure

Structuralist Analysis:

Textual surface structure → Textual deep structure → Cultural system of oppositions and relations → Universal structure of human consciousness

THE TWO DIRECTIONS OF TEXTUAL PRODUCTION AND STRUCTURALIST ANALYSIS

The interweaving of systems to form meaning brings with it the attendant assumption that texts have multiple meanings. Given the assumptions that texts have more than one code or structure,[15] that meaning is the product of relations, and that these codes and their relations can interact in many ways, texts cannot have a single meaning. Daniel Patte uses the phrase "meaning horizon" to refer to how a text does have a limit to what it can mean, but it doesn't have a limit to the number of meanings so long as they fit within the confines of this limiting horizon (see more below).[16] Historical criticism cut the text into more and more pieces to find a single meaning; structuralist criticism "trac[es] the connections outward in many directions in wider and wider circles."[17] It is not surprising, therefore, that so many biblical structuralists seem unconcerned that their structuralist analysis highlights a different meaning from that of another biblical structuralist working on the same passage.

A related assumption is that for structuralists, meaning is both arbitrary and determined. It is arbitrary insofar as meaning is entirely a matter of cultural convention. A smile in one culture might mean something entirely different in another. On the other hand, meaning is determined insofar as within that culture the given meaning is bound by those cultural conventions. A smile can't mean sadness in American culture because our culture dictates that it means happiness, though it may indicate sadness in another culture.[18]

Structuralism focuses on the latter aspect—namely, that the meaning of words and texts exists within a system. This system is specifically a cultural system of conceptual oppositions and their relations. These oppositions form the conceptual framework within which a story is told in a given culture. Only a culture that opposes sanity and insanity will find horror films such as *Psycho* and *The Shining* to be terrifying. Thus, textual meaning is produced in the following way: universal structure of human consciousness > cultural system of oppositions and relations > textual deep structure

---

15. On the concept of multiple textual codes, see Roland Barthes, *S/Z*, trans. Richard Miller (Oxford: Blackwell, 1990). On multiple textual structures, see Daniel Patte, "One Text: Several Structures," *Semeia* 18 (1980): 3–22.

16. Daniel Patte and Judson F. Parker, "A Structural Exegesis of Genesis 2 and 3," *Semeia* 18 (1980): 55.

17. Vern S. Poythress, "Structuralism and Biblical Studies," *JETS* 21 (1978): 231.

18. So-called ironic meanings, i.e., satiric meanings, are possible precisely because they exploit the normally fixed meaning within a culture. Saying "yeah, right" in the proper satiric tone of voice can only mean the opposite because they are normally words of assent.

> textual surface structure. Structuralist analysis, however, flows in the opposite direction, from surface structure, to deep structure, to the system of opposition and relation, to the universal structure of consciousness. It should be noted, however, that biblical structuralism usually stops short of the final step toward constructing a universal system of consciousness; it instead focuses on how the deep structure and system of opposition elucidates the meaning of the biblical text.

The emphasis on system leads to an intentional focus on synchrony (the study of something at a particular point in time) rather than diachrony (study oriented toward change/development over time). In other words, "The timeless, universal structures are pursued, not the ways in which meaning has been discovered in the past."[19] Secular and biblical structuralists alike approach texts "as is" rather than historically dissecting them and analyzing their constituent parts. Specific passages in the biblical text are most certainly discussed individually, but divisions are made structurally rather than historically. Paul Beauchamp, for example, breaks his structural analysis of the "creation myth" in Genesis 1–2 at Genesis 2:1 in part because, as the text exists *now*, a break exists after this verse.[20] It doesn't matter that no source or form critic would break the text there; historical development of the text doesn't matter, only the text in its present form.

Biblical structuralists are not as vehement in their focus on synchronous readings as secular structuralists are. For many biblical structuralists, the deep structures of the text are either implicitly or explicitly equated with the author's intention, thus allowing both interests to stand alongside each other. Brian Kovacs insists that the synchronic focus of structuralist criticism need not displace diachronic interests in the biblical text. In a 1978 article for *Semeia*, he argues for what he calls a "post-synchronic diachrony," by which he means that after the text has been examined synchronically, the exegete may then engage in the world of the author via the semantic universe reflected in the text as well as confront her own place in history by discerning the distance between the author's universe and her own.[21]

---

19. Carl Armerding, "Structural Analysis," *Them* 4, no. 3 (1979): 97.

20. Barton, *Reading the Old Testament*, 125.

21. Kovacs, "Philosophical Foundations," 85–105. At least, this is how I read his argument. Whether he was influenced by poststructuralism, Kovacs's comments depict an acute understanding of one of the major criticisms the latter discipline lobs at structuralism in general.

Finally, it should be noted that as a philosophy, structuralism is basically incompatible with other exegetical methodologies.[22] Because structuralism is an epistemology, not just an exegetical method, full adherence to structuralist philosophy requires acceptance of its "claim to provide a total *explanatory framework* for the whole of human culture."[23] Since most biblical structuralists do not adopt this philosophy, much of their work reflects the methodological eclecticism that is so common to biblical criticism. Moreover, when compared to the secular French structuralists who preceded them, many biblical structuralists appear methodologically sloppy or vague. This is not to say that biblical structuralism is inferior because much of it fails to adopt philosophical structuralism.[24] Rather, one may conclude that although it may have an organic connection to the French structuralist movement, because biblical structuralism diverged from its parent discipline in many ways, it should be distinguished from it insofar as the philosophical underpinnings are concerned. Just because a specific biblical scholar utilizes structuralist vocabulary and methodology does not in any way mean that he or she adheres to the belief that structuralism provides a way to look at the world rather than just the biblical text.

7.1.3 KEY CONCEPTS

More than any other discipline of biblical criticism, structuralism is burdened with a large amount of technical vocabulary (jargon) that can be quite daunting to learn. As Brian Kovacs put it, "They couch their work in an alien and impenetrable jargon, at once technical and highly metaphorical."[25] This is in part due to its basis in linguistics (the study of language) and semiotics (the study of meaning). It is also due to an effort, in

---

In most biblical structuralist articles, this self-conscious distinction between the initial synchronic research on the text and the secondary diachronic analysis is lacking. This results, I believe, in the equation of the deep structure with authorial intent.

22. Barton, *Reading the Old Testament*, 133.

23. Barton, *Reading the Old Testament*, 135. Emphasis original.

24. According to Armerding, "concern for stylistic research which does not build on French structuralism" would be better deemed style or rhetorical criticism. See Armerding, "Structural Analysis," 103.

25. Kovacs, "Philosophical Foundations," 85. In sharp contrast, Daniel Patte argues that "far from being gratuitous jargon, [technical vocabulary] constantly manifests that meaning is a mysterious relational happening and prevents the return to the false security of fossil-like images of meaning" ("One Text," 6).

its early years, to distinguish itself from other narrative disciplines due to the novelty of what was being discussed; a new methodology required a new vocabulary so as to avoid confusion. The following will cover the most common vocabulary encountered in structuralist studies, though it is by no means exhaustive.

7.1.3.a Deep and Surface Structures

As was briefly discussed above, the surface structure is the text itself as written—the words on a page. Analysis of surface structure includes plot summaries, descriptions of characters and actions, rhetorical analyses, and much of what is done in literary studies. In other words, surface structures deal with the questions of what a text says and how. This is also referred to as the syntagmatic aspect of the text.

The deep structure (also called the paradigmatic aspect), on the other hand, is the system of core semantic relationships and concepts that underlie texts and give rise to the surface structure. Deep structures answer the question of what a text means, but also, more importantly, *how* a text means. In theory, a relatively small number of deep structures are capable of producing an infinite number of surface structures, depending on how the concepts are related to one another and their organization. Deep structures are also called generative structures, or the system of deep values.

The easiest way to explain how these two concepts are related is by considering multiple versions of the same story. Take, for example, the fairy tale of Cinderella. This story exists in at least 1,500 different versions in both Europe and Asia.[26] Behind these various editions, one can posit a single story arc made up of the elements in the story (Cinderella herself, the stepmother, the ball, etc.) and their relations to one another. The various elements and their relations are the deep structure underlying the many surface instantiations of the story.

7.1.3.b Langue and Parole

In linguistics, parole refers to language as it is spoken by a specific individual in everyday life, while langue refers to the idealized language system as a

---

26. Chi-Yue Chiu and Ying-Yi Hong, *Social Psychology of Culture*, Principles of Social Psychology (New York: Routledge, 2013), 27.

whole.[27] English is a *langue*, but when you or I speak English, what is spoken is *parole*. The idea for this distinction between the underlying language system and its everyday manifestation in speech derives from Saussure.[28]

Literary structuralism argues that just as languages have an abstract ideal structure that governs individualized expression, so do texts. Whereas the textual *parole* is the individual text, the textual *langue* is the idealized textual structure that governs all text of a particular genre and, even more broadly, all genres of texts. Though it is not exactly the same, it can be useful to think of the textual *langue* as the collection of characteristics determined by the genre of the text, such as science fiction or creative nonfiction.[29]

In a sense, this distinction in literature may be perceived as an attempt to explain the reason that form criticism works. That discerning a text's genre is important to perceiving meaning is the fundamental tenet of form-critical analysis. *How* one can even begin to do that is the domain of structural analysis. Structural analysis also goes a step further than form criticism in assuming that distinctions in genre, which arise from deep structures, are the result of the cognitive processes in the brain and a reflection of universal shared structures.

7.1.3.c Signifier and Signified

This pair of terms is adapted from semiotics, the study of meaning. The signifier is the form that the sign takes, and the concept it represents is called the signified. For example, the word "cat" is the signifier for the concept of a small, domesticated feline (the signified). These two together—word

---

27. One may also see *langue* defined as a structure or code, with no change in meaning.

28. Ferdinand de Saussure, *Course in General Linguistics*, trans. Wade Baskin (New York: Philosophical Library, 1959), 9–15. In French, Saussure distinguishes *langue*, *langage*, and *parole*. *Langage* seems to be the umbrella term for the phenomena of human linguistic communication as a whole. *Langue* labels the abstract linguistic system of a particular language—the way the language works according to grammatical rules. *Parole* designates the language in actual use. Individual speakers may use language in inconsistent and innovative ways.

29. For example, science fiction differs from fantasy in that the cultures of the former are usually technologically advanced. In structuralism, plot or setting differences like these may be part of the surface structure, but in reality it is the deep structure that determines even these surface features. We recognize a story like that in The Lord of the Rings series to be fantasy because there is something about its deep structure that tells us it is not, say, historical fiction, nonfiction, an essay, etc.

and concept—form a sign, and the relationship between them is deemed signification.[30] These terms are used in the same way in structuralist theory, though they may also be used to refer to the text's deep and surface structures; the surface structure of the text corresponds to the signifier, and the deep structure to the signified. The textual sign would therefore be both the text's deep and surface structures.

7.1.3.d Binary Opposition

Binary opposition refers to how contrast creates meaning. A binary opposition is a pair of sounds, terms, or concepts with opposing meanings such as life/death, love/hate, female/male, or divine/human. While structuralism often focuses on direct opposites, the significant aspect of this concept is that meaning arises from contrast or choice. The choice may involve multiple possible expressions, not just two opposing terms. However, oppositions of various kinds can illustrate the contrasts more clearly. For example, distinguishing the English word "lip" from the word "rip" depends on how English uses *l* and *r* as contrasting sounds—the difference carries meaning. In Japanese, the difference between the sounds *l* and *r* is not meaningful.[31]

7.1.3.e Semiotic Square

A semiotic square is a tool of structuralist criticism used to visually depict the relationships between semiotic signs, especially binary opposites and the concepts relevant to these opposites.[32] One of the most common of the seemingly endlessly complicated diagrams that accompany structuralist exegesis, a semiotic square is typically composed of four terms: the positive *seme* ("seme" being the unit of meaning/concept), or X; a negative *seme*, or Y; and two other terms inferred from this initial pair: not-X and not-Y. This may seem a bit complicated, but an example will clarify. Take the binary

---

30. For further discussion, see Gregor Campbell, "Signified / signifier / signification," in *Encyclopedia of Contemporary Literary Theory: Approaches, Scholars, Terms*, ed. Irene R. Makaryk (Toronto: University of Toronto Press, 1993), 627.

31. Barry Kavanagh, "The Phonemes of Japanese and English: A Contrastive Analysis Study," *Journal of Aomori University of Health and Welfare* 8, no. 2 (2007): 288.

32. Scholars also refer to this as a "Greimas square," after notable development of this idea by prominent structuralist A. J. Greimas; see for example, Dino Franco Felluga, *Critical Theory: The Key Concepts* (London: Routledge, 2015), 123–26; and J. Holman, "Semiotic Analysis of Psalm cxxxviii (LXX)," in *In Quest of the Past: Studies on Israelite Religion, Literature and Prophetism*, ed. A. S. van der Woude (Leiden: Brill, 1990), 99.

concepts of "male" and "female." This opposition also generates the concepts of "not-masculine" and "not-feminine." From these options, one can further posit the concept of "both masculine and feminine" (bisexual or hermaphroditic) and "neither masculine nor feminine" (asexual). Thus, the binary pair "male-female" connotes more than just the surface opposition between the two sexes, and when this binary pair is part of the deep structure of the text, one, two, or all of the concepts may be relevant to analysis.

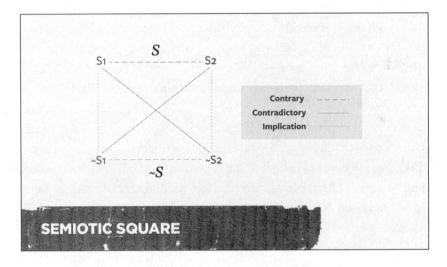

7.2 DEVELOPMENT OF STRUCTURAL CRITICISM

7.2.1 FERDINAND DE SAUSSURE AND STRUCTURAL LINGUISTICS

Although structural criticism reached its peak in the mid-twentieth century, it grew out of the posthumous publication of Ferdinand de Saussure's *Course in General Linguistics* in 1916. Saussure (1857–1913) argues that language consists in a universal system of relations that reflects the universal order of the human brain. For Saussure, studying language as system meant taking a synchronic approach instead of a diachronic approach (which was at that time the prevailing approach of philology). The diachronic approach considers how language changes over time, but a synchronic approach considers how the language as a system works as a whole (without regard for questions of historical development). Language is viewed as a closed system governed by a set of discernable rules that operate on the unconscious level and are universally applicable. The broader movement known as structuralism developed when Saussure's theories about structure and meaning were applied to other disciplines.

In the post-WWII years, as the philosophical center of Europe shifted away from Germany, French, Russian, and American linguists began to seek a way out of the seemingly atomistic approach to language that had dominated the pre-war years. Nikolai Trubetzkoy (1890–1938) and Roman Jakobson expanded Saussure's observations to phonology—the study of sounds in language—arguing that sounds have distinguishable meaning through a system of binary oppositions.[33] Jakobson applied the idea of binary opposition to cover all of language, not just phonology. He argued that languages are systems in which words have meaning based on their opposition and relation to other words. Blue, for instance, means what it does precisely because red, green, yellow, and black are also words used to represent colors. This nexus of ideas greatly influenced American linguist Noam Chomsky (1928–), the pioneer of transformational/generative linguistics, though he rejected strict binary opposition as an oversimplification. The distinction between surface and deep structures in linguistics (see above) is also attributed to him.[34] The trajectory from Saussure to the Russians to Chomsky is at the heart of linguistic structuralism, the methodology on which all other forms of structuralism are based.

7.2.2 CLAUDE LÉVI-STRAUSS AND STRUCTURAL ANTHROPOLOGY

While linguistic structuralism was gathering steam in America, in Europe, structuralist theory was beginning to affect other disciplines. French anthropologist Claude Lévi-Strauss (1908–2009) applied structuralist principles to anthropology and familial kinship structures in his work *Les structures élémentaires de la parenté* (1949).[35] This marked one of the first attempts to apply structuralist theory to a discipline other than linguistics. Although Lévi-Strauss argued more pervasively for the theory of binary opposition in his early years, later in life he came to argue that

---

33. For further discussion, see Edna Andrews, "Markedness," in *The Oxford Handbook of Tense and Aspect*, ed. Robert I. Binnick (Oxford: Oxford University Press, 2012), 213–14.

34. See for example, Robert Sklar, "Chomsky's Revolution in Linguistics," in *Noam Chomsky: Critical Assessments*, ed. Carlos P. Otero (London: Routledge, 1994), 3:30.

35. Claude Lévi-Strauss, *Les structures élémentaires de la parenté* (Paris: Presses universitaires de France, 1949), published in English as *The Elementary Structures of Kinship* (London: Eyre & Spottiswood, 1967).

opposition also included mediation—a concept or term that stood between the two opposing terms/concepts. Red/green on a stoplight, for example, is mediated by the yellow light, which stands between both "stop" and "go" as "slow down" or "caution." Thus, binary oppositions inherently include many levels of mediation, forming a network of meaning rather than a strictly binary structure.

Due to Lévi-Strauss's pioneering efforts toward applying structuralist ideas within other disciplines, it wasn't long until structuralism made its way into sociology, psychology, economics, architecture, and literary criticism, and from there into biblical criticism. Recall that structuralism was a philosophy that sought to explain how humans perceive and construct meaning. As such, it is understandable that it moved from a linguistic theory into an explanatory theory for various other subjects. It was only a matter of time before it was applied to literature.

7.2.3 VLADIMIR PROPP AND THE MORPHOLOGY OF A FOLKTALE

Vladimir Propp's (1895–1970) work on the narrative structure of folktales was also influential in the development of structuralism, especially once it was published in English in 1958.[36] Propp outlined the common narrative structure of Russian fairy tales, which he argued consisted of an initial situation and a combination of thirty-one distinct narrative functional units (e.g., abstention, mediation, struggle, victory, return).

Structuralism's emphasis on synchronicity and lack of concern for authorial intention works well for folktales, myths, and fairy tales since they are essentially authorless texts. Since the meaning of the tale cannot be traced back to the mind of a particular author, the meaning must be located somehow in the text itself and how the characters and actions relate to one another. Propp proposed that characters could be distilled into seven basic functions depending on their role in the narrative (e.g., villain, hero, helper, and sender/dispatcher) and that "all possible folktale plots may be generated by allowing characters to interact in certain specific ways."[37] He developed a formula for combining characters and

---

36. Alan Dundes, introduction to the second edition of *Morphology of the Folktale* (Austin: University of Texas Press, 1968), xi. Propp published his study in Russian in 1928.

37. Barton, *Reading the Old Testament*, 115.

actions. If a combination did not follow the formula, the audience would not recognize the story as a true folktale. Propp's work demonstrated that "folk-tales form a closed system" governed by a distinguishable set of rules.[38] Propp's work went largely unnoticed in the West until it was translated into English in 1958.[39]

7.2.4 ROLAND BARTHES AND SEMIOTIC CODES

Not long after, French literary theorist Roland Barthes (1915–1980) picked up on Propp's folklorist theory, but he sought to expand it by going "behind" the linear structure of the text. According to Barthes, texts, like languages, have surface and deep structures—meaning derives from the latter. He conceived of the goal of literary structuralist criticism as determining: (1) what relations the text establishes, (2) what the rules of organization are, and (3) how these two aspects allow for meaning to arise from the text itself. The text should be perceived as an utterance (*parole*) governed by a code (*langue*) that reflects the nature of the cultural system as present in the author's mind.

In his work *S/Z*, Barthes argues for the existence of five semiotic codes that interweave to form textual meanings: the hermeneutic code, the proairetic code, the semic code, the symbolic code, and the referential code.[40] The hermeneutic code is concerned with textual enigmas and their resolution, like plot events that are not immediately explained. Detective novels, for example, rely heavily on the hermeneutic code. The proairetic code refers to plot elements that imply further action; it is the origin of narrative momentum. The semic code encompasses characterizations of people, places, things, and events via the use of abstract concepts. Underlying these three codes are the symbolic code (the relationships between conceptual binary oppositions; see above) and the cultural code (the body of knowledge making up the cultural worldview of the author and the implied audience). Barthes argued that, like a choir, meaning in

---

38. Barton, *Reading the Old Testament*, 115.

39. See Hendrikus Boers, "Polarities at the Roots of New Testament Thought," in *Perspectives on the New Testament: Essays in Honor of Frank Stagg* (Macon, GA: Mercer University Press, 1985), 62–63.

40. Richard Howard, preface to *S/Z*, by Roland Barthes, trans. Richard Miller (Oxford: Blackwell, 1990), vii–viii.

texts arises from the blending and interweaving of these five voices, which allows for depth, richness, and a multitude of possible meanings.[41]

7.2.5 ALGIRDAS GREIMAS AND ACTANTIAL MODELS

Another prominent French structuralist, Algirdas Greimas (1917–1992), posited the existence of a semantic universe, which he defined as the sum of all possible meanings that can be produced by the value system of a given culture. Within particular texts, the semantic universe is brought into existence as the discourse universe; the resemblance of these two to surface and deep structures in linguistics is notable. Influenced by Propp, Jakobson, and Lévi-Strauss, Greimas argued for the existence of six distinct elements that make up a narrative: sequence, syntagm, statement, function, actant, and actantial model. The first three make up the narrative plot; the overarching sequence is broken down into smaller units of statements that can be broken into various syntagms, i.e., stylized individual actions.[42] Function refers to the technical category that each action belongs to, such as arrival, rejection, confrontation, etc.

More importantly, Greimas developed a system for classifying the roles of those who perform or are acted on by the various functions. These he deemed actants or actantial roles. Six such roles are outlined in his model: sender, receiver, subject, object, helper, and opponent. The relationship among these functional roles (the actantial model) is a large component of narrative development, and without one or more of the roles, the story may be perceived as incomplete. Moreover, combining one or more roles into a single character can create unique narrative tension or even perturbation.

---

41. Barthes is not the only structuralist to discuss multiple codes. Structuralists like their codes almost as much as they like their technical vocabulary. Boomershine's analysis of Gen 2–3 is replete with codes; see Thomas E. Boomershine, "The Structure of Narrative Rhetoric in Genesis 2–3," *Semeia* 18 (1980): 113–29. The same is true of Crespy's analysis of the good Samaritan, as he discusses the cultural, action, anagogic, semic, and hermeneutic codes embedded in the pericope. See Georges Crespy, "The Parable of the Good Samaritan: An Essay in Structural Research," *Semeia* 2 (1974): 27–50.

42. A more technical discussion of these terms is beyond the scope of this chapter. For further details, see A. J. Greimas and Joseph Courtés, *Semiotics and Language: An Analytical Dictionary*, trans. Larry Crist, Daniel Patte, et al. (Bloomington: Indiana University Press, 1982). It is a jargon-heavy tome and can be quite dense for those who have no prior experience or training in linguistics. Moreover, these three aspects of his theory are not as important for biblical structuralism as the final two—actant and actantial model (which is why these others are only given cursory discussion here).

This occurs in Genesis 32, when both the sender and opponent turn out to be none other than Yahweh (see further below).[43] Actantial roles, however, need not be filled by people; in the story of the good Samaritan (Luke 10:25–37), the wine, oil, and donkey may all be classified as filling the role of helper.[44] In the creation story, the role of opponent may be filled by chaos, as typified in the turbulent primordial waters that are held at bay by the Spirit (Gen 1).

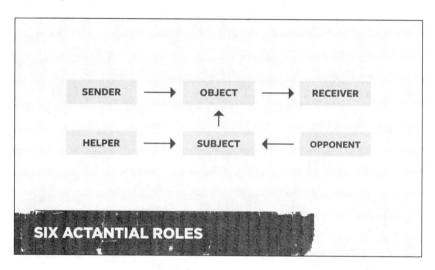

SIX ACTANTIAL ROLES

Greimas also developed the concept of the isotopy—that is, the repetition of a basic meaning trait. In the sentence "She drank some juice," both "drank" and "juice" refer to liquids.[45] Repetition of the reference to liquids creates an isotopy and allows for a more uniform interpretation of the sentence that would not be possible if, instead, it had read "She ate some juice." One could call this a "theme" or "motif." Overall, Greimas's greatest contribution to literary structuralism was the development of a comprehensive universal framework for narratives; his conceptualization of the actantial model, for instance, has been widely drawn on in biblical structuralism.

---

43. Barton, *Reading the Old Testament*, 117.

44. Vernon K. Robbins, "Structuralism in Biblical Interpretation and Theology," *The Thomist* 42 (1978): 361.

45. Patte and Parker define an isotopy as "a coherent set of deep values"; see Daniel Patte and Judson Parker, "A Structural Exegesis of Genesis 2 and 3," *Semeia* 18 (1980): 56.

Indeed, one could divide biblical structuralism into two parallel strands, one descended from Greimas and the other from Lévi-Strauss.

7.2.6 BIBLICAL STRUCTURALISM

So far, we have not mentioned biblical structuralism, but the preceding is a necessary prerequisite for understanding where biblical structuralism came from and how it modified structuralism to fit its own ends. Structural analysis of the Bible in particular finds its roots in Lévi-Strauss's essay "The Structural Study of Myth," which is one chapter of his larger work on structural anthropology (1958).[46] In it, he analyzes myths in terms of the relations between various actions and the paradigms produced by the combination of relations. Three years after its publication, Edmund Leach (1910–1989) published an essay titled "Lévi-Strauss in the Garden of Eden" (also known as "Genesis as Myth"), in which he attempted to provide a structural analysis of the first few chapters of Genesis.[47] Far from being an acceptance of the philosophy of structuralism, Leach's analysis was an attempt to apply the methodology of literary structuralism to the biblical text without the methodology's philosophical framework. Leach focused on the elements of redundancy (that many myths occur in multiple versions) and binary opposition, such as life/death, male/female, and human/divine. By applying Lévi-Strauss's methodology, Leach creates an elaborate diagram of the binary oppositions and their mediations in the biblical "creation myth," especially those of life/death and incest/procreation. Regardless of his conclusions and whether one finds them valuable, Leach inaugurated a new era of biblical criticism.

While Lévi-Strauss and Paul Ricoeur (1913–2005) doubted the applicability of literary structuralism to the Bible, others followed in Leach's footsteps, prioritizing structuralist method over structuralist philosophy.[48] Biblical scholars in the 1970s looked to structuralism to allow them to deal with new questions in a new way. Structuralism's focus on synchronicity

---

46. For a good summary of this article and its implications for the development of biblical structuralism, see Richard Jacobson, "The Structuralists and the Bible," *Int* 28 (1974): 146–64.

47. Edmund Leach, "Lévi-Strauss in the Garden of Eden: An Examination of Some Recent Developments in the Analysis of Myth," *Transactions of the New York Academy of Sciences (Series 2)* 23 (1961): 386–96.

48. David Greenwood, *Structuralism and the Biblical Text* (Berlin: Mouton, 1985), 16.

allowed them to take the biblical text "as is," circumventing the need to discuss the possible diachronic development of the text. Emphasis on structure, moreover, allowed for a greater freedom to focus on the unity and intertextuality of biblical themes. Narrative coherence was the focus, bracketing out discussion of sources, religious history, and textual disunity. Questions of what the biblical passage meant as a coherent text on its own terms unashamedly took center stage instead of being relegated to a back corner while historical criticism tore the text apart.

In 1972, Roland Barthes published a structuralist analysis of Genesis 32, the story of Jacob wrestling the angel at Peniel.[49] He discerned two different ways of reading the narrative that in a historical reading would most likely be attributed to different sources.[50] Taking the synchronic view, Barthes was able to assert that *both* ways of reading the story are exegetically valid. Thus, two different but equal structures can be distinguished and inter-woven to create meaning. Moreover, reading it against the backdrop of Propp's folktale formula, Barthes comes to the conclusion that this tale has an interesting twist on the roles Propp outlined: the originator of the quest (the one who commissions the hero's quest) and the opponent (the one who hinders the hero on his quest) are, in fact, the same character— Yahweh. Barthes's work presents a compelling account of why the text is so unsettling. The structure of folktales does not normally allow for the origi-nator and opponent to be the same character; that this is true for Genesis 32 creates a feeling of disorientation.[51] Thus, one can see how structuralism is capable of explaining how a text means, not just what it means.

In 1969, Paul Beauchamp published *Création et séparation*, a structural-ist study of Genesis 1-2.[52] In keeping with structuralism's ahistorical bent,

---

49. Roland Barthes, "The Struggle with the Angel: Textual Analysis of Genesis 32:23-33," in *Structural Analysis and Biblical Exegesis: Interpretational Essays*, trans. Alfred M. Johnson Jr. (Pittsburgh: Pickwick, 1974), 21-33.

50. White discusses the correspondences between these two ways of reading and Gunkel's sources ; see Hugh C. White, "French Structuralism and OT Narrative Analysis: Roland Barthes," *Semeia* 3 (1975): 99-127.

51. Barton, *Reading the Old Testament*, 118.

52. Paul Beauchamp, *Création et séparation. Étude exégétique du chapitre premier de la Genèse* (Paris: Aubier, 1969). The summary of Beauchamp's conclusions presented here is based on that of Barton, *Reading the Old Testament*, 122-27. For another account of Beauchamp's work, see Paul Ricoeur, *Figuring the Sacred: Religion, Narrative, and Imagination* (Minneapolis: Fortress, 1995), 135-39.

Beauchamp focused on the text itself rather than questions of historical composition; meaning, he argued, has more to do with the shape of the text and its internal relations—its literary syntax—than with the content it actually asserts.[53] In his analysis of Genesis 1:1–2:1, he breaks the text at Genesis 1:19, creating two almost exactly equal halves of 206 and 207 words apiece.[54] These two halves form a diptych contrasting inanimate creation, whose pinnacle is the creation of the luminaries, and animate creation, whose pinnacle is humanity; this structure underscores the theme of the status of humanity.[55] He also points out that there is a second narrative structure that interweaves with the first: the culmination of creation in the inauguration of the Sabbath day and worship, demarcated from the first half with the creation of the luminaries to mark the times and seasons.[56] Thus, the structure of Genesis 1:1–2:1 is twofold: one structure is concerned with the status of humanity, and the other is concerned with worship and the Sabbath. While neither of these themes is stated within the chapter as its explicit purpose (or focus), it is inescapable that Beauchamp has identified important thematic elements that are a part of the text. Beauchamp's analysis differs from that of Barthes in that Beauchamp's purpose was to delineate the structures of the text in front of him rather than to use what he found in that text as an example for more universal literary phenomena.[57]

In the following decade, structuralist analyses of the Bible increased significantly in America; the Society of Biblical Literature (SBL) Press published several collections of structuralist essays in its journal *Semeia* from 1972 to the early 1980s. More than anything, the proliferation of methodologies proved that there was more than one way to skin the structuralist cat. This, in part, was due to how biblical scholars derived their methodology from different nonbiblical structuralists, e.g., Algirdas Greimas and Claude Lévi-Strauss.[58] Those who followed Greimas focused more on actantial

---

53. Barton, *Reading the Old Testament*, 123.
54. Barton, *Reading the Old Testament*, 123.
55. Barton, *Reading the Old Testament*, 124.
56. Barton, *Reading the Old Testament*, 124.
57. Barton, *Reading the Old Testament*, 125.
58. That is not to say that these are the only two structuralists who influenced biblical structuralism. Rather, Greimas and Lévi-Strauss are representative of the two major methodological frameworks adopted in biblical structuralism. Biblical structuralists no doubt drew on concepts drawn from other structuralists such as Roman Jakobson and Vladimir Propp.

models and the concepts outlined in his narrative structure. Those who followed Lévi-Strauss emphasized binary oppositions and their mediations. This is complicated by how the analyses of biblical scholars interested in applying structuralist methods ended up being methodologically weaker due to the rejection of structuralist philosophy. The application of structuralist methodology was less consistent and tended to be interwoven with remnants of the biblical historical-critical method. Scholars with commitments to a specific interpretation of a passage might use structuralism to "prove" their preconceived notion of what the text meant rather than allowing the method to bring out meaning.[59] We can see this by examining how different scholars approach the same text (Gen 2–3) using a structuralist-based method.[60]

R. C. Culley rejected the philosophical tenets of French structuralism, specifically its ahistorical bent, but saw it as a useful tool to study biblical stories.[61] While accepting the usefulness of secular structuralism's synchronic analysis, he was openly interested in relating synchronic analysis to historical analysis, specifically form criticism. Like Lévi-Strauss, he was interested in how stories and story groups (i.e., genres) are related to one another, leading to an interest in biblical narratives that recur in one or more versions (like the sister-wife stories in Genesis). Given his rejection of structuralist philosophy, however, his methodology was less strict. Unable to let go of diachronic study entirely, he approaches the Genesis narrative as a composite text of "conjoined and subjoined narrative units in standard forms"—the interweaving of structuralism and form criticism is readily apparent.[62] The entire narrative structure is equivalent to the

---

59. The criticism that ideology drove structuralism rather than allowing the latter to change the former is not unique to biblical structuralism. It is, however, often more apparent that this is taking place in biblical structuralism, and critics of this propensity are often much louder when religious belief is at stake. One of the major criticisms of poststructuralism is precisely one's inability to be free of one's own preconceptions when interpreting any text.

60. *Semeia* 18, edited by Daniel Patte, presented a variety of structuralist interpretations of Gen 2–3 as well as scholarly critical responses. This survey of different approaches is based on the essays in that volume. The response essay by Kovacs is particularly helpful for his summary and critique of essays by Culley, Jobling, and Boomershine; see Brian Watson Kovacs, "Structure and Narrative Rhetoric in Genesis 2–3: Reflections on the Problem of Non-Convergent Structuralist Exegetical Methodologies," *Semeia* 18 (1980): 139–47.

61. Robert C. Culley, "Action Sequences in Genesis 2–3," *Semeia* 18 (1980): 25–33.

62. Kovacs, "Structure and Narrative Rhetoric," 142.

sum of the narrative structures present in the formal blocks of text. His methodological fuzziness leads to a problem: he fails to answer the question of what happens to the structure of a text when actantial units succeed one another or are interwoven.[63] In strict secular structuralist analysis, this would not be a problem because the diachronic, formal aspects of the text would be ignored.

David Jobling's analysis, on the other hand, lends itself more readily to the broader structuralist belief that texts reflect universal structures of consciousness.[64] Specifically, his focus on the spatio-temporal dimensions of the text can be perceived as human consciousness' perception and categorization of the world as either inside or outside. In Genesis 2–3, his interest in the spatio-temporal inside/outside opposition expresses itself in how humanity and Yahweh mediate these oppositions through their (potential) interactions with creation. In structuralist terminology, inside/outside is a fundamental binary opposition in this text's deep structure, an organizing principle for how the story unfolds, e.g., the implications of humanity being either inside or outside the garden. An important conclusion from his work is that this text is fundamentally "open," meaning that the possibility for multiple meanings is built into the deep structure of the text. Unlike Culley's, his analysis reads much more explicitly as structuralist and therefore has a cleaner method.[65]

Thomas Boomershine is heavily influenced by Freudian psychoanalysis—a common association in other structuralist disciplines—and therefore focuses on the latent sexual oppositions in the Genesis narrative.[66] Like Barthes, he deduces a series of codes (alimentary, animal, sexual, and life/death) that interweave to produce meaning.[67] Nevertheless, Boomershine cannot escape his interest in history—specifically, the historical cultural

---

63. Kovacs, "Structure and Narrative Rhetoric," 142–43.

64. David Jobling, "The Myth Semantics of Genesis 2:4b–3:24," *Semeia* 18 (1980): 41–49.

65. Jobling also wrote an article discussing three other biblical scholars' versions of structuralism. He, more than Culley, is aware that biblical structuralism takes on many forms based on the scholar's commitment to certain tenets of structuralist philosophy and methodology. See David Jobling, "Structuralism, Hermeneutics, and Exegesis: Three Recent Contributions to the Debate," *USQR* 34 (1979): 135–47.

66. Thomas E. Boomershine, "The Structure of Narrative Rhetoric in Genesis 2–3," *Semeia* 18 (1980): 113–29.

67. Boomershine, "Structure of Narrative Rhetoric," 126–28.

code of ancient Israel. He concludes his analysis of the deep structure by
positing an opposition between the fertility cult and Yahwism, which he
argues is a reflection of a fundamental opposition within the worldview of
ancient Israel.[68] Boomershine's reliance on Barthes's codes allows for this
kind of interweaving of history with the synchronic text. Note, however,
that by positing this opposition as part of the deep structure, Boomershine
is leaning toward a historical meaning of the text rather than a purely
synchronic one. This example reveals that no matter how much structuralists may try to avoid history, there are times when this simply cannot
be done (especially within historical texts that make historical claims).[69]
Boomershine's analysis also reveals the ways in which biblical structuralism differs depending on which structuralist the biblical scholar follows.
Boomershine is more indebted to Barthes, which makes his analysis that
much different from Culley's and Jobling's, who are both more indebted
to Lévi-Strauss.

Not all biblical structuralists are as methodologically fuzzy or eclectic
as these early examples. Even Jobling, who was more consistent in method
than Culley or Boomershine, did not construct a full-fledged structuralist
method for biblical criticism. Daniel Patte, on the other hand, did just that.
Patte is noted for his attempt to both understand and faithfully reproduce
the system of French structuralist thought in biblical studies, especially
that of Claude Lévi-Strauss. For Patte, the goal of biblical structuralism
is to elucidate the text's system of deep values, also known as the semantic universe. In their essay on Genesis 2–3, Patte and Judson Parker assert
that deep values are "elements of the vision of life and of the world held
as self-evident or revealed by the author or redactor (whether collective
or individual."[70] Deep values constitute the "meaning horizon" of the text
and should not be equated with either the central themes of the text or its
focus. They are the background against which the story is told, "the logical
and symbolic framework that underlies the other dimensions of the text

---

68. Boomershine, "Structure of Narrative Rhetoric," 127.

69. The poststructuralist critique of structuralism's ahistorical method is discussed in
§7.4 Limitations of Structural Criticism.

70. Daniel Patte and Judson F. Parker, "A Structural Exegesis of Genesis 2 and 3," *Semeia*
18 (1980): 55–56.

and through which they are articulated."[71] They provide the boundaries for textual meaning but are not themselves the meaning. In the book version of the *Wizard of Oz*, Dorothy and her companions discover that they only perceived the Emerald City to be green because they had been given a pair of green-tinted glasses when they entered the city. Patte's deep values can be compared to that set of green glasses: they provided the parameters through which Dorothy viewed the city; without them, she and her friends would have had a fundamentally different perception of what the city was like. Put another way, deep values are textual manifestations of the author's faith or worldview that provide the framework for meaning. Although the explanation may appear convoluted, Patte's "deep values" are no different from the deep structures discussed earlier in this chapter, just explained in another way.

According to Patte, deep values are reflected in the symbolic dimensions of the text and their metaphorical connotations (i.e., abstract concepts).[72] These, in turn, are expressed in the semantic (and thereby narratival) oppositions, a.k.a. binary oppositions. For example, Genesis 1 reflects a binary opposition between divided/undivided that is expressed literarily in the oppositions between sea and land, light and darkness, etc. The figurative content of the narrative is thus reduced into abstract categories and stated in terms of binary opposition. In sum, beneath any text is a system of deep values representing the worldview of the author and his culture. This system provides the necessary framework through which the story is told. Deep values are often expressed as abstract concepts, which are, in the narrative, manifested in a system of semantic oppositions expressed through figurative language. Like Barthes, Patte sees the text consisting of several structural systems that interweave to form meaning, though he does not equate them with Barthes's codes. The text does not have *a* structure; rather it has a plurality of structures. The linear progression of the narrative action takes its shape by means of this interweaving of systems.

Patte's version of biblical structuralism comes closest to applying the analytical style of French structuralism to the biblical text. The value of such a rigorous method for biblical structuralism is that Patte is able to

---

71. Glendon E. Bryce, "A Response to Patte and Parker," *Semeia* 18 (1980): 77.
72. Patte and Parker, "Structural Exegesis," 56.

explain why biblical texts produce a multiplicity of meanings. While the system of deep values provides the framework for meaning, it is not equivalent with a singular, absolute meaning of the text. As with the French structuralists, Patte believes that texts are inherently multivocal, meaning that they have more than one possible meaning. This is why he speaks of a "meaning horizon"—that is, a limit for potential meanings.[73] Unlike postmodern thought, in which texts can either mean anything or have no meaning other than what is "read in" by the reader, structuralists like Patte argue for multiple, but limited, meanings for a single text. The deep values provide the limits to possible meanings and, since they manifest the worldview of the author(s), a text cannot mean something contrary to or not conceived of in the text's semantic universe.

The preceding survey of biblical structuralism reveals a sharp divide between scholars who accept the fundamental philosophy of structuralism and those who see it as a useful methodology for exegesis but reject its all-encompassing philosophical structure. Yet even with this division there is a fundamental similarity in that biblical structuralism is far more text bound than secular literary structuralism. As originally conceived, the goal of literary structuralism was to illuminate the shared, universal structures of meaning that underlie every text in an attempt to understand how human beings construct meaning. The text was only useful insofar as it provided a particular manifestation of these structures. Because biblical structuralism was dealing with sacred text, it was far more interested in discussing the meaning of this text, and most biblical structuralism stopped short of analyzing the universal implications for how specific biblical texts produced meaning. This has led some to argue that biblical structuralism is not true structuralism at all, but rather a distortion of it, an application of method without accepting the philosophy that gave birth to it. Regardless, it is undeniable that biblical structuralism owes its entire existence to the Franco-Russian philosophy and its attendant methods.

7.3 APPLICATIONS OF STRUCTURAL CRITICISM

As exemplified in the historical survey, structuralist analysis is most readily applied to the narrative material of the Bible.

---

73. Patte and Parker, "Structural Exegesis," 56.

7.3.1 OLD TESTAMENT

Propp's study of the narrative structure of folktales provided a model for approaching "authorless" texts.[74] These are the stories a culture shares orally for generations before they start to write them down—their myths, legends, fables, and folklore. The affinities between this type of literature and the OT had been noted since at least the late nineteenth century.[75] Thus, moving from folklore to myth to biblical text made sense. The book of Genesis received the most attention, for it most readily fit into the mythic framework. Beauchamp's analysis of Genesis 1:1–2:1 was noted earlier, along with several analyses of chapters 2–3, and Roland Barthes's analysis of Genesis 32. Yet these are not the only chapters that received attention in structuralist methodology. Robert Polzin, for example, analyzed the three versions of the sister-wife narrative in Genesis 12, 20, and 26.[76] While novel, most of his analysis centers on the differences in surface structure instead of moving into the deep structure that might underlie all three versions. What he ends up with is more akin to rhetorical criticism than structuralist criticism. Polzin is distinct from other biblical structuralists in his interest in establishing the narrative structure of the entire book of Job.[77] Following Greimas and Jakobson, Polzin seeks to discern the framework, code, and message/meaning of the book. By breaking the text into functional units based on their mediation of oppositions or contradictions, Polzin distills a paradigmatic pattern that leads him to posit the semantic code underlying Job. His highly detailed analysis results in a deep structure that moves the reader from "equilibrium without insight" into "equilibrium with insight" by means of "the courageous integration of contradiction and resolution."[78] Although he openly disavows structuralist philosophy, his analysis more

---

74. See §7.2.3 Vladimir Propp and the Morphology of a Folktale.

75. For example, in 1895 Hermann Gunkel argued that Gen 1 was influenced by Babylonian mythology; see Hermann Gunkel, *Schöpfung und Chaos in Urzeit und Endzeit: Eine religionsges- chichtliche Untersuchung über Gen 1 und Ap Joh 12*, with contributions by Heinrich Zimmern (Göttingen: Vandenhoeck und Ruprecht, 1895). English translation: Hermann Gunkel, *Creation and Chaos in the Primeval Era and the Eschaton: A Religio-Historical Study of Genesis 1 and Revelation 12*, with contributions by Heinrich Zimmern, trans. K. William Whitney Jr. (Grand Rapids: Eerdmans, 2006).

76. Robert Polzin, " 'The Ancestress of Israel in Danger' in Danger," *Semeia* 3 (1975): 81–98.

77. Robert Polzin, "The Framework of the Book of Job," *Int* 28 (1974): 182–200.

78. Polzin, "Framework," 200.

closely approximates that of secular structuralism in his disavowal of historical research on the book of Job.

As exhibited by Polzin, not all structuralist exegesis focuses on discerning the structure of a specific chapter. R. C. Culley follows Lévi-Strauss in attempting to compare all examples of a specific type within a genre of literature, specifically miracle stories and deception stories.[79] His goal is to see what commonalities exist among the stories themselves and between the different groups of stories. In his analysis of miracle stories, he discerns the common structure problem/miracle/solution, which he contrasts with the structure of deception stories, problem/deception/solution. This leads him to propose a fundamental opposition between miracle stories and deception stories that manifests the opposition between Yahweh resolving a problem and human beings seeking to resolve a problem on their own.

Excepting Polzin and a few others, most structuralist exegesis of the OT has focused on discrete narrative units, whether individually or as a group typifying a specific genre. That many of the Pentateuchal narratives could be isolated from each other made structuralist analysis that much easier, but it left open the question of how one is to conceive of the larger structure of the Pentateuch (and the rest of the OT) if not as a concatenation of smaller units. This question has not yet sufficiently been answered within structural criticism.

This brief overview of the application of structuralist criticism to the OT has shown that there are many ways to "do" structuralist criticism. Unlike some other methods of biblical engagement, the process of biblical structuralist analysis is not monolithic—one does not always start at point A, proceed to point B, and end at point Z. To get a better idea of how structuralist analysis can work, we now survey Patte and Parker's analysis of Genesis 2–3 in more detail.[80]

Patte and Parker begin by noting the goal of structuralist analysis: "to elucidate the system of deep values, or semantic universe, presupposed by

---

79. Robert C. Culley, "Themes and Variations in Three Groups of OT Narratives," *Semeia* 3 (1975): 3–13.

80. Patte and Parker, "Structural Exegesis." This essay was chosen primarily because Daniel Patte is self-consciously attempting to adapt the French structuralist methodology to biblical studies rather than, say, using it as one method among others. This lends itself to a clearer, more concise, and more consistent methodology.

the text in its present form."[81] The determination of deep values is based on an analysis of the narrative organization of the text. The first step in analyzing the narrative organization is the determination of narrative levels. While they do not outline in detail how this is determined,[82] they distinguish between two kinds of *narrative levels*: (1) narrative development based on an opinion or interpretation by another character in the narrative, and (2) straightforward presentation of events without interpretation. On this basis, they divide Genesis 2–3 into two levels. The primary level, which reflects straightforward presentation of events, is Genesis 2:4–15 and Genesis 3:22–24; the secondary level, Genesis 2:16–3:21, rests on Yahweh's interpretation that the man must perform or refrain from certain actions in order to be in right relationship with the rest of creation. In other words, how the narrative unfolds in Genesis 2:16–3:21 is a direct result of the narrative assuming the perspective of one of the characters, Yahweh, and allowing his interpretation of the events to dominate how the story develops.

Patte and Parker then move on to discuss the system of transformations presupposed by each of the narrative levels. Their outline of the system of transformation is quite complex, and a full account is beyond the scope of this chapter. However, a few brief examples are noteworthy. In their system, the two methods of watering noted in Genesis 2:6b and 2:10b differentiate the garden from the rest of the land, creating an opposition between these two locales.[83] At the primary level, this distinction helps to spatially define the narrative insofar as the man is moved from outside the garden to within, and it is necessary that these be distinct spaces for that shift to be important. At the secondary level, they note that the narrative evinces a threefold structure that reflects the parallel actions and reactions related to Adam, the woman, and the serpent. A transformation at this level includes the shift from Adam and his wife not feeling shame (Gen 2:25) to their recognition of their nakedness and attempt to hide it after eating the fruit of the tree of knowledge (Gen 3:7). It is important to note that, while

---

81. Patte and Parker, "Structural Exegesis," 55.

82. They refer the reader to Daniel Patte's book coauthored with his wife for a detailed discussion of how one distinguishes narrative levels. See Daniel Patte and Aline Patte, *Structural Exegesis: From Theory to Practice* (Philadelphia: Fortress, 1978), specifically chaps. 2 and 3.

83. In Genesis 2:6b, the land (אֲדָמָה; *'ădāmâ*) is watered by אֵד (*'ed*; variously translated as "mists" or "subterranean streams"), wheras the garden in 2:10b is watered by river(s) (נָהָר; *nāhār*).

in their analysis transformations may include binary oppositions (such as the opposition between garden and land based on methods of watering), it also includes actions in the plot, such as the curses on man, woman, and serpent, each of which transforms their previous relationships (with each other, with their environment, and with Yahweh).

The next step in their analysis moves them to the "*symbolic* and *semantic organization* of the text," which is based on their analysis of the various transformations.[84] Pulling from Greimas, they assert, "to a *narrative opposition* (an opposition of narrative transformations) corresponds a *semantic opposition* (an opposition of semantic features manifested symbolically by the qualifications) *of contradiction* (the 'diagonal' of a semiotic square, such as A and non-A)."[85] In other words, narrative oppositions reflect semantic oppositions; the opposition between garden and land noted above is used to characterize the man based on his location in either sphere. Within the garden, he has creative agency (the power to increase the fertility of the land); prior to his move to the garden, he had no agency, and after he is expelled from the garden, this agency is severely diminished due to the curse in Genesis 3:17.

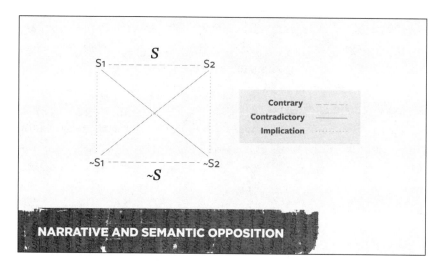

NARRATIVE AND SEMANTIC OPPOSITION

---

84. Patte and Parker, "Structural Exegesis," 62, emphasis added.
85. Patte and Parker, "Structural Exegesis," 62, emphasis original.

In the secondary narrative of Genesis 2:16–3:21, Patte and Parker contrast the narrative elements of the shameful couple hiding their nakedness (Gen 3:7) with the experience of the couple after they are clothed (Gen 3:21)—specifically, Adam's power to name and Eve's power as the mother of all living beings. They claim that this contrast at the narrative level reflects a symbolic opposition—namely, the different worlds in which the man and his wife attempt to define themselves. Their shame at their sexuality and attempt to cover themselves with leaves is viewed as their attempt to identify with the plant world. This is contrasted with the (appropriate?) view that they should be identified with the animal world, as is symbolized by their skin coverings and acceptance of their own sexuality in Genesis 3:21.

The next, and final, step in their analysis is the delineation of the system of deep values. According to Patte and Parker's method, the symbolic organization of the text directly reflects the system of deep values presupposed by the text. The opposition of physical space at the primary level, for example, reflects the fundamental opposition between divided and undifferentiated space.[86] Their analysis of the deep values underlying the opposition in Genesis 3:7 and 3:21 is much more elaborate, as it involves a full analysis of the anthropology that underscores the secondary narrative. However, they argue that this opposition reflects a deep value opposition between being alienated from the divine by being in the vegetal world and belonging to the world of living creatures, which places them in proper relationship to the deity.[87]

Finally, Patte and Parker close with the reminder that the system of deep values is not the focus of the text, but rather it is "what focuses the text and its thematic and figurative dimensions."[88] The deep value opposition between divided and undifferentiated space is necessary for the story to take the shape that it does, but it is not the *point* of the story. A summary of the steps in their method is: (1) determination of narrative levels, (2) determination of pertinent narrative transformations at each narrative

---

86. Patte and Parker use the notation X to refer to a concept that is a part of the system of deep values.

87. For a fuller discussion, see Patte and Parker, "Structural Exegesis," 74. This is part of a longer discussion of the deep value system that covers pages 63–74.

88. Patte and Parker, "Structural Exegesis," 75.

level, (3) determination of symbolic and semantic oppositions that underlie the narrative transformations, and (4) determination of deep values that provide the meaning horizon of the text. Not every biblical structuralist analysis proceeds in this manner, but most include one or more aspects of this analysis to varying degrees.

7.3.2 NEW TESTAMENT

Structuralism in the NT has focused primarily on the Synoptic Gospels, especially Jesus' parables. This is understandable given that, like folktales, parables are relatively brief and stylized and have a more readily apparent structure. There are enough of them to provide comparative data, but not so many as to be impossible to survey. The first volume in *Semeia* (1972) was entirely devoted to a structuralist approach to the parables, and the second (1973) to the parable of the good Samaritan (Luke 10:25–37). The interaction between John Dominic Crossan and Dan Via in the latter volume provides insight into the world of structuralism in NT studies.[89] While their arguments are too detailed to include here, their major disagreement concerns the nature of the actantial model that defines the structure of a parable. For Via, the story of the good Samaritan is not a parable because it is not a metaphor for the kingdom of God (a definition of parable that he accepts from Crossan). Moreover, the collapsing of the narrative's subject (the Samaritan) with the ordainer of the mission (also the Samaritan) violates the fundamental distinction between the two that is seen in the rest of Jesus' parables, where the ordainer is always Yahweh and the subject is a distinct character. Since the parable of the good Samaritan has a different deep structure from, say, the parable of the prodigal son, the two must belong to different genres and function in different ways. Crossan responds by promoting a different actantial model for parable stories in an effort to make the good Samaritan fit that mold. This brings to the forefront the problem of perception in structuralist analysis: structuralists

---

89. John Dominic Crossan, "Structuralist Analysis and the Parable of Jesus: A Reply to D. O. Via, Jr, 'Parable and Example Story: A Literary-Structuralist Approach,' *Semeia* 1 (1974)," *Semeia* 1 (1974): 192–221; Dan O. Via, "Parable and Example Story: A Literary-Structuralist Approach," *Semeia* 1 (1974): 105–33; and Dan O. Via, "A Response to Crossan, Funk, and Petersen," *Semeia* 1 (1974): 222–35.

may perceive the deep structure of the same text differently, resulting in different analyses.

One of the few structuralist analyses that attempts to provide a structure for an entire book of the NT is that of Jean Calloud.[90] Starting with selective pericopes, Calloud seeks to determine the deep structure of the entire book of Mark by comparing the deep structures of the smaller narrative units. His goal is to explain the seemingly random placement of narrative sequences in the life of Jesus. By working out the deep structure of a "micro-narrative," he is able to move into successively larger swaths of texts, which he compares to an archaeologist proposing a general hypothesis based on a localized excavation. In methodological terms, he adds an additional step to the method followed by Patte and Parker. After determining the deep structure of the smaller narrative, he then compares this to the deep structures of other narratives to determine their relationship with each other. He leaves it to others to verify whether his specific micro-narrative structure actually works for the entirety of the Gospel of Mark (which he was unable to cover in his article).

Little structuralist analysis has been done outside the Synoptic Gospels. Daniel Patte, for example, has applied his Lévi-Straussian analysis to Paul's Letter to the Galatians (specifically Gal 1:1-10).[91] His analysis focuses on the mediated opposites Paul utilizes as part of the universal semantic code, such as the opposition between "the gospel as teaching" and "the other gospel," which is mediated by the person and work of Paul himself.

7.4 LIMITATIONS OF STRUCTURAL CRITICISM

In his insightful article on biblical structuralism, Vern Poythress discerns four distinct ways that structuralism can be applied to literature and the unique limitations of each.[92] The first method involves the wholesale

---

90. Calloud, "Structural Analysis." Daniel and Aline Patte also provide a structuralist interpretation of the book of Mark in their book; see Patte and Patte, *Structural Exegesis*. For a good review of their book and methodology, see Elizabeth Struthers Malbon, "The Theory and Practice of Structural Exegesis: A Review Article," *PRSt* 3 (1984): 273-82.

91. Daniel Patte, *What Is Structural Exegesis?* (Philadelphia: Fortress, 1976), 59-75.

92. See Poythress, "Structuralism and Biblical Studies." Similarly, Patte distinguishes between five categories of structuralist analysis: (1) studies aimed at elucidating the structures in a specific text, (2) purely theoretical research aimed at uncovering universal structures, (3) studies that focus on the structure of specific texts to determine universal structures, (4) deductive analysis that verifies particular structuralist theories, and (5) studies that focus

adoption of linguistic categories to describe literature, best exemplified by Jakobson and Lévi-Strauss. The weakness of this method is that linguistic categories are insufficient to describe the depth and richness of literature, resulting in a rather truncated view of texts. The second method utilizes semiotic categories to describe narrative discourse, as in Greimas. The problem with using semiotics is that, as a theory, it tends to only find those aspects in literature that it specifically allows for; in other words, it is in danger of imposing a structure on the text that is not actually present in the text.

The third and fourth methods are connected insofar as they both extend and transform linguistic categories in order to apply them to texts, differing only in whether this method is applied to a single text or to literature as a whole. In other words, the third method focuses on the textual *parole* and the fourth on the literary *langue* (see above). The third methodology works well with texts that are closed systems and easily abstracted from their context, such as lyric poetry and psalms. However, even if one grants that these can be extracted from their literary context, it is difficult to extract them from the history of Israel and its theological development. The fourth method, on the other hand, tends to be reductive. In other words, it collapses all difference for the sake of universality.

The accusation of being reductive has, in fact, been leveled at structuralism as a whole.[93] The assumption of universal structures in literature coupled with the explicit goal of discerning those universal structures by means of specific texts is practically inherently reductive. The danger has been less extreme in biblical structuralism than in structuralism more broadly, but the danger is still there. The search for common structures can lead to the collapse of all difference for the sake of unity, which is especially

---

on how specific textual systems contribute to the overall meaning of a specific text (see Patte, "One Text," 7–9). This classification system was not chosen here for a few reasons. First, a few of his categories do not seem to apply to biblical structuralism, namely categories (2) and (4). Second, his distinction between categories (1) and (5) is vague and therefore unhelpful. Finally, Poythress's categorization of how structuralist methods are applied is a more helpful and thorough way to differentiate methodology than Patte's categorization based on the goal. The same methodological application can be used for any of Patte's goals.

93. For example, Allan Rodway, *The Craft of Criticism* (Cambridge: Cambridge University Press, 1982), 188.

dangerous for the analysis of sacred texts as it may blur each pericope's unique voice. Instead of a polyphonic choir, one ends up with a monotone.

Structuralism in general has also been criticized for its preoccupation with theory at the expense of practical application. In an effort to produce more and more reliable and "scientific" methods aimed at the elucidation of universal generative structures, the application of these methods to particular texts has fallen by the wayside. Again, this is not as much of a problem in biblical structuralism, given its focus on the exegesis of the biblical text. However, argument over theory and method is still a problem, as is the case with Crossan and Via.

The lack of agreement regarding the correct way to approach a text may appear to argue against the usefulness of structuralism in literary analysis—a problem Brian Kovacs addresses in his article on the nonconvergence of structuralist methodology in Genesis 2–3.[94] Kovacs argues that the variation among structural approaches "coincides with a difference in the location of structural grounding."[95] In other words, the fundamentally open character of most texts and the variety within structuralism as a methodology means that different people will begin at different places. Biblical structuralists have not constructed a universally applicable method that both allows for the polyvalent nature of texts to be apparent and can be used by different people to produce the same result.

Others, most notably poststructuralists, have argued that the inherently unstable nature of textual meaning is the real problem with structuralist approaches.[96] The nonconvergence of methodology is the result of the inherently paradoxical nature of texts and the reader's inability to free herself from both the text's and her own social, historical, and cultural context. This latter accusation deals a blow to one of the fundamental tenets of structuralist thought—namely, that one should approach the text ahistorically. In itself, this assumption can lead to the denial of the importance of history altogether: all texts exist in a universal present that need not have any reference to their culture or history. According to poststructuralism, synchronic reading is impossible. Readers perceive meaning in

94. Kovacs, "Structure and Narrative Rhetoric."
95. Kovacs, "Structure and Narrative Rhetoric," 147.
96. On poststructuralism, see chap. 8 of the present volume.

the text through the lens of their own sociocultural history, and the same is true for the text itself. It cannot be freed from its historical context and development, no matter how much structuralists wish it were otherwise.

This is not to say that structuralism is more fraught with difficulty than any other method of biblical criticism. Many of the accusations leveled at structuralism as a whole do not apply to the unique way that biblical structuralism developed. Its self-professed distance from the philosophy of French structuralism makes many structuralist exegeses of the Bible immune to the dangers of reductionism and preoccupation with theory. The poststructuralist critique of subjectivity is more pressing, but it can also add a healthy corrective to structuralism. Ideally, biblical criticism should pay attention to both the synchronic and diachronic aspects of the text, as poststructuralism helpfully reminds us.

Issues specific to biblical structuralism include the assumption of a polyvalent text. For structuralists, texts are inherently multidimensional and can have several "correct" meanings (as well as many wrong ones). The deep structure of the text provides the limits to meanings, but rarely, if ever, does it narrow the text so as to produce only one meaning. This has the potential to be problematic for many conservative biblical scholars who are convinced that the text has only one meaning. Similarly, focus on universals may allow for one to escape dealing with the particularities of biblical revelation.

Disregard for authorial intent in the creation of meaning also flies in the face of much recent history in biblical criticism. Certain traditions perceive the idea that the author has no say in the meaning of the text (because meaning is inherent in the text itself) as undermining the integrity and validity of the Bible.[97] By exposing the fundamentally human character of deep structures, some readers could perceive structuralism as denying divine biblical inspiration. On the other hand, by taking the text at face value, structuralism is able to investigate the richness and fullness of textual meaning while also allowing for a greater degree of intertextuality than was possible in the historical method that had dominated biblical criticism ever since its inception. Questions of sources, disunity, incremental

---

97. For further discussion, see chap. 1 of this volume.

diachronic accretions, and historicity can safely be ignored in order to more fully discern what, why, and how the biblical text means.

7.5 CONTEMPORARY INFLUENCE OF STRUCTURAL CRITICISM

While biblical structuralism was having its heyday in America in the 1970s, the structuralist philosophy was already facing extensive critique in France. In fact, Roland Barthes, one of the most prominent structuralists, became one of its strongest critics. This movement, which came to be known as poststructuralism, emphasized the limitations of human science and sought to de-center the meaning of texts from the author and text themselves to the reader. Supporters of this movement argued that meaning was always perceived by the reader and changed based on the reader's preconceptions, which are shaped by culture, class, race, sexual orientation, etc. Poststructuralists critiqued structuralism's synchronicity, asserting that cultural concepts themselves have historical development. Whereas structuralists had focused on how cultural concepts had been understood by the author(s) in his/their own time, poststructuralists focused on how those concepts are understood by the reader in the present. Poststructuralism also criticized the power dynamic implicit in many of the binary oppositions posited by structuralists, such as male/female and divine/human. Poststructuralism attempted to expose the latent hierarchical structuring in binary oppositions and underscore how the seemingly subservient term (the second term) shapes the definition of the first, dominant term rather than vice versa, as had been the focus of structuralism.

Poststructuralist critique reached the United States in the 1970s, but its influence was not felt in biblical criticism until the 1980s. By the late 1980s, deconstruction of texts, including biblical texts, had come to the forefront of literary biblical criticism. Roland Barthes revisited Genesis 32 and, rather than focusing on "how" the text means, he fixates on the ambiguities and unsolvable aspects of the text, its "undecidability." Genesis 32 is now an example of how all texts resist our attempts to make them coherent. Deconstruction of texts—an approach that sought to prove how texts undermine themselves—replaced the interest in deep structures and semantic universes. Structuralist essays on biblical texts with their charts and diagrams and precise, technical vocabulary, which were so common in the 1970s and 1980s, are now no longer to be found.

Even prior to the poststructuralist critique, many biblical scholars had professed unease with the use of structuralism in biblical criticism. Carl Armerding, for instance, argued that structuralism could not be extricated from its antihistorical foundations; he asserted that biblical critics who were drawn to the methodology

> have not been sufficiently willing to face this claim, though structuralists from Lévi-Strauss to Ricoeur have repeated it. Unless the Bible is to be seen as (mere) myth, rather than a record of the unique redemptive acts of God in the history of a particular people, I am not sure that the hermeneutical structures of the new analysis even apply.[98]

Those who desired to use structuralism to circumvent historical criticism, especially source criticism, had not faced the larger hermeneutical implications of the methodology they had adopted. Armerding again summarizes succinctly: "It is not simply a handy way to circumvent a given documentary hypothesis, but rather an entire system of hermeneutics."[99] Given that it faced criticism even while it was the dominant methodology, it is unsurprising that it fell out of favor not long after it was critiqued more widely in the global arena.

Structuralism has, however, left its mark on biblical criticism. Its interest in holistic, synchronic reading of texts still informs much of biblical criticism. Brevard Childs might protest the association, but his work on canonical criticism has much in common with structuralist criticism—especially his dissatisfaction with historical criticism and emphasis on taking the text "as is."[100] Moreover, while the technical vocabulary of structuralism may have fallen out of fashion, that need not preclude an interest in either the deep structure of the text or the deep values/worldview of

---

98. Armerding, "Structural Analysis," 103. Culley himself expressed doubts as to whether his analysis, which did not accept the broad framework of structuralist philosophy, qualified as structural analysis; see Robert C. Culley, "Structural Analysis: Is It Done with Mirrors?," *Int* 28 (1974): 169.

99. Armerding, "Structural Analysis," 104.

100. For example, Brevard S. Childs, *Biblical Theology of the Old and New Testaments: Theological Reflection on the Christian Bible* (Minneapolis: Fortress, 1992), 719-27.

the author(s). Interest in and exposition of these aspects may still be found today in biblical commentaries, and it is still worthwhile for the student of the Bible to read structuralist essays. Regardless of its having fallen out of favor, structuralism is still a useful tool in elucidating how texts come to mean certain things (as was the case for Barthes's essay on Gen 32), why a text has a certain effect on a reader, and how it achieves this end.

Most importantly, structuralism brought rhetorical analysis to the forefront of biblical criticism. Indeed, rhetorical analysis shares many similar interests with structuralist analysis, but it lacks the philosophical framework of structuralism. Both are interested in the narrative structure of the text and how the text produces meaning. Rhetorical criticism is more openly interested in intended effect (i.e., the meaning that the author[s] attempted to convey), but it also asks the question of *how* this meaning is conveyed by the structures of the text. It is, in one sense, what is left when one brackets out structuralist philosophy and assumptions with an added emphasis on how the author produces certain effects in his audience.[101] Free from the philosophical tenets of structuralism, it was spared poststructuralist critique and still maintains a strong presence in biblical criticism to this day.

7.6 RESOURCES FOR FURTHER STUDY

Armerding, Carl. "Structural Analysis." *Themelios* 4, no. 3 (1979): 96–104.

> This article is a concise overview of structural criticism in biblical studies and its roots in French structuralism. Although it is incomplete, it is a good introduction, especially when read alongside Jacobson, Kovacs 1978, and Poythress.

Barton, John. *Reading the Old Testament: Method in Biblical Study*. Revised and enlarged edition. Louisville: Westminster John Knox, 1996.

> This is a quite excellent introduction to the different kinds of OT criticism. He is erudite in both presenting and evaluating the

---

101. Committed structuralists would probably protest, arguing that rhetorical criticism is fundamentally concerned with the surface structure of the text. This may be true of some rhetorical criticism, but the interest in intended effect requires the understanding of at least the basics of deep structure, or, at the very least, some such conceptualization of the text.

various methodologies, though not always as comprehensive with respect to history and development.

Calloud, Jean. "Toward a Structural Analysis of the Gospel of Mark." *Semeia* 16 (1979): 133–65.

Though at times a bit dense, Calloud is an excellent example of structuralist analysis of a single book in the NT. He is also a good representative of the methodology that starts with small narratives (micro-narratives) and works outward to larger bodies of text. He provides an insightful explanation of the differences between his method and those of other structuralist scholars in the Synoptic Gospels.

Greimas, A. J., J. Courtés, and Michael Rengstorf. "The Cognitive Dimension of Narrative Discourse." *New Literary History* 7 (1976): 433–47.

If one is looking for a fuller definition of specifically Greimas's technical vocabulary, this is a good place to start. It is more approachable than his book *Semiotics and Language*, but it still covers all the most important aspects of his method.

Jacobson, Richard. "The Structuralists and the Bible." *Int* 28 (1974): 146–64.

This article offers an excellent introduction to those elements of structuralist interpretation that are relevant for biblical criticism. It is accessible to a wide audience, and Jacobson is careful to explain relevant technical jargon as well as provide a partial history of the historical development and its current (to him) use in biblical criticism. It should be read alongside Kovacs (1978), Armerding, and Poythress for a better understanding of how French and biblical structuralism are related.

Kovacs, Brian Watson. "Philosophical Foundations for Structuralism." *Semeia* 10 (1978): 85–105.

This article is an excellent introduction to structuralism as it was perceived by a practitioner of the discipline. He provides a concise and thorough examination of the philosophical foundations for biblical structuralism and its history, as well as overviewing perceived weaknesses with the method and how they can be potentially overcome. He is clearly a proponent of the method, and while at times he does not clearly define his terms, this is still one of the best overview articles of biblical structuralism to be found.

Patte, Daniel, and Judson Parker. "A Structural Exegesis of Genesis 2 and 3." *Semeia* 18 (1980): 56–75.

This is a good introduction to Patte's theory of deep values as applied to the narrative of Genesis 2–3. The theoretical and methodological discussion in the introduction is much easier to read than Patte and Patte. The structural analysis of Genesis is replete with diagrams and provides a window into the usage of semiotic squares and actantial models in biblical structuralism.

Patte, Daniel, and Aline Patte. *Structural Exegesis: From Theory to Practice.* Philadelphia: Fortress, 1978.

This book is the foundation for all Daniel Patte attempts to do in bringing a more thoroughgoing French structuralism to biblical criticism. Densely packed with his own unique vocabulary for biblical structural analysis, his and his wife's tome is not always an easy read. Those with a desire to see how biblical structuralism can be done in a methodologically precise way should consult this volume.

Poythress, Vern S. "Structuralism and Biblical Studies." *JETS* 21 (1978): 221–37.

This is an excellent discussion of the history, method, and potential problems of structuralism in biblical criticism. While his historical overview is not entirely complete, it is quite thorough, and his discussion of the hazards of structuralism for biblical scholars (as well as how they could be overcome) is eminently accessible and engaging to a wide audience. Kovacs 1978, Jacobson, and Armerding are all valuable resources, but this one is by far the best of the bunch.

8

POSTSTRUCTURAL CRITICISM

John DelHousaye

Poststructuralism is more of a philosophy than a type of literary criticism, but this stance toward reality has informed many of the literary approaches to Scripture in this volume. French philosopher Jacques
Derrida (1930–2004) coined the term "deconstruction," which has become
an alternative label.[1] Contrary to a popular misunderstanding, deconstructing a text is not an act of semantic destruction, but of love. Instead
of limiting its expression or forcing one's agenda on it, this way of reading
shows how texts are too meaningful for any final delimitation. There is
always a surplus of meaning.

Traditionally, before the rise of the historical-grammatical method,
with its emphasis on ascertaining a single true meaning, Jews and
Christians celebrated the Bible's potential for multiple meanings. They
would employ a fourfold reading strategy, the Garden (Hebrew *pardes*)
or the Chariot (Latin *quadriga*), which posits God as the ultimate author
of Scripture, who speaks afresh to each generation.[2] Yet these faiths also
struggled to find boundaries for interpretation that ensured continuity
with their tradition.

---

1. These terms are not synonymous, however. "Deconstruction" originates from within
structuralism as part of the movement toward poststructuralism, "within which deconstruction would be identified as a major force"; see Jonathan Culler, *On Deconstruction: Theory and
Criticism after Structuralism* (Ithaca, NY: Cornell University Press, 1982), 30.

2. Likewise, we should think of deconstruction as a plural, not singular, concept; Nicole
Anderson, "Deconstruction and Ethics: An (Ir)responsibility," in *Jacques Derrida: Key Concepts*,
ed. Claire Colebrook (London: Routledge, 2015), 50.

8.1 DEFINITION AND GOAL OF
POSTSTRUCTURAL CRITICISM

Gary Philips, a professor of religion who studied at *École Pratique des Hautes Études*, where Derrida was director of studies, offers this definition and goal:

> Poststructuralist criticism, in particular criticism owing to deconstructive thought, seeks to amplify the unvoiced and the unthought by demystifying the "natural," the "intuitive" and the "abstract" of criticism for what they are—institutionalized, cultural constructs which articulate very specific arrangements of power and control. With respect to biblical criticism, the non-theoretical and anti-theoretical complaints often muttered from traditional historical-critical corners represent institutionalized, empowered positions that experience themselves at risk.[3]

To "amplify" evokes the metaphor of a *loud*speaker, perhaps bringing to mind someone crying out like the Baptist in the wilderness (Matt 3:3). Derrida often focuses on a seemingly insignificant detail in a text that does not fit with a received interpretation or argument. In an unnumbered footnote, one of his interlocutors writes an academic commonplace, thanking someone for providing "valuable comments on an earlier draft of this paper; the errors that are present are the responsibility of the author." Derrida takes the message literally, thanking the author for acknowledging his errors.[4]

In the context of the journal *Semeia*, from which the above definition of deconstruction is taken, the critique seems to be towards "corners" of the Society of Biblical Literature—those who, according to the author, act to preserve their economic and social privilege. The goal of deconstruction, which emerged from the radical social movements in Paris in the 1960s, is intervention.[5]

---

3. Gary A. Phillips, "Editor's Introduction," *Semeia* 51 (1990): 2. I want to thank Don Randolph and Steven Baker for their input.

4. Jay Williams, preface to *Signature Derrida*, by Jacques Derrida, ed. Jay Williams (Chicago: University of Chicago Press, 2013), x–xi.

5. Françoise Meltzer, introduction to *Signature Derrida*, xvi–xvii.

8.1.1 RELATIONSHIP TO OTHER APPROACHES

As the adjective "poststructuralist" suggests, this criticism is related to structuralism, a twentieth-century approach to studying language that focuses on an underlying system rather than its manifestation in speaking and writing. Derrida established himself, in part, by deconstructing Ferdinand de Saussure's (1857–1913) *Cours de linguistique générale*, or *Course in General Linguistics*.[6] According to students of his who published their version of his lectures, Saussure understood words or signs by their relationship to one another. He distinguished between the "signifier" (French *signifiant*), or the form that a sign takes, and the "signified" (*signifié*), the concept it represents. This allowed him to ignore the referentiality of a word and to focus on language itself as a structure.

If we allow this distinction, signifiers are only meaningful in their relationship to others. This may be difficult for English-only speakers to grasp, because the language is not especially inflected. For example, when the King James Version reads "No man hath seen God at any time," the word "God" can be taken out of the verse and, say, used as a subject: "God is love." But in Greek, the word "God" in John 1:18 is marked through its spelling *theon* as the direct object of the transitive verb "hath seen." If it were functioning as a subject, it would be spelled differently—*theos*. Thus, in an inflected language such as Greek, the signifier takes on a form that is determined by its relationship to other signifiers in the same text. Saussure was a student of highly inflected languages like Greek. But what if, as Derrida argues in *Of Grammatology*, this binary distinction between signifier and signified is a construct, not a metaphysical reality? And what if there is no underlying structure?

Deconstruction is more than a critique of structuralism. Like Socrates before Plato, Derrida casts a light on cracks in the Western intellectual tradition, with its propensity for totalizing worldviews such as scholasticism or science. It is part of the intellectual weaponry that shut down the University of Paris, where Thomas Aquinas (1224–74) had lectured so

---

6. Ferdinand de Saussure, *Course in General Linguistics*, ed. and trans. Roy Harris (London: Bloomsbury, 2013).

confidently about the *liber scripturae* ("book of Scripture") and *liber natu-rae* ("book of nature").[7]

8.1.2 GUIDING ASSUMPTIONS

While poststructuralism is more of a philosophy than strictly an approach to literature, its guiding assumptions address how literature can be interpreted because they focus on the limitations and ambiguities inherent in language and society.

8.1.2.a Critical Self-consciousness

Deconstruction emphasizes the historical and social context of the interpreter. Derrida gave a famous paper for a conference at Johns Hopkins University that focused on the work of Claude Lévi-Strauss (1908–2009). Lévi-Strauss offered a structural analysis of myth that had traces of Hegel's dialectic: people think in binary oppositions, like death and life, which are then harmonized through ritual and myth.[8] For example, male and female become "one flesh" in marriage, or death and life are united in the crucified yet resurrected Lord Jesus. But Derrida showed how this interpretation was not outside its subject but within the same discourse that gave rise to mythology. There is no objective vantage point for analysis.[9]

Interpreters should approach a text with a critical self-consciousness of their own theoretical perspective and their own social and historical contexts. Academics who study the Bible now often confess their background or social location. So, for example, I (perhaps not surprisingly) am a white, middle-class, North American male who has been afforded some leisure to write such things. Who, then, has shouldered the burden of this privilege—women, minorities, the conscripted poor in economically developing nations? What skin do I have in the game?

---

7. The expression goes back to Bonaventure (1221–74), but it is a fair representation of Aquinas's approach to reality. Francis Bacon (1561–1626) calls them "the book of God's Words" and "the book of God's Works."

8. On structuralism as developed by Lévi-Strauss and others, see chap. 7 on structuralist approaches to biblical interpretation.

9. A lack of an objective vantage point is not the same as claiming "everything is relative." Rather, poststructuralism rejects privileged readings of the text, though objectivity of a sort is possible within poststructuralist interpretation when based, for example, on a code of a reading community.

8.1.2.b The Death of the Author

Like some other literary approaches, poststructuralism does not take an author's intent into account in interpretation.[10] Poststructuralists tend toward a notion of human nature in which the self or ego is not metaphysically autonomous from its environment, contra René Descartes (1596–1650). Rather, our concept of self is genetically pre-constructed and largely co-constructed by sociocultural dynamics. This presupposition leads to Roland Barthes's 1967/8 essay "La mort de l'auteur" ("The death of the author"), in which he argues: "The text is a tissue of quotations, descended from culture's thousands of sources."[11] From this perspective, texts are like the crest of a single wave of discourse, not the singular expressions of an ego. Barthes declares the death of the author to draw attention to the role of the reader in interpretation, concluding that "a text's unity lies not in its origin but in its destination ... [and that] the birth of the reader must be at the cost of the death of the Author."[12]

8.1.2.c The Instability of Meaning

Poststructural interpretation assumes inherent instability in the relationship between a word ("signifier") and what it represents (the "signified"). If the signified is a mental concept, as Saussure maintains, how does it relate to those in the minds of others or to what it might refer to in the real or imagined world? A reader cannot get into the mind of the author: as the Bible teaches, only God knows the heart (Psa 44:20-21; 1 Cor 2:11). A community may use a common word, like "justice," but people may be using it to point to different things. Ancient Athenian philosopher Cratylus gave up on the capacity of language to convey meaning because, like a river, it is always changing, limiting his communication to finger pointing.[13] Rivers are no foundation for structure. (Ludwig Wittgenstein attempted this early

---

10. In this volume, see §1.2 The Relationship of Author, Text, Reader, and Context; §1.3.3 Reading Fallacies.

11. Roland Barthes, *Image, Music, Text*, trans. Stephen Heath (New York: Hill and Wang, 1977), 146. The French is *Le texte est un tissue de citations, issues des mille foyers de la culture.* Barthes claims singular authorship is a modern concept.

12. Barthes, *Image, Music, Text*, 148.

13. Aristotle, *Metaphysics*, 1010a10-14.

in his career, but gave up the pursuit in his *Philosophical Investigations*.)[14] Writers and readers cannot depend on a stable union between the signifier and the signified, but are caught up in the stream of discourse.

Derrida acknowledges that we cannot do without language, but metaphysical terms like "nature" are always already (*toujours déjà*) embedded culturally and are therefore context-dependent. Such terms are put under erasure (*sous rature*) as a reminder of their provisional meaning: "nature."[15] He treats any transcendental signifier (God, Truth, Reason, Being) as a *deus ex machine* (that is, a sudden introduction of a perhaps contrived means to solve a difficult problem), invoked to maintain the status quo.

8.1.2.d Power and Social Inequality

Another assumption guiding postmodern (or poststructural) thinking is that power derives from social institutions, such as churches, schools, and government, and that the possession of power creates an imbalance between the empowered and the marginalized. Michel Foucault (1926–84) popularized the view of knowledge as a form of social control. National stories naturalize. Language can be used to support or subvert existing power structures. (In my context, Phoenix, Arizona, we have discussed the difference between referring to those who informally cross the border as "illegal aliens" or "undocumented workers.") Julia Kristeva (1941–) shows how oppression can be uncovered through careful attention to what falls between the cracks of naturalizing or normalizing discourse in culture.[16]

---

14. The thought of the "early Wittgenstein" is characterized by his *Tractatus*, first published in 1921. His later thought culminated in the *Philosophical Investigations*, first published in 1953, two years after his death; see Ludwig Wittgenstein, *Tractatus Logico-Philosophicus*, trans. D. F. Pears and B. F. McGuinness (London: Routledge, 1974); see also Ludwig Wittgenstein, *Philosophical Investigations*, 4th ed., ed. and trans. P. M. S. Hacker and Joachim Schulte (Oxford: Wiley-Blackwell, 2009).

15. Donald R. Burleson, *Lovecraft: Disturbing the Universe* (Lexington: University Press of Kentucky, 1990), 9.

16. Julia Kristeva, *Tales of Love*, trans. Leon S. Roudiez (New York: Columbia University Press, 1987).

8.1.3 KEY CONCEPTS

Différance. The Derridean neologism plays with the dual sense of the French verb *différer*—to "differ" and "defer."[17] The pun incorporates the structuralist fascination with meaning through difference—such as male and female, black and white, up and down—but also critiques the false delimitation. This way of reading finds openness behind the seeming closure of a text. Towards the end of his career, Derrida confessed: "However old I am, I am on the threshold of reading Plato and Aristotle. I love them and I feel I have to start again and again."[18] For those who approach Scripture as God's Word, this is perhaps all the more the case.

Différance has a family resemblance to "overdetermination" (German *Überdeterminierung*). Sigmund Freud (1856–1939) popularized the observation of multiple causes behind a single effect.[19] People may seek a divorce to be happy, isolating the cause of their unhappiness to their spouse. But after the divorce, they remain unhappy, suggesting there is more than one cause for the effect. Deconstruction challenges positivism.[20] Paul writes:

> And concerning the greatness of the revelations, therefore, that I may not be puffed up with pride, a thorn (lodged) in the flesh was given to me, an angel from Satan, that it would torment me, so that I may not be puffed up with pride. (2 Cor 12:7)[21]

The expression "was given" is probably a divine passive: God gave the thorn to prevent pride. But the apostle also attributes his suffering to "an angel from Satan." What caused the apostle's thorn? His own propensity toward arrogance, God, the malevolent angel, or Satan? The informed

---

17. The term is used in his 1963 paper; see Jacques Derrida, "Cogito et histoire de la folie," *Revue de métaphysique et de morale* 68 (1963): 460–94.

18. John D. Caputo, ed., *Deconstruction in a Nutshell: A Conversation with Jacques Derrida* (New York: Fordham University Press), 9.

19. Graham Frankland, *Freud's Literary Culture* (Cambridge: Cambridge University Press, 2000), 122.

20. Positivism is a complex philosophical concept that, at its root, suggests understanding human issues is an "illegitimate" enterprise if one goes "beyond 'observational,' evidential, empirical criteria." One goal of positivism is to bring the rigor and structure of natural sciences to areas of study that are in some ways not like the natural sciences (such as theology or economics); see Anthony C. Thiselton, *A Concise Encyclopedia of the Philosophy of Religion* (Oxford: Oneworld, 2002), 232–33.

21. Author's translation.

reader may hear an echo of Jesus' crown of thorns, especially because both pray for deliverance three times (1 Cor 12:8) and yet yield to the divine will, and may also hear an echo to the suffering of Job.[22] Perhaps Paul suffered as proof of his faith and union with Christ. The text resists any simplistic explanation for suffering, not unlike when the disciples asked Jesus whether the blind man had sinned or his parents—a binary, limited way of thinking (John 9:2).

Codes. Readers bring a network of references to the text, which shape their interpretation.[23] A personal illustration may be helpful. The rock group Led Zeppelin recorded "When the Levee Breaks" in 1971. When I heard the song as a child, it made little impression on me. I probably did not hear it again until 2006, after Hurricane Katrina, when several levees broke, devastating New Orleans. The words took on a fresh meaning because my grandfather came from the city. Later I learned the lyrics were written in 1929 by two African American blues artists, Kansas Joe McCoy and Memphis Minnie, who, like my grandfather, had left the vulnerable region rich in culture but poor in power: "I works on the levee, mama both night and day / I works so hard, to keep the water away."[24] The dates—1929, 1971, and 2006—anticipate, by a year or two, economic hardships for the majority of Americans. This meaning may not be significant to others, who bring their own experiences to the song.

Double binds. Popularized by English polymath Gregory Bateson (1904-80), a double bind describes the (often distressing) effect of receiving what appear to be conflicting messages, like in Paul's letters, which recommend singleness for widows (1 Cor 7:39-40) but then marriage (1 Tim 5:14), or women praying and prophesying in church (1 Cor 11:5), but then silence (1 Cor 14:34; 1 Tim 2:12).[25] Those with personal investment in women speaking or remaining silent in the church have tended to prioritize one of the

---

22. Noticing the echoes of one text in another is sometimes called "intertextuality"; see the chapter in this volume on "Inner-Biblical Interpretation and Intertextuality."

23. See Caputo, ed., *Deconstruction in a Nutshell*, 101.

24. http://www.mccoybrotherstribute.com/joe.html.

25. Gregory Bateson, *Steps to an Ecology of Mind* (Chicago: University of Chicago Press, 1972), 206–12.

binary options, contributing to a polarization. Instead of privileging one message over the other—avoid marriage, remain silent—poststructuralists hold them in tension, waiting for another option. These examples remind us that Paul's letters are occasional, addressing shifting circumstances, from the first to the twenty-first century: "For everything there is a season, and a time for every delight under heaven ... a time to speak and a time remain silent ... a time to marry and a time to be single" (Eccl 3:1, 7, 8).[26]

A double bind may be communicated through a pun, like *différance*. According to the English Standard Version, Jesus says, "The wind blows where it wishes, and you hear its sound, but you do not know where it comes from or where it goes. So it is with everyone who is born of the Spirit" (John 3:8). However, the Greek may also be translated, "The Spirit (*to pneuma*) breathes (*pnei*) where it wills. And you are hearing its voice. But you do not know where it comes from and where it goes. In the same way, it is for everyone who has been born of the Spirit (*to pneuma*)." Native Greek-speakers probably heard both senses at once. Instead of choosing one avenue for translation, Jesus' disclosure may be enriched by both. In addition to the mystery yet ordinariness of the wind, Jesus attributes an evangelistic voice to the Spirit, who also "breathes" life into people like God did at the first creation (Gen 2:7; see Heb 3:7; 10:15).

8.2 VARIETIES OF
POSTSTRUCTURAL CRITICISM

Poststructuralism informs reader-response criticism as well as feminist and postcolonial readings. With the polyvalence and ambiguity of discourse, readers must respond to the text by continually filling in the picture in their mind's eye. So, for example, Paul writes about his thorn in a veiled way, so that readers seem to be invited to fill the image with their own suffering.[27] Reader-response critics seek to bring this often unconscious aspect of reading into the open. Before poststructuralism, at least in the academy, reading into the text (eisegesis) was treated as problematic—something to be overcome through objective exegetical methodology.

---

26. Author's translation.

27. There seem to be as many interpretations of Paul's thorn as there are readers: partial blindness, malaria, pride, same-sex attraction, depression, enduring guilt, and so forth.

Readers have always come to texts with specific interests, but there has been a shift in biblical studies toward foregrounding these agendas, looking to expose patriarchal, homophobic, or colonial ideology. With the poststructuralists, the discussion often focuses on power and its misuse.

8.3 APPLICATIONS OF POSTSTRUCTURAL CRITICISM

Poststructuralism is not so much a method as an interest in how a text plays with convention. Practitioners look for logical gaps, double binds, puns, fissures in the narrative, unexpressed cultural assumptions, and, with translations, the ways not taken. (Learning biblical Greek and Hebrew is a helpful tool because translations used in churches are often done by academics from a limited cultural background.)

In this section, we will move from the OT to the NT, through a typology between Jonah and Jesus, and then from the NT to the OT, through a reading of Moses by Jesus against the Sadducees.

8.3.1 OLD TESTAMENT

Jewish theologian Neil Gillman notes the paradox of Jonah as "the only successful biblical prophet" who "feels that he has failed."[28] Prophets normally preach to God's people and are rejected. Jonah speaks to the people of Nineveh, the traditional enemies of Israel, and they repent. God gives the traditional prophetic message to Jonah, to promise judgment: "Yet forty days, and Nineveh will be overthrown" (Jonah 3:4).[29] But the prophet flees from God's presence because he knows God is "gracious," "merciful, slow to anger and abounding in steadfast love, and relenting from disaster" (Jonah 4:2, ESV). He alludes to Exodus: "The Lord passed before [Moses] and proclaimed, 'The Lord, the Lord, a God merciful and gracious, slow to anger, and abounding in steadfast love and faithfulness' " (Exod 34:6, ESV). The self-disclosure occurs after Israel commits idolatry.[30] Yet God

---

28. Neil Gillman, *The Way into Encountering God in Judaism* (Woodstock, VT: Jewish Lights, 2000), 115.

29. Unless noted otherwise, the Scripture quotations used in this chapter are ESV.

30. Michael Widmer, *Moses, God, and the Dynamics of Intercessory Prayer: A Study of Exodus 32–34 and Numbers 13–14* (Tübingen: Mohr Siebeck, 2004), 183.

reverses the order of an earlier self-disclosure, which occurred before their disobedience:

> I the Lord your God am a jealous God, visiting the iniquity of the fathers on the children to the third and fourth generation of those who hate me, but showing steadfast love to thousands of those who love me and keep my commandments. (Exod 20:5-6, ESV)

The point is not to reject one of the self-disclosures: both are true yet partial revelations of divine mystery. Nevertheless, God emphasizes his mercy. For this reason, the second revelation is cited and reflected on throughout the Psalms (86:15; 103:8; 145:8-9).[31] Following the reference in Psalm 145:8, the psalmist says: "The Lord is good to all, and his mercy is over all that he has made" (Ps 145:9).

However, God's self-revelation puts Jonah in a double bind. On the one hand, he knows God is just and therefore ultimately has to take care of evil. But he also knows God will forgive anyone who repents, and Jonah hates the people of Nineveh. God's mercy would seem to be good news to the bad and bad news to the good.

Jonah was from Gath-hepher, a village in Galilee, not far from Nazareth (2 Kgs 14:25). Jesus began his public ministry in the same region, offering God's mercy to the repentant. However, unlike the people of Nineveh, Jesus encounters resistance:

> Then some of the scribes and Pharisees answered him, saying, "Teacher, we wish to see a sign from you." But he answered them, "An evil and adulterous generation seeks for a sign, but no sign will be given to it except the sign of the prophet Jonah. For just as *Jonah was three days and three nights in the belly of the great fish,* so will the Son of Man be three days and three nights in the heart of the earth. The men of Nineveh will rise up at the judgment with this generation and condemn it, for they repented at the preaching of Jonah, and behold, something greater than Jonah is here." (Matt 12:38-42, emphasis added; see also 16:1-4)

---

31. See also Joel 2:13; Neh 9:17.

Jesus focuses on an ambiguity in the biblical story. Although the narrator says Jonah prays "from the belly of the fish," the prophet cries "from the belly of Sheol," the place of the dead (Jonah 2:1–2, ESV). The prayer implies Jonah died, but was also saved. Jesus exploits the ambiguity to foreshadow his death and resurrection.

Jesus also makes a judgment: "Something greater than Jonah is here." This is seen in the stilling of the storm:

> And as he got into the boat, his disciples followed him. And behold, there arose a great storm on the sea, so that the boat was being swamped by the waves; but he was asleep. And they went and woke him, saying, "Save us, Lord; we are perishing." And he said to them, "Why are you afraid, O you of little faith?" Then he rose and rebuked the winds and the sea, and there was a great calm. And the men marveled, saying, "What sort of man is this, that even the winds and the sea obey him?" (Matt 8:23–27)

There is continuity and discontinuity with Jonah. We have a similar storm threatening to sink the ship. Like the prophet, Jesus is asleep. The disciples act like the desperate captain and crew. But instead of crying out to God, "O LORD, let us not perish" (Jonah 1:14), they say to Jesus, "Save us, Lord; we are perishing." And then, instead of being thrown off the boat, Jesus takes God's role by commanding the winds and the sea—literally, a lake—into submission. He is not running away from God, but is crossing over to the Gentile side of Galilee, the Decapolis, where he is asked to leave.

In a sense, Jonah was sacrificed in place of the sailors, who pray, "Do not put innocent blood on us" (Jonah 1:14).[32] The request is ironic because of Jonah's disobedience. However, after Jesus' death and resurrection, the language takes on a fresh meaning. Jesus lovingly dies in the place of his enemies, so that his innocent blood may cover their evil.

8.3.2 NEW TESTAMENT

The Synoptic Gospels record an encounter between Jesus and the Sadducees. Here is Mark's version:

---

32. Author's translation.

And Sadducees came to him, who say that there is no resurrection. And they asked him a question, saying, "Teacher, Moses wrote for us that *if a man's brother dies* and leaves *a wife, but leaves no child* [Deut 25:5-6], the *man must take the widow and raise up offspring for his brother* [Gen 38:8]. There were seven brothers; the first took a wife, and when he died left no offspring. And the second took her, and died, leaving no offspring. And the third likewise. And the seven left no offspring. Last of all the woman also died. In the resurrection, when they rise again, whose wife will she be?" (Mark 12:18-23, emphasis and additional references added)

The Sadducees were part of the cultural elite, drawing power from their control of the temple, which, for many Jews, was the center of the universe (Acts 4:1-2; 5:17). The high priest Caiaphas was a Sadducee.[33] The group is remembered primarily for denying the general resurrection of the dead.[34] According to Jewish historian Josephus, they presumed souls died with the body.[35]

The Sadducees cite from Deuteronomy and Genesis—a device in Hebrew called *gezerah shavah*—because they only accepted positions that were grounded in the Mosaic Law, the first five books of the OT or Hebrew Bible.[36] (*Gezerah shavah* anticipates intertextuality: If two Scriptures share a word or phrase or are analogous in some other way, they may be joined regardless of their placement in the canon.)[37]

The citation and scenario function as a polemic against the resurrection: If the first brother and husband will be resurrected someday, why must Levirate marriage be performed, which presumes he lives on through the child? Moses does not talk about eternal life or the resurrection.

---

33. No text explicitly claims Caiaphas was a Sadducee, but the relationship is likely because his brother-in-law was a Sadducee (Josephus, *Antiquities*, 20.199) and Luke associates him and his father-in-law, Annas, with the group (Acts 4:1; 5:17). See Helen K. Bond, *Caiaphas: Friend of Rome and Judge of Jesus?* (Louisville: Westminster John Knox, 2004), 165.

34. Matt 22:23; Luke 20:27; Acts 4:1-2; 23:6-8.

35. Josephus, *Antiquities*, 18.16.

36. Josephus, *Antiquities*, 13.297.

37. See Susan A. Handelman, *The Slayers of Moses: The Emergence of Rabbinic Interpretation in Modern Literary Theory* (Albany: State University of New York Press, 1982), 57.

So we have those in power seeking to maintain their social position by attempting to delegitimize an alternative interpretation of reality. They do this, in part, by attempting to limit the meaning of the Mosaic Law. Jesus responds with a twofold rebuttal:

> Is it not for this reason that you are deceived: You know neither the Scriptures nor God's power?[38] For when they are raised from those who are dead, they [husbands] neither marry, nor are they [wives] given in marriage. But they are like angels in the heavens. Now concerning those who are dead—that they are raised—have you not read in the book of Moses, near the thorn-bush, how God said to him, saying: *I am the God of Abraham and the God of Isaac and the God of Jacob*? [Exod 3:6]. He is not the God of the dead, but of the living. You are greatly deceived. (Mark 12:24-27)

After God created the woman from Adam's rib, according to Genesis, he gave her to him in marriage. So Jesus introduces a discontinuity, presuming the resurrected are transfigured in nature, something more akin to an angelic being. Having children is a mode of physical immortality, but after the resurrection, the human transfiguration into a new mode of being, procreation will no longer be necessary.

This is God's power as Creator. The Sadducees assumed the resurrection was fictitious, but their rejection of the claim was grounded in a faulty conception of its nature—essentially, that the new heavens and earth would be *just* like the first creation. They were stuck in the status quo.

Jesus criticizes the Sadducean position from within their worldview by amplifying an incommensurable detail in the Mosaic Law. "Have you not read" is ironic in light of the paradigmatic role of the passage. Of course, the Sadducees knew the story, like any Jew who ever frequented the synagogue. However, for Jesus, there is a hermeneutical dimension to reading: Do they understand what the words signify? He then focuses on a seemingly insignificant detail, the implied present-tense verb "I am."[39] When God said this, the patriarchs had been dead for centuries. The unstated

---

38. Author's own translation. Translations often read "wrong," but the verb *planaō* more naturally refers to being led astray from a path or the truth.

39. There is no verb in the Greek. Such elisions are common with the emphatic personal pronoun *egō* ("I").

premise, which is derived from the Sadducees' example of marriage, is that death annuls a covenant.[40] Since the death of the patriarchs would have released God from his covenantal obligations, God's faithfulness implies their continual existence. (Moses himself appeared at the Mount of Transfiguration.)

On the one hand, Jesus seems to go beyond the literal sense of the text. One could read God as merely relating himself to the patriarchs in Exodus. But he employs a hyperliteral interpretation, something like what the rabbis called *kivyakhol* and not unlike Derrida's response to his interlocutor.[41]

8.4 LIMITATIONS OF POSTSTRUCTURAL CRITICISM

Would-be practitioners of this reading strategy may find themselves in double binds. On the one hand, poststructuralism seeks to expose power without a transcendent viewpoint, like prophets without gods, but the criticism is part of the discourse it critiques, like when postcolonial readings (most of which are university dissertations) footnote Western intellectuals to legitimate their positions.[42] Derrida, a professor, knew this irony and encouraged the academy to own up to it. The Bible is read better in a faith community that listens for God while testing the interpretations.

On the one hand, deconstruction attempts to level the playing field by deferring all interpretation. But most people read the Bible for wisdom, seeking a better understanding of God, their faith, and how to live with others. They believe God is the ultimate author of Scripture, intending and communicating in any way God chooses. God is not a structure, but a person who calls people to repentance. To defer such interpretations is like Jonah's disobedience.

Derrida has rightly focused on the difficulties of interpretation. As Paul notes, "We see in a mirror dimly [or in a riddle]" (1 Cor 13:12). (Unlike modern mirrors, the apostle refers to one made of bronze, which offered

---

40. B. R. Trick, "Death, Covenants, and the Proof of Resurrection in Mark 12:18–27," *NovT* 49 (2007): 232–56.

41. Michael A. Fishbane, *The Garments of Torah: Essays in Biblical Hermeneutics* (Bloomington: Indiana University Press, 1992), 26.

42. See, for example, David M. Crump, review of Israel Kamudzandu, *Abraham Our Father: Paul and the Ancestors in Postcolonial Africa*, *Review of Biblical Literature* (2014).

a distorted outline of the face.) Within the letter of this citation, the apostle expresses frustration over being misunderstood, as Derrida does with his interlocutors.[43] However, they both believe that misunderstanding can be partially overcome through humility and love. Slaughtering the author for one's ideology and burying them voiceless in a sea of discourse is cruel and unloving.

8.5 CONTEMPORARY INFLUENCE OF POSTSTRUCTURAL CRITICISM

Poststructuralism has influenced the humanities, particularly in North America, so that a generation of those who were able to attend university have had some exposure to it. Its influence can be seen in particular manifestations, like the Occupy Wall Street Movement (2011), but perhaps also in a broader cynicism toward organized religion and centralized government. The discourse seems to be moving in a localized yet global direction. People are becoming more aware of being situated. We are all looking at the same things differently. This hermeneutical turn can be seen in shows like *Anthony Bourdain: Parts Unknown*. Derrida, towards the end of his life, described Christianity as the most "plastic" of the faith options in a global context and therefore open to transformation—an "unpredictable earthquake."[44]

8.6 RESOURCES FOR FURTHER STUDY

Beardslee, William A. "Poststructuralist Criticism." Pages 253–67 in *To Each Its Own Meaning: An Introduction to Biblical Criticisms and Their Application*, edited by Steven L. McKenzie and Stephen R. Haynes. Rev. and enl. ed. Louisville, KY: Westminster John Knox, 1999.

William A. Beardslee, professor at Emory University and director of the Process and Faith Program at the Claremont School of Theology, contributed this sympathetic yet critical chapter shortly before his death (2001).

---

43. See 1 Cor 5:9–13.
44. "Jacques Derrida On Religion": http://www.youtube.com/watch?v=gyOWAcpIaB8.

Longman, Tremper, III. *Literary Approaches to Biblical Intepretation.*
   Foundations of Contemporary Interpretation 3. Grand Rapids:
   Zondervan, 1987.

   Tremper Longman III studied at Yale when and where
   poststructuralism was at its zenith. He offers a nuanced critique.

Meltzer, Françoise. Introduction to *Signature Derrida,* by Jacques Derrida.
   Chicago: University of Chicago Press, 2013.

   Meltzer coedited the journal *Critical Inquiry,* which published
   several essays by Derrida. She provides context for the
   philosopher's work and some personal insight.

BIBLIOGRAPHY

Abrams, M. H., and Geoffrey Galt Harpham. *A Glossary of Literary Terms*. 9th ed. Boston: Wadsworth, 2009.

Ackerman, James S. "Jonah." In *The Literary Guide to the Bible*, edited by Robert Alter and Frank Kermode, 234-43. Cambridge, MA: Belknap, 1987.

Agamben, Giorgio. *The Time That Remains: A Commentary on the Letter to the Romans*. Stanford, CA: Stanford University Press, 2005.

Alter, Robert. "Psalms." In *The Literary Guide to the Bible*, edited by Robert Alter and Frank Kermode, 244-62. Cambridge, MA: Belknap, 1987.

———. *The Art of Biblical Narrative*. Rev. and updated ed. New York: Basic Books, 2011.

———. *The Art of Biblical Poetry*. New York: Basic Books, 1985.

———. *The World of Biblical Narrative*. New York: Basic Books, 1992.

Alter, Robert, and Frank Kermode, eds. *The Literary Guide to the Bible*. Cambridge, MA: Belknap, 1987.

Anderson, Bernhard W. "The New Frontier of Rhetorical Criticism: A Tribute to James Muilenberg." In *Rhetorical Criticism: Essays in Honor of James Muilenburg*, edited by Jared J. Jackson and Martin Kessler, ix-xvii. Pittsburgh: Pickwick, 1974.

Anderson, Nicole. "Deconstruction and Ethics: An (Ir)responsibility." In *Jacques Derrida: Key Concepts*, edited by Claire Colebrook. New York: Routledge, 2015.

Anderson, R. Dean, Jr. *Ancient Rhetorical Theory and Paul*. Rev. ed. Leuven: Peeters, 1998.

———. *Glossary of Greek Rhetorical Terms: Connected to Methods of Argumentation, Figures and Tropes from Anaximenes to Quintilian.* Leuven: Peeters, 2000.

Arend, Walter. *Die Typischen Scenen Bei Homer.* Berlin: Weidmann, 1933.

Aristotle. *Poetics.* Translated by Stephen Halliwell. Cambridge, MA: Harvard University Press, 1999.

———. *Problems, Books 32–38, and Rhetorica Ad Alexandrum.* Translated by W. S. Hett and H. Rackham. Cambridge, MA: Harvard University Press, 1937.

———. *Rhetoric.* Translated by J. H. Freese. Medford, MA: Harvard University Press, 1926.

———. *The "Art" of Rhetoric.* Translated by John Henry Freese. Cambridge, MA: Harvard University Press, 1975.

Armerding, Carl. "Structural Analysis." *Themelios* 4, no. 3 (1979): 96–104.

Auerbach, Erich. *Mimesis: The Representation of Reality in Western Literature.* Translated by Willard R. Trask. Princeton, NJ: Princeton University Press, 1971.

Augustine. "On Christian Doctrine." In *St. Augustin's City of God and Christian Doctrine*, edited by Philip Schaff. Translated by J. F. Shaw. Buffalo, NY: Christian Literature Company, 1887.

Aune, David E. "Literary Criticism." In *The Blackwell Companion to the New Testament*, edited by David E. Aune, 116–39. West Sussex: Wiley-Blackwell, 2010.

Bal, Mieke. *Narratology: Introduction to the Theory of Narrative.* Translated by Christine van Boheemen. 2nd ed. Toronto: University of Toronto Press, 1997.

Ball, Edward, ed. *In Search of True Wisdom: Essays in Old Testament Interpretation in Honour of Ronald E. Clements.* Sheffield: Sheffield Academic Press, 1999.

Bann, Stephen, and John E. Bowlt, eds. *Russian Formalism: A Collection of Articles and Texts in Translation.* Edinburgh: Scottish Academic Press, 1973.

Barbiero, Gianni. *Song of Songs: A Close Reading.* Leiden: Brill, 2011.

Bar-Efrat, Shimon. *Narrative Art in the Bible.* Sheffield: Almond, 1989.

Barker, Kit. "Speech Act Theory, Dual Authorship, and Canonical Hermeneutics: Making Sense of *Sensus Plenior*." *Journal of Theological Interpretation* 3, no. 2 (2009): 227-39.

Barr, David. *Tales of the End: A Narrative Commentary on the Book of Revelation*. Santa Rosa, CA: Polebridge, 1998.

Barr, James. *Bible and Interpretation: The Collected Essays of James Barr*, edited by John Barton. 3 vols. Oxford: Oxford University Press, 2013.

———. *The Concept of Biblical Theology*. Minneapolis: Fortress, 1999.

———. *Holy Scripture: Canon, Authority, Criticism*. Philadelphia: Westminster Press, 1983.

Barrera, Julio Trebolle. *The Jewish Bible and the Christian Bible: An Introduction to the History of the Bible*. Translated by Wilfred G. E. Watson. Leiden: Brill, 1998.

Barthes, Roland. "An Introduction to the Structural Analysis of Narrative." *New Literary History* 6, no. 4 (1975): 237-72.

———. *Image, Music, Text*. Translated by Stephen Heath. New York: Hill and Wang, 1977.

———. *S/Z*. Translated by Richard Miller. Oxford: Blackwell, 1990.

———. "The Struggle with the Angel: Textual Analysis of Genesis 32:23-33." In *Structural Analysis and Biblical Exegesis: Interpretational Essays*, translated by Alfred M. Johnson, Jr., 21-33. Pittsburgh: Pickwick Press, 1974.

Bartholomew, Craig G., Scott Hahn, Robin Parry, Christopher R. Seitz, and Al Wolters, eds. *Canon and Biblical Interpretation*. Grand Rapids: Zondervan, 2006.

Bartholomew, Craig G., and Heath A. Thomas, eds. *A Manifesto for Theological Interpretation*. Grand Rapids: Baker, 2016.

Barton, John. "Canon and Old Testament Interpretation." In *In Search of True Wisdom: Essays in Old Testament Interpretation in Honour of Ronald E. Clements*, edited by Edward Ball. Sheffield: Sheffield Academic Press, 1999.

———. "History and Rhetoric in the Prophets." In *The Bible as Rhetoric: Studies in Biblical Persuasion and Credibility*, edited by Martin Warner, 51-64. London: Routledge, 1990.

————. *Reading the Old Testament: Method in Biblical Study.* Rev. and enl. ed. Louisville, KY: Westminster John Knox, 1996.

Bateson, Gregory. *Steps to an Ecology of Mind; Collected Essays in Anthropology, Psychiatry, Evolution, and Epistemology.* San Francisco: Chandler, 1972.

Beardslee, William A. *Literary Criticism of the New Testament.* Philadelphia: Fortress, 1970.

————. "Poststructuralist Criticism." In *To Each Its Own Meaning: An Introduction to Biblical Criticisms and Their Application,* edited by Steven L. McKenzie and Stephen R. Haynes, rev. and enl. ed., 256–67. Louisville, KY: Westminster John Knox, 1999.

Beauchamp, Paul. *Création et séparation. Étude exégétique du chapitre premier de la Genèse.* Paris: Aubier, 1969.

Becking, Bob. "No More Grapes from the Vineyard? A Plea for a Historical Critical Approach in the Study of the Old Testament." In *Congress Volume: Oslo, 1998,* edited by André Lemaire and Magne Sæbø, 123–41. Leiden: Brill, 2000.

Bennema, Cornelis. *Encountering Jesus: Character Studies in the Gospel of John.* 2nd ed. Minneapolis: Fortress, 2014.

Ben-Porat, Ziva. "Intertextuality." *Ha-Sifrut* 34 (1985): 170–78.

Berlin, Adele. *Poetics and Interpretation of Biblical Narrative.* Winona Lake, IN: Eisenbrauns, 1994.

Betz, Hans Dieter. *Galatians: A Commentary on Paul's Letter to the Churches in Galatia.* Hermeneia. Philadelphia: Fortress, 1979.

Billings, J. Todd. *The Word of God for the People of God: An Entryway to the Theological Interpretation of Scripture.* Grand Rapids: Eerdmans, 2010.

Birch, David. *Language, Literature and Critical Practice: Ways of Analysing a Text.* London: Routledge, 1989.

Black, C. Clifton. *The Rhetoric of the Gospel: Theological Artistry in the Gospels and Acts.* 2nd ed. Louisville, KY: Westminster John Knox, 2013.

Blenkinsopp, Joseph. *Prophecy and Canon: A Contribution to the Study of Jewish Origins.* Notre Dame, IN: University of Notre Dame Press, 1986.

Boda, Mark J., and Michael H. Floyd, eds. *Bringing Out the Treasure: Inner Biblical Allusion in Zechariah.* London: T & T Clark, 2003.

de Boer, Martinus C. "Narrative Criticism, Historical Criticism, and the Gospel of John." *JSNT*, no. 47 (September 1, 1992): 35-48.

Boers, Hendrikus. "Polarities at the Roots of New Testament Thought." In *Perspectives on the New Testament: Essays in Honor of Frank Stagg,* edited by Charles H. Talbert. Macon, GA: Mercer University Press, 1985.

Bond, Helen K. *Caiaphas: Friend of Rome and Judge of Jesus?* Louisville, KY: Westminster John Knox, 2004.

Boomershine, Thomas E. "The Structure of Narrative Rhetoric in Genesis 2-3." *Semeia*, no. 18 (1980): 113-29.

Booth, Wayne C. *The Rhetoric of Fiction.* Chicago: University of Chicago Press, 1983.

———. *The Rhetoric of Rhetoric: The Quest for Effective Communication.* Oxford: Blackwell, 2004.

Bowman, Richard G. "Narrative Criticism: Human Purpose in Conflict with Divine Presence." In *Judges and Method: New Approaches in Biblical Studies,* edited by G. A. Yee, 2nd ed., 19-45. Minneapolis: Fortress, 2007.

Brett, Mark G. *Biblical Criticism in Crisis?: The Impact of the Canonical Approach on Old Testament Studies.* Cambridge: Cambridge University Press, 1991.

Brodie, Thomas L. *The Gospel according to John: A Literary and Theological Commentary.* New York: Oxford University Press, 1993.

Brooks, Peter. *Reading for the Plot: Design and Intention in Narrative.* Cambridge, MA: Harvard University Press, 1992.

Brown, J. Dickson. "Barton, Brooks, and Childs: A Comparison of the New Criticism and Canonical Criticism." *Journal of the Evangelical Theological Society* 36 (1993): 481-89.

Brown, Jeannine K. "Narrative Criticism." In *Dictionary of Jesus and the Gospels,* edited by Joel B. Green, Jeannine K. Brown, and Nicholas Perrin, 2nd ed. Downers Grove, IL: InterVarsity, 2013.

Broyles, Craig C. *Interpreting the Old Testament: A Guide for Exegesis.* Grand Rapids: Baker Academic, 2001.

———. "Traditions, Intertextuality, and Canon." In *Interpreting the Old Testament: A Guide for Exegesis*, edited by Craig C. Broyles, 157–76. Grand Rapids: Baker Academic, 2001.

Brueggemann, Walter. "On Trust and Freedom: A Study of Faith in the Succession Narrative." *Interpretation* 26 (1972): 3–19.

Bryce, Glendon E. "A Response to Patte and Parker." *Semeia*, no. 18 (1980): 77–81.

Buhl, Frants. *Canon and Text of the Old Testament*. Edinburgh: T&T Clark, 1892.

Bultmann, Rudolf. *Jesus Christ and Mythology*. New York: Scribner, 1958.

Burleson, Donald R. *Lovecraft: Disturbing the Universe*. Lexington: The University Press of Kentucky, 1990.

Burnett, Richard. "Historical Criticism." In *Dictionary for Theological Interpretation of the Bible*, edited by Kevin J. Vanhoozer. Grand Rapids: Baker, 2005.

Callaway, Mary C. "Canonical Criticism." In *To Each Its Own Meaning: An Introduction to Biblical Criticisms and Their Application*, edited by Steven L. McKenzie and Stephen R. Haynes, rev. and exp. ed., 142–55. Louisville, KY: Westminster John Knox, 1999.

Calloud, Jean. "Toward a Structural Analysis of the Gospel of Mark." *Semeia*, no. 16 (1979): 133–65.

Campbell, Barth L. *Honor, Shame, and the Rhetoric of 1 Peter*. Atlanta: Scholars Press, 1998.

Campbell, Gregor. "Signified/Signifier/Signification." Edited by Irene R. Makaryk. *Encyclopedia of Contemporary Literary Theory: Approaches, Scholars, Terms*. Toronto: University of Toronto Press, 1993.

von Campenhausen, Hans. *The Formation of the Christian Bible*. Translated by J. A. Baker. Philadelphia: Fortress, 1972.

Caplan, Harry, trans. *Rhetorica ad Herennium*. Cambridge, MA: Harvard University Press, 1954.

Caputo, John D., ed. *Deconstruction in a Nutshell: A Conversation with Jacques Derrida*. New York: Fordham University Press, 1997.

Carr, David M. *The Formation of the Hebrew Bible: A New Reconstruction*. Oxford: Oxford University Press, 2011.

————. "The Many Uses of Intertextuality in Biblical Studies: Actual and Potential." In *Congress Volume: Helsinki 2010*, edited by Martti Nissinen, 505-36. Leiden: Brill, 2012.

Carson, D. A. *The Gospel According to John.* Pillar New Testament Commentary. Grand Rapids: Eerdmans, 1991.

Ceresko, Anthony R. "A Rhetorical Analysis of David's 'Boast' (1 Samuel 17:34-37): Some Reflections on Method." *CBQ* 47 (1985): 58-74.

Chapman, Stephen B. "Collections, Canons, and Communities." In *The Cambridge Companion to the Hebrew Bible/Old Testament*, edited by Stephen B. Chapman and Marvin A. Sweeney, 28-54. New York: Cambridge University Press, 2016.

————. "The Old Testament Canon and Its Authority for the Christian Church." *Ex Auditu* 19 (2003): 125-48.

Chapman, Stephen B., and Marvin A. Sweeney, eds. *The Cambridge Companion to the Hebrew Bible/Old Testament.* New York: Cambridge University Press, 2016.

Charlesworth, James H. "The Pseudepigrapha as Biblical Exegesis." In *Early Jewish and Christian Exegesis: Studies in Memory of William Hugh Brownlee*, edited by Craig A. Evans and William F. Stinespring, 139-52. Atlanta: Scholars Press, 1987.

Chatman, Seymour. *Story and Discourse: Narrative Structure in Fiction and Film.* Ithaca, NY: Cornell University Press, 1978.

Childs, Brevard S. *Biblical Theology of the Old and New Testaments: Theological Reflection on the Christian Bible.* Minneapolis: Fortress Press, 1992.

————. *Introduction to the Old Testament as Scripture.* Philadelphia: Fortress, 1979.

————. *The New Testament as Canon: An Introduction.* London: SCM Press, 1984.

————. "Review of *Holy Scripture: Canon, Authority, Criticism* by James Barr." *Interpretation* 38 (1984): 66-70.

————. "The 'Sensus Literalis' of Scripture: An Ancient and Modern Problem." In *Beiträge zur Alttestamentlichen Theologie: Festschrift für Walther Zimmerli zum 70 Geburtstag*, edited by Herbert Donner, Robert Hanhart, and Rudolf Smend, 80-96. Göttingen: Vandenhoek & Ruprecht, 1977.

Chiu, Chi-yue, and Ying-yi Hong. *Social Psychology of Culture*. New York: Routledge, 2013.

Cicero. *The Orations of Marcus Tullius Cicero*. Translated by C. D. Yonge. London: Henry G. Bohn, 1853.

Clarke, M. L. *Rhetoric at Rome: A Historical Survey*. Edited by D. H. Berry. London: Routledge, 1996.

Classen, Carl Joachim. *Rhetorical Criticism of the New Testament*. Tübingen: Mohr Siebeck, 2000.

Clifford, Richard J. *Fair Spoken and Persuading: An Interpretation of Second Isaiah*. New York: Paulist, 1984.

Clines, David J. A. "Deconstructing the Book of Job." In *The Bible as Rhetoric: Studies in Biblical Persuasion and Credibility*, edited by Martin Warner, 65–80. London: Routledge, 1990.

Cohan, Steven, and Linda M. Shires. *Telling Stories: A Theoretical Analysis of Narrative Fiction*. London: Routledge, 1988.

Collins, John J. *Introduction to the Hebrew Bible: An Inductive Reading of the Old Testament*. Minneapolis: Fortress Press, 2004.

Coloe, Mary L. "Woman of Samaria: Her Characterization, Narrative, and Theological Significance." In *Characters and Characterization in the Gospel of John*, edited by Christopher W. Skinner, 182–96. London: Bloomsbury, 2013.

Connolly, Joy. "Virile Tongues: Rhetoric and Masculinity." In *A Companion to Roman Rhetoric*, edited by William Dominik and Jon Hall, 93–94. Oxford: Blackwell, 2007.

Cosgrove, Charles H., ed. *The Meanings We Choose: Hermeneutical Ethics, Indeterminacy and the Conflict of Interpretations*. London: T & T Clark, 2004.

Crespy, Georges. "Parable of the Good Samaritan: An Essay in Structural Research." *Semeia*, no. 2 (1974): 27–50.

Crossan, John Dominic. "Structuralist Analysis and the Parables of Jesus." *Semeia*, no. 1 (1974): 192–221.

Crowley, Sharon, and Debra Hawhee. *Ancient Rhetorics for Contemporary Students*. 3rd ed. New York: Pearson Longman, 2004.

Crump, David M. "Review of Israel Kamudzandu, Abraham Our Father: Paul and the Ancestors in Postcolonial Africa." *Review of Biblical Literature*, 2014. http://www.bookreviews.org.

Culler, Jonathan. *The Pursuit of Signs: Semiotics, Literature, Deconstruction.* London: Routledge, 2001.

———. *On Deconstruction: Theory and Criticism After Structuralism.* Ithaca, NY: Cornell University Press, 1982.

Culley, Robert C. "Action Sequences in Genesis 2-3." *Semeia*, no. 18 (1980): 25-33.

———. "Structural Analysis: Is It Done with Mirrors?" *Interpretation* 28, no. 2 (1974): 165-81.

———. "Themes and Variations in Three Groups of Old Testament Narratives." *Semeia*, no. 3 (1975): 3-13.

Culpepper, R. Alan. *Anatomy of the Fourth Gospel.* Philadelphia: Fortress, 1983.

Damrosch, David. "Leviticus." In *The Literary Guide to the Bible*, edited by Robert Alter and Frank Kermode, 66-77. Cambridge, MA: Belknap, 1987.

Danto, Arthur C. *Narration and Knowledge: Including the Integral Text of Analytical Philosophy of History.* New York: Columbia University Press, 1985.

Davies, Philip R. *In Search of "Ancient Israel": A Study in Biblical Origins.* Sheffield: Sheffield Academic Press, 1992.

Davis, Todd F., and Kenneth Womack. *Formalist Criticism and Reader-Response Theory.* Transitions. New York: Palgrave, 2002.

DeMaria, Robert Jr. "The Ideal Reader: A Critical Fiction." *PMLA* 93 (1978): 463-74.

Dempster, Stephen G. "The Canon and Theological Interpretation." In *A Manifesto for Theological Interpretation*, edited by Craig G. Bartholomew and Heath A. Thomas, 131-48. Grand Rapids: Baker, 2016.

———. *Dominion and Dynasty: A Theology of the Hebrew Bible.* Downers Grove, IL: InterVarsity, 2003.

Derrida, Jacques. "Cogito et Histoire de La Folie." *Revue de métaphysique et de morale* 68 (1963): 460-94.

———. *Of Grammatology.* Translated by Gayatri Chakravorty Spivak. Baltimore, MD: Johns Hopkins University Press, 1974.

———. *Of Grammatology.* Translated by Gayatri Spivak. Corrected ed. Baltimore, MD: Johns Hopkins University Press, 1976.

————. *Signature Derrida*. Edited and with a preface by Jay Williams. Introduction by Françoise Meltzer. Chicago: University of Chicago Press, 2013.

DeSilva, David A. "What Has Athens to Do with Patmos? Rhetorical Criticism of the Revelation of John (1980–2005)." *Currents in Biblical Research* 6, no. 2 (2008): 256–89.

Dicken, Frank, and Julia Snyder, eds. *Characters and Characterization in Luke-Acts*. London: Bloomsbury, forthcoming.

Dionysius of Halicarnassus. *On Literary Composition: Being the Greek Text of the De Compositione Verborum*. Edited by W. Rhys Roberts. London: Macmillan, 1910.

Dominik, William, and Jon Hall, eds. *A Companion to Roman Rhetoric*. Oxford: Blackwell, 2007.

Donner, Herbert, Robert Hanhart, and Rudolf Smend, eds. *Beiträge zur alttestamentlichen Theologie: Festschrift für Walther Zimmerli zum 70 Geburtstag*. Göttingen: Vandenhoeck & Ruprecht, 1977.

Dozeman, Thomas B. "Inner-Biblical Interpretation of Yahweh's Gracious and Compassionate Character." *JBL* 108 (1989): 207–23.

Dundes, Alan. Introduction to *Morphology of a Folktale*, by Vladimir Propp, xi–xvii. 2nd ed. Austin: University of Texas Press, 1968.

Eagleton, Terry. *Literary Theory: An Introduction*. Anniversary ed. Minneapolis: University of Minnesota Press, 2008.

————. *The Event of Literature*. New Haven, CT: Yale University Press, 2012.

Eco, Umberto. *The Role of the Reader: Explorations in the Semiotics of Texts*. Bloomington, IN: Indiana University Press, 1979.

Edenburg, Cynthia. "How (Not) to Murder a King: Variations on a Theme in 1 Sam 24; 26." *SJOT* 12 (1998): 65–70.

Ellis, E. Earle. *The Old Testament in Early Christianity: Canon and Interpretation in the Light of Modern Research*. Eugene, OR: Wipf and Stock, 2003.

Empson, William. *Seven Types of Ambiguity*. London: Chatto and Windus, 1930.

Engnell, Ivan. *Gamla Testamentet: En Traditionshistorisk Inledning*. Vol. 1. Stockholm: Svenska Kyrkans Diakonistyrelses Bokförlag, 1945.

Enkvist, Nils Erik. "Context." In *Literature and the New Interdisciplinarity: Poetics, Linguistics, History*, edited by Roger D. Sell and Peter Verdonk, 45–60. Amsterdam: Rodopi, 1994.

Eriksson, Anders, Thomas H. Olbricht, and Walter Übelacker, eds. *Rhetorical Argumentation in Biblical Texts: Essays from the Lund 2000 Conference*. Harrisburg, PA: Trinity Press International, 2002.

Eslinger, Lyle. "Inner-Biblical Exegesis and Inner-Biblical Allusion: The Question of Category." *VT* 42 (1992): 47–58.

———. *Kingship of God in Crisis: A Close Reading of 1 Samuel 1–12*. Sheffield: Almond, 1985.

Estes, Douglas. "Biblical Narrative." *Lexham Bible Dictionary*. Edited by John D. Barry. Bellingham, WA: Lexham Press, 2016.

———. *The Questions of Jesus in John: Logic, Rhetoric and Persuasive Discourse*. Leiden: Brill, 2013.

———. *The Temporal Mechanics of the Fourth Gospel: A Theory of Hermeneutical Relativity in the Gospel of John*. Leiden: Brill, 2008.

Estes, Douglas, and Ruth Sheridan, eds. *How John Works: Storytelling in the Gospel of John*. Atlanta: SBL Press, 2016.

Exum, J. Cheryl, and David J. A. Clines, eds. *The New Literary Criticism and the Hebrew Bible*. Sheffield: Sheffield Academic Press, 1993.

Fahnestock, Jeanne. *Rhetorical Style: The Uses of Language in Persuasion*. Oxford: Oxford University Press, 2011.

Felluga, Dino Franco. *Critical Theory: The Key Concepts*. New York: Routledge, 2015.

Fewell, Danna Nolan, ed. *The Oxford Handbook of Biblical Narrative*. Oxford: Oxford University Press, 2016.

Fish, Stanley. *Is There a Text in This Class? The Authority of Interpretive Communities*. Cambridge, MA: Harvard University Press, 1980.

Fish, Stanley E. "Interpereting the 'Variorum.'" *Critical Inquiry* 2, no. 3 (1976): 465–85.

Fishbane, Michael. *Biblical Interpretation in Ancient Israel*. Oxford: Clarendon, 1985.

———. "Inner Biblical Exegesis: Types and Strategies of Interpretation in Ancient Israel." In *Midrash and Literature*, edited by Geoffrey

H. Hartman and Sanford Budick, 19–37. New Haven, CT: Yale
University Press, 1986.

———. *The Garments of Torah: Essays in Biblical Hermeneutics.*
Bloomington, IN: Indiana University Press, 1992.

———. "The Hebrew Bible and Exegetical Tradition." In *Intertextuality
in Ugarit and Israel*, edited by Johannes C. de Moor, 15–30. Leiden:
Brill, 1998.

———. "Types of Biblical Intertextuality." In *Congress Volume: Oslo
1998*, edited by André Lemaire and Magne Sæbø, 39–44. Leiden:
Brill, 2000.

Floyd, Michael H. "Deutero-Zechariah and Types of Intertextuality." In
Bringing Out the Treasure: Inner Biblical Allusion in Zechariah 9–14,
edited by Mark J. Boda and Michael H. Floyd, 225–44. London:
T & T Clark, 2003.

Fokkelman, J. P. "Exodus." In *The Literary Guide to the Bible*, edited
by Robert Alter and Frank Kermode, 56–65. Cambridge, MA:
Belknap, 1987.

———. "Genesis." In *The Literary Guide to the Bible*, edited by Robert Alter
and Frank Kermode, 36–55. Cambridge, MA: Belknap, 1987.

———. *Narrative Art and Poetry in the Books of Samuel.* 4 vols. Assen: Van
Gorcum, 1981.

———. *Narrative Art in Genesis: Specimens of Stylistic and Structural
Analysis.* Assen: Van Gorcum, 1975.

———. *Reading Biblical Narrative.* Louisville, KY: Westminster John
Knox, 1999.

Forster, E. M. *Aspects of the Novel.* New York: Harcourt, Brace, and
World, 1927.

Fox, Michael V. "The Rhetoric of Ezekiel's Vision of the Valley of the
Bones." *HUCA* 51 (1980): 1–15.

Frankland, Graham. *Freud's Literary Culture.* New York: Cambridge
University Press, 2000.

Frei, Hans W. *The Eclipse of Biblical Narrative: A Study in Eighteenth and
Nineteenth Century Hermeneutics.* New Haven, CT: Yale University
Press, 1974.

Frye, Northrop. *Anatomy of Criticism: Four Essays.* Princeton, NJ:
Princeton University Press, 1957.

———. *The Great Code: The Bible and Literature*. New York: Harvest, 1983.

Gadamer, Hans-Georg. *Truth and Method*. Translated by Joel Weinsheimer and Donald G. Marshall. 2nd rev. ed. London: Continuum, 2004.

Gaines, Robert N. "Roman Rhetorical Handbooks." In *A Companion to Roman Rhetoric*, edited by William Dominik and Jon Hall, 163–80. Oxford: Blackwell, 2007.

Geiger, Abraham. *Urschrift Und Uebersetzungen Der Bibel in Ihrer Abhängigkeit von Der Innern Entwickelung Des Judenthums*. Breslau: Julius Hainauer, 1857.

Genette, Gérard. *Narrative Discourse: An Essay in Method*. Translated by Jane E. Lewin. Oxford: Basil Blackwell, 1980.

———. *Narrative Discourse Revisited*. Translated by Jane E. Lewin. Ithaca, NY: Cornell University Press, 1988.

Gignilliat, Mark S. *A Brief History of Old Testament Criticism: From Benedict Spinoza to Brevard Childs*. Grand Rapids: Zondervan, 2012.

Gillman, Neil. *The Way into Encountering God in Judaism*. Woodstock, VT: Jewish Lights, 2000.

Gitay, Yehoshua. "A Study of Amos's Art of Speech: A Rhetorical Analysis of Amos 3:1–15." *CBQ* 42 (1980): 293–309.

———. *Prophecy and Persuasion: A Study of Isaiah 40–48*. Bonn: Linguistica Biblica, 1981.

Good, Edwin M. *Irony in the Old Testament*. Sheffield: Almond, 1981.

Graff, Gerald. "Determinacy/Indeterminacy." In *Critical Terms for Literary Study*, edited by Frank Lentricchia and Thomas McLaughlin, 2nd ed. Chicago: University of Chicago Press, 1995.

Grant, Jaime A. *The King as Exemplar: The Function of Deuteronomy's Kingship Law in the Shaping of the Book of Psalms*. Atlanta: Society of Biblical Literature, 2004.

Green, Joel B. "Narrative Criticism." In *Methods for Luke*, edited by Joel B. Green, 74–112. Cambridge: Cambridge University Press, 2010.

———. *The Gospel of Luke*. NICNT. Grand Rapids: Eerdmans, 1997.

Greenwood, David. *Structuralism and the Biblical Text*. Berlin: Mouton, 1985.

Greimas, A. J., and Joseph Courtés. *Semiotics and Language: An Analytical Dictionary*. Translated by Larry Christ, Daniel Patte, James Lee,

Edward McMahon II, Gary Phillips, and Michael Rengstorf. Bloomington, IN: Indiana University Press, 1982.

Greimas, A. J., and Michael Rengstorf. "The Cognitive Dimension of Narrative Discourse." *New Literary History* 7 (1976): 433–47.

Gros Louis, Kenneth R. R., James S. Ackerman, and Thayer S. Warshaw, eds. *Literary Interpretations of Biblical Narratives.* Nashville, TN: Abingdon, 1974.

Gunkel, Hermann. *Creation and Chaos in the Primeval Era and the Eschaton: A Religio-Historical Study of Genesis 1 and Revelation 12.* With contributions by Heinrich Zimmern. Translated by K. William Whitney, Jr. Grand Rapids: Eerdmans, 2006.

———. *Schöpfung Und Chaos in Urzeit Und Endzeit: Eine Religionsgeschichtliche Untersuchung Über Gen 1 Und Ap Joh 12.* Göttingen: Vandenhoeck and Ruprecht, 1895.

Gunn, David M. "Narrative Criticism." In *To Each Its Own Meaning: An Introduction to Biblical Criticisms and Their Application*, edited by Steven L. McKenzie and Stephen R. Haynes, rev. and exp. ed., 201–29. Louisville, KY: Westminster John Knox, 1999.

———. "New Directions in the Study of Biblical Hebrew Narrative." In *New Directions in the Study of Biblical Hebrew Narrative*, edited by Paul R. House, 412–22. Winona Lake, IN: Eisenbrauns, 1992.

Habib, M. A. R. *Literary Criticism from Plato to the Present: An Introduction.* Malden, MA: Wiley-Blackwell, 2011.

Habinek, Thomas. *Ancient Rhetoric and Oratory.* Oxford: Blackwell, 2005.

Hafemann, Scott J., ed. *Biblical Theology: Retrospect and Prospect.* Downers Grove, IL: InterVarsity Press, 2002.

Hahn, Scott W. *Kinship by Covenant: A Canonical Approach to the Fulfillment of God's Saving Promises.* The Anchor Yale Bible Reference Library. New Haven, CT: Yale University Press, 2009.

Handelman, Susan A. *The Slayers of Moses: The Emergence of Rabbinic Interpretation in Modern Literary Theory.* Albany: State University of New York Press, 1982.

Haydon, Ronald. *"Seventy Sevens Are Decreed": A Canonical Approach to Daniel 9:24–27.* Winona Lake, IN: Eisenbrauns, 2016.

Hays, Richard B. "Can Narrative Criticism Recover the Theological Unity of Scripture?" *Journal of Theological Interpretation* 2, no. 2 (2008): 193–211.

———. *Echoes of Scripture in the Letters of Paul*. New Haven, CT: Yale University Press, 1989.

Heard, R. Christopher. "Narrative Criticism and the Hebrew Scriptures: A Review and Assessment." *Restoration Quarterly* 38, no. 1 (1996): 29–43.

Heath, Malcom. "The Substructure of Stasis-Theory from Hermagoras to Hermogenes." *Classical Quarterly* 44, no. 1 (1994): 114–29.

Hengel, Martin. *The Four Gospels and the One Gospel of Jesus Christ: An Investigation of the Collection and Origin of the Canonical Gospels*. Translated by J. Bowden. Harrisburg, PA: Trinity Press International, 2000.

Herman, David. *Basic Elements of Narrative*. Oxford: Wiley-Blackwell, 2009.

Hester, James D., and J. David Hester. *Rhetorics in the New Millennium: Promise and Fulfillment*. London: T & T Clark, 2010.

Henze, Matthias. *A Companion to Biblical Interpretation in Early Judaism*. Grand Rapids: Eerdmans, 2012.

Hirsch, E. D., Jr. *Validity in Interpretation*. New Haven, CT: Yale University Press, 1967.

Holman, J. "Semiotic Analysis of Psalm Cxxxviii (LXX)." In *In Quest of the Past: Studies on Israelite Religion, Literature, and Prophetism*, edited by A. S. van der Woude. Leiden: Brill, 1990.

House, Paul R., ed. *Beyond Form Criticism: Essays in Old Testament Literary Criticism*. Winona Lake, IN: Eisenbrauns, 1992.

Howard, David M., Jr. "Rhetorical Criticism in Old Testament Studies." *BBR* 4 (1994): 87–104.

Howard, Richard. Preface to *S/Z*, by Roland Barthes, translated by Richard Miller. Oxford: Blackwell, 1990.

Hunt, Steven A., D. Francois Tolmie, and Ruben Zimmermann, eds. *Character Studies in the Fourth Gospel: Narrative Approaches to Seventy Figures in John*. Tübingen: Mohr Siebeck, 2013.

Hurvitz, Avi. "Can Biblical Texts Be Dated Linguistically? Chronological Perspectives in the Historical Study of Biblical Hebrew." In

Congress Volume: Oslo, 1998, edited by André Lemaire and Magne
  Sæbø, 143–60. Leiden: Brill, 2000.

Iser, Wolfgang. *Prospecting: From Reader Response to Literary Anthropology.*
  Baltimore: Johns Hopkins University Press, 1989.

———. *The Implied Reader: Patterns of Communication in Prose Fiction
  from Bunyan to Beckett.* Baltimore: Johns Hopkins University
  Press, 1978.

———. *The Range of Interpretation.* New York: Columbia University
  Press, 2000.

Iverson, Kelly R., and Christopher W. Skinner, eds. *Mark as Story:
  Retrospect and Prospect.* Atlanta: Society of Biblical Literature, 2011.

Jackson, Leonard. *The Poverty of Structuralism: Literature and Structuralist
  Theory.* London: Longman, 1991.

Jacobson, Richard. "The Structuralists and the Bible." *Int* 28, no. 2
  (1974): 146–64.

Jakobson, Roman. *Main Trends in the Science of Language.* London: Allen
  & Unwin, 1973.

Jobling, David. "Structuralism, Hermeneutics, and Exegesis: Three
  Recent Contributions to the Debate." *USQR* 34, no. 3 (1979): 135–47.

———. "The Myth Semantics of Genesis 2:4b–3:24." *Semeia*, no. 18
  (1980): 41–49.

Jost, Walter, and Wendy Olmstead, eds. *A Companion to Rhetoric and
  Rhetorical Criticism.* Oxford: Blackwell, 2004.

Kalafenos, Emma. "Toward a Typology of Indeterminacy in Postmodern
  Narrative." *Comparative Literature* 44, no. 4 (1992): 380–408.

Kavanagh, Barry. "The Phonemes of Japanese and English: A Contrastive
  Analysis Study." *Journal of Aomori University of Health and Welfare*
  8, no. 2 (2007): 283–92.

Kelber, Werner. *Mark's Story of Jesus.* Philadelphia: Fortress, 1979.

Kennedy, George A. *A New History of Classical Rhetoric.* Princeton, NJ:
  Princeton University Press, 1994.

———. *Greek Rhetoric under Christian Emperors.* A History of Rhetoric 3.
  Princeton, NJ: Princeton University Press, 1983.

———. *Invention and Method: Two Rhetorical Treatises from the Hermogenic
  Corpus.* Atlanta: Society of Biblical Literature, 2005.

———. *New Testament Interpretation through Rhetorical Criticism.* Chapel Hill: University of North Carolina Press, 1984.

Kennedy, George A., trans. *Progymnasmata: Greek Textbooks of Prose Composition and Rhetoric.* SBLWGRW 10. Atlanta: Society of Biblical Literature, 2003.

———. *The Art of Persuasion in the Greece.* A History of Rhetoric 1. Princeton, NJ: Princeton University Press, 1963.

———. *The Art of Rhetoric in the Roman World: 300 B.C.–A.D. 300.* A History of Rhetoric 2. Princeton, NJ: Princeton University Press, 1972.

Kermode, Frank. *The Genesis of Secrecy: On the Interpretation of Narrative.* Cambridge, MA: Harvard University Press, 1979.

———. *The Sense of an Ending: Studies in the Theory of Fiction.* New York: Oxford University Press, 2000.

Kessler, Martin. "A Methodological Setting for Rhetorical Criticism." In *Art and Meaning: Rhetoric in Biblical Literature*, edited by David J. A. Clines, David M. Gunn, and Alan J. Hauser, 1–19. Sheffield: JSOT Press, 1982.

———. "Rhetorical Criticism of Genesis 7." In *Rhetorical Criticism: Essays in Honor of James Muilenburg*, edited by Jared J. Jackson and Martin Kessler, 1–17. Pittsburgh: Pickwick, 1974.

Kingsbury, Jack Dean, ed. *Gospel Interpretation: Narrative-Critical and Social-Scientific Approaches.* Harrisburg, PA: Trinity Press International, 1997.

———. *Matthew as Story.* Philadelphia: Fortress, 1986.

———. "Reflections on the 'Reader' of Matthew's Gospel." *NTS* 34 (1988): 442–60.

Klarer, Mario. *An Introduction to Literary Studies.* 2nd ed. London: Routledge, 2004.

Klerk, Johannes C. de. "Situating Biblical Narrative Studies in Literary Theory and Literary Approaches." *R&T* 4 (1997): 190–207.

Klink, Edward W., III. "The Bridegroom at Cana: Ignorance Is Bliss." In *Character Studies in the Fourth Gospel: Narrative Approaches to Seventy Figures in John*, edited by Steven A. Hunt, D. Francois Tolmie, and Ruben Zimmermann, 233–37. Tübingen: Mohr Siebeck, 2013.

Kloppenborg, John S., and Judith Hood Newman, eds. *Editing the Bible: Assessing the Task Past and Present*. Atlanta: Society of Biblical Literature, 2012.

Knight, Douglas A. *Rediscovering the Traditions of Israel*. 3rd ed. Atlanta: Society of Biblical Literature, 2006.

Knight, Mark. "Wirkungsgeschichte, Reception History, Reception Theory." *JSNT* 33, no. 2 (2010): 137–46.

Kort, Wesley A. *Story, Text, and Scripture: Literary Interests in Biblical Narrative*. University Park: Pennsylvania State University Press, 1988.

Kovacs, Brian W. "Philosophical Foundations for Structuralism." *Semeia*, no. 10 (1978): 85–105.

———. "Structure and Narrative Rhetoric in Genesis 2–3: Reflections on the Problem of Non-Convergent Structuralist Exegetical Methodologies." *Semeia*, no. 18 (1980): 139–47.

Kristeva, Julia. *Desire in Language: A Semiotic Approach to Literature and Art*. Edited by Leon Roudiez. Translated by Thomas Gora, Alice Jardine, and Leon Roudiez. New York: Columbia University Press, 1980.

———. *Tales of Love*. Translated by Leon S. Roudiez. New York: Columbia University Press, 1987.

Kugel, James L. "The Bible's Earliest Interpreters." *Prooftexts: A Journal of Jewish Literary History* 7 (1987): 269–83.

———. *The Idea of Biblical Poetry: Parallelism and Its History*. New Haven, CT: Yale University Press, 1981.

Kurz, W. J. "Narrative Models for Imitation in Luke-Acts." In *Greeks, Romans, and Christians: Essays in Honor of Abraham J. Malherbe*, edited by David L. Balch, Everett Ferguson, and Wayne A. Meeks, 171–89. Minneapolis: Fortress, 1990.

Lamarque, Peter. "The Intentional Fallacy." In *Literary Theory and Criticism: An Oxford Guide*, edited by Patricia Waugh. Oxford: Oxford University Press, 2006.

Lampe, Peter. "Rhetorical Analysis of Pauline Texts—Quo Vadit? Methodological Reflections." In *Paul and Rhetoric*, edited by J. Paul Sampley and Peter Lampe, 3–21. New York: T & T Clark, 2010.

———. "Theological Wisdom and the 'Word About the Cross': The Rhetorical Scheme in 1 Corinthians 1-4." *Int* 44 (1990): 117-31.

Lanham, Richard A. *A Handlist of Rhetorical Terms*. 2nd ed. Berkeley: University of California Press, 1991.

Lawlor, John I. "Theology and Art in the Narrative of the Ammonite War." *Grace Theological Journal* 3 (1982): 193-205.

Leach, Edmund. "Lévi-Strauss in the Garden of Eden: An Examination of Some Recent Developments in the Analysis of Myth." *Transactions of the New York Academy of Sciences (Series 2)* 23 (1961): 386-96.

Leiman, Shnayer Z. *The Canonization of Hebrew Scripture: The Talmudic and Midrashic Evidence*. Hamden, CT: Published for the Academy by Archon Books, 1976.

Leithart, Peter J. *Deep Exegesis: The Mystery of Reading Scripture*. Waco, TX: Baylor University Press, 2009.

Lemaire, André, and Magne Sæbø, eds. *Congress Volume: Oslo 1998*. Leiden: Brill, 2000.

Lentricchia, Frank, and Thomas McLaughlin, eds. *Critical Terms for Literary Study*. 2nd ed. Chicago: University of Chicago Press, 1995.

Levinson, Bernard M. *Deuteronomy and the Hermeneutics of Legal Innovation*. New York: Oxford University Press, 1997.

———. *Legal Revision and Religious Renewal in Ancient Israel*. New York: Cambridge University Press, 2008.

Lévi-Strauss, Claude. *Les structures élémentaires de la parenté*. Paris: Presses universitaires de France, 1949.

———. *The Elementary Structures of Kinship*. London: Eyre & Spottiswood, 1967.

Lewis, David. *On the Plurality of Worlds*. Oxford: Basil Blackwell, 1986.

Libanius. *Libanius's Progymnasmata: Model Exercises in Greek Prose Composition and Rhetoric*. Translated by Craig A. Gibson. Atlanta: Society of Biblical Literature, 2008.

Litz, A. Walton, Louis Menand, and Lawrence Rainey, eds. *The Cambridge History of Literary Criticism*. Vol. 7, *Modernism and the New Criticism*. Cambridge: Cambridge University Press, 1985.

Long, Frederick. *Ancient Rhetoric and Paul's Apology: The Compositional Unity of 2 Corinthians*. Cambridge: Cambridge University Press, 2004.

Longman, Tremper, III. *Literary Approaches to Biblical Interpretation.*
    Grand Rapids: Zondervan, 1987.

Lowe, N. J. *The Classical Plot and the Invention of Western Narrative.*
    Cambridge: Cambridge University Press, 1985.

Lowenthal, David. *The Past Is a Foreign Country.* Cambridge: Cambridge
    University Press, 1985.

Lowth, Robert. *Lectures on the Sacred Poetry of the Hebrews.* Translated by
    G. Gregory. 3rd ed. London: Thomas Tegg & Son, 1835.

Lukács, George. *The Theory of the Novel: A Historico-Philosophical Essay
    on the Forms of Great Epic Literature.* Translated by Anna Bostock.
    Cambridge, MA: MIT Press, 1971.

Lundbom, Jack R. *Jeremiah.* Anchor Bible 21A–C. New York:
    Doubleday, 1999.

———. *Jeremiah: A Study in Ancient Hebrew Rhetoric.* Missoula, MT:
    Scholars Press, 1975.

Lyons, William John. *Canon and Exegesis: Canonical Praxis and the
    Sodom Narrative.* JSOTSupp 352. Sheffield: Sheffield Academic
    Press, 2002.

Macherey, Pierre. *A Theory of Literary Production.* Translated by Geoffrey
    Wall. London: Routledge & Kegan Paul, 1978.

Malbon, Elizabeth Struthers. "Narrative Criticism: How Does the Story
    Mean?" In *Mark and Method: New Approaches in Biblical Studies,*
    edited by J. C. Anderson and S. D. Moore, 23–49. Minneapolis:
    Fortress, 1992.

———. "Structuralism, Hermeneutics, and Contextual Meaning." *JAAR* 51,
    no. 2 (1983): 207–30.

———. "The Theory and Practice of Structural Exegesis: A Review
    Article." *PRSt* 11, no. 3 (1984): 273–82.

Man, Paul de. *Blindness and Insight: Essays in the Rhetoric of Contemporary
    Criticism.* 2nd ed. Oxford: Oxford University Press, 1971.

———. *The Rhetoric of Romanticism.* New York: Columbia University
    Press, 1984.

Mangum, Douglas, and Amy Balogh, eds. *Social and Historical Approaches
    to the Bible.* Lexham Methods Series 3. Bellingham, WA: Lexham
    Press, 2017.

Mason, Rex. "The Use of Earlier Biblical Material in Zechariah 9–14: A Study in Inner Biblical Exegesis." In *Bringing Out the Treasure: Inner Biblical Allusion in Zechariah 9–14*, edited by Mark J. Boda and Michael H. Floyd, 245–59. London: T & T Clark, 2003.

McConville, J. Gordon. "Old Testament Laws and Canonical Intentionality." In *Canon and Biblical Interpretation*, edited by Craig G. Bartholomew et al., 259–81. Grand Rapids: Zondervan, 2006.

McDonald, Lee Martin. *The Biblical Canon: Its Origin, Transmission, and Authority*. 3rd ed. Peabody, MA: Hendrickson, 2007.

———. *The Formation of the Christian Biblical Canon*. Peabody, MA: Hendrickson, 1995.

McDonald, Lee Martin, and James A. Sanders, eds. *The Canon Debate*. Peabody, MA: Hendrickson, 2002.

McWhirter, Jocelyn. *The Bridegroom Messiah and the People of God: Marriage in the Fourth Gospel*. Cambridge: Cambridge University Press, 2006.

Meltzer, Françoise. Introduction to *Signature Derrida*, by Jacques Derrida, edited by Jay Williams. Chicago: University of Chicago Press, 2013.

Merenlahti, Petri. *Poetics for the Gospels?: Rethinking Narrative Criticism*. London: T & T Clark, 2002.

Meynet, Roland. *Treatise on Biblical Rhetoric*. Translated by Leo Arnold. Leiden: Brill, 2012.

Mihaila, Corin. *The Paul-Apollos Relationship and Paul's Stance Toward Greco-Roman Rhetoric: An Exegetical and Socio-Historical Study of 1 Corinthians 1–4*. New York: T & T Clark, 2009.

Mikics, David. *A New Handbook of Literary Terms*. New Haven, CT: Yale University Press, 2007.

Milgrom, Jacob. *Numbers*. JPS Torah Commentary. Philadelphia: The Jewish Publication Society, 1990.

Miller, J. Hillis, ed. *Aspects of Narrative: Selected Papers from the English Institute*. New York: Columbia University Press, 1971.

Mitchell, Margaret M. *Paul and the Rhetoric of Reconciliation: An Exegetical Investigation of the Language and Composition of 1 Corinthians*. Louisville, KY: Westminster John Knox, 1993.

Moore, Stephen. "A Modest Manifesto for New Testament Literary Criticism: How to Interface with a Literary Studies Field That Is Post-Literary, Post-Theoretical, and Post-Methodological." *Biblical Interpretation* 15 (2007): 1–25.

Moore, Stephen D. *Literary Criticism and the Gospels: The Theoretical Challenge*. New Haven, CT: Yale University Press, 1989.

Muilenburg, James. "A Liturgy on the Triumphs of Yahweh." In *Studia Biblica et Semitica*, edited by W. C. van Unnik and A. B. van der Woude, 233–51. Wageningen: H. Veenman en Zonen, 1966.

———. "Form Criticism and Beyond." *JBL* 88 (1969): 1–18.

———. "The Book of Isaiah: Chapters 40–66." In *The Interpreter's Bible*, edited by George Arthur Buttrick, 5:381–773. New York: Abingdon, 1956.

Murphy, James J., and Richard A. Katula. *A Synoptic History of Classical Rhetoric*. 3rd ed. Mahwah, NJ: LEA, 2003.

Myers, Alicia D. *Characterizing Jesus: A Rhetorical Analysis on the Fourth Gospel's Use of Scripture in Its Presentation of Jesus*. London: T & T Clark, 2012.

Nadeau, Ray. "Classical Systems of Stases in Greek: Hermagoras to Hermogenes." *NovT* 52 (2010): 355–75.

Nickelsburg, George W. E. "Tobit, Genesis, and the Odyssey: A Complex Web of Intertextuality." In *Mimesis and Intertextuality in Antiquity and Christianity*, edited by Dennis R. MacDonald, 41–55. Harrisburg, PA: Trinity Press International, 2001.

Nissinen, Martti, ed. *Congress Volume: Helsinki 2010*. Leiden: Brill, 2012.

Noble, Paul. "Esau, Tamar, and Joseph: Criteria for Identifying Inner-Biblical Allusions." *VT* 52 (2002): 219–52.

Nogalski, James D. "Intertextuality and the Twelve." In *Forming Prophetic Literature: Essays on Isaiah and the Twelve in Honor of John D. W. Watts*, edited by James W. Watts and Paul R. House, 102–24. Sheffield: Sheffield Academic Press, 1996.

Noth, Martin. *A History of Pentateuchal Traditions*. Translated by Bernhard W. Anderson. Chico, CA: Scholars Press, 1981.

Nurmela, Risto. *Prophets in Dialogue: Inner-Biblical Allusions in Zechariah 1–8 and 9–14*. Åbo: Åbo Akademi University Press, 1996.

———. "The Growth of the Book of Isaiah Illustrated by Allusions in
Zechariah." In *Bringing Out the Treasure: Inner Biblical Allusion
in Zechariah 9-14*, edited by Mark J. Boda and Michael H. Floyd,
245-59. London: T & T Clark, 2003.

O'Connor, Michael P. *Hebrew Verse Structrue*. Winona Lake, IN:
Eisenbrauns, 1980.

Olmstead, Wendy. *Rhetoric: An Historical Introduction*. Oxford:
Blackwell, 2006.

Oswalt, John N. "Canonical Criticism: A Review from a Conservative."
Journal of the Evangelical Theological Society 30 (1987): 317-25.

Paris, Christopher T. *Narrative Obtrusion in the Hebrew Bible*.
Minneapolis: Fortress, 2014.

Parrish, V. Steven. *A Story of the Psalms: Conversation, Canon, and
Congregation*. Collegeville, MN: Liturgical Press, 2003.

Patrick, Dale, and Allen Scult. *Rhetoric and Biblical Interpretation*.
Sheffield: Almond, 1990.

Patte, Daniel. "One Text: Several Structures." *Semeia*, no. 18 (1980): 3-22.

Patte, Daniel, and Judson Parker. "A Structural Exegesis of Genesis 2 and
3." *Semeia*, no. 18 (1980): 55-75.

Patte, Daniel, and Aline Patte. *Structural Exegesis: From Theory to Practice*.
Philadelphia: Fortress Press, 1978.

Pavel, Thomas G. *Fictional Worlds*. Cambridge, MA: Harvard University
Press, 1986.

Pearson, Brook W. R. "New Testament Literary Criticism." In *Handbook
to Exegesis of the New Testament*, edited by S. E. Porter, 241-66.
Leiden: Brill, 1997.

Perelman, Chaïm. *The New Rhetoric: A Treatise on Argumentation*.
Dordrecht: D. Reidel, 1979.

Perelman, Chaïm, and Lucie Olbrechts-Tyteca. *The New Rhetoric: A
Treatise on Argumentation*. Notre Dame, IN: University of Notre
Dame Press, 1969.

Perry, Menakhem, and Meir Sternberg. "The King through Ironic Eyes:
Biblical Narrative and the Literary Reading Process." *Poetics Today*
7 (1986): 275-322.

———. "The King through Ironic Eyes: The Narrator's Devices in the
    Story of David and Bathsheba and Two Excurses on the Theory of
    the Narrative Text." *Ha-Sifrut* 1 (1968): 263–93.

Perry, T. Anthony. "A Poetics of Absence: The Structure and Meaning of
    Genesis 1:2." *JSOT* 58 (1993): 3–11.

Petersen, David L. "Zechariah 9–14: Methodological Reflections." In
    Bringing Out the Treasure: Inner Biblical Allusion in Zechariah 9–14,
    edited by Mark J. Boda and Michael H. Floyd, 210–24. London:
    T & T Clark, 2003.

Petersen, Norman. *Rediscovering Paul: Philemon and the Sociology of Paul's
    Narrative World*. Philadelphia: Fortress Press, 1985.

Petersen, Norman R. *Literary Criticism for New Testament Critics*.
    Philadelphia: Fortress Press, 1978.

Phelan, James, and Peter J. Rabinowitz, eds. *A Companion to Narrative
    Theory*. Oxford: Blackwell, 2005.

Phillips, Gary A. "Editor's Introduction." *Semeia*, no. 51 (1990): 1–5.

Plato. *Gorgias*. Translated by W.R.M. Lamb. Medford, MA: Harvard
    University Press, 1967.

Plett, Heinrich F., ed. *Intertextuality*. Berlin: Walter de Gruyter, 1991.

Polzin, Robert. "Deuteronomy." In *The Literary Guide to the Bible*, edited
    by Robert Alter and Frank Kermode, 92–101. Cambridge, MA:
    Belknap, 1987.

———. "'The Ancestress of Israel in Danger' in Danger." *Semeia*, no. 3
    (1975): 81–98.

———. "The Framework of the Book of Job." *Int* 28, no. 2 (1974): 182–200.

Pontifical Biblical Commission. "The Interpretation of the Bible in
    the Church." *Pontifical Biblical Commission - Documents*, April 15,
    1993. http://www.vatican.va/roman_curia/congregations/cfaith/
    pcb_doc_index.htm.

Porter, Stanley E., ed. *Handbook of Classical Rhetoric in the Hellenistic
    Period: 330 B.C.–A.D. 400*. Leiden: Brill, 1997.

Porter, Stanley E., and Thomas H. Olbricht. *Rhetoric and the New
    Testament: Essays from the 1992 Heidelberg Conference*. Sheffield:
    Sheffield Academic Press, 1993.

Porter, Stanley E., and Dennis L. Stamps, eds. "Rhetorical and
    Narratological Criticism." In *Handbook to Exegesis of the New
    Testament*, 219-39. Leiden: Brill, 1997.
———, eds. *Rhetorical Criticism and the Bible: Essays from the 1998 Florence
    Conference*. London: Sheffield Academic Press, 2002.
Powell, Mark Allan. "Narrative Criticism." In *Hearing the New Testament:
    Strategies for Interpretation*, edited by Joel B. Green, 2nd ed.,
    240-58. Grand Rapids: Eerdmans, 2010.
———. "Narrative Criticism: The Emergence of a Prominent Reading
    Strategy." In *Mark as Story: Retrospect and Prospect*, edited by K.
    R. Iverson and Christopher W. Skinner, 19-43. RBS 65. Atlanta:
    Society of Biblical Literature, 2011.
———. "Types of Readers and Their Relevance for Biblical
    Hermeneutics." *TSRev* 12 (1990): 19-34.
———. *What Is Narrative Criticism?* Minneapolis: Fortress, 1990.
Poythress, Vern S. "Structuralism and Biblical Studies." *JETS* 21, no. 3
    (1978): 221-37.
Prince, Gerald. "Narrative Analysis and Narratology." *New Literary
    History* 13, no. 2 (1982): 179-88.
———. *Narratology: The Form and Functioning of Narrative*. Berlin:
    Mouton, 1982.
Propp, Vladimir. *Morphology of the Folktale*. Edited by Louis A. Wagner.
    Translated by Laurence Scott. 2nd ed. Austin: University of Texas
    Press, 1968.
Quine, W. V. *Word and Object*. Cambridge, MA: MIT Press, 1960.
Quintilian. *Institutio Oratoria*. Edited by Harold Edgeworth Butler.
    Medford, MA: Harvard University Press, 1920.
Rabinowitz, Peter J. "Against Close Reading." In *Pedagogy Is Politics:
    Literary Theory and Critical Teaching*, edited by Maria-Regina
    Kecht, 230-43. Urbana: University of Illinois Press, 1992.
Rad, Gerhard von. *Genesis: A Commentary*. Translated by John H. Marks.
    OTL. Philadelphia: Westminster, 1961.
———. *The Problem of the Hexateuch and Other Essays*. Translated by E. W.
    Trueman Dicken. Edinburgh: Oliver & Boyd, 1966.
Ransom, John Crowe. *The New Criticism*. Norfolk: New Directions, 1941.

Resseguie, James L. *Narrative Criticism of the New Testament: An Introduction.* Grand Rapids: Baker, 2005.

———. *Revelation Unsealed: A Narrative Critical Approach to John's Apocalypse.* Leiden: Brill, 1998.

Rhoads, David M. "Narrative Criticism and the Gospel of Mark." *JAAR* 50, no. 3 (1982): 411–34.

———. "Narrative Criticism: Practices and Prospects." In *Characterization in the Gospels: Reconceiving Narrative Criticism,* edited by David M. Rhoads and Kari Syreeni, 264–85. Sheffield: Sheffield Academic Press, 1999.

Rhoads, David M., and Kari Syreeni, eds. *Characterization in the Gospels: Reconceiving Narrative Criticism.* Sheffield: Sheffield Academic Press, 1999.

Rhoads, David, and Donald Michie. *Mark as Story: An Introduction to the Narrative of a Gospel.* Philadelphia: Fortress, 1982.

Rhoads, David, Donald Michie, and Joanna Dewey. *Mark as Story: An Introduction to the Narrative of a Gospel.* 3rd ed. Minneapolis: Fortress, 2012.

Richards, I. A. *Practical Criticism: A Study of Literary Judgment.* London: Kegan Paul, Trench, Trubner, 1930.

———. *Principles of Literary Criticism.* New York: Harcourt Brace, 1961.

———. *Science and Poetry.* New York: W. W. Norton, 1926.

Richardson, Brian. *Narrative Dynamics: Essays on Time, Plot, Closure, and Frames.* Columbus: Ohio State University Press, 2002.

Ricœur, Paul. *Figuring the Sacred: Religion, Narrative, and Imagination.* Edited by Mark I. Wallace. Translated by David Pellauer. Minneapolis: Fortress Press, 1995.

Ricoeur, Paul. *History and Truth.* Translated by Charles A. Kelbley. Evanston, IL: Northwestern University Press, 1965.

Rimmon-Kenan, Shlomith. *Narrative Fiction: Contemporary Poetics.* London: Routledge, 1994.

Ritterspach, A. D. "Rhetorical Criticism and the Song of Hannah." In *Rhetorical Criticism: Essays in Honor of James Muilenburg,* edited by Jared J. Jackson and Martin Kessler, 68–74. Pittsburgh: Pickwick, 1974.

Robbins, Vernon K. *Jesus the Teacher: A Socio-Rhetorical Interpretation of Mark.* Minneapolis: Fortress, 1992.

———. "Structuralism in Biblical Interpretation and Theology." *The Thomist* 42 (1978): 349–72.

Robertson, David A. *Linguistic Evidence in Dating Early Hebrew Poetry.* Missoula, MT: Society of Biblical Literature, 1972.

Rodway, Allan. *The Craft of Criticism.* Cambridge: Cambridge University Press, 1982.

Ronen, Ruth. *Possible Worlds in Literary Theory.* Cambridge: Cambridge University Press, 1994.

Rosenberg, Joel. "Meanings, Morals, and Mysteries: Literary Approaches to the Torah." *Response: A Contemporary Jewish Review* 9 (1975): 67–94.

Rosenzweig, Franz. "Die Einheit Der Bibel: Eine Auseinandersetzung Mit Orthodoxie Und Liberalismus." In *Die Schrift Und Ihre Verdeutschung*, edited by Martin Buber and Franz Rosenzweig. Berlin: Schocken, 1936.

Rothschild, Clare K. *Luke-Acts and the Rhetoric of History: An Investigation of Early Christian Historiography.* Tübingen: Mohr Siebeck, 2004.

Rubinelli, Sara. *Ars Topica: The Classical Technique of Constructing Arguments from Aristotle to Cicero.* Dordrecht: Springer, 2009.

Ryken, Leland. "The Bible as Literature: A Brief History." In *A Complete Literary Guide to the Bible*, edited by Leland Ryken and Tremper Longman III, 49–68. Grand Rapids: Zondervan, 1993.

Ryken, Leland, and Tremper Longman III, eds. *A Complete Literary Guide to the Bible.* Grand Rapids: Zondervan, 1993.

———. "Introduction." In *A Complete Literary Guide to the Bible*, edited by Leland Ryken and Tremper Longman III, 15–39. Grand Rapids: Zondervan, 1993.

Ryle, Herbert Edward. *The Canon of the Old Testament: An Essay on the Gradual Growth and Formation of the Hebrew Canon of Scripture.* 2nd ed. London: Macmillan, 1914.

Sailhamer, John H. "Biblical Theology and the Composition of the Hebrew Bible." In *Biblical Theology: Retrospect and Prospect*, edited by Scott J. Hafemann, 25–37. Downers Grove, IL: InterVarsity Press, 2002.

————. *Introduction to Old Testament Theology: A Canonical Approach.* Grand Rapids: Zondervan, 1995.

Sampley, J. Paul, and Peter Lampe, eds. *Paul and Rhetoric.* New York: T & T Clark, 2010.

Sanders, James A. "Canonical Context and Canonical Criticism." *Horizons in Biblical Theology* 2 (1980): 173–97.

————. *From Sacred Story to Sacred Text: Canon as Paradigm.* Eugene, OR: Wipf and Stock, 2000.

————. "Review of *Holy Scripture: Canon, Authority, Criticism,* by James Barr." *Journal of Biblical Literature* 104 (1985): 501–2.

————. *Torah and Canon.* Philadelphia: Fortress, 1972.

Sarna, Nahum M. "Abraham Geiger and Biblical Scholarship." In *New Perspectives on Abraham Geiger: An HUC-JIR Symposium,* edited by Jakob Josef Petuchowski. Cincinnati: Hebrew Union College, 1975.

————. "Psalm 89: A Study in Inner Biblical Exegesis." In *Biblical and Other Studies,* edited by Alexander Altmann. Cambridge, MA: Harvard University Press, 1963.

Saussure, Ferdinand de. *Cours de linguistique générale.* Edited by Charles Bally, Albert Secheye, and Albert Reidlinger. Paris: Payot, 1916.

————. *Course in General Linguistics.* Edited by Charles Bally, Albert Secheye, and Albert Reidlinger. Translated by Wade Baskin. New York: Philosophical Library, 1959.

————. *Course in General Linguistics.* Translated and annotated by Roy Harris. London: Bloomsbury, 2013.

Scalise, Charles J. *Hermeneutics as Theological Prolegomena: A Canonical Approach.* Macon, GA: Mercer University Press, 1994.

Schellenberg, Ryan S. *Rethinking Paul's Rhetorical Education: Comparative Rhetoric and 2 Corinthians 10–13.* Atlanta: Society of Biblical Literature, 2013.

Schneidewind, William. "'Are We His People or Not': Biblical Interpretation During Crisis." *Biblica* 76 (1995): 540–50.

Scholes, Robert. *Structuralism in Literature: An Introduction.* New Haven, CT: Yale University Press, 1974.

Schultz, Richard L. "Intertextuality, Canon, and 'Undecidability': Understanding Isaiah's 'New Heavens and New Earth' (Isaiah 65:17–25)." *Bulletin for Biblical Research* 20 (2010): 19–38.

Schweitzer, Albert. *The Quest of the Historical Jesus*. Translated by W. Montgomery. Mineola, NY: Dover, 2005.

Seeley, David. *Deconstructing the New Testament*. Leiden: Brill, 1994.

Segal, Gabriel. "Four Arguments for the Indeterminacy of Translation." In *Knowledge, Language and Logic: Questions for Quine*, edited by Alex Orenstein and Petr Kotatko, 131–39. Dordrecht: Springer, 2000.

Seitz, Christopher R. "The Canonical Approach and Theological Interpretation." In *Canon and Biblical Interpretation*, edited by Craig G. Bartholomew et al., 58–110. Grand Rapids: Zondervan, 2006.

———. *The Character of Christian Scripture: The Significance of a Two-Testament Bible*. Studies in Theological Interpretation. Grand Rapids: Baker Academic, 2011.

———. *The Goodly Fellowship of the Prophets: The Achievement of Association in Canon Formation*. Grand Rapids: Baker Academic, 2009.

———. *Prophecy and Hermeneutics: Toward a New Introduction to the Prophets*. Studies in Theological Interpretation. Grand Rapids: Baker Academic, 2007.

———. "Tribute to Brevard Childs at the International SBL Meeting in Vienna, Austria." In *The Bible as Christian Scripture*, edited by Christopher R. Seitz and Kent Harold Richards, 1–8. Atlanta: Society of Biblical Literature, 2013.

Seitz, Christopher R., and Kent Harold Richards, eds. *The Bible as Christian Scripture: The Work of Brevard S. Childs*. Atlanta: Society of Biblical Literature, 2013.

Selden, Raman, ed. *The Cambridge History of Literary Criticism*. Vol. 8, *From Formalism to Poststructuralism*. Cambridge: Cambridge University Press, 1995.

Selden, Raman, Peter Widdowson, and Peter Brooker. *A Reader's Guide to Contemporary Literary Theory*. 5th ed. Harlow, UK: Pearson, 2005.

Shen, Dan. "What Narratology and Stylistics Can Do For Each Other." In *A Companion to Narrative Theory*, edited by James Phelan and Peter J. Rabinowitz. Oxford: Blackwell, 2005.

Sherwood, Yvonne. "Jacques Derrida and Biblical Studies." *SBL Forum*, 2004. sbl-site.org/Article.aspx?ArticleID=332.

Shklovsky, Viktor. "The Resurrection of the Word." In *Russian Formalism: A Collection of Articles and Texts in Translation*, edited by Stephen Bann and John E. Bowlt. Edinburgh: Scottish Academic Press, 1973.

Sider, John W. "Nurturing Our Nurse: Literary Scholars and Biblical Exegesis." *ChrLit* 32 (1982): 15–21.

Skinner, Christopher W. "Characterization." In *How John Works: Storytelling in the Gospel of John*, edited by Douglas Estes and Ruth Sheridan, 115–32. Atlanta: SBL Press, 2016.

———, ed. *Characters and Characterization in the Gospel of John*. London: Bloomsbury, 2013.

Sklar, Robert. "Chomsky's Revolution in Linguistics." In *Noam Chomsky: Critical Assessments*, edited by Carlos P. Otero, Vol. 3. London: Routledge, 1994.

Smith, Morton. *Palestinian Parties and Politics That Shaped the Old Testament*. New York: Columbia University Press, 1971.

Smith, Robert W. *The Art of Rhetoric in Alexandria: Its Theory and Practice in the Ancient World*. The Hague: Martinus Nijhoff, 1974.

Sommer, Benjamin D. *A Prophet Reads Scripture: Allusion in Isaiah 40–66*. Stanford: Stanford University Press, 1998.

———. "Allusions and Illusions: The Unity of the Book of Isaiah in Light of Deutero-Isaiah's Use of Prophetic Tradition." In *New Visions of Isaiah*, edited by Roy F. Melugin and Marvin A. Sweeney, 156–87. Sheffield: Sheffield Academic Press, 1996.

———. "Exegesis, Allusion and Intertextuality in the Hebrew Bible: A Response to Lyle Eslinger." *VT* 46 (1996): 479–89.

Spellman, Ched. *Toward Canon-Conscious Reading of the Bible: Exploring the History and Hermeneutics of the Canon*. Sheffield: Sheffield Phoenix, 2014.

Stanley, Christopher D. *Arguing with Scripture: The Rhetoric of Quotations in the Letters of Paul*. London: T & T Clark, 2004.

Stein, Robert H. "The Benefits of an Author-Oriented Approach to Hermeneutics." *JETS* 44, no. 3 (2001): 451–66.

Sternberg, Meir. "The Bible's Art of Persuasion: Ideology, Rhetoric, and Poetics in Saul's Fall." *HUCA* 54 (1983): 45–82.

———. *The Poetics of Biblical Narrative: Ideological Literature and the Drama of Reading*. Bloomington, IN: Indiana University Press, 1985.

Stone, Timothy J. *The Compilational History of the Megilloth: Canon, Contoured Intertextuality and Meaning in the Writings*. Tübingen: Mohr Siebeck, 2013.

Stowers, Stanley K. *The Diatribe and Paul's Letter to the Romans*. Chico, CA: Scholars Press, 1981.

Sundberg, Albert C. *The Old Testament of the Early Church*. Cambridge, MA: Harvard University Press, 1964.

Sweeney, Marvin A. "Form Criticism." In *To Each Its Own Meaning: An Introduction to Biblical Criticisms and Their Application*, edited by Steven L. McKenzie and Stephen R. Haynes, rev. and exp. ed., 58–89. Louisville, KY: Westminster John Knox, 1999.

Swirski, Peter. *Literature, Analytically Speaking: Explorations in the Theory of Interpretation, Analytic Aesthetics, and Evolution*. Austin: University of Texas Press, 2010.

Tai, Nicholas H. F. *Prophetie Als Schriftauslegung in Sacharja 9-14: Traditions- Und Kompositionsgeschichtliche Studien*. Stuttgart: Calwer, 1996.

Tannehill, Robert C. *The Narrative Unity of Luke-Acts: A Literary Interpretation*. 2 vols. Philadelphia; Minneapolis: Fortress, 1986.

Tanner, Beth LaNeel. *The Book of Psalms through the Lens of Intertextuality*. New York: Peter Lang, 2001.

Thielman, Frank. *Theology of the New Testament: A Canonical and Synthetic Approach*. Grand Rapids: Zondervan, 2005.

Thiselton, Anthony C. *A Concise Encyclopedia of the Philosophy of Religion*. Oxford: Oneworld, 2002.

———. "Introduction: Canon, Community and Theological Construction." In *Canon and Biblical Interpretation*, edited by Craig G. Bartholomew et al., 1–30. Grand Rapids: Zondervan, 2006.

Tite, Philip L. *The Apocryphal Epistle to the Laodiceans: An Epistolary and Rhetorical Analysis*. Leiden: Brill, 2012.

Todorov, Tzvetan. *Introduction to Poetics*. Translated by Richard Howard. Sussex: Harvester, 1981.

Tolbert, Mary Ann. *Sowing the Gospel: Mark's World in Literary-Historical Perspective*. Minneapolis: Fortress, 1989.

Tompkins, Jane P., ed. *Reader-Response Criticism: From Formalism to Post-Structuralism*. Baltimore: Johns Hopkins University Press, 1980.

Treier, Daniel J. *Introducing Theological Interpretation of Scripture: Recovering a Christian Practice*. Grand Rapids: Baker, 2008.

Trible, Phyllis. *Rhetorical Criticism: Context, Method, and the Book of Jonah*. Minneapolis: Fortress, 1994.

Trick, B. R. "Death, Covenants, and the Proof of Resurrection in Mark 12:18–27." *NovT* 49 (2007): 232–56.

Tull, Patricia K. "Rhetorical Criticism and Intertextuality." In *To Each Its Own Meaning: An Introduction to Biblical Criticisms and Their Application*, edited by Steven L. McKenzie and Stephen R. Haynes, rev. and exp. ed., 156–180. Louisville, KY: Westminster John Knox, 1999.

Ulrich, Eugene. "The Evolutionary Composition of the Hebrew Bible." In *Editing the Bible: Assessing the Task Past and Present*, edited by John S. Kloppenborg and Judith H. Newman, 23–40. Atlanta: Society of Biblical Literature, 2012.

———. "The Notion and Definition of Canon." In *The Canon Debate: On the Origins and the Formation of the Bible*, edited by Lee Martin McDonald and James A. Sanders, 21–35. Peabody, MA: Hendrickson, 2002.

Vanhoozer, Kevin J. *The Drama of Doctrine: A Canonical-Linguistic Approach to Christian Theology*. Louisville: Westminster John Knox Press, 2005.

———. *Is There a Meaning in This Text? The Bible, the Reader, and the Morality of Literary Knowledge*. Grand Rapids: Zondervan, 2009.

Vanhoozer, Kevin J., ed. *Dictionary for Theological Interpretation of the Bible*. Grand Rapids: Baker Academic, 2005.

Via, Dan O., Jr. "A Response to Crossan, Funk, and Petersen." *Semeia*, no. 1 (1974): 222–35.

———. "Parable and Example Story: A Literary-Structuralist Approach." *Semeia*, no. 1 (1974): 105–33.

Vickers, Brian. *In Defence of Rhetoric*. Oxford: Clarendon, 1988.

Vorster, Willem S. "Readings, Readers, and the Succession Narrative." *Zeitschrift Für Die Alttestamentliche Wissenschaft* 98 (1986): 351–62.

Waltke, Bruce K. *An Old Testament Theology: An Exegetical, Canonical, and Thematic Approach*. With Charles Yu. Grand Rapids: Zondervan, 2007.

Watson, Duane F. *Invention, Arrangement, and Style: Rhetorical Criticism of Jude and 2 Peter*. Atlanta: Scholars Press, 1988.

Watson, Duane F., and Alan J. Hauser. *Rhetorical Criticism of the Bible: A Comprehensive Bibliography with Notes on History and Method*. Leiden: Brill, 1994.

Watson, Francis. "The Fourfold Gospel." In *The Cambridge Companion to the Gospels*, edited by Stephen C. Barton, 34–52. Cambridge: Cambridge University Press, 2006.

Waugh, Patricia, ed. *Literary Theory and Criticism: An Oxford Guide*. Oxford: Oxford University Press, 2006.

Webb, Ruth. *Ekphrasis, Imagination and Persuasion in Ancient Rhetorical Theory and Practice*. Surrey: Ashgate, 2009.

Webster, John. "Canon." In *Dictionary for Theological Interpretation of the Bible*, edited by Kevin J. Vanhoozer. Grand Rapids: Baker, 2005.

Weima, Jeffrey A. D. "What Does Aristotle Have to Do With Paul : An Evaluation of Rhetorical Criticism." *Calvin Theological Journal* 32, no. 2 (1997): 458–68.

Weitzman, Steven. "Allusion, Artifice, and Exile in the Hymn of Tobit." *Journal of Biblical Literature* 115 (1996): 49–61.

Westminster John Knox Press. An Interview with Brevard S. Childs (1923–2007), 2000. https://web.archive.org/web/20160413191537/ http://www.philosophy-religion.org/bible/childs-interview.htm.

White, Hugh C. "French Structuralism and OT Narrative Analysis: Roland Barthes." *Semeia*, no. 3 (1975): 99–127.

Widdowson, Peter. *Literature*. The New Critical Idiom. London: Routledge, 1999.

Widmer, Michael. *Moses, God, and the Dynamics of Intercessory Prayer: A Study of Exodus 32–34 and Numbers 13–14*. Tübingen: Mohr Siebeck, 2004.

Wildeboer, Gerrit. *The Origin of the Canon of the Old Testament: An Historico-Critical Enquiry*. Translated by B. W. Bacon. London: Luzac, 1895.

Williams, Jay. Preface of *Signature Derrida*, by Jacques Derrida, edited by Jay Williams. Chicago: University of Chicago Press, 2013.

Williamson, H. G. M. "Isaiah 62:4 and the Problem of Inner-Biblical Allusions." *JBL* 119 (2000): 734–39.

Wimsatt, W. K. *The Verbal Icon: Studies in the Meaning of Poetry*. Lexington, KY: University of Kentucky Press, 1982.

Winsor, Ann Roberts. *A King Is Bound in the Tresses: Allusions to the Song of Songs in the Fourth Gospel*. New York: Lang, 1999.

Witherington, Ben, III. "'Almost Thou Persuadest Me ...': The Importance of Greco-Roman Rhetoric for the Understanding of the Text and Context of the New Testament." *Patheos.com*, December 19, 2012. http://www.patheos.com/blogs/bibleandculture/2012/12/19/the-sbl-in-chicago-a-potpourri-of-things-part-one/.

———. *New Testament Rhetoric: An Introductory Guide to the Art of Persuasion in and of the New Testament*. Eugene, OR: Cascade, 2009.

Wittgenstein, Ludwig. *Philosophical Investigations*. Edited and translated by P. M. S. Hacker and Joachim Schulte. 4th ed. Oxford: Wiley-Blackwell, 2009.

———. *Tractatus Logico-Philosophicus*. Translated by D. F. Pears and B. F. McGuinness. London: Routledge, 1974.

Wood, Michael. "William Empson." In *The Cambridge History of Literary Criticism*, edited by A. Walton Litz, Louis Menand, and Lawrence Rainey, Vol. 7, *Modernism and the New Criticism*. Cambridge: Cambridge University Press, 2000.

Worthington, Ian, ed. *Persuasion: Greek Rhetoric in Action*. London: Routledge, 1994.

Zakovich, Yair. *"And You Shall Tell Your Son ...": The Concept of Exodus in the Bible*. Jerusalem: Magnes, 1991.

———. "Inner-Biblical Interpretation." In *A Companion to Biblical Interpretation in Early Judaism*, edited by Matthias Henze, 27–63. Grand Rapids: Eerdmans, 2012.

Zunz, Leopold. *Die Gottesdienstliche Vorträge der Juden: Historisch Entwickelt*. Berlin: A. Asher, 1832.

SUBJECT INDEX

SCRIPTURE INDEX

Old Testament

New Testament